politics

A Brief Inquiry into
the Conceptual Language
of Political Science

THE FREE PRESS   NEW YORK
COLLIER-MACMILLAN LIMITED   LONDON

The Free Press   A DIVISION OF THE MACMILLAN COMPANY
866 Third Avenue, New York, New York 10022

Collier-Macmillan Canada Ltd., Toronto, Ontario

Library of Congress Catalog Card Number: 71–142363
Printing Number 1 2 3 4 5 6 7 8 9 10

This book is dedicated to Dorothy,
who knows what it means
and what it has meant.

Contents

Preface, ix

1

Metapolitics, 1

2

On Science and
the Study of Politics, 17

3

On the Meaning of
"Meaning" and
"Truth," 42

4

On Semantics
and Syntactics, 77

5

On Concept Formation,
Conceptual Schemata,
and Generalizing
Knowledge Claims, 119

6

On Laws,
Theories, and Models, 160

7

On Explanation, 198

8

On Understanding
and Knowing, 238

9

On Normative
Discourse, 282

10

On Noncognitive
Discourse, 315

11

Conclusion, 343

Glossary, 366

Index, 383

Preface

This book was originally undertaken to satisfy what I felt to be a serious pedagogical and professional need. It is intended to be an introduction to a range of problems central to political inquiry—an introduction accessible to both upper division undergraduate and beginning graduate students. It is a book devoted almost exclusively to analytic and conceptual concerns and, as a consequence, makes no pretense of enhancing substantive knowledge about political science.

It must be said that this work is the result of long deliberation, much effort, and a heart-felt conviction. I am convinced that political science is an informal discipline and that many, if not most, of its problems are the consequence of linguistic (or if one would like, conceptual) confusion. Political inquiry is pursued, by and large, with the analytic and logical machinery of ordinary language, and there has been, unfortunately, little sustained effort within the discipline to standardize linguistic usage or systematize theoretical procedures. As a result one is never quite sure what claims are being advanced by participants in the enterprise, what criteria of adequacy to employ in judging them, and what evidence conditions putative knowledge claims are expected to satisfy.

What this book attempts is a preliminary move in the direction of more sophisticated language use—in order that we ourselves, and our students, may begin to appreciate what it is that we and they are about in tendering knowledge claims about political affairs. The formulations suggested in this text are not, I believe, privative. I believe that responsible work in the areas of traditional political theory, empirical theory, quasi-experimental, experimental, and mathematicological inquiry can be conducted, without loss and with some profit, in the proposed language style and with the proffered conceptual machinery. Through their use, moreover, both students and practitioners might attain a more enduring and compelling sense of the continuity and radical compatibility that I believe characterizes our discipline. The forthcoming analyses should help dissipate some of the fictive distinctions between fields and subfields in political science that have been productive of little other than dissension and confusion. One of the fondest aspirations with which this book is launched is that it might provide for students, and perhaps colleagues alike, an account of political science that permits an accommodation of all responsible cognitive pursuits—and convey a sense of the radical unity of the discipline.

In the last decade a number of efforts have been made to explore the linguistic and epistemological bases of political science—and almost all have something to recommend them. But I shall argue that there remains a considerable gap in the literature at a reasonably sophisticated language and conceptual level that has not as yet been filled. This book is a first effort in filling that gap. If some small portion of it survives critical appraisal, if some students and/or colleagues find *some* merit in any of it, my efforts will be more than repaid.

The book does make demands on its readers. Much of its vocabulary is that of the philosophy of science—and is, as a result, unfamiliar to the student of political inquiry. In an effort to assist the reader I have appended a glossary of terms that may be found useful. Furthermore, to relieve some of the tedium, I would suggest that those students and colleagues not interested in, or who have reason to believe that they would not profit from, a relatively elementary analysis of semantic and syntactical truth, skip Chapter Four, "On Semantics and Syntactics." Colleagues in whom I have every confidence have lamented the necessity of reading it. I have considered suppressing it. On the other hand, I believe it does convey some information concerning language employments that is useful to the student attempting to understand the role of reconstructed language in political inquiry—and I think some discussion of formal language is useful for the subsequent discussion of partial axiomatization and computer applications. I would suggest that the student skip Chapter Four until the remainder of the book has been read, and possibly return to it should he feel so disposed.

If this short book does anything to make those interested in the systematic study of political matters more sensitive to the obligations they at least implicitly assume in undertaking a relatively specialized cognitive activity, it will have accomplished as much as could be expected of any work of this nature. Even if every analysis is found wanting, the overall effect should be therapeutic—the faulted analyses will, hopefully, compel others to formulate countertheses with more precision and specificity than is presently the case. In effect, I an suggesting that in success or failure, the subsequent chapters should have *some* beneficent influence in the development of our discipline—I am arguing that the book was worth writing and merits reading. Writing the book has, of course, put me in debt to many students and colleagues. My students, both undergraduate and graduate, in the courses I have taught in both philosophy and political science, have always provided stimulation and insight. I am indebted to the most indigent and uninspired among them. My colleagues, on the other hand, have given of their time and acumen without stint. More than that, they have provided an atmosphere rich in intellectual and human qualities unmatched, I am convinced, anywhere else in the world. Everyone in the discipline is aware of the academic and research accomplishments of men like Aaron Wildavsky, Nelson Polsby, Carl Rosberg, Ernst Haas, Paul Seabury, and Ralph Retzlaff—what could not be as well appreciated is their generosity, integrity, and affability. These qualities, as much as their intellectual gifts, have made this work possible. To Michael Shapiro, Peter Sperlich, Lois Gold, and Todd La Porte I owe special insights and the excision of errors that would have otherwise afflicted the text. That so many errors and shortcomings remain is compelling evidence that, in the final analysis, this work is my very own.

I am indebted to Mrs. Michael McGrath for her patience and diligence in preparing this manuscript for publication. She has assisted me in more ways than I could enumerate. Finally, to my wife, Dorothy, to whom this book is dedicated, I owe all manner of good things so necessary to protracted study and scholarly effort.

Berkeley, California   A. JAMES GREGOR

1

Metapolitics

Any serious human activity begets a "meta-activity," individual brooding or talk among a group. This is as true about hunting or gambling or house-building as it is about politics; and such talk always "feeds back" in some sense into the original activity itself. The talk is itself an activity, time-killing, pleasant, sometimes exciting; people talk about politics (engage in "meta-politics") because they like it, as fishermen talk about fishing (Izaak Walton is the complete meta-angler?).

W. J. M. Mackenzie

It has become a commonplace in our own time to say that the study of politics has entered into crisis. *When* it entered into crisis is problematic—Arnold Brecht identifies the turn of the century, while David Easton identifies the period of the Second World War, as marking its commencement[1]— but that political inquiry is in fact in the throes of crisis appears to be generally admitted. Identifying the loci of tension within political inquiry is a tiresome and frequently fruitless task. Some insist it is a consequence of normative malaise; some maintain it is the consequence of the impact of either methodological over- or undersophistication. Some conceive it to

1

be the consequence of ideological confusion and some conceive it to be a consequence of the conjunction of all such factors. Whatever factors conspired to produce the crisis, the crisis is painfully manifest to the professional practitioners and the students of political inquiry embroiled in it. What seems equally clear is that a variety of other distinguishable academic pursuits share, or have shared, some of the same species attributes of intellectual ferment characterized in popular parlance as "crisis."

Within the last fifty years a variety of disciplines have evinced the same syndrome of pathic traits. Contemporary experimental psychologists find very little to talk about with clinical psychologists; "empirical" sociologists assiduously avoid "speculative" sociologists; "analytic" philosophers have painfully little patience with "existential" philosophers; and historians who conceive their craft as having "scientific" pretensions mock those who construe the enterprise as essentially an art form. Among those preoccupied with political inquiry, political "scientists" have, with alarming frequency and increasing emotional salience, broken off communication with their political "theorist" confreres. Departments are riven by a disjuncture that all too often ceases to respect even the most elementary academic proprieties, entire institutions are beset by apparently irrepressible differences, and students are more and more frequently caught up in the slackening of all conventions and a general abrogation of rules—that ultimately produces only intellectual anarchy. In exacerbated instances escape is sought, by professional thinkers and their charges alike, in a pernicious form of irrationalism that seeks to displace critical intelligence with mystic and fideist elements through which one attempts to find the lost security and sense of order of a time gone by. The cure becomes manifestly worse than the disease.

Like innocence, the security and sense of order once lost can no longer be simply conjured up. If security and the sense of order are to be restored, they can no longer be the unproblematic and somewhat naive security and order that prevailed in that now lost time.

In the untroubled past it was generally assumed that the professional thinker in matters political was charged with the responsibility of demonstrating (in some significant sense of that term) that one variety of political organization was particularly praiseworthy and that any alternative was, in varying measure and degree, defective. In effect, the study of politics was essentially a moral pursuit and political "scientists" were conceived to be essentially, if not exclusively, practicing moralists issuing appraisive assessments and prescriptive advice.

The "Revolution" in Political Science

At some time in the twentieth century, a group of "Young Turks" began to insist that the function of political inquiry was to attempt adequate description, seek out appropriate typologies and classificatory schemata, and formulate lawlike propositions calculated to further the explanation and prediction of political phenomena.

They maintained that political inquiry should be a "scientific" inquiry, concerned with the formulation of defensible lawlike statements that would provide leverage in the comprehension and prediction of political events. Since the advent of these iconoclasts political inquiry has no longer been the same. In the space of a single generation the entire complexion of political inquiry has changed. And it continues to change at a remarkable rate. Hardly a year passes that fails to find a new, oft-times exotic, research method or technique added to the armarium of political inquiry. We find colleagues and students enmeshed in game-theory and Markoff processes, factor analyses and regressive statistics. Conceptual schemata are borrowed from biology and sociology in terms of organismic or general systems "theory" or its cognate functionalism—psychoanalytic schemata resurface with somewhat tedious regularity—psychological concepts proliferate and are unself-consciously exploited. Students run t tests and talk knowingly about platykurtic distributions and *rho* values. Anyone who cannot negotiate Chi squares, assess randomization, statistical significance, and standard deviations is less than illiterate; he is preconscious.

For all its merits (and there are many), there is something amiss in all this frenetic activity. Irrespective of its substantive merits (or its substantive defects), there appears to be something grievously wrong with the way in which this patrimony of funded knowledge and available technique is conveyed to students. Generally, and at its best, the procedure pursues something like the following process: the student, as an undergraduate, takes a rag-bag of political inquiry courses, perhaps two or three political "theory" courses, a very loosely structured descriptive course generally called "Comparative Political Systems," another on "American Institutions" or its analogue, and finally, courses devoted to "area studies" in which the student is exposed to "The Political Systems of East Africa" or "Western Europe" or their equivalents. All of these are conceived as satisfying the requirements for majoring in political science as an academic discipline. That the student develops a pervasive sense of the discontinuity, of the sometimes irrelevance and fragmentariness of the discipline, is a predictable result.

On their entry into advanced studies and in the effort to find continuity and order, graduate students generally pursue one relatively narrow line of inquiry with but nodding acquaintance and tangential interest in alternate areas of political inquiry. Those in area studies know relatively little about traditional political theory, those in political theory systematically avoid anything in which numbers are used for any other purpose than to identify the pages of a book or manuscript, students in international relations employ a fashionable language style that has come to characterize their pursuit, and almost all are innocent of any systematic awareness of a community of concerns that sustains political inquiry as a discipline. Traditional political theorists are spoken of, with perhaps less than polite disdain, as "political theologians," those of behavioral persuasion as "prisoners of methodology," those preoccupied with axiomatic systems and analytic conceptual schemata as concerned with "generating empty systems and playing language games."

The Language of Political Science

The fact is that the universe of political discourse has at least three constituent, mutually interpenetrative and radically compatible, *cognitive* domains, the analytic, the synthetic and the normative—a fact to which the student, under present circumstances, is given but minimal exposure. Not only do all these cognitive linguistic elements find a place in the discipline, but all are essential to the collection, processing, interpretation, storage, and use of significant and reliable information about politics. Until those concerned with political inquiry develop a minimum awareness of this fact, the discipline appears fragmentary and ill-contrived. Those concerned with typologies and classificatory and axiomatic schemata will continue to talk of "general theories," "models," and "approaches." Those concerned with inductive generalizations and the collection of data will speak of "investigations," "observations," and "facts," and those preoccupied with the "significance" of it all for human activity will speak of "recommendations" and "posting warnings."

Utterances, we will be reminded, serve other purposes, of course, than making cognitive assertion—whether those assertions are analytic, synthetic, or normative. Utterances can be instances of ritual or ceremonial language use (as when we say "Good morning," or "How are you?") and constitute occasions for appropriate exchanges of etiquette that we all anticipate in the patterned expectations which sustain daily life. Utterances can be performative (as when we say "I do" during a marriage ceremony, "I promise" when we take up an obligation, or "I declare" when we certify a decision made). Utterances can be expressive (as when we use invective or declaim). All of which is transparently true, but these and other noncognitive uses of language (utterances which cannot be assigned truth status) can, however, be accommodated within the three domains of cognitive discourse. As students of politics we can inquire what the circumstances might be that govern the appropriate use of ritual, ceremonial, or symbolic language. We can synthesize such employments as elements in an analytic conceptual scheme and characterize them as partially satisfying the "integrative functional requisite," or we can assess their normative import in the interpersonal behavior of moral agents. We can search out the conditions which make promising and declaring appropriate; we can begin to understand the function of promising, declaring, and declaiming; we can effectively classify such utterances in schemata; we can see the value in them. We can investigate their function, specify conditions governing their use, and evaluate their occurrence.

In effect, the student of politics concerns himself inextricably with signs and the linguistic vehicles in which they are lodged—linguistic entities—employed to make significant and reliable utterances about political matters. The speech acts which will be admitted into the class of utterances identified as "political" will depend upon stipulations concerning language use advanced and argued by each serious political practitioner. What counts as "political" will continue to remain problematic, for the concept, like all serious empirical concepts in an informal discipline like political science, is open-textured. The stipulative definitions advanced to define the denotative scope of politics will vary from author to author and student to student.

To attempt to provide a necessary and sufficient definition of the term "politics" is a useless preoccupation. Such definitions are manifestly appropriate in formal systems, analytic schemata, and axiomatized reconstructed languages; they are unnecessarily restrictive in informal or minimally formalized disciplines. At best we find "range or criterial definitions" for concepts like "politics." Such a definition is given in terms of a set of overlapping criteria, membership in the class being the consequence of the possession of one or another or several of the criterial attributes that license entry. All that is logically required is that at least one criterial attribute, but no specific one, be manifest. Politics is spoken of as activity having to do with government, or with organized power, the institutions of command and control, or with the study having to do with the shaping and sharing of power, or the "authoritative allocation" of values, or a "form of activity centering around the quest for competitive advantage conditioned by the fact that it occurs in a situation of change and relative scarcity." Or it is "the process of applying systematic intelligence to the adjustment of group conflicts and to control of force that is shared by both leaders and citizenry in a politically organized society," or more simply, "political science is the study of men related by authority," or "who gets what, when and how."

For one purpose or another a scholar or student may stipulate a definition, and vindicate such stipulation by indicating that it leads to greater rigor, hence increased reliability, in treating elements within the universe of discourse, or it leads to greater theoretical yield because of its increased scope and range. To know what a construct like "politics" means is to study its employments, to characterize what has loosely been called its "grammar," to exhibit its use, role, or function with respect to other cognitive signs in the language matrix.

To begin to operate with some competence within the universe of discourse of any discipline is to understand something of the vehicle in which information is encoded and the process by virtue of which information so encoded is, in principle, decoded by information recipients. In effect, to deal significantly with the information products of any reasonably systematic knowledge enterprise is to know something of the process of information gathering, processing, interpretation, storage, recall, and use. All such processing involves techniques and methods, but all such techniques and processes and the products in which they result are inescapably embodied in language which is their common substance. The products of science are linguistic entities; the processes of science are themselves explicated and justified in complex linguistic products. The products of art are no less symbols and signs which themselves constitute nonlinguistic sign use, that satisfy the minimal requirements of rule governance—and they are appraised in language. Human knowledge and understanding are embodied in systematic symbol and sign use; language is their public vehicle.

Linguistic Analysis and Political Inquiry

At least since the commencement of the twentieth century language itself, and semiotics as the general science of signs, has occupied a central place in the analysis and deliberation of those concerned with man's efforts to understand himself and his world. The twentieth century is characterized as the "age of analysis," a characterization made manifest in increasing self-consciousness about the employments of language—and signs in general. More and more frequently analytic concerns have focused on talk about the propositions in which substantive knowledge claims are made. The talk is *about* the talk of science, aesthetics, theology, philosophy. It operates on a different logical level than the substantive propositions formulated by practitioners of any specific universe of discourse.

Rudolf Carnap has spoken of a language as a system of signs and/or symbols employed for the purposes of cognitive communication, to influence actions, decisions, or thoughts, and to perform tasks like promising or declaring. Languages can be spoken, written, or gestural; they can be spoken of, simply, as sign *systems*.

If one studies, analyzes, and describes a language, the language used for studying, analyzing, and describing the object language is a *metalanguage*.[2] It is talk about language. Any language, any system of signs, may be taken as the object language and the language containing expressions suitable for studying, analyzing, and describing the object language is the metalanguage. When mathematicians are concerned not with the formulae of mathematics, but with talk in a metalanguage about the formal system, calculus, the system of axioms which constitutes the foundation of mathematical talk, they occupy themselves with *metamathematics*,[3] i.e., talk about mathematical talk. A *metatheorum,* for example, would be a truth about a formal system which is not a truth in the system. It is arrived at by reasoning in a metalanguage about the characteristics and properties of the formal system.[4] Logicians, in turn, who engage in metalinguistic talk about the talk of formal logic identify their concern as *metalogic.*[5] Philosophers who concern themselves not with the substantive propositions, the products, of science, but with the examination, analysis, and description of the language of science, occupy themselves with *metascience.*[6] The ethicist who is not concerned with issuing prescriptions and proscriptions, approbations and disapprobations, that is to say who is *not* concerned with making ascriptive value judgments that could be characterized as "normative," and who focuses his attention on the explicit and careful analysis of the language with which such ascriptive claims are made and the truth conditions governing them, is concerned with *metaethics.*[7] Recently Joseph Murphy has suggested that students of politics more concerned with an examination of the *procedures* that subtend the formulation and issuance of recommendations and prescriptions which characterize the language of traditional political theory than with those recommendations and prescriptions themselves are concerned with *metatheory*.[8]

Some years ago A. J. Ayer introduced T. D. Weldon's, *The Vocabulary of Politics,* with the characterization of the effort as being unconcerned with the argued defense or the enumeration of deficiencies of any one or another political system, but with the effort "to exhibit the logic of the statements which . . . figure in discourse about politics."[9] Earlier still, Margaret Macdonald concerned herself with "The Language of Political Theory."[10] She was occupied with the language employments of political theorists and not their substantive claims as such. More recently, a spate of books has appeared that concern themselves with the use of scientific language in the formulation of propositions in political inquiry. They are broadly characterized as "methodological" or "analytic" to distinguish them from substantive inquiries which are additive to the sum of knowledge possessed about politics. They speak of themselves as applying the philosophy of science, metascience, to political inquiry.[11] But it is clear by their inclusion of normative considerations that they are preoccupied with more than the application of metascience to political inquiry. They are undertaking metaethical analysis as well. In effect, their object language is the language of politics, and their concern is both metascientific and metaethical. Their efforts could appropriately be identified as metalinguistic. Their *universe* of discourse is that of politics, their analysis concerns itself with analytic, synthetic, and normative *domains* of that universe at various linguistic and epistemic *levels*. Their systematic, analytic, and descriptive accounts can be classed under the generic rubric *"metapolitics,"*[12] metalinguistic talk about the analytic, synthetic, and normative language of political inquiry and politics itself.

All those who feel compelled to "get on with the business of politics," and who feel obliged by some special mandate to "add to the sum of political wisdom" find such metalinguistic activities tedious and unrewarding. It is only when they find themselves confused, or lament the confusion they find in others in the inability to distinguish a definition from a factual claim, an analytic conceptual scheme from an empirical theory, a mathematical model from a heuristic analogy, a description from an injunction, that they begin to see the significance of the talk about the talk of politics and political inquiry.

Only when they begin to comprehend the different truth conditions which govern the various domains of discourse, and the fact that their colleagues and their students fail to make elementary distinctions between typologies and testable hypotheses, between normative ideals and empirically determined organizational requisites and prerequisites, do they begin to concern themselves with the implicit and explicit rules governing language use.

All of us have had occasion to hear colleagues maintain that their *analytic* schemata *explain* political phenomena and have felt embarrassed for them. All of us have had exposure to counterfeit arguments and bogus truth warrants. Prudence suggests that we be prepared to identify the sometimes elementary linguistic confusions which generate mysteries about "meaning" and "truth," about "understanding" and "explanation," which confound the resolution of problems and compound obscurities. Concern for our own integrity requires the avoidance of fallacy and error; concern for ourselves and our students recommends the provision of reasonably adequate tools of analysis and critical appraisal. What this entails is at least a preliminary, even if relatively superficial, inquiry into the language which is the intersubjective vehicle for all of our substantive and analytic claims.

Hopefully what results is conceptual therapy, a dissolution of linguistic confusions. What may result, moreover, is an appreciation of the unity of a discipline as old as man's thinking itself. No less a luminary than Aristotle, a systemizer of logic, an empiricist of sorts, and an ethicist and metaethicist of the first rank as well, saw in political inquiry a "master art," a unity of analytic, synthetic, and normative concerns.

Metapolitics and Political Inquiry

In itself, metapolitics is a broadly gauged methodological concern with the political science enterprise. To characterize its concern as "broadly gauged" is a move in the effort to distinguish metapolitics from the perfectly legitimate concern with procedures or techniques involved in the accumulation, processing, and interpretation of political science data (a concern characterized as "methodological-empirical"). Books dealing with such matters in behavioral and political science are almost legion. Books entertaining a broader concern, concentrating upon the more theoretical aspects of political and social science research, in general, are becoming more frequent (a concern characterized as "methodological-theoretical").[13] Nonetheless, such works frequently confine themselves to the methodological foundations for "viable *empirical* research," a "yardstick against which the *empirical* achievements of the various disciplinary areas can be estimated . . . ," an important, complex, and legitimate preoccupation. It is generally recognized, however, that such efforts "require a companion stress on *normative* issues and their methodology."[14]

Books that do complement such a focus with a discussion of metaethics are generally too broad in scope for the purposes of the student of political inquiry. Abraham Kaplan's volume, *The Conduct of Inquiry,* which has done yeoman service in introductory political science courses, includes in its range all the behavioral sciences.[15] Books like those of Eugene Meehan and Vernon Van Dyke are appropriate in range, restricted as they are to political inquiry, but are for one reason or another still not adequate to the purposes of an introduction to metapolitics. Van Dyke's book is flawed by a privative and anachronistic metaethics: the theory of ethics entertained by the emotivists of the nineteen thirties.[16] Meehan's books, while certainly not defective in this manner, and whose range is relatively well confined to the political universe of discourse, operate at a somewhat higher epistemic level than would serve as an introduction to the language of politics and political inquiry. Metapolitics is a concern which commences with an analysis of the most primitive of fundamental knowledge claims upon which the edifice of political inquiry rests.

Political inquiry rests upon an analytically primitive language base. Its language is characterized, even at that level, by the governance of rule and the possession of linguistic properties which can be shown to obtain even in the most complex political argument and most intricate political research. Sophisticated political argument and political research are governed by linguistic norms, evidence conditions, and have linguistic properties substantially parasitic on those which characterize the language of political inquiry at its most primitive levels. When we consider the ordinary and theoretical language employed in the study of politics, we become aware that complex linguistic structures like axiomatic systems, analytic conceptual schemata, and typologies share common properties with simple and analytically true propositions. Theories, heuristic schemata, unrestricted, restricted, and accidental generalizations, theoretic concepts and constructs display properties shared by simple observation sentences.

At the more complex levels of language employment—characterized by varying degrees of standardization and formalization—we find enormously complex linguistic artifacts like theories, justificatory arguments, vindications, appraisals, and recommendations. To catalogue and analyze some of these, to exhibit the relationship to more elementary linguistic products, is a metalinguistic concern—and constitutes a brief introduction to metapolitics.

In this sense metapolitics gravitates to and explores a lower epistemic and linguistic level than the interesting and stimulating books provided by Meehan. Metapolitics concerns itself with the specification of linguistic domains which can be isolated in the language of political inquiry and addresses itself to the most general kinds of truth conditions which govern each of them. It is a systematic concern with language use within a specific linguistic universe, that universe which is the province of activity of practicing political scientists.

To begin to unpack the problems which collect around issues which have become urgent for the behavioral sciences in general, and political science in particular, it is necessary to begin somewhere near the beginning. Problems like the "sociology of knowledge," the putative distinction between the methodology of the natural as distinct from the methodology of the social sciences, the nature of intrinsic norms governing the descriptive and explanatory efforts of standard science, and the nature of "facts," "observations," and "explanations," can be effectively dealt with only if one knows something of the rudiments of language use. No single piece of work can reasonably hope to effectively deal with all these issues. All that one can hope to accomplish is to lay down the outlines of what seems to be a fruitful pursuit.

The proper conduct of political inquiry has become an increasingly sophisticated occupation. Techniques that ten years ago would have staggered the imagination and intellect of established experimental scientists and scholars are now deployed by graduate students, and yet how frequently the most elementary confusions about the use of language persist. How frequently students fail to understand the most elementary rationale for the use of the techniques they administer. How frequently their perspective is narrowed by the confines of the techniques and methods with which they have developed proficiency. How frequently has the employment of a special tool cut them off from effective communication with others occupied in the same field of endeavor.

An analytic concern with the language of political inquiry is calculated to provide some insight not only into the constituents that enter into complex theoretical structures, but into their rationale as well. It also suggests something about the fundamental unity of the discipline. There is a fundamental similarity between the most primitive analytic truths and the most complex calculus—just as there obtains a fundamental similarity between the simplest empirical utterance and the most impressive lawlike assertion. There is a substantial kinship between the vindication of an individual course of action and the rationale for a political *Weltanschauung*—and that *Weltanschauung* will contain, as constituents, the most complex as well as the most simple analytic and descriptive components. The most comprehensive theories will evince an analytic structure in which empirical generalizations find a place, or they will constitute calculi mapped on an appropriate universe which has directly or indirectly observable things as primitives—and the entire undertaking will be sustained by on-going extrinsic or intrinsic values. Exhibited in their most elementary form, these linguistic elements become almost transparent. We understand a great deal about them by characterizing their simplest uses. This is what metapolitics attempts to be about. It is the metalanguage in which one expresses what one wishes to say about politics and political inquiry as an object language.

It is as though one were speaking in English about a foreign language and one wished to ventilate the syntactical rules governing the structure of that language, and one wished to understand something of the semantic conditions which made its conventional signs meaningful and true. It is as though one wished to tender criticism of the narrative prose and poetry of an alien tongue. One would have to speak of analysis and criteria, of description and evaluation, of the language in question. Similarly metapolitics would analyze and investigate, suggest norms and exhibit the rule rudiments and extended logic of political discourse. Metapolitics is concerned with the description, analysis, and justificatory norms governing the linguistic practices of those employing the language of politics and political inquiry. It is not concerned with substantively employing that language itself. It will generate no new substantive truths. Everything will be pretty much the same as it was before—perhaps without the confusion. Certain questions, long conceived to be problems, will presumably no longer command attention. New questions might well be posed. False starts might be avoided—and a great deal of the emotion which is still generated at certain junctures in the enterprise will, hopefully, be dissipated.

Metapolitics is a critical and analytic concern with the conceptual language of political inquiry. That such a concern is of vital cognitive consequence can be suggested by a preliminary treatment of some of the issues which occupy much of contemporary discussion: the nature of science and its relationship to political inquiry. What will become fairly obvious will be the fact that without more systematic treatment of a collection of interrelated concepts no adequate resolution of these issues can be forthcoming. At certain critical junctures the discussion must invoke concepts which themselves require analysis. In effect what the account in the next chapter is calculated to produce is a recognition that wherever one choses to commence in the serious assessment of the epistemological issues vital to contemporary political inquiry one finds oneself faced with the necessity of embarking upon conceptual analysis—a metalinguistic inquiry into the language of political science.

Notes

1 A. Brecht, *Political Theory* (Princeton: Princeton University, 1959), "Introductory"; D. Easton, "Alternative Strategies in Theoretical Research," in D. Easton (ed.), *Varieties of Political Theory* (Englewood Cliffs, N.J.: Prentice-Hall, 1966), pp. 1f. Cf. also M.B. Parsons, "Perspective in the Study of Politics," in M.B. Parsons (ed.), *Perspectives in the Study of Politics* (Chicago: Rand McNally, 1968), p. 9; R. A. Dahl, "The Behavioral Approach in Political Science," reprinted in *Politics and Social Life* eds. N. W. Polsby, R. A. Dentler, and P. A. Smith, (Boston: Houghton Mifflin, 1963), pp. 15–25.

2 R. Carnap, *Introduction to Semantics* (Cambridge, Mass.: Harvard, 1948), pp. 3f.

3 Cf. F. Waismann, *Introduction to Mathematical Thinking* (New York: Harper, 1951), p. 77; R. Carnap, *The Logical Syntax of Language* (New York: Humanities, 1951), pp. 325ff.

4 J. M. Anderson and H. W. Johnstone, *Natural Deduction* (Belmont, Calif.: Wadsworth, 1962), p. 293.

5 Carnap, *Logical Syntax of Language,* p. 9.

6 M. Bunge, *Metascientific Queries* (Springfield, Ill.: Thomas, 1959), pp. 3–6.

7 P. W. Taylor, "Introduction," in *The Moral Judgment,* ed. P. W. Taylor (Englewood Cliffs, N.J.: Prentice-Hall, 1963), pp. xiv, xv.

8 J. S. Murphy, *Political Theory: A Conceptual Analysis* (Nobleton, Ontario: Dorsey, 1968), p. xi.

9 A. J. Ayer, "Editorial Foreword," in T. D. Weldon, *The Vocabulary of Politics* (Baltimore: Penguin, 1953), p. 7.

10 M. Macdonald, "The Language of Political Theory," in *Logic and Language,* ed. A. Flew (Garden City, N.Y.: Anchor, 1965), pp. 174–194.

11 V. Van Dyke, *Political Science: A Philosophical Analysis* (Stanford: Stanford University, 1960), p. vii.

12 I know of only two instances (other than in the quote which heads this chapter) where "metapolitics" has been used in the literature of political inquiry— and in both cases it has been used either as a simple pejorative, as a reference to a broad, vague and pernicious kind of political speculation, or to suggest that

"empirical political science" be supplemented by a kind of political poetry. (Cf. P. Viereck, *Metapolitics: The Roots of the Nazi Mind* [New York: Capricorn, 1961], and N. O. Brown, "Love Mystified: A Reply," in H. Marcuse, *Negations: Essays in Critical Theory* [Boston: Beacon, 1968], p. 246.) W. J. M. Mackenzie uses the term to refer to the talk about the talk of politics. It is this use of the term that is here intended.

[13] Cf. E. J. Meehan, *The Theory and Method of Political Analysis* (Homewood, Ill.: Dorsey, 1965), *Contemporary Political Thought* (Homewood, Ill.: Dorsey, 1967); G. Sjoberg, R. Nett, *A Methodology for Social Research* (New York: Harper and Row, 1968).

[14] R. T. Golembiewski, W. A. Welsh, and W. J. Crotty, *A Methodological Primer for Political Scientists* (Chicago: Rand McNally, 1969), pp. 2, 4, 6.

[15] A. Kaplan, *The Conduct of Inquiry: Methodology for Behavioral Science* (San Francisco: Chandler, 1964).

[16] Van Dyke, *op. cit.,* p. 9.

Suggested Readings

Plamenatz, J. "The Use of Political Theory," in *Political Philosophy,* edited by A. Quinton. London: Oxford University, 1967.

Weldon, T. D. *The Vocabulary of Politics.* Baltimore: Penguin, 1953.

Wilson, J. *Language and the Pursuit of Truth.* Cambridge, England: Cambridge University, 1956.

2

On Science and the Study of Politics

Thou shalt not sit with Statisticians nor commit a Social Science.

W. H. Auden

For at least a generation the putative differences that have separated the "behavioralists" and the "anti-behavioralists" in political science have been a public scandal. Robert Dahl's urbane and sanguine anticipation concerning immanent rapprochement in the discipline[1] has not been, in fact, realized, if one measures it against the abundance and the exacerbated quality of the critiques of "behavioralism" that have appeared in a variety of places. The critiques of Russell Kirk, Mulford Sibley, and the collective criticisms contained in Herbert Storing's *Essays on the Scientific Study of Politics* followed close on the heels of Dahl's account.[2] The relatively recent publication of critical assessments like that of Christian Bay and K. W. Kim, conveniently bound in a volume dedicated to "a critique of behavioralism,"[3] indicates that the issues that divide "behavioralists" and "nonbehavioralists" are far from resolved. This material, conjoined with earlier critiques like those collected by Helmut Schoeck and James Wiggins,[4] provides a broad and loosely jointed collection of objections to the "behavioral approach" in the contemporary study of politics. These objections range from suggestions that behavioralists are, in some vague sense, crypto-Marxists and/or "characterized by

17

conservatism"[5]—that they practice a science predicated on a "dogmatic atheism" and/or that they invoke a science that lacks "even
dogmatic atheism to fall back upon"[6]—that they are incorrigibly
"holistic" or "collectivistic" and/or that they are irretrievably
"methodological individualists"[7]—to the insistence that they be
more "unscientific" and less rigorously scientific in their inquiries
and/or that they are *too* unscientific, and fail, as a result, to be
"scientific."[8]

The fact that such objections enjoy evident popularity and that
the charges with which they are freighted recur with such insistent
regularity indicates that the strife between "behavioral" and "non-
behavioral" persuasions has hardly diminished since Dahl's
hopeful assessment of almost a decade ago. That many of the charges
are mutually exclusive, indicates that the discussion is beset by
regular equivocation and/or analytic and interpretive error.

The principal contention of this book will be, implicitly, that
once certain critical concepts are at least moderately well characterized, most of the putative issues dividing parties in the exacerbated
debate dissipate themselves; they are in a real sense "pseudo-prob-
lems," the consequence of linguistic, analytic, conceptual, and procedural confusions. In effect, once terms like "science," "truth,"
"knowledge," "understanding," "philosophy," "meaning," and
"values" are specified with minimal precision, few, if any, substantive issues remain to divide our discipline into dysfunctional
factions.

Science and "Behavioralism"

The fact that both the critics and protagonists of "behavioralism"
have rarely attempted to explicate concepts critical to the discussion
of the relation of "science" to political inquiry is, at best, curious.
It is curious because much of the criticism turns upon the employment
of such terms. For example, "anti-behavioralists" frequently simply and flatly oppose the application of the "scientific approach"
to the study of politics, or by entailment insist that its study be
pursued by auxiliary "unscientific" techniques.[9] As a matter of
fact, what such critics frequently adduce as evidence that political

science requires "unscientific" adjuncts are select instances of research that are trivial or scientifically impoverished. Under such
circumstances the criticism that political science requires "unscientific" supplements collapses into a confused admonition that political
scientists should apply only responsible, accredited, and appropriate scientific techniques to the study of politics. In order to make
such criticism coherent, what would be required is an antecedent
discussion of what "science" is understood to be. Before anyone
can recommend supplements to "science," it seems reasonable that
he should offer some account of what he conceives himself to be
supplementing.

There is yet another reason for undertaking some preliminary
effort to characterize what "science" might be. If one seeks to identify those political scientists that are understood to be "behavioralists,"
it becomes immediately obvious that the term is painfully vague.
At best, the term can be given a range or criterial definition in terms
of a set of overlapping and interacting criteria by virtue of which
the members of the class might be identified.[10] To be admitted to
class membership, an instantial case must be in possession of at
least one of the requisite criteria for admission, but the possession
of no one specific trait is necessary for entrance. Any one of a
number of possible traits would seem to qualify one for entrance
into the class of "behavioralists." The range or criterial definition
of the term reflects the complexity and continuous variability of
the membership criteria as well as the lack of specific class bounda-
ries.

"Behavioralists" have been identified by the possession of any
one of a number of traits. A "behavioralist" has been identified as
a political scientist who 1) publishes in relatively specialized jour-
nals such as *Public Opinion Quarterly, World Politics, American
Behavioral Scientist,* and *Behavioral Science;* and/or 2) enjoys
membership or participation in the Social Science Research Council's
Committee on Political Behavior and the Committee on Comparative Politics; and/or 3) is preoccupied with the study of small
group and voting behavior; and/or 4) undertakes research efforts
conducted with a concern (*a*) for searching out regularities, discover-
able uniformities in political behavior expressed in lawlike state-

ments that could be, ideally, systematically interrelated to produce explanatory and predictive accounts, (*b*) for establishing appropriate verification techniques, (*c*) for rigorous scrutiny of procedures involved in the collection, processing, and interpretation of data, (*d*) for quantification whenever possible, relevant, and meaningful, (*e*) for maintaining the logical distinction between factual knowledge claims and normative prescription and proscription, (*f*) for a self-conscious and systematic interrelationship of theory and research, (*g*) for the development of explanatory and predictive theory as a necessary antecedent to applications, and (*h*) for the integration of the findings of political science with those of the related social sciences.[11]

The possession of any one of these characterizing traits would admit one into the class of "behavioralists." The "paradigm behavioralist" would be one who exemplified *all* these characteristics. There are, of course, few such political scientists. In general, a political scientist identified as a "behavioralist" would display only some one or some combination of these traits and the traits most generally taken to characterize the class are, in fact, those associated with a research concern directed toward discovering regularities governing political behavior, regularities that might be articulated into a systematically related collection of propositions having explanatory and predictive yield. Since just such concerns have been understood to loosely characterize "science," it seems that the disposition to employ the scientific method has been generally assumed to characterize "behavioralism" and "behavioralists." If such is the case—all the more reason to attempt some assessment of what "science" and its "method" might be reasonably understood to be.

Some of the critical issues that seem to divide political science as a discipline into factions turn on what science is understood to be. First, the suggestion that "unscientific" methods are essential to political inquiry requires that we have at least some understanding of what "science" might be—and secondly, the identification of "behavioralists" seems, generally, to turn on the disposition of some political scientists to attempt to employ the methods of science in their work. Science, and the methods of science, should be, therefore, the first objects of analysis if one wishes to assess the cognitive merits of the "behavioralist-non-behavioralist" dispute.

The effort to unpack the concept "science" and to offer a summary account of "the scientific method," is beset, of course, with innumerable difficulties. The term "science" obviously has persuasive force, either positive or negative as the case might be. It has also enjoyed a long history. Its specific cognitive meaning is, as a result, difficult to isolate, not only because of the persuasive employments of the term, but because the term has had a long and confused philological history. It has been deployed throughout the history of its use over such a variety of activities and such disparate collections of methods and putative truths that any significant characterization must, of necessity, be at least substantially stipulative and historically contextual.

Once this qualification is made, it can be argued that the term "science" has taken on a relatively (but not undisputed) specific contemporary meaning: it refers to those *procedures,* which, as a matter of historic fact, have provided a systematically articulated and comprehensive body of *maximally reliable knowledge claims* that afford men survival and adaptive advantage by affording explanatory and predictive leverage.[12] Such an explication thus includes both a consideration of "science" as *process* (that is to say, the term refers to methods and procedures invoked to provide for maximally reliable truth ascriptions) and "science" as *product* (that is to say, the term has as referent that corpus of linguistic entities to which truth can be ascribed with maximal domain variant reliability). The former is commonly spoken of as the "scientific method," and the latter "scientific knowledge." Both are historic products and both are historically relative.

What this implies is that neither specific observational nor experimental procedures, nor methods of generalization, nor specific logi-codeductive strategies, nor any collection of procedural assumptions or presuppositions, nor any technique of measurement or instrumentation is *absolutely essential* to the method of science. Furthermore, no single existential assertion delivered by scientists, nor any conjunction of such assertions, is *absolutely essential* to the corpus of science. Science is neither a specific collection of procedures nor a specific body of essential truths. Every truth warranting procedure and every truth claim remains, in principle, subject to review—none are specific to science.

Mathematicians do not make observations; geographers are but little concerned with formulating lawlike generalizations; astronomers undertake few, if any, experiments; meteorologists make only the poorest predictions and botanists rarely measure—and yet all are scientists. The products of science have, at various times, characterized our world as being composed of an infinite number of qualitatively identical, irreducible, variously shaped, ceaselessly moving, impenetrable particles, and at other times as being composed of enormously complicated systems of discontinuous positive and negative electrical charges in Hilbert multidimensional space. Science has conceived our spatial environment as Euclidean and then sometimes as non-Euclidean, our local celestial environment as geocentric and then again as heliocentric. Science has argued that man himself is an intricate reflex mechanism, and again (at the same or at other times) that he is an autogenically motivated complex of physical and psychic needs.

In effect, processes and products are identified as "scientific" only by virtue of that system of overlapping and interacting criteria that evidence the complexity and the changing substance of the object of inquiry.

The one feature that we have gradually come to realize as constitutive of science in whatever form it has taken, a feature pervasive of science both as process and product, is its necessary concern with reliability. Without minimal reliability science is impossible, because without minimal reliability interpersonal communication becomes all but inconceivable. Without reliability argument and deliberation cannot proceed. Knowing anything becomes impossible.

Only when a descriptive term is deployed over particulars reliably can we understand assertions about its past, present, and future employments. Without reliability, explaining the past, organizing the present, and anticipating the future becomes impossible and rationality itself is, for all intents and purposes, abandoned. It has been the insistent awareness of these considerations, the recognition of the critical function of reliability, that has motivated the search for verification procedures of *maximal reliability* with respect to *descriptive* claims and *absolute reliability* with respect to *formal* truth claims. In the continuing effort to maximize still further the reliability assigned to descriptive claims and expand the power, range, and effectiveness of our logical apparatus, the procedures employed by science will be constantly subject to review—and with them their linguistic products and the truth status attributed to them.

Our preoccupation with reliability is dictated by the generic human concern with adapting to, and controlling, our complex and changing environment. We find it necessary to anticipate futures—and we do that best by exercising the imagal trial-and-error techniques, and their subtending rationale, that we identify as rational behavior. That behavior necessitates a sensitive awareness of verification procedures for empirical knowledge claims and an appreciation of the formal and informal logic of cognitive discourse.

Science as "Ideology"

Once science is so understood, as a dynamic and self-corrective concern for reliability in procedures and in cognitive yield, it becomes evident that the disposition on the part of some commentators to refer to science as an "ideology," the equivalent of any alternate "ideology" (an equivalence which is a calculated criticism of science), leads not only to confusion, but to serious error as well.

An "ideology," understood in any meaningful sense, is a system of argued beliefs having both specific empirical content and normative intent. Certainly science, at any particular time, constitutes an argued belief system, but science is intrinsically *self-corrective* and has no *essential* substantive content. Not only *can* science alter both its procedures and its products and still remain science—it *must* do so on pain of ceasing to be science. An "ideology" possessed of the same properties would simply not be an ideology. For every ideology there is some particular set of substantive propositions without which it would cease to be *that* ideology. If one rejected, for example, the thesis that race was a significant historical, social, and political variable in any sense, one could not entertain a National Socialist ideology. If one rejected class as a serious historic, social, and political variable, one could hardly entertain a Marxist ideology.

An ideology contains at least some identifiable descriptive propositions that *are* essential to its continued existence as *that* ideology.
Without that specific content the ideology would cease to be that
ideology.

Science, on the other hand, is committed to the recognition that
each and every descriptive proposition, no matter how well-entrenched in contemporary science, is nonetheless, in principle, corrigible
—and is therefore *not* essential to the continued existence of science.
In this sense, science cannot be an ideology. Science is, in principle,
animated by *any* method that can show itself to be maximally
reliable, and composed of all and any linguistic products that are
the consequences of the application of those methods. If intuitions,
mystic insights, the dialectic, phantasy, or whispered intelligences
from God proved to be maximally reliable in permitting men to
empirically adapt to and effectively control their environment, they
would become, *ipso facto,* constituent procedures of science.

The "objectivity" of science implies no more than the employment
of techniques that assign maximally reliable truth status to propositions. Its propositions are "objective" insofar as they are the consequent products of the employment of those techniques. Objectivity
means maximal reliability with respect to empirical truth claims
and demonstrative certainty with respect to formal or analytic
claims. Intersubjective observations, direct or indirect, have provided, in fact, the most reliable warrants for the first, and valid arguments the validating warrant for the second. Children and primitive
peoples very quickly learn the advantages of intersubjective checks
on subjective impression. Intersubjectivity, in effect, was one of the
first and remains one of the necessary conditions of reliability.
Intersubjective observation, direct or indirect, has entrenched itself
as the maximally reliable method of empirical truth determination.
Among all candidate alternatives it has minimized the likelihood
of error. Empirical inquiry is not the kind of pursuit in which error
can be made logically impossible. We can never attain *absolute*
reliability concerning any material truth. But we can maximally
reduce the possibility of empirical or factual error—and intersubjective observation is the necessary condition for accomplishing precisely that.[13]

When propositions are articulated into arguments, the best defense we have developed against flawed conclusions is the employment of the techniques of formal logic. Every child who awaits to have his identifications confirmed or corrected, every scientist who awaits experimental replication and confirmation of his findings by suitably trained peers, has committed himself to the consistency criteria of contemporary logic, and *consistency* reveals itself as the necessary condition of reliability—a domain invariant requirement.

Knowledge claims can only be made in a natural or reconstructed language and language use, when employed for cognitive purpose, is rule governed. As early as antiquity the first efforts were made to standardize just those rules. Aristotelian syllogistic logic was the first major effort to codify them. It was understood that if language was to be used with cognitive intent, consistency in use was a minimal, but necessary, requirement. If prediction was to be of some effect, if generalizations were to serve orientation and adaptation, the general terms which denoted identifiable classes of particulars *had* to evince consistency. If generalizations held conjointly with some specific and specifiable particulars were to provide explanatory and predictive leverage, those procedures which permitted licit transit from premises to valid conclusions had to be specified. Aristotle's syllogistic was the first systematic effort to provide a science of the implications of sentential forms. His efforts were supplemented by the Megarians and the Stoics who delivered what is now sometimes called "sentential logic," the study of logical connectives, particles such as "and" and "or" by virtue of which sentences could be legitimately combined to form new sentences while preserving their truth status. The irregular development of logic proceeded throughout the medieval period until Gottlob Frege developed, at the end of the nineteenth century, the logic of functions or predicate logic, the study of all logical particles.[14]

Since then the developments in logic have provided science with a rigorous technique for insuring consistent articulation and valid derivation without which contemporary physics and computer employments, for example, would be impossible. Formal logic has grown into a science of which the old traditional logic forms only a

fragment. It is now a science of such enormous scope, rigor, and fertility that the most reliable and productive efforts of contemporary science would be faulted without its governance.

Science is maximally reliable because it has at its disposal two progressively refined techniques which provide independent checks upon its claims: 1) observations which elicit involuntary recognitions irrespective of the commitment of the men, individual or collective, involved in inquiry, and 2) tests of internal consistency and licit derivation provided by the rigorous techniques of formal logic. These are the intrinsic devices of self-correction which make science something more than an ideology. Any ideology possessed of the independent techniques of self-correction, cognizant of the corrigibility of its descriptive or substantive claims, and subject to the consistency criteria of formal logic, is no longer an ideology in the generally accepted meaning of the term.

What has been argued is that science is a unique cognitive activity; it is the most reliable method for warranting both empirical and formal truth claims. The necessary conditions involved in establishing maximal reliability invoke direct or indirect appeal to unproblematic assertions about the nonlinguistic object world and tests of logical consistency and licit derivation. Science has no essential content, but is composed, at any specific period, of the collection of assertions that individually enjoy maximal credibility and collectively have the greatest measure of internal and mutually supportive strength.

Against this account there has arisen, in the recent past, a counter thesis that sees science as only one of several "ideological" devices for producing conformity in the young, suppressing dissidence within the knowledge enterprise, and licensing the status quo. Science is not seen as a technique for providing responsible truth ascription, but as a device which is in and of itself essentially non-rational—a device calculated to insure the sovereign privilege of one or another group or groups. Science, in effect, does nothing to certify the truth of propositions, science assigns truth because of extraneous and noncognitive commitments.[15] Science is part of the "Establishment's" calculated efforts to dominate men's minds.

Such a thesis has won considerable support among the disaffected and the professionally disadvantaged. As a thesis it is paradoxical at best. Its central argument is that science cannot make reliable truth ascriptions, that science is, in a radical sense, subjective, unreliable, serving special interests, and that its truths are so characterized only because they serve those special interests. And yet, for all that, those who advance the thesis have themselves discovered the truth that science cannot discover truth.

Science and Objective Truth

The question is, if science cannot certify truth, what certifies the truth of the thesis that science cannot certify truth? Is there a method independent of science that provides more reliable truth ascriptions? If so then *that* method is science and the objects of criticism are but the semblance of science. If the thesis is that there is *no* method for responsibly assigning truth status to propositions, the argument is self-stultifying, since the thesis itself is composed of propositions which individually and collectively claim truth status. One simply cannot have it both ways—but whichever way one chooses to have it, science is restored as the only method available for responsibly assigning maximally reliable truth status.

One way out of the obvious dilemma is to opt for a specially gifted segment of the community that escapes interest-bound "ideology." This is, of course, the escape recommended by Karl Mannheim. Truth is attainable, but it is the privilege of a small community of declassed intellectuals. This "relatively classless stratum" has the advantage of true objectivity. It can discover and license truth because it is relatively untrammelled by prevailing interests.[16]

When the thesis is advanced in this fashion, it simply means that science requires a specific and specifiable technique that would invariably identify instances of individual and collective bias in any pursuit of responsible knowledge about the natural and social world. The evidence of bias might manifest itself, for instance, in the neglect of anomalies unexplained or unattended by research scientists and/or scholars, or by flawed logic in the articulation of arguments. In effect, what such a thesis ultimately culminates in is an admonition that the methods of science should be applied more *rigorously* than has been the case to date—an admonition one can only applaud. We can only identify truth, whatever its source, if we have independent standards which characterize it. That the "relatively classless stratum" is best equipped with such standards and is thus more capable of identifying truth is itself an empirical claim—to be certified by the techniques of standard science which certify *any* descriptive claim.

An alternate, recent, and well-known attempt to throw into question the entire concept of the objectivity of science has been that undertaken by Thomas S. Kuhn. His challenging monograph, *The Structure of Scientific Revolutions,* has been employed by some to discredit any effort to attain objective truth in the field of social and political inquiry. It is at least doubtful that whatever Kuhn says about the natural sciences is transferable without supplementary and special arguments to political inquiry, but for the sake of discussion such a transfer can be countenanced.

Kuhn begins his argument by suggesting that there is something called a "paradigm" which governs activities which he, in turn, calls "normal science." He seems to conceive "paradigms" as involving something like a special and specific research tradition embracing "law, theory, application, and instrumentation together" (Kuhn, *Structure of Scientific Revolutions* [Chicago: University of Chicago, 1962], p. 10). In "preparadigm" periods a science characteristically involves only random research and *ad hoc* scholarly efforts. During its "preparadigm" stages the pursuit of knowledge in a specific universe of inquiry is unsystematic and relatively unstructured. A "paradigm" develops by some "inscrutable" happenstance and constitutes the "promise of success" in some selected and incomplete ranges of concern (pp. 23f., 89). On the appearance of a "paradigm" a science is transmogrified. Once the "paradigm" becomes the dominant research orientation, "normal science" becomes a "puzzle-solving activity," an activity that fulfills the promise, and is in the service, of the paradigm. The paradigm, Kuhn seems to argue in some places, provides not only the "puzzles" to be solved, but the *rules* and *criteria* governing the scientific enterprise itself (p. 42). Science is conceived to be, in some sense, intrinsically paradigm dependent. A paradigm comes to dominate a universe of inquiry by a process that Kuhn seems to feel is remarkably like religious conversion. The scientist gives his "allegiance" to the prevailing or a contending paradigm (p. 150) and to opt for one paradigm rather than another is to make a "transition between incommensurable," like opting for Methodism rather than Roman Catholicism. When paradigms compete for "allegiance," there seems to be "no point at which" resistance to one or the other paradigm becomes "illogical or unscientific" (p. 158). A decision to opt for a contending paradigm "can only be made on faith" (p. 157). The decision to transfer allegiance from one paradigm to another does not involve matters "of proof or error"—"the transfer of allegiance . . . is a conversion experience that cannot be forced" (p. 150).

This kind of reading can be given, unfortunately, to Kuhn's interesting monograph—and there has been a disposition, among some political scientists, to so read it. As a matter of fact a more generous interpretation of Kuhn's account can be provided and, once some of the more hyperbolic utterances Kuhn permits to escape are deflated, his narrative collapses into a variation (still interesting and important) of the standard account of scientific procedures.

First of all, it is not absolutely clear what Kuhn understands by a paradigm. On some occasions in referring to "paradigms," he simply talks of "conceptual schemata."[17] "Paradigms" obviously perform all the functions that we shall see can be attributed to a variety of linguistic entities which can be collectively referred to as "conceptual schemata." Conceptual schemata, as we shall argue, perform all the functions Kuhn attributes to his "paradigms": 1) they provide a schematic guide to research because they are composed of 2) broad theoretical or speculative hypotheses about the object world. Because they characterize the object world in a broad but relatively distinct fashion, they 3) provide the occasion for determining what will count as significant data of observation and, finally, they 4) afford the categories in which relevant data are classified, catalogued, stored, and retrieved. But we shall argue that no one linguistic entity performs *all* these tasks. The schemata involved are many and they all differ in character and degree of sophistication. Kuhn seems disposed to telescope all these schemata under the generic rubric "paradigm." But it is clear that the various linguistic entities housed under this rubric are substantially heterogeneous. On one occasion, for instance, Kuhn speaks of a paradigm "taken from some fraction of everyday discourse" (p. 126). This could hardly be a paradigm that could guide the specific "puzzle-solving" research of the most unsophisticated "normal science."

We shall refer to such conceptual schemata as "ordinary language schemata." They are the artifacts of ordinary language and are beset by all its linguistic vagueness and ambiguity. Only when a scientist shifts to a more sophisticated linguistic level can such a schema begin to function as a "framework," or a "conceptual model," that provides an initial definition of his field of inquiry. Such "frameworks" shall be referred to in the subsequent discussion as "preliminary conceptual schemata"—they suggest speculative hypotheses and begin to isolate certain elements in experience as significant. Certain variables are understood to have causal relevance in the analysis of experience. In the effort to provide evidence for the hypotheses suggested by these preliminary conceptual schemata, a social scientist will be compelled to specify the semantic meaning of critical terms in his hypotheses and reduce the syntactical vagueness of his formulations. As we shall suggest, the result is partial standardization and formalization. What subsequently develops is a partially or fully axiomatized system. In some cases a calculus develops and, once conjoined with coordinating definitions which relate the calculus to the object world, we have a partially or fully articulated standard theory. Such a theory can operate as a "paradigm." Such "paradigms" are to be found in the formalized sciences like physics and chemistry. Political science simply has no "paradigm" of *this* kind (Kuhn seems to recognize this; cf. p. 15 of his text). Political scientists are not involved in "puzzle-solving," because "puzzle-solving" implies, as is clear in Kuhn's account, a viable *theory* covering at least a substantial range of phenomena within a specific universe of inquiry. Political science has no "general theory" of politics that could pass as a "paradigm." At best, even by Kuhn's account, political science is "preparadigmatic."

But more interesting for our purposes here is the analysis of his account of "paradigm-switching" which could be construed as "subjectivistic"—denying to standard science the objectivity which makes it what it is.

If the account of conceptual schemata offered in the foregoing account is correct, then "rules," "standards," and "criteria" which establish the truth of the propositional constituents of a paradigm (or theory) can hardly be by-products of the paradigm itself. Paradigms develop because scholars and research scientists pursue the methods of science . . . and those methods are "trans-paradigmatic." The methods produce paradigms; it is not paradigms that produce methods, rules, standards, or criteria.

Kuhn seems to recognize as much. He regularly refers to "anomalies" which cannot be "explained" within a prevailing paradigm (pp. 6, 33f., 52, 56f., 62, 65, 74f., 81f., 86). These irrepressible anomalies are intersubjective and unproblematic *observations* recognized by practitioners "within" the paradigm—they persist no matter how strong the "allegiance" to the established paradigm. In effect, the acceptance of a paradigm is *contingent*—the measure of its acceptability is a function of its ability to explain and predict the phenomena recognized in critical ordinary observations which must of necessity, be "extraparadigmatic." With the increment in the number of anomalies unexplained by the regnant paradigm, scientists begin to contemplate alternate ways of structuring, in theory, their experience. An alternate paradigm, which is actually an alternate preliminary conceptual schema, is advanced because it is conceived as offering solutions to the problems unresolved by the prevailing paradigm. It is neither "accepted," nor does one give "allegiance" to it. It is advanced as a *candidate* (as yet informal) *theoretical sketch*. To be accepted it would have to go through the stages which we shall characterize more fully in the forthcoming account. Its speculative and loosely worded hypotheses would have to be reformulated into test hypotheses and evidence accumulated that would satisfy intersubjective tests of adequacy. And those tests are not "paradigm dependent."

The "observations" which are referred to as "protocol statements," or "observation statements" do function, at least in part, within the compass of ordinary language, but they are *not* dependent upon the paradigm under scrutiny. The very fact that "anomalies" develop within the prevailing paradigm indicates that not all observations are "paradigm dependent"—if they were, such anomalies would never appear and every paradigm would be forever insulated against empirical disconfirmation. All of which means that paradigms simply cannot be conceived as *sui generis* and incommensurable. Their acceptability is governed by their ability to more effectively explain and predict publicly observable phenomena. Kuhn, himself, says as much in a number of places. A new paradigm *does* succeed in explaining the anomalies that plagued the old paradigm—and predicts those unsuspected by the antecedent paradigm (pp. 152f.). The new paradigm is more fruitful in opening up new areas for detailed inquiry (pp. 10, 103). This indicates that the rules governing *empirical* evidence, explanation, and prediction are "transparadigmatic"—they are the rules of evidence, explanation, and prediction governing standard science—and they are substantially independent of any paradigm.

At various places in his treatment Kuhn, himself, further indicates that rules of evidence and the criteria governing *consistency and logical derivation* are "paradigm independent." He indicates, in fact, that paradigms are measured against logical criteria of consistency and simplicity (pp. 153f.). All of which indicates, if it indicates anything, that *logic* and *empirical evidence criteria* subtend science *in general* and are *not* paradigm specific.

What Kuhn seems to be arguing is that an *initial conceptual* schema cannot meet the test of evidence and yet is advanced on the *supposition that it will resolve the logical and observational perplexities* which infect an antecedent paradigm. That such a preliminary schema is offered and acted upon, he describes, unhappily, in terms of acting "on faith." But such an "act of faith" is similar to an "intuition" or an "insight," which suggests a particular manner of conceiving problems. No "intuition" is born in "faith." It is the result of long familiarity with the procedures of standard science.[18] "Intuitions" are elaborate "hunches," guided largely by what one has learned about a particular universe of inquiry. It is true that each candidate preliminary schema is offered in the *hope* that it will facilitate the resolution of problems, provide the schematic guide for research, suggest test hypotheses, afford taxonomies and classificatory schemata serviceable to the identification, storage, and retrieval of information, and constitute a mnemonic convenience to the cataloguing of information. But a preliminary conceptual schema, one logical level removed from the schemata that inhabit ordinary language, cannot hope to "prove" its utility. Only a fully articulated *theory* can do that.

To call all schemata "paradigms" is to obscure the many and significant differences between a variety of linguistic artifacts each having different evidence conditions and theoretical yield. When a fully articulated *theory* meets the evidence criteria of standard science, it is unreasonable *not* to accept it. And this is precisely what Kuhn says (pp. 30, 146, 157). He says that the Newtonian paradigm was finally accepted by the scientists of the eighteenth century—and that they "had every reason to do so" (p. 30). Similarly, in his volume on the Copernican revolution, Kuhn argues that the Ancients refused to countenance the heliocentric conception of the universe advanced by Aristarchus and, because of its *prima facie* implausibility, the lack of confirming evidence, its inability to predict phenomena, and its logical peccability, they had "every reason to do so."[19] If men have "every reason" to accept or reject alternate paradigms, one wonders what "conversion" or "opting on faith" have to do with the cognitive process of discriminating between alternative paradigms. The fact is that the evidence requirements for accepting a *preliminary conceptual schema* are different than those for entertaining a *formal theory*. Newton offered a reasonably well-articulated *theory;* Aristarchus offered, at best, a *preliminary conceptual schema*. The fact that the highly modified analogue of Aristarchus' heliocentric conception ultimately proved acceptable to the scientific community means that "brilliant insights," "intuitions" and "hunches" *may* be true—just as the evolutionary notions of pre-Socratic and Lucretian speculation have proved more akin to contemporary conceptions of the evolution of species that the Aristotelian and Linnean concepts of persistence of species. But a clear distinction must be made between preliminary conceptual schemata, often brilliant and suggestive, but too vague and general to be confirmed or disconfirmed—and extensively formalized theories which are subject to logical and empirical truth conditions. To call all the linguistic entities advanced by thinkers "paradigms" is to obscure fundamental differences between them. Where no distinctions are made—anything can be said . . . unfortunately with little cognitive profit.

One can admit therefore almost everything Kuhn says and yet not submit to his notion that paradigms cannot be subject to "transparadigmatic" evidence conditions. As has been suggested, the fact that anomalies develop within prevailing paradigms is clear evidence that observations are made with relative independence of them. Furthermore, that paradigms are subjected to logical scrutiny indicates that not only critical observations, but logical procedures, have an independence of paradigms.

It is clearly the case that "faith," "interests," and "parascientific commitments" figure in the acceptance and rejection of alternate conceptions of man and society. This is an interesting and significant *sociological* and *psychological* fact. But such considerations have nothing whatever to do with the analysis of the admissibility conditions governing truth ascriptions. The fact that men permit non-cognitive concerns to influence their judgments is a well-known and generally acknowledged fact; but that it is, *in principle,* impossible to isolate those influences is a claim that has *not* been established. A distinction must be recognized between *performance* and *competence.* Many natural and social scientists, indeed whole political cultures, admit "truths" only if they conform to some religious, political, or philosophical prejudice. But the fact that men so perform does not constitute evidence that they can *only* so perform.[20] Kuhn's indisposition to make the necessary distinction between the *logic of discovery*—how men have tended, in fact, to argue about alternate interpretations of nature and man—and the normative and prescriptive *logic of justification* thwarts analysis and confuses issues (cf. pp. 8f.).

We accept a proposition, or an articulated collection of propositions, not on impulse, intuition, or faith—if we pretend to be rational—but rather because it fits coherently within a system of funded credibilities, themselves warranted, individually and collectively, directly and indirectly, by best evidence. Best evidence for *empirical* claims refers to assertions about matters of fact that survive the scrutiny of intersubjective assessment. These are the "protocol utterances" of natural language. The import of such utterances is always directly or indirectly referential. We anticipate futures through them. We utter them because some experiential cues tell us that we have an instance of some identifiable class of objects before us. If our anticipations concerning them are fulfilled, we say our utterance was confirmed. If we fail to satisfy anticipations, we review the system of credibilities in which that utterance is lodged and which contributed to its articulation. The ultimate purpose of all this activity is to permit us greater reliable leverage on life and experience. We understand because we can predict and explain. We can predict and explain because we can make significant and recurrent discriminations in practice. We guide this activity with formal and informal logic and inductive procedures. The entire program is that of standard science.

Science, Ethics, and Political Science

There is no intrinsic reason why this program cannot include ethical concerns. Matters of ethical moment, for example, can be studied as the subject matter of empirical science. Ethical utterances can become the first-order constituents of a second-order scrutiny (when we analyze ethical language in metaethics), and we can seek out the meaning and implications of ethical "principles" using standard techniques of analysis, descriptive and probability assessment. All these activities are eminently cognitive—and it is doubtful if there are any human concerns which are irreducibly and forever outside their ken.

Political inquiry is an informal discipline. Much of its research and scholarly activity is fragmentary and seemingly random. Individuals and groups of individuals pursue some special concern with the techniques suitable to their purpose. There are those preoccupied with axiomatizing some or another area of inquiry—and their preoccupations are essentially analytic. There are those who are concerned with how participants in the political processes actually do behave, or they are concerned with how they might behave under certain initial conditions. Their activity concerns itself with adequate description and, more frequently than not, low-level prediction. Their concerns are essentially descriptive. There are those who focus on the values men harbor or pretend to harbor. They seek out the vindications that men might offer to support one or another vision of the world and of men and their society. They are concerned with the issuance and support of normative utterances. This is perhaps one of the least understood areas of political concern. But the efforts that characterize this activity are essentially cognitive and science, broadly conceived, constitutes its substance.

To have characterized these distinct domains of concern is not to suggest that they are mutually exclusive even if exhaustive of the preoccupations that animate political inquiry. There is a complex and important interaction between these analytically discrete domains. Very frequently those concerned with analytic preoccupations hold naive and irresponsible normative commitments—and succeed in drawing, as a consequence, illicit conclusions from their inquiries. Similarly, and more frequently, this is the case with empirical political scientists who claim that their undertakings are "value free" in some vague and unspecified sense. On the other hand, many political theorists, who claim special competence in the normative domain of inquiry, simply lapse into confusion and conjure up a new obscurantism which reduces serious concern for political issues to a contest between "ultimate values" which are the gift of "faith," "phantasy" and/or the "dialectic."

Political science is a coherent and unified concern with political life. Because it is informal, minimally standardized, and possessed of only a restricted inventory of confirmed generalizations and can exhibit no general theory which covers its universe of discourse, its inquiries, for the foreseeable future, will be defined in a variety of ways and its pursuits will be, in large measure, significatly influenced by the personal concerns of individual scholars and research personnel. But subtending all this activity are implicit rules governing truth ascription—rules which make the activity coherent and its results cumulative. The task of making those rules explicit is arduous, sometimes thankless, and in a substantial sense endless.

Those rules originate in the life process itself—and life is an ongoing activity. In attempting to characterize that protean activity we employ language and we do not, and cannot, have an ideally anti-septic language that fails to give rise to confusions and creates no paradoxes. But this does not constitute an argument that because natural language is vague and the source of confusion and paradox—vagueness, confusion, and paradox are to be embraced as truths truer than true.

Political science is, at best, a partially formalized and standardized science, a corrigible and self-corrective pursuit of propositions of maximal reliability concerning political matters (however defined). It is a pursuit governed by the reasonably well understood *domain invariant criteria of logic* and the *domain variant criteria of empirical research, theory construction, and ethics.* Its successes, by whatever standards, have been relatively modest—but whatever successes it has enjoyed have been achieved through the use of standard science broadly conceived. Neither the addiction to linguistic magic nor the advent of a new obscurantism can confound that fact. We do know a great deal more about man's political life and his political behavior today than we did a generation ago. Our future success will be contingent on our ability to effectively employ the corrigible methods of contemporary science, on our ability to refine those methods, and on our capacity to more cognitively assess our needs, aspirations, and conflicting desires as human beings. There are no magic formulas nor guarantees of success. There is only the prospect of hard and collaborative enterprise.

Science, Political Inquiry, and Metapolitics

If there is any merit in the preceding discussion, it trafficks on an analysis of several key concepts: "science," "objectivity," and "conceptual schemata" among the most critical. It is equally evident that the issues involved and the concepts employed require far more substantial treatment if the analysis is to be convincing. The point of this introductory essay into the issues that seem to invoke so much contemporary energy is to convey an appreciation of the fact that before the student of political inquiry can address himself to the "significant" concerns that beset the discipline, it is necessary to gain a foothold on the rudiments of cognitive activity itself. In order to accomplish that, it is necessary to unpack terms in common currency—terms whose meaning seems to be intuitively understood but whose meaning seems to become more variable in direct proportion to the frequency of their use.

There is, in fact, a catalogue of terms that the student of political inquiry employs, each of which has a variable, vague, and ambiguous meaning. The term "meaning," itself, has variable, vague, and ambiguous meaning. Similarly, terms like "truth," "law," "theory," "explanation," "model," "understanding," "knowing," "normative," and "noncognitive," have elusive and fugitive meanings. Before meaningful discussion can take place between participants in the enterprise we identify as political inquiry, some initial moves must be made to reduce the variance that characterizes too much of our talk.

What this means is that linguistic analysis is a necessary preliminary to political inquiry if we are to attempt any adequate assessment of the diffuse and complex issues that agitate political inquiry. If we are to more competently pursue any of the issues joined in this introductory discussion, we shall have to address ourselves to the conceptual language with which such a discussion must be conducted. In effect we shall employ a metalanguage to discuss the language of political inquiry. Hopefully what will result will be insight into the implicit and explicit rules governing man's most distinctive and successful cognitive activities. It will be, at best, a foray into a vast and poorly charted territory—a brief introduction to metapolitics.

Notes

[1] R. Dahl, "The Behavioral Approach in Political Science: Epitaph for a Monument to a Successful Protest," *American Political Science Review, 55* (December, 1961), 763–771, reprinted in N.W. Polsby, R. A. Dentler, and P. A. Smith (eds.), *Politics and Social Life* (Boston: Houghton Mifflin, 1963), pp. 15–25 (subsequent citations will be made to this republication).

[2] R. Kirk, "Segments of Political Science not Amenable to Behavioristic Treatment," and M. Sibley, "The Limitations of Behavioralism," in J. C. Charlesworth (ed.), *The Limitations of Behavioralism in Political Science* (Philadelphia: American Academy of Political and Social Science, 1962), pp. 49–67 and pp. 68–93. Kirk's article has been reprinted in N. P. Guild and K. T. Palmer, *Introduction to Politics* (New York: Wiley, 1968), pp. 290–305, and Sibley's in J. C. Charlesworth (ed.), *Contemporary Political Analysis* (New York: Free Press, 1967), pp. 51–71 (subsequent references will be made to these republications). H. J. Storing (ed.), *Essays on the Scientific Study of Politics* (New York: Holt, Rinehart and Winston, 1962).

[3] Cf. C. A. McCoy and J. Playford, *Apolitical Politics: A Critique of Behavioralism* (New York: Crowell, 1967).

[4] H. Schoeck and J. Wiggins (eds.), *Scientism and Values* (New York: Van Nostrand, 1960).

[5] "In essence . . . the typical behaviorist's idea of justice is a vulgarized Marxism." Kirk, *op. cit.,* p. 299. McCoy and Playford, *op. cit.,* p. 3. With respect to the putative Marxist origins of behavioralism, see the criticisms of the Storing volume by J. Schaar and S. Wolin, "Essays on the Scientific Study of Politics: A Critique," *American Political Science Review, 57,* 1 (March, 1963), p. 139.

[6] L. Strauss, "An Epilogue," in Storing, *op. cit.,* p. 322. Cf. Kirk, *op. cit.,* pp. 294ff.

[7] Cf. H. S. Kariel, "Social Science as Autonomous Activity," in Schoeck and Wiggins, *op. cit.,* pp. 239f., 244; L. von Bertalanffy, "The Psychopathology of Scientism," *Ibid.,* p. 205; K. W. Kim, "The Limits of Behavioral Explanation in Politics," in

McCoy and Playford, *op. cit.*, p. 39.

8 Sibley insists that some of the fundamental questions concerning politics "cannot be answered scientifically." Answers must be sought in a combination of imaginative and "unscientific" reconstruction of the past. Sibley, *op. cit.*, p. 66. That behavioralistic political science fails to be sufficiently "scientific" is the principal thrust of articles like that of R. Strausz-Hupé, "Social Science Versus the Obsession of 'Scientism,'" in Schoeck and Wiggins, *op. cit.*, pp. 219–234, particularly p. 227.

9 Cf. "Preface" to Storing, *op. cit.*, p. v, and Sibley, *op. cit.*, n. 8.

10 For a more extensive treatment of "range" or "criterial definitions," cf. M. Black, *Problems of Analysis: Philosophical Essays* (Ithaca: Cornell University, 1954), pp. 24–27; cf. also M. Scriven, "Definitions, Explanations, and Theories," in H. Feigl, M. Scriven and G. Maxwell, *Minnesota Studies in the Philosophy of Science* (Minneapolis: University of Minnesota, 1958), III, pp. 105f.

11 D. Easton, "The Current Meaning of 'Behavioralism,'" in Charlesworth, *Contemporary Political Analysis*, pp. 14–17. These are essentially the criterial attributes identified by R. Dahl and V. Van Dyke, *Political Science: A Philosophical Analysis* (Stanford: Stanford University, 1960), p. 159.

12 Cf. M. Black, "The Definition of Scientific Method," *Problems of Analysis: Philosophical Essays* (Ithaca: Cornell, 1954), p. 13; R. Rudner, *Philosophy of Social Sciences* (Englewood Cliffs: Prentice-Hall, 1966), pp. 76f.

13 Cf. R. Rudner, *Philosophy of Social Science*, pp. 73–83.

14 Cf. W. Kneale and M. Kneale, *The Development of Logic* (Oxford: Clarendon Press, 1962).

15 Cf. 1. Scheffler, *Science and Subjectivity* (New York: Bobbs-Merrill, 1967), chap. 4.

16 K. Mannheim, *Ideology and Utopia* (New York: Harcourt Brace, 1936), pp. 154f.

17 T. S. Kuhn, *The Copernican Revolution* (New York: Random House, 1959), p. 41.

18 Cf. Kuhn, *The Copernican Revolution*, pp. 41f.

19 *Ibid.*, pp. 42f.

20 Cf. I. Sheffler, *Science and Subjectivity*, pp. 88f.

Suggested Readings

Bunge, Mario. *Intuition and Science.* Englewood Cliffs, N. J.: Prentice-Hall, 1962.

Murphy, Joseph. *Political Theory: A Conceptual Analysis.* Homewood, Ill.: Dorsey Press, 1968. Chapter seven.

Sheffler, Israel. *Science and Subjectivity.* New York: Bobbs-Merrill, 1967.

3

On the Meaning of "Meaning" and "Truth"

For a *large* class of cases—though not for all—in which we employ the word "meaning" it can be defined thus: the meaning of a word is its use in the language.

Ludwig Wittgenstein

No words in our language are abused with such abandon and with such frequency as "meaning" and "truth." Few are put to more persuasive uses. Few invoke more emotions and deploy more approbation. Without "meaning" words are mere sounds, sentences are vacuous, enterprises are demeaned, life has no substance. All become the objects of polite disdain and urbane or less urbane opprobrium. "Meaning" and "truth" are two of the most frequently exploited terms of general commendation—following only "good" and "nice" in frequency and range of employment—but there are perhaps few in ordinary discourse that have less specific or specifiable meaning. So systematically ambiguous are the terms in ordinary usage that their meaning is less than diaphanous; they seem to enjoy less substance than "idea"—appear more infinitely variable than "conceptual"—yet command as much positive emotional salience as "virtue" or "honor." As obscure as the terms "meaning" and "truth" are, they nonetheless appear with predictable regularity in the literature of political inquiry. Even a modest concern for our intellectual obligations recommends that some attempt at analysis be undertaken, for any activity that does not pretend to give issue to "meaning" and "truth" is no activity at all.

The Various Meanings of "Meaning" and "Truth"

Early in the present century C. K. Ogden and I. A. Richards indicated that the term "meaning" enjoyed at least sixteen separately identifiable meanings, among the most prominent being the connotation of a word; an activity projected into an object; an event intended, or a volition, or intention; the practical implications of a thing for future experience; the theoretical implications implied by a statement; the emotion elicited by anything; the associations invoked by a stimulus; what a sign, symbol, or stimulus suggests; that to which the sign or symbol refers; that to which the sign user should be referring; that to which a sign user believes himself to be referring; and finally (though not exhaustively) the function of something.[1] C. E. Osgood, G. J. Suci, and P. H. Tannenbaum, in attempting to summarize the various meanings of "meaning," restrict their considerations to 1) meaning as characterized by the formal or structural relation of signs to other signs (rather than the denotative meaning of the signs themselves) in the rule-governed relations of a language (*syntactical meaning*); 2) denotative, referential, or designative meaning (*semantic meaning*); and 3) the relation of signs to psychosociological situations and behaviors *(pragmatic meaning)*.[2]

Syntax concerns itself with formal or structural aspects of language: the formation rules that specify the catalogue of available signs, indicate what combinations of signs are permissible as well-formed sentences, and transformation rules—those rules that govern which signs can be substituted for alternate signs without changing the meaning or truth of a sentence and which tell us which sentences may be derived from others. A syntactical concern ideally occupies itself with the formal properties of sentences rather than their descriptive content. It will be restricted to a study of formation and transformation rules, activities which identify prototypic sentences, the form of true sentences and their permissible derivations. *Semantics,* in turn, concerns itself with those implicit or explicit rules that make it possible to assign descriptive or designative meaning to signs and sign-complexes and exhibit the truth conditions for empirical assertions. *Pragmatics,* finally, directs its attention to the investigation of language as a human activity, not only its specific cognitive uses, but also its emotional, volitional, and other essentially private psychological effects. Pragmatics also concerns itself with the action, circumstances of the action, and outcomes which obtain on the occasion of linguistic use.

This triune typology seems not only to characterize the categories to which "meaning" can be assigned, to illuminate most of the characteristic uses of ordinary language, but to follow the stipulative and explicative usage suggested by semiotics (or semiology), the science of signs, as well.[3]

"Truth," in turn, has entertained a similar multiplicity of meanings. It has been understood 1) to signify a relationship between an utterance and an eternal and immutable "form"; 2) to signify a state of mind, an intuition, or a demonstration; 3) to refer to the "coherence" or logical consistency of a body of propositions; and finally 4) to signify a relationship between an utterance and some "state of affairs."

Only by attempting to sort out the meanings of "meaning" and "truth" that attend the various and varying uses of the terms can we begin to seriously understand interpersonal utterances. Expressions like, "You don't know what the overthrow of Nkrumah *meant* to me," "Do you have any idea what nuclear proliferation *means?*" and "Did you understand the *meaning* of the *Communist Manifesto?*" indicate that "meaning" and its derivatives have a variety of distinguishable and intelligible meanings for students of politics—all subject to different truth conditions. In general we know how to entertain, respond to, question, and assess such employments. It is only when we abandon the scrutiny of its various employments and give ourselves over to the search for *the* putative "Meaning" (spelled with a suitable capital) that subtends all the token uses of the sign that we lapse into unintelligibility. On the other hand, when we use the term expressively rather than cognitively, for example, when we speak of "*the* meaning of it *all*" or in similar uses, intelligible meaning escapes us. Upon such occasions, the Wittgensteinian might say, language goes on holiday.

The judgmental "true" is similarly deployed over a variety of linguistic entities: "McCarthy's political instincts were *true*," "It is *true* that the sense of political alienation increases with the complexity of the political infrastructure," and "The conclusion that '6' follows from '3+3' is *true*."

We shall see that unqualified and/or corrigible truth ascriptions can be made and warranted in the case of analytic and synthetic statements—and we all intuit something of the meaning, and can assign some measure of truth, to sentence types in which expressions like "*true* blue," "his aim was *true*," "he had *true* instincts," and "tried and *true*" appear. In such circumstances we seek to appreciate the use or function of such signs in the language. It is only when we make our concern the discovery of *the* "Truth" (spelled with a capital T) that we find ourselves embroiled in mystery.

It is as though someone wished to know the "meaning" of the word "time" in our language, and was informed that the word was used in complete sentences to solicit responses which referred to the various positions taken by the hands of a watch, shadows on sundials, the distribution of sand in hourglasses, dates on calendars, or the movements of planetary and sidereal bodies in one or another reference system—what the sign "time" means in some logically related set of propositions—or that it was used metaphorically in expressions like "giving him the time of day"—and having heard such an explication were to ask, "Yes, but what does 'Time' (spelled with the honorific capital) mean?" "Time" means, in terms of *signification,* nothing more and nothing less than the adequate characterization of its public employments as a sign in the language. Whatever else "time" "means" to each individual in terms of private and variable significance is treated as part of its pragmatic meaning, its subjective psychological import. The failure to appreciate the fact that words have *public meaning* insofar as they have a *public use,* an intersubjective role in the language, and truth insofar as they have such meaning, has been father to any number of fictive problems which want not solution but dissolution.

The various uses of "meaning" and "truth" can be explicated—

the meaning of "Meaning" and "Truth" (spelled with capitals) cannot. When we are asked what the advent of George Wallace to the Presidency of the United States might mean, there are a number of licit "meanings" that might appropriately be attributed to such a query. We might take it to mean that he would become "Chief Executive" of the United States. Such a determination would follow *analytically*—by definition—from the fact that he had become "President." The transformation rules governing the sign "President" in our language permit the substitution of the sign "Chief Executive" without loss of meaning or impairment of truth status in any sentence in which the sign "President" functions. Intuitively, however, we generally take such a question to concern itself with the *descriptive implications* of his advent to that office. The advent of Wallace to the Presidency might be construed as making highly probable an increase in racial strife or, among other possibilities, the passing of the traditional two-party system. Such judgments would constitute *synthetic claims,* predictions made with as much confidence as the evidence which warrants them. Finally an utterance like, "What is *the* meaning of his election?" might constitute a simple personal lament, the issuance of an expressive statement which calls for no response, but is calculated to elicit from us a doleful sigh or a lugubrious "Oh God!" What may be requested of us on such occasions is not so much an answer to a cognitive query, but empathic commiseration.

Linguistic Competence and Linguistic Performance

In effect, if we recognize a question about meaning to be *cognitive* rather than *expressive,* we attempt to search out some indication of the public function of the sign in a specific sign vehicle, or the public function of the sign complex itself, in some reasonably specific context. *Knowing something of their public function, we would know something of the rules governing their intersubjective meaning and the conditions which might warrant their truth.* If their function is one which can appropriately support truth ascription, we attempt to characterize the rules governing that ascription. If the use *is* cognitive, some rules would have to be forthcoming if we are to establish meaning and assign truth responsibly. If "meaning" is to be accorded a new or new meanings, it is incumbent upon those who would so employ it to give some indication of the rules governing its use and the ways of establishing truth when meaning is so conceived.

Signs and sign complexes have varied and various meanings. "Meaning," itself, has various meanings. As we shall suggest, even social scientists frequently telescope the explicative, definitional, implicative, explanatory, and psychological meanings of "meaning"—to their own and everyone else's confusion. Badly formulated and loosely jointed arguments, freighted with obscure, vague, and ambiguous meanings strung into exotic sentences— whatever their noncognitive functions—do little to assist in the intellectual enterprise.

Implicit in such suggestions is a distinction between linguistic *competence* and linguistic *performance*. We are all lamentably familiar with gross confusions which result from the failure to felicitously employ the language. Locutionary acts can be faulted, in fact and in principle, in a variety of ways. They can be undone by dispositions (entertained for whatever reason) to obscure, confuse, titillate, gull, incense, and manipulate. They can be faulted by psychic disabilities such as stupidity, disinterest, fallibility, impaired perception, as well as by intercultural and interpersonal contextual variation, socialization, and tacitly held presuppositions and auxiliary assumptions. Attempts at semantic, syntactic, and pragmatic rigor are calculated to produce criteria for characterizing linguistic *competence*—ideally independent of such extraneous dispositional, psychological, and contextual variables.

The more clearly such measures of competence are formulated, the more specific the interaction of these several and individual factors can be, in principle, isolated. Moreover, the more rigorously the standards of competence are specified, the more evident will be whatever obscurity, imprecision, and inappropriateness attend them. The indisposition to search for and specify the public criteria for linguistic competence and attendant truth ascription is not therefore (as it is sometimes characterized) a defense of "creativity" or "freedom of expression"—but a conscious or unconscious abdication to caprice and obscurantism. Not only is cognitive communication and truth ascription impossible outside the context of rule-governed speech acts, but the most compelling and precious products of the knowledge enterprise and human creativity are those that have been consequent upon the systematic efforts to reduce the vaguenesses, reifications, tense obscurities, and ambiguities that afflict ordinary speech and understanding. The most characteristic feature of those linguistic entities we identify as "contemporary science," for example, is a systematic reduction of semantic and syntactic variance through at least partial standardization and formalization of language use. The discovery, accumulation, processing, interpretation, storage, communication, and use of reliable knowledge requires the publicity and neutrality of specified or specifiable rules of successful employment. The creativity exhibited in such performances is evidence of *competence*. Creative language use requires common rules that afford infinitely varied permutations of sign elements and a specification of their interrelations and referents in determinate contexts. Only then is the product both creative and cognitive. The specific measure of such successful performance is provided through a conscious appreciation of the semantic, syntactic, and pragmatic rules common to the language community.

We have no reason to expect that all men will respect the implicit or explicit rules of proper linguistic employments, but we have a moral and intellectual obligation not to be duped or confused by their defective performance or to characterize such performances as "creative."

The Meaning of "Meaning" and "Truth"

For the purposes of our discussion we shall employ the following working definition of "meaning": "the meanings of signs and sign-complexes are to be revealed in how one characterizes their employments, or variously, their use or function."[4] This leaves the specific "meaning" of specific signs to be determined by the circumstances governing instances of their respective uses. What one has offered is a *procedural rule* rather than a characterizing definition.

The virtues that recommend such a preliminary move in the effort to explicate the concepts "meaning" and "truth" include 1) its evident tolerance, and 2) its economy, for the generality of the procedural rule explicating meaning covers all signs employed in the language—including "truth" as well. If we wish to determine the meaning of "truth," we can begin by observing how *it* is deployed in the language. We seek to establish *its* meaning.

One of the most unproblematic instances of its use is when we assign the ascription "true" to utterances which make no reference to any conceivable state of affairs. To say that the assertion "There are four prime numbers greater than 1, between 1 and 10" is true is to say that there are true statements whose truth requires no appeal to evidence statements which have as their referents any state or states of affairs in the object world. The truth status of such assertions depends on the *definitions* of "prime" and "number." Assertions which depend for their truth status on explicit and recursive definition constitute a special class of candidates for truth ascription. Any descriptive signs they contain function vacuously. They are true because they are substitution instances of logical truths— utterances which we can loosely describe as "true by definition"— true because of the transformation rules governing language use rather than any substantive, descriptive claims they make.

One does not certify the truth of the assertion that "all four-sided figures are quadrilaterals" by making observations on the world. Such assertions are true "by definition."[5] One says nothing about the object world by asserting that "all four-sided figures are quadrilaterals." *If* there are any four-sided figures in the world—they are quadrilaterals—by definition. Similarly if a political scientist defines "system" as "any aggregate of interactions that we choose to identify" and then tells us that "society" or the "polity" is a "system,"[6] he has told us very little about the world. *He has told us how he employs some signs in the language.* If there is a "society" or a "polity" (and it would be hard to conceive a "society" or a "polity" anything less than "any aggregate of interactions"), then that "society" is, by definition, a "system." Such assertions are true, but they are true because of some linguistic properties they exhibit and not because they inform us in any significant sense about the object world.

The meaning of "true" in such employments is revealed in how the term functions in the language. Some assertions are true because they possess certain linguistic properties—when, for example, whatever is asserted in the predicate of the sentence is already implied in the subject. "All four-sided figures are quadrilaterals" is true because having said "four-sided figures" one has implicitly said "quadrilaterals." For some political scientists, similarly, to say "society" is to say, by definition, "system." Such truths are commonly spoken of in the literature as *analytic truths,* assertions whose truth is determined by a consideration of sign meanings, rather than any observations made on the world. Analytic truths are truths determined by inspection of the formal or structural relation of signs to other signs (rather than any empirical meaning the signs may have). In that sense analytic truths are syntactical. To determine the syntactical meaning of a sign or sign-complex is to appreciate the evidence conditions for certifying its truth—and the evidence for such truths is found in the intralinguistic properties of the assertion itself and the signs it harbors.

One of the standard uses of the term "true" is that ascription made to "logical truths," truths determined by the rules governing language use itself.

Conjoined with such use is another standard use to which the term "true" is put—when the ascription "true" is credited to descriptive assertions, statements which make some knowledge claim about the object world. When a political scientist claims that "The more rigid the stratification of the society, the more likely it is that class-orientated parties will emerge," and he defines "stratification" *independently* of "class-orientated parties," he is making a substantive (descriptive or empirical) knowledge claim. Its truth or falsity is not determined by the linguistic properties of the assertion itself, but is determined, to speak in the language of ordinary discourse, by a relationship presumed to obtain between the assertion and some state of affairs in the object world. The political scientist is claiming that where a complex something characterized by intersubjectively observable properties ("rigid stratification") obtains, it is highly probable that something else independently defined by characterizing properties ("class-orientated parties"), will "emerge."

The first condition for making truth ascription in such a case is establishing what constitutes its empirical confirmation or disconfirmation. Truths warranted by observations made on the object world are "synthetic truths." The truth of such assertions is warranted by specifying the semantic meaning of the signs used to refer to the objects under scrutiny and then confirming the requisite "state of affairs." The objects under scrutiny can be *concreta,* directly observable physical entities (like persons, tables, chairs); *constructs,* construed entities not directly observable, but which are characterized by observable properties (objects like "the state," "the government," "classes," "class-orientated parties," "society," "stratified societies," and so forth); or *theoretical entities,* which are not directly observable, but are only possessed of indirectly observable properties (like Freud's "Id" or "Superego"). If we can determine the semantic meaning of such signs and sign complexes, we can anticipate what will count as evidence for the truth status of sentences which contain them. The determination of semantic meaning is indispensable in determining the synthetic truth of substantive propositions.

In effect, the responsible scrutiny of truth warrants for single assertions or collections of assertions requires a technique for distinguishing between at least two classes of truth claims, each class occupying, for the sake of analysis, a distinct domain: the analytic and synthetic.[7] The truth of an assertion is certified by its warrant—and there can be *genuine* or *counterfeit* warrants. The analytic/synthetic distinction is indispensable in the inspection of truth claims. Some of the difficulties that afflict the literature of political inquiry exemplify the consequences of a failure to make this distinction. Analytic truth is established by inspecting the logical properties of assertions in which they appear. Only descriptive (i.e., empirical or synthetic) truth claims can be verified by observations; analytic claims are validated by inspecting their linguistic properties. Descriptive claims are probability statements—of a high or low order of probability—but probability statements nonetheless. They remain forever *corrigible*. Analytic truths are *necessarily true*—but they purchase their certainty at the expense of content. When the political scientist, preoccupied with formalization, identifies a "set" as "a number of things (names, numbers, objects, symbols, species . . . in fact, entities of any kind, countable or uncountable, real or imaginary) taken together for any reason"—he has not succeeded in telling us anything about the object world. He has informed us about a specific linguistic employment. To identify a number of things taken together for any reason as a "set" is "true" insofar as it is true by stipulative definition. Why such strategies are invoked will become more apparent in the course of our account. For the time being our purpose is to identify a peculiar order of truth—that characteristic of the formal domain of discourse. Any collection of things taken together for any reason can be felicitously called a "set" because such use accords itself with the stipulative rules governing the use of the term. The *definiens* (the defining phrase) can be consistently substituted for the *definiendum* (the term, sign, or sign complex to be defined) without loss of meaning or truth. Analytic assertions are irretrievably about the language and, although they are true, assert nothing, necessarily, about the properties of the extralinguistic world.

Empirical assertions, on the other hand, contribute to funded knowledge of the object world. Empirical or "substantive" propositions pretend to tell us something about the "external" world. While the subsequent discussion of such truths will accede to ordinary usage by making the truth of a descriptive assertion the function of the "correspondence" between the assertion and "facts" or "states of affairs" in the object world, it should be borne in mind that such truths might be more defensibly characterized not as a "correspondence" between some assertion, P, and some state or states of affairs in the object world, but rather by saying that the warrant for the truth status of the assertion, P, is the expression of an observation statement, S, or observation statements, $S_1 \ldots S_n$ — the explicit *assertion* of it or them in some language.

When a descriptive assertion is true, there is, of course, a state of affairs which makes it true and which is necessarily distinct from the putative truth claim about it, but one can only *describe that state in language*. A true assertion is warranted (or more appropriately expressed, evidenced) by the occasion of a descriptive utterance or utterances. To speak about a "state of affairs" is a compendious way of *talking* about the world—which means we never compare truth claims with the "world" (whatever that might mean). What we compare are *truth claims* and *assertions elicited by perceptual activity* (the identification of empirical *indicators*). The sentence used in asserting the truth claim is true if, and only if, the assertion which expresses a factual condition holds. To say that the assertion which expresses a factual condition "holds" is to indicate, minimally, that *intersubjective confirmation* of some specific observations is forthcoming: under unproblematic contextual conditions some specifiable perceptual stimuli would elicit the same confirming assertion from any similarly circumstanced observer. Which means that not only is material (or empirical) truth (as distinct from formal or logical truth) forever corrigible, it is also *mediate*—it is mediated by language, for only assertions, locutionary acts, can be true or false, and only confirming utterances can be their warrant. The world itself does not harbor truth or falsity—truth and falsity is predicative of linguistic assertions.

Language and Observation

It is important to appreciate the significance of such (admittedly imprecise) considerations, for they provide insights into the character of contemporary analytic philosophy, the philosophy of science, and metapolitics itself. Assertions are made only in language, and without the conceptual apparatus afforded by language any "experience" and "observation" is impossible. There is *naive* observation, and *sophisticated* observation, that is to say, descriptive assertions in ordinary language and assertions in *standardized* or *partially standardized* (assertions in which semantic variance is reduced) and *formalized* or *partially formalized* (assertions in which syntactical variance is reduced) languages. The naive observer "sees" traces on a photographic plate; the sophisticated observer "sees" *electron* traces. Each operates at a different linguistic and epistemic level (and in a different context). Physicists might well say, and feel warranted in saying, "The creation of two electron-positron pairs was *observed*," while the college freshman could only report he hadn't *observed* anything like *that*. Observation statements are inevitably assertions conjointly determined by the impact of physical stimuli on receptor or proprioceptor organs *and* the structure of the natural or reconstructed language in which they find expression.[8]

What this means is that assertions about the "object world" are inevitably mediated by language. Charles Sanders Peirce early suggested that the meaning of a descriptive sign or symbol having an empirical referent consists of the total of all general expectations which, conditionally upon *all the possible different circumstances,* are implied in entertaining the sign or symbol.[9] One set of possible circumstances governing meaning in this sense is the language in which the assertion is formulated. That is to say, as Ogden and Richards insisted as early as 1923, that every assertion about the object world involves some measure of interpretation. The "sign-situation" involves perceptual stimuli encoded, recorded, stored, decoded, and communicated in and by language.[10] Even the most insistent "objectivists," those who insist that true empirical assertions "correspond" to some objective features of the external world, have understood that

> Sentences and sequences of sentences of ordinary language correspond only to vaguely delineated areas of experience, just as do single words; the question of the "precise, complete, truly objective" meaning of a sentence contradicts the fundamentals of linguistic usage.[11]

Language is a historic deposit. Signs and sign complexes are indispensable tools in man's effort to orientate himself in a world, on the one hand, filled with hazards, and on the other, possessed of the potential to satisfy his material and intellectual needs. As such, language has an essentially pragmatic function and it is maximally adaptable to altered circumstances.

> Language originates in and has its primary reference to everyday life; it refers above all to the reality I experience in wide-awake

consciousness, which is dominated by the pragmatic motive (that is, the cluster of meanings directly pertaining to present or future actions) and which I share with others in a taken-for-granted manner. Although language can also be employed to refer to other realities . . . it even then retains its rootage in the commonsense reality of everyday life. . . . Language provides me with a ready-made possibility for the ongoing objectification of my unfolding experience. Put differently, language is pliantly expansive so as to allow me to objectify a great variety of experiences coming my way in the course of my life. Language also typifies experiences, allowing me to subsume them under broad categories in terms of which they have meaning not only to myself but also to my fellowmen. As it typifies, it also anonymizes experiences, for the typified experience can, in principle, be duplicated by anyone falling into the particular category in question.[12]

As early as the turn of the century Peirce insisted that making an assertion consists, implicitly, in *taking responsibility for some future experiences* having bearing on the conduct of life and is thus context dependent. Because of their life-circumstances, for example, Laplanders "observe" twenty different varieties of ice where urban Europeans "observe" only ice. Bedouins "observe" at least ten varieties of sand where urban Europeans "observe" only sand.[13] The knowledge that descriptive assertions are context variant and language dependent is a commonplace among empiricists and semanticists concerned with descriptive utterances.

What is more interesting, and the source of egregious confusion, are the illicit inferences drawn from such considerations. That members of various language communities can be said to "observe" different "facts," that is, tender significantly different utterances to characterize "the same" stimulus situation and warrant the truth of factual assertions, does not render "facts" irreducibly "subjective." The Laplander can *teach* the urban European to identify the varieties of ice by specifying the evidence conditions which intersubjectively identify what we shall hereafter call the symptomatic *recognitors* that provide entrance into each discrete class. "Recognitors" refer to the percepts which afford the defining characteristics used in sorting out identifiable classes of phenomena. We shall see that the effort to identify the recognitors that are taken to characterize members of an identifiable class of phenomena constitutes the essence of "operationalizing" concepts in political inquiry.

The rules for the cognitive use of any conventional sign, S, used to identify a member of a specific object class, Y, specify that that sign will be felicitously employed only upon the intersubjective characterization of specific recognitors—and that those recognitors function as reliable symptoms of Y. The meaning of the sign for a specific variety of ice unfamiliar to the urban European, for example, is unpacked in terms of some finite set of unproblematic intersubjective experiences that act as confirmations of truth, indicators of meaning and guides to expectation. The sign, S, is given "operational meaning."

Such an analysis permits us to argue from analogy: it is not true that Marxists "observe" instances of capitalist oppression unobservable to non-Marxists, and anti-Semites "observe" instances of Jewish connivance unobservable to others. The Marxist or anti-Semite, concerned in any way with the truth status of his claims, is obliged to instruct us in identifying instances of capitalist oppression or Jewish connivance, just as the Bedouin or Laplander is obliged to, and in principle able to, instruct us in properly identifying, respectively, the various categories of sand or ice— categories we had not been hitherto prepared to recognize. Such problematic truth claims must be unpacked, ultimately, in terms of unproblematic intersubjective recognitors, empirical indicators (available to all similarly circumstanced observers) that identify some reasonably specific experience as evidence for some specific claim. When an empirical truth claim is tendered, and refers to a complex social or political "fact," what is minimally required is the production of at least a partial catalogue of perceived or anticipated recognitors that mark out some aspects of intersubjective experience as the evidence conditions for the claim.

This elementary analysis suggests how the search, among analytic philosophers, for "protocol sentences," through which complex or obscure sign complexes could be, in principle, evidenced might be most generously understood. Analytic philosophers were not necessarily seeking some special class of experiences which were "pure," unalloyed with extraneous conceptual or ideational material. "Protocol sentences" were spoken of as "dealing with statements having immediate, present events as their subject."[14] This characterization of "protocol or observation statements" suggests something of the use to which they were to be put. They were to be the kind of descriptive utterance whose truth status could be determined in the most unproblematic intersubjective fashion, those assertions which referred to experiences which would most immediately elicit confirming expressions from *any* observer. They were understood to be the assertions which would enjoy the widest possible intersubjective confirmation, for they demanded the least possible interpretaion.

Thus Moritz Schlick spoke of "protocol statements" as those assertions to which we unproblematically assent, as the "registering of simple data of observation" and Hans Reichenbach referred to the "immediate concreta we observe just at that moment." Observable characteristics are spoken of as those characteristics which "under *suitable circumstances* . . . can be ascertained through direct observation." Observation predicates refer to the unproblematic observable characteristics of things (in terms of "sense data" or "thing-language"). Observation sentences assert that one or more specifically named objects possess or fail to possess some specified observable property or share some relation (their operational meaning in terms of recognitors). Thus in *Testability and Meaning* Rudolf Carnap spoke of "observation terms" as those signs which refer to an observable quality and whose determination must be subject to confirmation by the observer in a relatively short time period and with a high degree of intersubjective agreement. In the "Methodological Character of Theoretical Concepts," he maintained that "An observable property may be regarded as a simple special case of a testable disposition: for example, the operation for finding out whether a thing is blue or hissing or cold consists simply in looking or listening or touching the thing, respectively."

Irrespective of their recognition of the role of "observation sentences" in truth determination and meaning, philosophers of science nonetheless regularly remind us of the contextual dependency of knowledge claims (what Ogden and Richards referred to as the "sign situation"). "Observation," Morris Cohen and Ernest Nagel early insisted, "is not so simple a matter as is sometimes believed. . . . Even apparently random observation requires the use of hypothesis to interpret what it is we are sensing."[15] *All* language therefore is "theory loaded," even the ordinary language of the primitive or the layman. But each language and each language level is freighted with a *different* theory load. The analysis of linguistic meaning and truth determination does not require a disinterment of "pure experience" (whatever that might be), but is, rather, a systematic effort to substantially isolate the interpretive or theoretical elements in language so that the least problematic rational technique for warranting the truth status of descriptive or empirical truth claims can be most reliably established. Without some specification of what is to count, at least initially, as the unproblematic evidence for truth status, no discrimination between knowledge claims could begin—and the entire cognitive enterprise would collapse. Recently George Mandler and William Kessen characterized these considerations in the following manner:

> However complex theories may be, they all rest on statements of evidence, on the protocol sentences of a science. This is so homely and obvious that several important implications of the special nature of protocol statements may be missed. . . . Human communication, and most especially scientific communication, depends on the existence of a shared language about which there is relatively little argument, a foothold in ignorance which will permit us to start any investigation. Just as the common language of a cultural group serves communication among members of the group, so the protocol language of a science is the shared reference point for systematic research. It is not putting it too strongly to maintain that protocol language, the statement of relations among terms in the basic vocabulary, is the irreducible minimum of empirical science. . . . [Protocol] statements represent the end point of intersubjective agreement—

whatever arguments may exist on more abstract levels of scientific
language, there must be no argument about protocol statements
or else a science cannot exist.[16]

What seems clear, in our own time, is that what analytic philosophers (of whatever persuasion) were concerned with was establishing
what might constitute the unproblematic evidence conditions governing material or empirical truth ascription. When a cognitive problem
arises, we want to know what constitutes a *reliable* method of truth
determination. Reliability here can be construed as meaning that
the use of one method of truth determination is, in fact, less subject
to error than any other candidate method. We seek for *maximally*
reliable methods of truth ascription in the empirical, and for *absolutely* reliable methods in the formal, sciences. Rationality implies a systematic search for reliable knowledge—and the most reliable
knowledge available to men has been forthcoming when men measure their truth claims against intersubjective evidence conditions.
Methods such as the appeal to authority, appeals to the conviction
that attends "intuitive" insights or psychological "certainty,"
have all displayed their manifest unreliability.[17] They have all sired
serious errors and rationality counsels their abandonment. Reliance
on intersubjective experience has proved maximally reliable in
providing mankind with the knowledge which permits effective
orientation and negotiation in a complex and recalcitrant material
environment.

What analytic philosophers have sought to provide is a basic
language which would be maximally unproblematic and provide
for maximally reliable truth ascription. They sought to maximally
reduce the ideational, inferential, or conceptual elements of experience to unproblematic observations in order to maximally reduce
the range of conceivable objection and consequently the problem
potential of any truth ascription. Assertions like "I experience a
patch of red now," seem to constitute "atomic sentences," maximally innocent of interpretation, that might function as unproblematically true utterances. In some cases such utterances were
conceived as a final answer to the question "How do you know?"
A knowledge claim was understood as certified when it could be
shown to follow from truths which could not be seriously doubted.[18]

The most generous interpretation of the entire analytic enterprise is that which construes it to have been an effort to reveal how descriptive or empirical truth claims could be warranted under conditions *minimally* context and language dependent. This would reduce the occasion for challenge, challenge which makes truth ascription problematic. Such efforts, mistaken in many respects, did have significant yield. We know far more today concerning the truth conditions governing the various language domains than we did half a century ago.

We no longer conceive geometry, mathematics, and uninterpreted calculi, for example, as informing us about the *world*. Such linguistic entities are analytic—they do not inform us about the world or its properties. Thus their truth is determined by procedures other than making observations upon the world and the things in it. They are true "by definition." Only synthetic, or empirical, truth claims are warranted by observations—and such observations have proven to be most reliable when undertaken under circumstances that are minimally context and language dependent. For that reason analytic philosophers have attempted to formulate artificial *sense-data, phenomenalistic* or *thing-predicate languages*— to maximally reduce context and language dependence. The choice between sense-data language, phenomenalistic or "thing" language is not made as a result of some special ontological insight (that only "sense-data" or "things" truly "exist"), but is a consequence of judgments concerning the maximally unproblematic character of the assertions they permit. The effort at specifying what is to count as a "primitive" in any warranting procedure is a consequence of judgments about the accessibility of unproblematic intersubjective experience and the reliability with which they can be characterized. What we have with respect to our descriptions about the real world are partial and logically defective justificatory strategies, but strategies which answer many important questions concerning the confidence with which we can entertain assertions and what is to count as substantial evidence.[19]

Systematic empirical knowledge claims require an attempt to specify the conditions governing the most reliable truth ascriptions in terms of the fewest possible and best *entrenched* (most unproblematically intersubjective) predicates. Determining what are to constitute "observation sentences" may be reduced to the question of choosing the basic predicates of a rationally reconstructed language. Such a conception is unconcerned with the issue of ontological fidelity—it offers no judgments concerning what the objects of experience "really" are. (That can be conveniently left to speculative philosophy.) *The problem that confronts the empirical knowledge enterprise is to determine the best way to warrant reliable descriptive claims.* The choice between alternative sense-data, phenomenalistic or thing-language primitives is a choice among alternative justificatory strategies.

Which is the most useful, logically precise, and least problematic technique for discovering reliability most economically and with least obscurity? It is clearly less problematic to refer to sense-data—cold, hot, solid, or objects—trees, dogs and tables, than it is to refer to electron pairs or chromosomes. The use of signs like "cold," "hot," "solid," "trees," "dogs," and "tables" has to be learned, but the ideational component in such cases is manageable and certainly less theory loaded than the employment of signs like "electron" and "chromosome." Trying to unpack the meanings of these latter signs involves entering upon a reconstruction of their conceivable warrant. What is produced is an artificial language in which complex terms are unpacked in terms of easily understood terms—which any ordinary person or ordinary science never has occasion to use. What the analyst has attempted is to show something of the strategy of reliable truth ascription. He is unconcerned with how faithfully his language reflects "Reality" in itself (whatever that means).

Observation Language and "Objectivity"

It is clearly not the case that men start out with pure sense-data and subsequently "construct" things, relations, and processes on this primitive base. Men learn a specific natural language by spontaneous mimicry, negative and positive affective reinforcements; we learn a language by living in the world. That language is possessed of signs which refer to conceptual elements which do, in fact, direct and influence the focus of our attention. If we are Laplanders, our life space requires a reliable discrimination between various kinds of ice because our safety and survival depend on such discrimination. If we have been raised in a Marxist environment, we tend to "observe" facts in some respects singularly different from observers accustomed to a different political environment.

Language is a historical patrimony, the funded wisdom of our historic, cultural, and biological progenitors. As long as we operate in a relatively static ecological and cultural niche, our language constitutes an unproblematic and efficient adaptive instrument, and when we wish to warrant empirical truth, we make ready reference to unproblematic observations. But when unproblematic observations become problematic, we seek recourse to the most elementary intersubjective experiences. This occurs when as Europeans we meet Laplanders or Bedouins who "open our eyes" to simple observations hitherto unnoticed—or when a Marxist calls our attention to observations we have not attended. The urgent question that faces us in such problematic situations is to determine a strategy which, in principle, permits the most reliable resolution of doubt concerning the truth status of claims tendered.

Analytic philosophers have generally understood this. Their enterprise can hardly be conceived as offering an account of how language actually develops or has developed. They cannot be seriously understood to have argued, for example, that we start out with pure sense data from which all *ideata* are absent, but rather to have sought a rational reconstruction of sign use in which what might constitute reliable warrants for empirical truth ascriptions made in any language, and in any sphere of language, and under the most problematic circumstances, could be determined.

When we assert of something that it is "red," the term "red" functions as an unproblematic *conventional* sign—it might equally well have been *"Rot"* or *"rosso."* Its meaning is revealed in its use. We employ the conventional signs "red," "green," and all the other color terms to refer to some enjoyed or expected experience of which all members of the language community will unproblematically assert "red" or "green" or what-have-you (once they have learned the conventions). We have, in effect, "operationalized" the sign.

The color-blind individual provides a counterinstance of confirmatory utterance. He will not deploy "red" or "green" in accordance with ordinary use. The context in which color predicates are customarily used becomes problematic. This cannot be understood to mean that knowledge claims are "subjective"—and that color distinctions can come to be known only by individuals possessed of unimpaired color discrimination. The individual with impaired vision can be "shown" that *some* difference obtains between red objects and green objects by a variety of means. The hitherto unproblematic context (generally referred to in science through the use of the "all things being equal," the *ceteris paribus,* clause) has now become problematic. Certain auxiliary assumptions can no longer be entertained. We now can no longer *ostensively* convey the meaning of "red" or "green." We have recourse to other conveyances of meaning; we refer our unfortunate to *other* experiences which would be unproblematic. We might show him that snow melts more rapidly around one object rather than another even though both objects are for him (since he cannot distinguish colors) otherwise "identical." He *sees* a difference. We explain this by relating color predicates to the theory of electromagnetic waves. Colors differentially reflect electromagnetic waves, the frequency of red being different from the frequency of green; wave frequency being associated with heat. Alternately we might provide him with meter readings which are unproblematically conceived as evidencing differential wave frequency. He *sees* the difference in the pointer readings. We employ a different strategy from that which is "normal," because we understand that the evidence conditions which obtain in an unproblematic context no longer can be effectively employed as a warrant for the same material assertion in a now problematic context.

What this discussion is intended to suggest is that characterizing the "meaning" of the simplest signs in our language is a complex affair. We *can* teach the color-blind person the *referential meaning* of the term "red" by providing him with suitable unproblematic observations (meter readings and so forth). We *can* teach the color-blind person the *systemic meaning* of "red," by showing how, in theory, wave frequencies can be understood to give rise to the perception of red among color-normal persons. In effect, we *can* provide him with *cognitive appreciation* of such sign use—even though we *cannot* convey to him the private *psychological meaning* of "red"—the personal internal reaction to exogenous stimuli. Similarly, we can discuss the private motives, intentions, and desires of madmen in terms of their *referential meanings* (the behaviors which evidence their possession) and in terms of their *systemic meanings* (the implications of attributing such motives, intentions, and desires to actors), even though we may never enjoy, personally, the motives, intentions, and desires of madmen. We nonetheless license ourselves to speak of the meaning and truth of assertions through which we refer to them. We license our assertions by meeting the *intersubjective* evidence conditions which warrant them. We identify motives, intentions, and desires in terms of overt behavioral acts—speech acts and performances—and we employ such ascriptions to make public predictions and proffer explanations.

Moreover, the discussion ventilated above alludes not only to the fact that "meaning" has semantic, syntactical, and pragmatic dimensions, but that there is a potential for infinite regress intrinsic in the assessment of any empirical knowledge claim. Every sophomore has learned the trick of converting every reason given for a knowledge claim into a question. The person who makes any epistemic judgment assumes the obligation of producing adequate intersubjective evidence upon demand, but he does *not* commit himself to satisfying *every* question that can be generated by converting his reasons into questions. Such an enterprise is an exercise in futility. The very corrigibility of *descriptive* knowledge claims, does, in fact, imply the *possibility* of infinite regress. When we assert we have adequate warrant for knowing X to be the case, this entails that at least *some* things are unproblematic. But the recognition that *all* truth claims make *some* assumptions does not produce an argument which licenses the conclusion that *nothing* can be shown to be true.

What this latter argument involves is a confusion of criteria. The criteria governing truth ascription in the *formal* domain provide for *certainties ;* the criteria governing the *descriptive* domain provide for *reliabilities*. When we have seen, touched, smelled, and tasted the apple pie, we are licensed to say "We know it is apple pie." There does remain the *logical* possibility of error, but we engage no real doubt. We *may* be suffering delusion, episodic or systematic; we *may* be in a dream state; but until we can provide some *reason* for believing this to be the case, we entertain no real doubt. All such descriptive assertions are ventilated in contexts where *some* things are held to be unproblematically known. When the sceptic insists that we have no right to entertain *any* such epistemic judgments, it is incumbent upon him to indicate *why not*. To insist that there is always a *logical* possibility of error is to say no more than has already been conceded. *Every* descriptive claim is in principle corrigible, but we have no *reason* to doubt confirmed warrant statements for descriptive epistemic claims unless we can produce an argument *other* than the *logical* possibility of error.

What this means is that without recourse to some special pragmatic considerations (for example, the functions of language in orienting one in the social and natural environment), an indication of what criteria are domain invariant and which are domain variant, and without a recognition of different linguistic levels (varying unproblematic contexts), no knowledge claims can effectively be made. But the fact that such considerations are not always recognized, and confusions between domain invariant and domain variant criteria are sometimes tolerated, and diverse and divergent language levels are frequently confounded, can hardly pass for evidence that we possess *no* knowledge. We know a great many things about the world, its structure, its organization, and the diachronic and synchronic regularities which govern it. We understand the processes of organic evolution—we have unleashed the enormous potential of the atom—we have deciphered the genetic code by virtue of which animal traits are transmitted. Only incorrigible ignorance and irrepressible obscurantism deny that man possesses *reliable* knowledge of himself and his world and *certain* formal knowledge which exhibits truth by virtue of its structure.

Pragmatics

Ultimately specific and public pragmatic considerations determine what will constitute a warrant for any epistemic claim. Considerations of *utility* (a special class of pragmatic concern) *vindicate* criteria governing truth ascription. In a substantial, if necessarily compendious, sense, criteria are justified by the *purposes* they serve. *If* one opts to speak at all, he is confined by the most elementary principles of logic explicitly recognized as binding since at least Socratic times. *If* one chooses to survive, he must accept some material knowledge claims (some "facts" and "laws") as reliable guides to survival. Historically man *commences* his enterprise with just such survival and welfare considerations. *Subsequently* he pursues systematic knowledge at language levels one or several removes from the natural language appropriate to the survival and welfare concerns which initially occupy him. He pursues a systematic appreciation of aesthetic, ethical, religious, and scientific wisdom. Each concern involves him in a language shift, a move into troubled and problematic linguistic levels. In each context the untroubled assumptions governing some other are questioned—standards are altered—meanings are obscured or refined—and truths are jettisoned or reargued. But at no point can *all* explicit and implicit procedural assumptions, and presuppositions be questioned. The universal sceptic produces only self-stultifying arguments. If "all things are doubtful," for example, the assertion "all things are doubtful" is itself doubtful; if "all the world's an illusion"—the assertion "all the world's an illusion, " being part of the world, is equally illusory. By maintaining that *all* things are doubtful and *all* things are illusory, the universal sceptic cannot entertain any nonvacuous contrast between doubt and certainty, illusion and reality—and his criticisms telescope into absurdity.[20]

When we employ the term "dead" in ordinary language, we perform eminently well. We never (under normal circumstances) mistake a dead man for a living one. We have a vague sense of criterial attributes which permit us to identify members of the class. We need no greater precision because our purpose in the unproblematic context of ordinary life is to be in a position to distinguish the living from the dead. In ordinary circumstances we make few errors of any magnitude. Our awareness of what qualifies something as dead, however, is vague and unspecific, but for ordinary purposes, perfectly functional.

When men find themselves thrust into an environment in which their unproblematic knowing no longer functions appropriately—when as lawyers they must transfer the estate of a man who has disappeared, when as surgeons they must transplant a heart, when as medical practitioners they must decide when a patient is, in fact, dead—specific criteria (characterizing recognitors—operational indicators) must be selected to identify members of the requisite class. We then find ourselves talking about "legally dead" men, men who are "clinically dead," and men who are "biologically deceased." The hitherto unproblematic context, in which ordinary language was perfectly appropriate, becomes problematic in any number of ways. What results is an enterprise characteristic of science in general. There is recourse to stipulative standardization of semantic meaning—so that the sign "dead" will be used with specific denotation. As a consequence what we as purveyors of ordinary language signs might count as "dead," would not be "dead" for the clinician and the surgeon. We will have occasion to observe the same developments in political inquiry as research and study become increasingly specialized and our attention turns to problematic and unusual contexts.

In ordinary language we have inherited a quasi-scientific meaning for the sign "dead"; we also employ the sign metaphorically as when we refer to "dead weight," "dead head," and "dead end." All these uses are felicitous when we can give an indication of the observation utterances which make their use functional. But all such uses refer directly or indirectly to observations made on the world and the utterances they elicit. A lawyer, clinician, or surgeon must make a deliberate attempt to specify the observations (the symptomatic recognitors) which permit entry into the class of objects to be characterized as "dead"—since such an admission has impressive consequences. Nonetheless, the descriptive attributes which permit entry into the class are not different in logical type from those we employ in ordinary language to warrant the truth of our ascriptions. To determine the meaning and truth of descriptive utterances one must make appeal to observations which, in principle, can be intersubjectively enjoyed.

Meaning, Truth, and Linguistic Precision

When an assertion is tendered, we have the right and obligation to demand both an indication of meaning and an indication of how one might undertake a determination of truth. We have already alluded to the kinds of generic meanings with which we are concerned in attempting to establish truth status. We speak of semantic meaning when we attempt to convey the referential meaning of a term— for example, when we attribute an attitude, a disposition, or a sentiment to an individual or group. In undertaking such ascriptions we assume responsibility for a discrete collection of anticipations. If we characterize an individual as "a right-wing Republican," we tender a prediction, among other things, concerning his behavior in political discussions, his performance in elections, and his party loyalties. Such behaviors provide the evidence conditions which confirm the truth status of the ascription. Such public observations, involving unproblematic behaviors, evidence not only the truth of the claim, but its meaning as well. When we attribute "functions" to some institution operative within some reasonably well defined "system," the meaning of the attribution is unpacked in terms of expectations made evident by inspecting an entire collection of logically related propositions. We provide systemic or theoretic meaning to the subject proposition. In order to appreciate the meaning of such a claim we must be in a position to rehearse an entire collection of propositions and indicate some testable results that are logically implied. Finally, and in some instances, we attribute private states of mind to an individual—a state to which only that individual has immediate access. We may insist that we know something of that private state by analogy with similar states we have enjoyed or suffered—but such meanings constitute a subset of pragmatic meaning—and while they have private human "significance," they are tangential to the business of science.

One can concern himself with the consideration of what it "means" to be a Fascist (or a Communist, a member of the "New Left" or a "pluralist"). Such a concern can occupy itself either with 1) referential meaning—the implication of such an ascription for overt behaviors; or 2) systemic meaning—the implicit meaning of such an ascription within the context of a relatively elaborate collection of propositions having ultimate empirical implications; or 3) an aspect of private pragmatic meaning—the significance of such a state of mind for the individual himself.

Science directs its attention to referential and systemic meanings (essentially semantic and syntactic concerns)—the "signification" of terms, complex terms, and the propositions which host them. The "significance" of such terms, as long as one is preoccupied with "psychological significance," is of minimal scientific concern. Only when such "significance" betrays itself in public actions, becomes subject to explanation and prediction, is it of scientific concern. In effect, one need never have experienced "being a Fascist" to "understand" Fascists, that is to say, to have attained some predictive and explanatory leverage on their behavior. Similarly, one need never have been a ghetto dweller to "understand" ghetto dwellers—if one means by "understanding" having predictive and explanatory insight into their behavior. One comprehends the signification of the term—its private significance may forever elude one.

Perhaps it is true that to *empathize* with Fascists, revolutionaries, and ghetto dwellers, it may be necessary to have been a Fascist, a revolutionary, or a ghetto dweller. And having been a Fascist, a revolutionary, or a ghetto dweller may provide one with certain heuristic advantage. One *might* be in an advantaged position in formulating speculative hypotheses or preliminary conceptual schemata. But the *confirmation* of such insights always awaits *public* confirmation—the satisfaction of public evidence conditions. The individuals who know most about Fascists, revolutionaries, and ghetto dwellers may, in fact, never have been Fascists, revolutionaries, or ghetto dwellers any more than the individuals most knowledgeable about criminals or cancer victims may never have been criminals or cancer ridden. We may never know what being a ghetto dweller "meant" to John in the sense of the inner workings of his personal sentiments—for such "meaning" may be completely idiosyncratic. But when we make public attributions to him of dispositions, attitudes, and intentions, conceived to be the consequence of his life experience—such claims refer to referential and systemic meaning—and they must be, ultimately and in principle, subject to public evidence conditions.

The relationship between "meaning" and "truth" has become increasingly evident, and the transparency of the relationship is largely the product of the work of analytic philosophers. The initial preoccupation of the early "positivists" was to distinguish meaningful from meaningless utterances. Derivatively, they sought to excise from the language a class of utterances characterized as "metaphysical." The concerns of contemporary analytic philosophy are not calculated to perform such cognitive surgery. They are, rather, homeopathic and therapeutic.[21] The meaning of signs and sign-vehicles can only be determined by a scrutiny of their uses in the language. Living language performs far too many functions to attain the rigor of specialized and formalized languages. But this is not to say that when someone tenders knowledge claims, he can, when challenged, seek refuge in vague and ambiguous language and equivocation. Any inferential knowledge claim for example, and as we shall see, cannot offer as warrant a set of propositions which involve a literal contradiction. Any set of propositions containing a contradiction is truth functionally sterile. Within such a collection of utterances no distinction can be drawn between truth and falsity. Hence no such collection of propositions can count as warrant for any knowledge claim.

Consistency is a necessary (domain invariant) condition for truth ascription in inferential knowledge claims. The effort to avoid fallacy does, in fact, drive language in the direction of formalization (syntactical invariance) which makes explicit the logic governing sign and complex sign use. Language users are driven in the direction of standard and standardized sign use (semantic invariance) in the effort to avoid equivocation (the inability to identify the class under scrutiny) and the consequent faulting of demonstrative or problematic proof. Formalization and standardization are the consequence of attempting to meet the evidence conditions for *any* epistemic claim. Vague and ambiguous terms and obscure syntax, as we shall argue, make any knowledge claim suspect. When, for example, a sociologist or political scientist maintains that "anomie" is a "special problem" in our society, or that man's "alienation" increases with the measure of civilization, we entertain a vague intuitive feeling that we understand what is meant. But if we are asked to produce the warrant for such assertions, we will find it necessary to offer some stipulative, if complex, definition of "anomie" and "alienation," "society" and "civilization," as well as some indices that serve as standards of temporal increment or decrement of "anomie" and "alienation." What we embark upon is the effort to produce at least the minimal rigor that has come to characterize significant discourse. We expose the signification of such expressions. Each science has, in significant measure, produced its standardized language by virtue of which referential and systemic meaning is conveyed and defensible truth ascriptions are made. What will count as significant usage will be determined by the uses to which a sign or sign-complex is to be put in the nonproblematic context of that science. What will count as evidence for such usage will be similarly determined. The ultimate test of meaning and truth is the *reliability* of the knowledge enterprise—and this necessitates an account of public evidence conditions.

Reliability maximally enhances man's ability to understand and control his evironment through the attainment of systematic and intersubjective *knowledge,* defined as 1) warranted conclusions about the more or less extensive uniform conditions under which natural events take place and 2) valid conclusions within the domain of formal concerns. Science has most effectively met the requirements governing the knowledge enterprise. Aestheticians, moralists, and theologians are, nonetheless, enjoined by the same obligations. If a theologian conceives himself as contributing to the knowledge enterprise, it is incumbent upon him to convey meaning and offer criteria for the admissibility of his utterances as true. He has made the knowledge claim—and thus has assumed the burden of producing its warrant. He is not obliged to meet *our* standards, but he must meet *some* intersubjective standards.

His efforts must, in effect, be pedagogical. He is obliged (as is the Laplander, the Bedouin, the Marxist, or the anti-Semite) to teach us how he uses the language, i.e., what he conceives the rules of felicitous use might be. If the putative referents of his assertions are "supernatural" entities of whatever kind, he must have some determinate way of conveying the meaning of the signs he employs. If he wishes to maintain that his utterances are true, he must indicate what is to count as a legitimate, as distinct from a counterfeit, warrant for their truth.

In extensively standardized and formalized scientific disciplines, the truth warrants for assertions or collections of assertions can be produced with minimal confusion. The rules governing language use in such reconstructed language is maximally specific. In a discipline like political inquiry, in which overlapping and intersecting concerns render analysis and appraisal particularly difficult, any assessment of meaning and truth involves an appreciation of the various functions of language. How a word is used in an informal discipline is a guide to its meaning and an exhibition of what is taken to provide the conditions for certifying its truth.

Political inquiry is a minimally formalized and standardized enterprise. It occupies an intermediate locus in the continuum that extends from the maximally formalized and standardized sciences like applied physics, through the formal sciences like geometry, to the minimally formalized and standardized pursuits like aesthetics and theology. Political inquiry shares, in fact, the species traits of history and clinical psychology. The reliability of knowledge claims made in such disciplines, like the reliability of claims made in political science, stands in inverse relation to the degree of vagueness, ambiguity, reification, and tense obscurity that attend the language they employ. The reduction of semantic and syntactical variance is the first responsibility of such pursuits in their effort to increase the reliability of their truth claims. A minimal appreciation of the semantic and syntactical rules and pragmatic considerations governing language use is a necessary preliminary to the responsible assessment of the knowledge enterprise in general, and political inquiry in particular.

Notes

1 C. K. Ogden and I. A. Richards, *The Meaning of Meaning* (New York: Harcourt, Brace, 1923), pp. 186f.

2 C. E. Osgood, G. J. Suci, and P. H. Tannenbaum, *The Measurement of Meaning* (Urbana: University of Illinois, 1967), pp. 2f. Cf. R. Carnap, "Foundations of Logic and Mathematics," in J. A. Fodor and J. J. Katz, *The Structure of Language* (Englewood Cliffs, N. J.: Prentice-Hall, 1966), pp. 420f.

3 Cf. C. W. Morris, *Signs, Language, and Behavior* (New York: Prentice-Hall, 1946); G. Klaus, *Semiotik und Erkenntnistheorie* (Berlin: VEB, 1963).

4 Cf. L. Wittgenstein, *Philosophical Investigations* (New York: Macmillan, 1953), §§1, 10, 11, 20, 30, 43, 50, 122, 421; G. Pitcher, *The Philosophy of Wittgenstein* (Englewood Cliffs, N.J.: Prentice-Hall, 1964), chap. 10; G. Hallett, *Wittgenstein's Definition of Meaning as Use* (New York: Fordham University, 1967); H. Feigl, "Some Major Issues and Developments in the Philosophy of Science of Logical Empiricism," in *Minnesota Studies in the Philosophy of Science,* eds. H. Feigl and M. Scriven (Minneapolis: University of Minnesota, 1956), 1, 5.

5 For a brief but serviceable glossary of such terms, cf. A. Pap, *Semantics and Necessary Truth* (New Haven: Yale University, 1958), pp. 423–39. For a discussion of the distinction between tautologies, analytically true propositions, and *a priori* truths, cf. A. Pap, *Introduction to the Philosophy of Science* (New York: Free Press, 1962), chap. 6.

6 D. Easton, *A Framework for Political Analysis* (Englewood Cliffs, N.J.: Prentice-Hall, 1965), p. 27.

7 The criticism of the synthetic/analytic distinction, made prominent by W. V. Quine, can be construed as a criticism of the failure, on the part of some analysts, to make the necessary distinction between the analysis of *artificial* and *reconstructed* languages—in which semantic variance is eliminated or maximally reduced by the substitution of undefined variables for conventional speech signs and syntactical variance is eliminated by explicit transformation rules—and dynamic natural languages in which semantic and syntac-

tical variance remains a problem. Recently Jerrold Katz has attempted to formulate the synthetic/analytic distinction for natural languages (cf. J. Katz, *The Philosophy of Language* [New York: Harper and Row, 1966], chap. 5). For our purposes, it is sufficient to indicate that even granting the vaguenesses and ambiguities that occur in natural languages there are rule-governed (and context dependent) synonymies of signs that provide for the analyticity of specific assertions. What frequently happens is that ordinary language is standardized (or partially standardized) and formalized (or partially formalized) for the purposes of scientific precision by the commonly understood techniques of casuistic and logical analysis, the use of descriptive and logical signs rendered systematic by the elaboration of the syntactic, semantic and pragmatic rules governing their use. Descriptive signs are defined with some precision and rules of synonomy (or equivalence) are formulated with some specificity. Without such efforts (which are often tedious to those who wish to "get on" with the subject matter) one cannot decide what kind of knowledge claim is being tendered. One has no sure way of determining whether the claims are bona fide descriptive claims or concealed analytic assertions.

Without such a preliminary determination one cannot know whether the warrant for a specific assertion is provided by references to the world or by an inspection of the language—whether we are occupied with necessary or problematic inference (deduction or induction).

8 For an interesting and competent exposition of these considerations, cf. F. Cowley, *A Critique of British Empiricism* (New York: St. Martin's, 1968), chaps. 15–17.

9 C. S. Peirce, *Collected Papers of Charles Sanders Peirce,* eds. C. Hartshorne and P. Weiss (Cambridge, Mass.: Harvard, 1931–1935), V, §438.

10 Ogden and Richards, *op. cit.,* pp. 50f.

11 R. von Mises, *Positivism* (New York: Dover, 1951), p. 40.

12 P.L. Berger and T. Luckmann, *The Social Construction of Reality* (Garden City, N.Y.: Anchor, 1967), pp. 38f.

13 Cf. E. Albrecht, *Sprache und Erkenntnis* (Berlin: VEB, 1967), chap. 5.

14 Von Mises, *op. cit.,* p. 92; cf. P. Caws, *The Philosophy of Science* (Princeton: Van Nostrand, 1965), pp. 73f.

15 M. Cohen and E. Nagel, *An Introduction to Logic and Scientific Method* (New York: Harcourt, Brace, 1934), p. 215; cf. A. Kaplan, *The Conduct of Inquiry* (San Francisco: Chandler, 1964), p. 58.

[16] G. Mandler and W. Kessen, *The Language of Psychology* (New York: John Wiley, 1959), pp. 166f.

[17] Cf. C. S. Peirce, "The Fixation of Belief," in *Philosophical Writings of Peirce,* ed. J. Buchler (New York: Dover, 1955), pp. 5–22.

[18] In a sense this was conceived, certainly by some, to provide the necessary constituent elements for the *demonstrative* warrants for descriptive knowledge claims. Truth claims concerning *things* were conceived warranted by analytically valid arguments based on unimpeachable premisses. Some seemed to have argued that in some sense the propositions which constituted the premisses of the justificatory argument employed to warrant descriptive knowledge claims and the conclusion of that argument were conceived as sharing an *entailment.* In effect, it seems that some analysts construed the standard of *validity,* appropriate to *formal* discourse, to be domain invariant, that is, applicable to empirical as well as to formal claims. Descriptive assertions were to meet the *same standards* of truth certification as *formal* language acts. The problems that ensued are now part of the history of analytic philosophy.

It is generally recognized, in our own time, that the propositions advanced as "true," in ordinary life and science, are frequently of a *different logical type* than their truth warrants. We predict, for example, the *future* by employing *past* and *present* data. We attribute *attitudes, dispositions* and *character* to people and cite *behaviors* as evidence. We assert descriptive claims about the *past* and cite *present* traces as evidence. The discrepancy between logical types that frequently characterizes descriptive claims has been recognized to obtain between our assertions about *"things"* and the collection of assertions about *sensory experiences* which we cite as their evidence warrant. *Any* collection of propositions elicited by sensory experience fails to *entail* a conclusion which has an "objective physical thing" as its referent. And yet we are confident in our knowledge of at least some physical things however subject we are, in principle, to the *logical* possibility of error. What such considerations mean is that descriptive assertions cannot reasonably be conceived as falling under the requirement of meeting *analytic* truth conditions in our search for their legitimate warrant. Cf. S. Toulmin, *The Uses of Argument* (London: Cambridge University, 1964), pp. 217–223.

[19] Cf. in this respect N. Goodman, *The Structure of Appearance* (New York: Bobbs-Merrill, 1966), pp.

136–142; R. Carnap, *Meaning and Necessity* (Chicago: University of Chicago, 1956), pp. 206f.

[20] Kaplan, *op. cit.,* pp. 86f.

[21] For an urbane treatment of these issues, see the discussion in F. Waismann, *How I See Philosophy* (New York: St. Martin's, 1968), chap. 1.

Suggested Readings

Alston, W. P. *Philosophy of Language.* Englewood Cliffs, N. J.: Prentice-Hall, 1964.

Morris, C. *Signification and Significance.* Cambridge, Mass.: MIT, 1964.

Pole, D. *The Later Philosophy of Wittgenstein.* London: Athlone, 1958.

Wartofsky, M. W. *Conceptual Foundations of Scientific Thought.* New York: Macmillan, 1968. Chap. 5.

4

On Semantics and Syntactics

All life comes back to the question of our speech—the medium through which we communicate.
Henry James

Language is at once a commonplace and a great puzzlement. It is the principal vehicle of communication, an indispensible mnemonic aid in the collection, storage, and retrieval of information and a superlative creative tool—and yet it is a treacherous source of confusion and error as well. We employ language to tender *knowledge claims* as well as produce their warrant. We report, opine, and predict—and we describe, deduct, induct, and explain. We employ language to *express* and *persuade*. We exult, lament, expostulate, approve, disapprove, thank, and congratulate—we recommend, propose, petition, reprove, evoke, invoke, and exhort. We employ language to *perform*. We admit, inquire, proclaim, declare, command, request, confess, and promise.

All such locutionary acts can be performed successfully or unsuccessfully in one and/or a number of ways. We might conjoin words in such a fashion that what results is unintelligible—"few tree and are the go"—and our effort is neither cognitive, expressive, persuasive nor performative. We might produce a well-formed sentence, one that meets the minimal syntactical requirements of English—"procrastination devours triangularity"—and fail to convey meaning, thereby faulting the entire effort. Or we might advance a legitimate knowledge claim (or embark on a performatory act) and produce in its support only the semblance of warrant (or fail to comply with the conditions for successful performance).

There are therefore (for the purposes of our introductory discussion) various ways in which we can abuse the language: *semantically,* by violating the rules which render signs and sign complexes meaningful and establish their descriptive truth status; *syntactically,* by violating the rules governing the organization, transformation, and truth conditions involved in formal sign employments; and *pragmatically,* by failing to meet the minimal conditions for felicitous persuasive, performative, and/or expressive employment or by neglecting the sociopsychological contexts or effects which attend language use. [1]

Natural languages are vehicles for communication which, employing sets of public signs or symbols arranged in accordance with syntactic, and governed by semantic, rules, permit meaningful exchanges between language users. To qualify as meaningful, any language must minimally involve the use of some publicly observable symbols, either acoustic, tactile, or visual, whose syntactic and semantic rules permit a speaker or writer to encode and a listener, listeners, reader, or readers to decode the speaker's or writer's thoughts or impressions. It is evident therefore that in some significant sense the users of a natural language tacitly or explicitly employ a system of rules. Moreover, human beings understand each other not only because they encounter and recognize in their exchanges signs and sign complexes that they have previously encountered (animals do as much), but also because they possess knowledge of a finite if indeterminate set of syntactic and semantic rules governing the creation and interpretation of new and hitherto unencountered signs and sign complexes.

The number of sentences a human being can produce, for example, is potentially infinite; for the longest sentence produced in the natural language a longer one can be generated by adding, in accordance with the formation rules of the language, an appropriate qualifier or clause. Any such hitherto unencountered sentence, as long as it obeys the syntactic and semantic rules governing sign employments, is meaningful and can, in principle, be understood. One's mastery of the rules governing language, and most characteristically in the case of formal languages like mathematics, is established not by performing well with problems in whose solutions one has been trained, but by performing well in solving problems to which one has never before been exposed. We can all so perform and our performance can be adjudged successful or unsuccessful so long as our language community shares with us a common system of rules. We are understood to reason together. Evaluations of such reasonings can gain a foothold only where criteria of correct and incorrect usage obtains. Outside the governance of such reasonably well understood rules no nonvacuous cognitive distinction can be drawn between meaningful and meaningless, correct and incorrect reasonings.

The Felicitous Use of Signs

Natural language can be employed meaningfully and meaninglessly, correctly and incorrectly in a variety of perplexing ways. Words have a variety of senses and uses and take on various meanings in different contexts. The noun "dog," for instance, is ordinarily used *descriptively* to inform, as when we utter, "A dog is barking." The sign "dog" can have an equally intelligible use when it is employed *appraisively* to convey negative evaluation in sentences of the sort, "My date turned out to be a real dog." In either case the use of the sign is governed by specified or specifiable, tacit or explicit, rules of use. Should we concern ourselves with the cognitive merits of either employment, we are intellectually obliged to seek a specification of those rules.

The first move in the direction of such specification is to offer verbal *definitions* for the sign or sign complexes under scrutiny. This involves the provision of alternate signs or sign complexes as substitution instances of the obscure sign or sign complex. The rule covering such substitutions would involve exhibiting a sign or sign complex S_1 that could be employed to communicate the same cognitive information as the sign or sign complex S. Such a technique, "giving a definition," is commonplace among fairly sophisticated language users. But there comes a point at which such verbal substitutions break down. In effect, what is required is a method for breaking out of the language circle. This is effected by exhibiting criteria for use that make direct or indirect reference to the nonlinguistic material world, by indicating at least some of the observable characteristics, recognitors, something must display if a sign or sign complex is to be used referentially. Thus when, as students of political inquiry, we attempt to employ the term "set" for any substantive purpose, it becomes incumbent upon us to specify what entities in the object world we intend to count among elements of our set. When such characterization is given, we lay down semantic, or meaning, rules governing the use of the sign, and lay down rules of evidence which allow one to pass from the statement containing the sign to others that describe some real or potential observation or observations.

When we study some aspects of the political system, we concern ourselves with a set of elements, human beings (unproblematically characterized by some finite set of recognitors), who share some relations among them. A system is defined as a set of elements related in some way. The elements of the formal set are identified, via meaning rules, as human actors—and their relations characterized. The relationship may be one of binary opposition, that is, the system is one of mutually exclusive and exhaustive elements. The elements in the system, for example, either vote or they do not. The voting or not voting, like the elements of the system, is characterized by intersubjective recognitors. The formal definitions of "set" and "system" are related to the object world through meaning or semantic rules.

In such circumstances, to ask for the meaning of a sign or sign complex is to ask, in the last analysis, for *formal rules governing its intralinguistic use* (a formal definition) and *meaning rules which provide for its extralinguistic referents*. To concern oneself with the positive or negative truth status of a descriptive assertion would be to imply, minimally, that some confirming or infirming observational utterance or utterances in terms of recognitors has or have, or will be made. The conditions governing comprehensible language use in such instances reveal both the formal and substantive rules implicit or explicit in its employment, its "grammar," or "function."

When one concerns oneself exclusively with its extralinguistic use, one is preoccupied with its "reference" or "designatum."

This is not to be construed to mean that any sign in the natural language employed to signal extralinguistic referents has a fixed and unalterable reference or designation. A word is a sign and a sentence is a sign vehicle having *conventional* public uses. A descriptive sign can be given novel employment, but its use can be characterized as intelligible and correct only if its reference and use is, to some degree, exhibited. Signs, simple or complex, require such specification if they are to be used for any cognitive purpose. Such specification indicates what is to count as evidence of empirical meaningfulness, correct use and truth—each new descriptive sign requires new rules that provide for its felicitous employment.

Semantic Meaning

Semantic rules for the specification of meaning effectively operate when signs appear in syntactically ordered linguistic entities called "well formed sentences." Such sentences accord themselves with the rules of formation of the natural language. Only in such contexts is it possible to specify which meaning rules govern the signification of the sign. Only if they occur in a context will it be possible to determine what differences obtain between "dog" (when it is used to identify members of a class and hence used descriptively), "dog" (when it is used to indicate disapproval and hence is used appraisively), and "dog" (when it is used as a proper name to indicate, for example, the Dog Star Sirius or Procyon). Meaning, then, is something that can be assigned with some assurance only to a word appearing in a well-formed sentence. In context we narrow the range of conceivable alternate meanings (the *sign type,* "dog," is employed in a specific instance and we refer to each specific use of the sign or word type as a *sign* or *word token* use).

We understand the meaning of a sentence, in turn, if we know the meaning of the individual words (now specified as sign tokens in context) and its grammatical structure. Truth, in turn, is a function of the meaning of such sign tokens as they appear in complete sentences, in assertions. To say that we know a sentence to be true requires that we comprehend the signification of the sentence. To establish that we know the signification of a descriptive sentence is to describe the circumstances under which we would be prepared to ascribe to it positive truth status.

We certify the meaningfulness of a descriptive utterance by giving the rules of evidence that specify what is to count as its truth conditions. *The criteria of meaningfulness indicate the conditions of truth.* Notice that it is not necessary to commit oneself to the truth of a statement before one conceives it as meaningful. All that is necessary is to describe a manner by virtue of which evidence for its truth could be, in principle, forthcoming. Designative, descriptive or "empirical" signification is, in this restricted sense, a function which conventional signs acquire, ultimately, by being conceived as enjoying some correspondence, through appropriate language use, with some real or fancied, direct or indirect extralinguistic reference (via recognitors). A descriptive meaning, the *signification* of a sign, is attached to a term when we know the semantic rules governing its use. Descriptive generic signs like "dog," "chair," "the state," "the nation" are employed to range over some class of recurrent collections of observations. The sentence, "This is a chair," characterized by the indexical "this," is accounted true when we, in fact, enjoy the spatially and temporally determinate observations conceived as its confirmation. In this sense, to know what would count as its confirmation is to warrant the claim that one knows what a sentence means.[2] One has "operationalized" the term. One is apprized of its signification, its *public* meaning. Whatever *private* significance a sign or sign complex may have (because of idiosyncratic experience) can only enter into public meanings when intersubjective rules governing its employment are exhibited.

Recently Hans Morgenthau tendered the following complex truth claim concerning the "cold war." ". . . One realizes that [the cold war] has not been the result of willful machinations of certain individuals or groups of individuals but that it arose inevitably out of objective conflicts of interests which could not be accommodated by the diplomatic means which both sides were willing to use."[3] Before one could embark upon an assessment of the claim's truth, one construal of its meaning would make it necessary to know what the author might mean by "willful machinations"—since, intuitively, the notion of "objective conflicts of interests" would seem to imply that participants would be aware of their interests and would be expected, consequently, to act in ways appropriate to their defense—actions that produced the cold war. In ordinary language "to machinate" means "to contrive or devise, artfully and/or with evil purpose" and "machinations" refers to the acting out of "crafty schemes, plots and intrigues." When individuals pursue their "objective interests" and those interests "conflict" with those of other conscious agents—one can legitimately wonder if any of their behaviors could be conceived as "machinations." If acting consciously in one's own interests excludes "machinating," it would seem that the truth claim harbors a sophisticated and perhaps normative distinction between "willful machinations" and "consciously pursuing one's own interests" in a situation involving an "objective conflict of interest."

The candidate truth exhibited in the quotation from Morgenthau is a densely packed linguistic entity that requires considerable analysis before one can confidently search his subsequent (or antecedent) exposition for evidence that would successfully warrant it. The first move would be in the direction of reducing the semantic variance, the vagueness that surrounds ordinary language concepts. Only if the vagueness is reduced can one certify whether the claim is, in this case, only seemingly paradoxical, or in fact contradictory (i.e., that is to say, acting in one's own objective interest may involve "machinating"—if so, the antecedent clause would contradict the subsequent clause—and the performance would be irredeemably faulted). One can tender such a judgment only when semantic meaning is specified with sufficient precision to determine whether the class of behaviors that fall under the characterization "machinations" includes no member that could fall under the implied willful acts undertaken in the pursuit of one's own, or one's nation's, objective interests.

To identify what is to count as "machinations" is to identify the recognitors that license entry into the class. When some determinate piece of behavior evidences those recognitors, it will count as "machinating" and fix the public meaning of the term.

In scrutinizing the claims made in the literature of political inquiry, one is obliged to attempt an analysis of all claims critical to the author's exposition. Implied in the illustrative quotation from Morgenthau are public meanings for complex concepts. There are, for example, "objective conflicts of interests" which "could not be accommodated by diplomatic means which both sides were willing to use"—which implies not only that such interests could be identified, but that the means by which they could be "accommodated" might well be identified, and that there was an indisposition on both sides to employ them. Such claims involve far more than simple referents to warrant their truth. They involve negative truth claims (the cold war was *not* the result of willful machinations of certain individuals or groups of individuals), deterministic truth claims (the cold war arose *inevitably* out of objective conflicts of interests), and dispositional truth claims (both sides were *willing to use only* certain diplomatic means to attempt the accommodation of such conflicts).

Nonetheless, to commence analysis one must attempt some determination of semantic meaning—to identify the extralinguistic referents of any descriptive terms employed in tendering the truth claim.

Syntactical Meaning

Such concerns are limited, of course, to the *designative* or *referential* use of signs both simple and complex, descriptive and theoretical. They are obviously too restricted to tap all the dimensions of meaning. There are, for example, special signs in natural language which are meaningful and yet have no referential function, that is to say, which cannot be analyzed *semantically*. Pronouns, prepositions, adverbs, articles, and conjunctions, "I," "on," "the," "and," "no," "all," and "but" are meaningful terms and yet have no specific referents, they refer to no *specific* conceivable extralinguistic states of affairs. They do not have *specific* extralinguistic referents, but intralinguistic uses, uses within the structure of language. Pronouns, for example, do not have a specific extralinguistic referent, but supplant gestures of pointing to any number of things. Prepositions are used to indicate something general about the *relations* obtaining between elements in our experience and cannot be employed to "name" anything (a relation, for example, is not an element in a set). The meaning of such terms is, literally, their special *intra-linguistic* function. We establish their meaning by giving the rules for operating with them within the confines of language rather than confirming them simply by reference in terms of recognitors in the object world.

Such parts of speech are of special importance, for although they themselves are never objects of truth ascription, their presence in an assertion has bearing on the conditions governing its truth status. The assertion, "The cat is *on* the mat," is obviously governed by different truth conditions than the assertion, "The cat is *under* the mat." Similarly the indexical signs, "this" and "that," invoke different truth conditions.

Deductive Logic

A special class of such intralinguistic signs has been the subject of scrutiny since antiquity, for such signs govern the ways in which parts of sentences and sentences (or the propositions they express) can be related and truth status assigned independently of the meaning of any descriptive sign which occurs in them—and consequently independent of any experience with the world. We are all prepared to grant that the statements "A dog is a dog," "A system is a set of elements related in some way," "All bachelors are unmarried," and "An individual either votes or he does not" are, in a significant sense, meaningful and true. The singular feature about such statements is that their truth or falsity can be determined by inspection of their form and the substitutability of the signs employed to express them quite independent of any observations made upon the world. The statement, "A dog is a dog," has the form "A = A" and is hence a "self-evident" or logical truth. Similarly the statements, "All bachelors are unmarried," and "A system is a set of elements related in some way," are seen to instantiate the same form when once it is revealed that their respective predicates are, by definition, contained in their respective subjects.

Such statements can be seen to be self-evidently true by substituting synonyms for synonyms and then inspecting the resultant sentence. Thus the definition of "bachelor" is "any unmarried adult male." The sentence, "All bachelors are unmarried" can now be read as "All unmarried adult males are unmarried," the truth of which is as evident as it is uninformative. In order to determine its truth we need not even know what the descriptive signs "bachelor" and "unmarried adult male" mean—only that they constitute substitution instances of each other. The same results could be obtained by substituting uninterpreted symbols for "bachelor" and "unmarried adult male." The reduction of such sentences to logical truths can be effected by exploiting the opportunities provided by the conjoint use of definitions (a subset of syntactical transformation rules governing the substitution of synonymous terms in the language) and the rules governing one sense of the verb "is." Similarly, the truth of the sentence "A system is a set of elements related in some way," even if more unfamiliar (although David Easton has familiarized us with it), is true for the same reasons "All bachelors are unmarried" is true. If we know that "is" provides for definitional equivalency, then to say that "A system is a set of elements related in some way" is reducible, via transformation rules, to "A = A."

The truth of the sentence "An individual either votes or he does not," is true for the same reason that "It will either rain or not rain" is true. Neither assertion makes a prediction. When we understand the transformation rules governing the use of the disjunctive sign "or," such a sentence reveals itself to be self-evident. The prototype of such a sentence has the form "p or not p" where "p" functions as a sentential variable. A compound sentence which is an instance of such a prototype is true irrespective of whether the component "p" is true or false, for the rules governing the disjunctive sign "or" provide that the truth of a compound disjunctive statement is established if *either* of its disjuncts is true. Thus any sentence instantiating the form "p or not p" must necessarily be true, for if "p" is true then "p or not p" is true and yet if "p" is false "p or not p" nonetheless remains true.

The class of statements that instantiate the form "p or not p"

is called tautologous—and statements that are members of this class are always *true* irrespective of their content and any conceivable state of affairs.

Two Orders of Cognitive Truth

We have therefore at least two kinds of statements which can be assigned truth status ("truth status" understood to cover the truth, falsity and indeterminate status of a statement): 1) statements whose meaning and truth are a function of their relationship to utterances invoked by some extralinguistic state or states of affairs; and 2) some statements whose truth is a function of their intra-linguistic "form," the *syntactical* rules governing the connectives and signs employed in them.

The first class of meaningful statements are characterized as "contingent," descriptive, synthetic, or empirical and the second "necessary," formal or logical. Contingent statements are those statements whose meaning and truth requires reference to some utterances about some conceivable state or states of affairs that constitute their truth conditions. The most direct way of defending a truth claim about contingent truths is to refer to observations about some state of affairs that is its confirmation. Such a specification, it has been suggested, provides what has been loosely called "rules of evidence" or "truth conditions," that is, some indication of what will count for and against the truth of a contingent statement. It must be recognized that to commit ourselves to the contention that the evidence for the truth of statement p is provided by statements $S_1, S_2 \ldots S_{\hat{n}}$ which describe some recognitor states is not to say that p is *identical* with any finite collection of such evidential statements. Such an identification would require that the finite set of evidential statements *entailed p*, and p would serve as a stenographic formulation for the set of statements that constitute evidence of its truth. As has been suggested, this could clearly not be the case. When one utters the statement "This is a table," confirming evidence is forthcoming in descriptive symptomatic statements of the sort that report visual and tactile sense experience—but such warranting experience is not the logical equivalent of the original assertion.

There is a point at which we would normally say that we are prepared to admit the *practical* certainty that the assertion "This is a table" is true—and yet we all know that some possible future experience might compel us to withdraw or modify our truth claim. We are not prepared to commit ourselves to its *logical* certainty. The ascription might have been made in a dream, or we might have been under the influence of drugs or hypnosis when we enjoyed the confirming experience. Such descriptive truth claims remain always less than absolute; they remain corrigible or fallible. They are, in effect, contingent; their truth warrant is experiential, and since experience is forever ongoing and there is no way in which we can be certain what future experience will bring, all such claims remain, in principle, corrigible.[4]

Necessary truths, analytic truths, and tautologies, enjoy, on the other hand, a truth status of a special sort. They are true by virtue of the rules governing the substitution of descriptive terms and logical connectives. Thus the assertion "All societies are systems" does not require recourse to experience for the certification of its truth. Its truth has become definitional for a number of political scientists employing a stipulative definition of the sign "system." It is absolutely true that "All societies are systems," not because something is true of the world, but because in the special language of some political scientists the class "systems" ("a set of elements related in whatever fashion") includes, by definition, the subclass, "societies." Such an assertion does not provide information about the world, but about the language employed by some political scientists. The word "society" entails "system" in the language of some political scientists and anyone who believes that evidence must be collected to confirm such an assertion has woefully misconstrued one important aspect of the knowledge enterprise. Once the stipulative definition of "system," as, for example, "any interactive aggregate," is accepted, *any* "society" (defined as any "organization" of persons, i.e., "elements" related by whatever relations) *must* be a system. It is an assertion that can be reduced to a logical truth by employing the substitution rules governing synonymous terms.

Similarly, tautologies will remain necessarily true and contradictions necessarily false irrespective of what extralinguistic experiences we enjoy. In this sense the truth ascribed to necessary truths both analytic and tautological is syntactical.[5] The truths ascribed to contingent statements, on the other hand, are governed by semantic (and, as we have suggested, pragmatic) truth conditions, conditions which specify a putative correspondence between an assertion and some determinate state of affairs (within some unproblematic context).

Statements like "The Soviet Union is a one-party state," and "China is a dictatorship" require, for their cognitive truth, a specification of semantic meaning—and an indication of the truth conditions governing their responsible assertion as well, for nothing in the signs "Soviet Union" or "China" implies "one-party state" or "dictatorship" the same way "system" implies "a set of related elements." Contingent truths concern the world as we experience it; they assert something of it. Such truths, identified as "synthetic," or "descriptive," contribute to funded knowledge and are required to refer, directly or indirectly, to experience as their ultimate warrant. Necessary truths are, on the other hand, concerned with the uses of special parts of speech and the rules governing their use, and whatever truths they assert, are purely formal, devoid, in and of themselves, of descriptive or synthetic content.

Any effort to bring order into either realm of truth ascription within the confines of ordinary language involves a host of difficulties which could hardly be adequately treated within the limits of this initial discussion. But it is evident that if some class of statements is to be accorded truth status by virtue of the syntactical rules of the language, those rules require a specificity not readily exemplified in ordinary language use. Ordinary language is singularly characterized by semantic and syntactical variance. Words frequently do not enjoy standard meanings, and the uses of ordinary language connectives like "or" and "is" are sufficiently diverse to engender confusion.

"Or," in ordinary language, for example, is a sign that can signify either inclusion or exclusion. Thus a complex sign over a door saying "Faculty *or* Students" means that both faculty and students and anyone who is both a faculty member and a student may enter.

On the other hand the assertion, "You can have a hamburger *or* a frankfurter," exemplifies the exclusive sense of "or." You can have one or the other, but not both. Similarly the verb "to be" enjoys at least three distinct employments in ordinary speech. "Is" may be used, for example, to indicate identity as in the case of "America *is* this country," or "is" may be used to predicate a property as in the case, "America *is* a democracy." Finally the verb may function as an indication of unqualified existence, as in the case, "America *is*" (that is to say, "America exists").

Obviously, if consistency is to govern the use of such connectives, a greater specificity of the rules governing their function is to be forthcoming. Such precision obtains within the confines of formal logic and marks a transition to a higher level of language employment. Logic systematizes the use of such connectives, thereby reducing the *syntactical variance* that characterizes ordinary speech. To further reduce the variance of ordinary language which obscures the systematic employment of connectives, formal logic introduces certain conventions. In propositional logic, sentence variables and sentence formulae are provided to take the place of sentences (or more properly the propositions they express). Stripped of descriptive content, the syntactical relationships that bind sequences of sentences into arguments are afforded maximum exposure. These and similar devices eliminate semantic considerations and permit the logician to occupy himself exclusively with the formal properties of reasoning, the syntactical properties of an idealized or reconstructed language.[6] The logician can be said to concern himself essentially with the nature of systemic intralinguistic truth, *validity,* rather than with the *verification* of any truth which requires extralinguistic referents.

Validity and Soundness in Argument

Thus, to say that a systematically related set of propositions expressed by sentences is formally *valid* is to say nothing about the material world. An argument is formally valid if and only if it belongs to a valid argument type which instantiates a valid logical forms. Its *validity* depends exclusively on its syntactical form, the rules governing the use of logical connectives. All arguments which are substitution instances of the same form are valid irrespective of any substitution in their nonlogical constituents. The *soundness* of an argument depends, on the other hand, not only on its valid form but on the truth of the premises which enter into it, premises which may contain nonlogical constants which give them extralinguistic reference.

Thus the sequence, "All democracies in which classes exist are dictatorships; America is a democracy in which classes exist; therefore America is a dictatorship," instantiates the valid argument form: "All A's are B; C is an A; therefore, C is a B." Such a sequence is formally valid. But any such argument is clearly not compelling. Technically speaking the argument is valid, but it may not be *sound*. It may be unsound because two of its constituent propositions, its premises, are suspect. They may be *empirically* false. In order to make such an argument sound as well as valid one would have to have empirical evidence that it is the case that all "democracies" (whatever that might mean) in which "classes" (whatever that means) exist are "dictatorships" (whatever that means). Moreover, one would have to evidence the assertion that classes exist in America. Only after the descriptive and corrigible truth of the two premises is confidently established and the premises found to inhabit a valid argument form, could the argument be characterized as sound. To establish the soundness of an argument one is driven to undertake a confirming or warranting strategy different from that which certifies its validity alone.

The study of the *formal* validity of arguments is singularly oblivious of their factual content. The preceding arguments can thus best be construed as a conditional: "If it is the case that all democracies in which classes exist are dictatorships; and further if it is the case that American democracy possesses classes; then it must follow (if one understands anything about the logic of the connectives 'all' and 'is') that America is a dictatorship." Whether any such hypothetical applies to any case under scrutiny involves a *factual* or *empirical* judgment, a decision with which logic alone cannot assist us. Thus the mathematical formula "$2+2=4$" expresses (given the logistic interpretation of mathematics) a logical truth. Whatever is contained (explicitly) in the predicate is already contained (implicitly) in the subject. If we understand what "2" means and what "+," "=," and "4" mean, to say that "2 + 2 = 4" is to assert that to say that there are two and two is to say that there are four. To say "two plus two" and to say "four" is to say the same thing. But to have said that is not to say that "two" or "four" or "2 + 2 = 4" applies to anything in the real world at all. Such formal statements reflects syntactical concerns: the equivalence of the symbols and an explication of the use of connectives.

Whether such a formula applies to anything extralinguistic will be the consequence of an empirical judgment. We would not normally apply such a formula, for example, to two drops of water and two drops of water. The union of two drops of water and two drops of water is not four drops. Such a formula as "2+2=4" is simply inapplicable under such circumstances. This will be true whenever certain empirical conditions governing appropriateness of application do not obtain. The entities to which numbers can be made to apply must, for example, be in some empirical sense discrete and retain their "individuality" in combination. This is obviously not the case with drops of water or clouds. Similarly, if two hungry lions are brought into proximity with two lambs the result would be two less hungry lions rather than four entities. We could only save the truth of the formula "2 + 2 = 4" by arbitrarily insisting that the two lambs continued to exist as discrete entities in the stomachs of the lion (until they were digested?).

In any event it becomes obvious that such applications turn on empirical decisions concerning how some mathematical terms are to be given *semantic referents* since such mathematical terms, in themselves, could not serve to *unambiguously* describe *any* features of the empirical world. Mathematics cannot tell you what will happen if you mix two quarts of any liquid with two quarts of any liquid. In the case of the mixture of gasoline and water what results from the mixture of two quarts of gasoline and two quarts of water is, in *fact*, something less than four quarts. Mixing two quarts of substance A with two quarts of substance B could produce, in fact, incalculable results. The results might well be an explosion

—to have said that four quarts would result from the mixing of any two quarts of one substance and any two quarts of another would have been *factually* false. Having less than the four units of volume that the mathematics of "2 + 2 = 4" might lead one to expect, is the only one of a variety of empirically possible outcomes. To apply logical truths to the world of politics, for example, in the search for material truth, involves restoring all the binding ligaments of semantic (and pragmatic) character from which they were, for the sake of analysis, abstracted. In principle, logic (and by implication mathematics and statistics) is concerned with the study of relations between certain abstract and uninterpreted symbols independent of any particular natural language. Once the symbolic notation is related to a natural language by interpreting the symbols that stand in the place of descriptive nouns, predicates and verbs, questions of semantics (and pragmatics), of meaning and material truth, are raised.[7]

When political scientists assign numerical values to extralinguistic entities, behaviors or expressions of attitudes or values, for example, the most urgent issues which engage critical attention are not whether numbers can be effectively handled, whether statistical treatment is intrinsically responsible, but whether the assignments have been made appropriately. When an attitude, for instance, is expressed by one respondent—is it equivalent to a seemingly similar attitude expressed by another? If one undertakes a content analysis of Hitler's speeches and finds that reference is made to war with a certain frequency—and it is subsequently found by similar analysis that the same references recur with the same frequency in the speeches of Mao Tse-tung—in what sense can it be said that numbers were assigned appropriately? Do the numbers count the same things in both cases? How and in what sense?

Numbers can be dealt with in a formal and systematic manner. Numbers inhabit a formal system. The application of numbers to the object world, however, involves complex semantic and pragmatic issues. However one interprets logical truths, and number systems as subsets of logical truths, there is general agreement that logical truths are purely formal, universal formulae devoid of descriptive constants or statements in which such nonlogical constants occur vacuously, and whose truths are therefore, in and of themselves, independent of any reference to the world of experience. Such logical truths purchase their status as necessary truths, insulated from falsification by any empirical facts, at the cost of being empty of any incorrigible correspondence with the world of observation. A logically true proposition contains no descriptive constant or if any such constants occur their occurrence is vacuous, that is, the truth value of the proposition does not change if any other syntactically admissible descriptive constant is substituted consistently throughout. The truth of a logically true proposition, or a valid argument, follows from the uses and deployment of the logical constants alone. The test of their logical truth is the result of formal calculation rather than empirical discovery. We know that the proposition asserted by means of the sentence, "All bachelors are unmarried," is true because it can, via the definition "A bachelor is an unmarried man" be translated into a logical truth: "All unmarried men are unmarried," or the form: "A = A." To recognize its truth it is not necessary that we understand the semantic meaning of the terms "bachelor" or "unmarried man." All we need to know is that the signs are subject to a transformation rule which renders them substitution instances of each other. Any synonymous signs (for example, "interactive elements in a set" and "system") could occupy the places in the formula and the formal truth value of the assertion would be preserved.

The systematic concern with the presence or absence, respective locations and functional use of logical signs, signs which have no "meaning" in isolation, like "and," "if," "is" and "therefore," and terms such as "all," "some," "not," "no," and formulae such as "both . . . and . . . ," "either . . . or . . . ," and "if . . . then . . ." has been the traditional preoccupation of *deductive* logic. Deductive logic has been concerned with how such connectives (and terms such as "not" have been construed as "connectives") can be understood to permit the transition from collections of premises to *unimpeachable conclusions*. A valid argument produces a *necessarily true conclusion*, a conclusion from which there is no appeal if one does not wish to assert a contradiction. In effect, formal deductive logic operates as a regulative, as a systematic and rigorous technique for avoiding contradiction—and non-contradiction is a domain invariant condition for any truth.

Logical analysis, in the formal sense, requires an abstraction from all descriptive content and focuses attention on the *form* of argument. Thus the sequence "All men are political animals; Socrates is a man; therefore Socrates is a political animal" is reduced to the form "All A's are B; C is B; therefore C is A" and reveals the same argument form as "All democracies in which there are classes are dictatorships; there are classes in American democracy; therefore America is a dictatorship." Both arguments are valid because both instantiate a valid argument form; they are syntactically isomorphic, sharing the same formal structure. Knowing the rules governing the use of "all," "are," "is," and "therefore," we know that in all arguments having the same formal structure, given the premises, the conclusion must logically follow. The *economy* of such a device is an obvious recommendation.

The practice, in logic, of substituting ordinary descriptive elements by uninterpreted symbols, simplifies any argument so that its logical form is revealed without the distractions generated by content. It also permits the logician to occupy himself with rules having general validity rather than having to scrutinize, individually, each argument that exemplifies the general form. Finally semantic vagueness and ambiguity are eliminated by the substitution of uninterpreted signs so that syntactical rigor is, in principle, possible.

Formal validity and invalidity are functions of the logical connectives as they operate between the conclusion and the premises on which it is purportedly based. Valid arguments are not, as has already been indicated, necessarily sound. This is indicated by the contemporary logician's disposition to couch arguments of the sort "All *A*s are *B*s; *C* is *A*; therefore *C* is *B*" in terms of a conditional, "If all *A*s are *B*s and *C* is *A*, then *C* is *B*." The conclusion which results is necessarily the case *given the antecedents*. The argument that "All power corrupts; Hitler was powerful; therefore Hitler was corrupt" is valid insofar as it exemplifies a valid argument form. Given the premises, the conclusion follows. We could not *consistently* accept the premises and disaffirm the conclusion. To legitimately resist the conclusion would require an examination of the *material* truth of the premises. The proposition that all power corrupts, however, pretends to advance a legitimate *synthetic* or *descriptive* knowledge claim—as does the characterization of Hitler as powerful. But any assessment of the truth status of such propositions requires recourse to semantic meaning and truth, concerns outside the confines of formal logic *per se*. Nonetheless, the putative general truth of the conclusion of any argument based on any collection of propositions of this order must meet the minimal domain invariant criterion of validity.[8]

Logic, Precision, and Heuristics

In the development of a science there comes a time when the inventory of truth claims becomes unmanageably large. Then there is a disposition to cull the set, to eliminate redundancies and reduce the catalogue to more manageable proportions. At such a juncture precise definition, substitution rules, are employed to identify and eliminate redundancies. But no matter how carefully a collection is so culled, every inventory of propositions entertained by a science requires, if for no other reason than mnemonic convenience, an ordering of some sort. One can simply provide *a seriatim* list of the propositions—as has been done by the authors of *Voting* and by Bernard Berelson and Gary Steiner in *Human Behavior: An Inventory of Scientific Findings*. But more efficient modes of ordering an inventory of propositions recommend themselves. One of the most interesting and significant ways of ordering propositions is *partial axiomatization,* which can take a variety of forms, but which most frequently appears as *definitional* and *proposition reduction*. Hans Zetterberg illustrates how definitional reduction proceeds by "reducing" a set of propositions borrowed from political sociology.[9] The inventory, for the sake of illustration, contains 1) three propositions, a set characterized as a "consensus list," propositions advanced as "findings" by empirical scientists in their study of their universe of inquiry; and 2) a list of definitions of critical concepts:

Prop. 1
Groups have less turnover than publics;

Prop. 2
Publics show less emotion than crowds;
Prop. 3
Groups show less emotion than masses.

The key terms in the list are defined in the following manner:

Def. A Groups are social aggregates interacting in terms of specified roles
with a common leader (e.g., a voluntary association).

Def. B Masses are social aggregates interacting (if at all) in terms of
unspecified roles but with a common leader (e.g., a radio audience).

Def. C Publics are social aggregates interacting in terms of specified
roles but without a common leader (e.g., a market).

Def. D Crowds are social aggregates interacting in terms of unspecified
roles and without a common leader (e.g., milling in Times Square).

Such a definitional reduction is normally conducted informally
by the researcher in the course of his work, but making the reduction
explicit has several merits: 1) it makes transparent the semantic
rules for tying the definition to the extralinguistic world (it will
be noticed that all these "aggregates" are, by definition, "sets" and
"systems"), and 2) it clarifies the concepts housed in the propositions. Such an effort reduces semantic variance. Such an effort
constitutes an initial move in the direction of axiomatization, and
instances of such strategy are to be found in any text devoted to
political inquiry in which categories are defined.

Such strategy has, furthermore, a more interesting theoretical
yield. By undertaking such reduction the theorist reveals *implications* interred in less explicitly formulated inventories.

Once some of the key terms employed in the propositions are
reasonably well defined, it is revealed that the original three "consensus" propositions provided by Zetterberg can be reduced to
two:

Theoretical Prop. 1 If a social aggregate has a common leader, then
its turnover is low (a group is a "social aggregate" having a "common
leader"—which follows by definition—conjoined with the original
proposition 1 which maintains that "Groups have less turnover than
publics").

Theoretical Prop. 2 If a social aggregate interacts in terms of specified
roles, then its level of emotion is low (which follows from the definitions

of "publics," "crowds," "groups," and "masses"—conjoined with the truth of the original propositions 2 and 3).

Moreover, if we accept theoretical proposition 1 and definition B, we can formulate a *novel* hypothetical proposition: "Masses have less turnover than crowds," a proposition *not* contained in the original consensus list. By employing reductive definition and rudimentary logic, a *new* proposition is generated. Thus partial axiomatization provides not only a mnemonic convenience, a specification of meaning rules and linguistic precision, but constitutes a heuristic technique (specifically, a method of suggesting novel research propositions) as well. What is required to effect partial axiomatization is semantic and syntactical invariance—a disposition to employ the language with semantic precision and logical consistency.

A more potentially interesting method of partial axiomatization is that which involves a reduction in the inventory of propositions by identifying some select subset of propositions as *postulates,* or axioms, and generating the remainder of the set by logical derivation. Strickland, Wade, and Johnston in their *Primer of Political Analysis,* provide such partial axiomatization by advancing a list of eight "assumptions" from which they purport to logically generate a finite class of derived propositions (theorems).[10] Zetterberg likewise provides an illustrative sample of a partial axiomatization.

Such an exercise is recommended to the political scientist by its potential yield. The most immediate consequence of the effort is to force the theorist to clarify vague and ambiguous concepts. Vagueness and ambiguity readily reveal themselves when efforts are made to logically relate propositions. But more than that, such an enterprise reveals how propositions are related to each other—what propositions are most basic to a system of thought—how the evidence from one proposition might support a number of entailed propositions and how, conversely, the abandonment of a basic proposition impairs the integrity of a subset of related propositions. In effect, as we shall see, even rudimentary axiomatization moves the theoretician on the way toward serious theory construction. The precision with which concepts must be specified if logical operations are to be undertaken with them, produce the conceptual specificity that reduces the semantic variance of ordinary language. Semantic meaning rules become explicit and specific—and what is to count as confirmatory evidence is increasingly revealed. Finally, the necessity of employing logical operations compels the theoretician to recognize the logical rules governing his enterprise, thereby reducing the syntactical variance characteristic of the locutions of ordinary language.

These are benefits similar to those which attend more extensive computer employments in political science. Computer programming has both sharpened our descriptive categories and compelled respect for the operative logic of electronic systems. Under such impetus even processes which were hitherto conceived as intuitively understood have turned out to require much more explicit statement once computer operations were anticipated. With the increased precision required by computer employment has come new understanding and still further precision and unexpected research hypotheses.

The relationship between logic and descriptive statements is still easier to countenance. The mathematics employed in the treatment of political science data is derivative of the basic axioms of set theory—logical operations. Mathematics, as we have already suggested, must be mapped on the nonlinguistic universe to serve the purposes of inquiry. This can only be accomplished by characterizing the elements of that universe with sufficient specificity so that mathematics (statistics, probability, and calculus) can be unambiguously employed. No one any longer doubts the efficacy of statistics and probability in analyzing, explaining and predicting occurrences in the object world of politics. The fact is that the theoretical yield of their employment rests on the joint employment of logic and semantic specificity.

The profit which attends the conjoint use of these techniques: the partially axiomatized propositions of a given consensus list, the specific identification of recognitors that define categories, the use of funded statistics—is illustrated in research efforts like the Simulmatics Project of Ithiel de Sola Pool and Robert Abelson.[11] The project employed the partially axiomatized propositions of cross-pressure theory, advanced empirical recognitors for the identification of "voter types" and "issue clusters," thereby categorizing the universe of elements under scrutiny, and exploited funded statistics in order to undertake a computer simulation of the 1960 Presidential election. The simulation produced a product-moment correlation over states between the Kennedy index on the simulation and the actual Kennedy vote in the national election of .82, an anticipation significantly better than any alternative approximation.

The Simulmatics Project is only one of those undertaken by political scientists sensitive to the demand for strategies that reduce semantic and syntactical variance—capable of employing sophisticated research strategies and hardware in the effort to better comprehend the political process. Computer employments require linguistic precision in order to provide the empirical categories upon which formal logic will operate. Logic is not only a study of valid argument forms, it is the foundation of mathematics as well. Moreover, it is a method for extracting implicit information from linguistic formulations. Logic certifies, minimally, that the necessary condition of truth ascription, consistency, has been met. Furthermore, it provides for an economical storage of information by eliminating redundancies. Finally, it is a heuristic device of incomparable yield, displaying entailments that subtend any collection of propositions as clearly and conclusively as the nature of the case allows. But logic, in and of itself, is devoid of empirical significance unless it is mapped over categories, sets and subsets in the universe of inquiry, defined in terms of direct and/or indirect recognitors.

Computer simulations in political science frequently reveal the strategy of logical employments: a set of axioms or "assumptions" are programmed into a computer—which performs a chain of deductive operations for the investigator, yielding implications that would otherwise have remained hidden—or a variety of programs are invoked in order to isolate that set of axioms which best yield a known set of implications. The latter strategy increases the power and generality, and unambiguously reveals the logical structure of theory. Supportive evidence, which might have otherwise escaped identification, is isolated.

Political science has only begun the effective employment of formal logic in theory construction. Its potential is obviously far greater than its current minimal yield. Computer simulation, with its semantic and syntactical requirements, affords a device for unpacking and assessing intuitively understood verbal theories, for drawing out implications, and for testing direct and implicit test hypotheses.

Inductive Logic

As has already been argued, the rigor of formal logic is purchased at a price. Its truths are incorrigible simply because they are insulated from experience—they are, in fact, formal, and tell us, in and of themselves, nothing of the material world. Formal logic concerns itself with linguistic transformations, the drawing out of implications contained in linguistic artifacts. The incorrigibility exemplified in valid arguments refers only to the connections that obtain between a conclusion and the premises on which it is based. If the premises contained in a valid argument are to refer to the material world, their truth must be established independently of formal logic. But since our knowledge of the material world is always contingent and inferential, every assertion about the world harbors a corrigible argument. This is implied by what was said about contingent statements. From immediate experience, visual and tactile, one asserts a simple proposition, "There is a table," or a complex proposition, "There are 52 issue clusters governing the voting preferences of a constituency." But such assertions are based on immediate or mediate evidence which, in itself, is never capable of establishing the *absolute* truth of either assertion (since it could, logically, be faulted by some conceivable future experience, i.e., we suddenly awaken from a dream or new evidence makes itself available). The assertions, "There is a table" or "There are 52 issue clusters . . ." are *probable inductive inferences*. We say, for ordinary purposes, that we are *certain* that the assertion "There is a table" is true. But the truth value we ascribe has the virtue of *practical* certainty—not *logical* certainty. Complex assertions are similarly and more obviously corrigible.

The point of such remarks is not to provide grist for the sceptic's mill, but merely to indicate 1) that all synthetic or empirical knowledge claims, regardless of semantic precision, are in principle corrigible, because 2) all such claims are in a significant sense inferential, and consequently 3) logic (although not necessarily *deductive* logic) enters into all, including our most pedestrian, deliberations. Thus it becomes clear that the logic which has occupied us thus far, formal deductive logic, provides a guide to the analysis of a special class of arguments: those that involve conclusions strictly entailed by their antecedent premises. Most of our ordinary knowledge claims do not involve a logic of this sort. They produce their warrant employing *inductive* logic.

To argue from visual and tactile experience to the instantial proposition affirming the existence of a table or the prevalence of "issue clusters" is to produce an argument of non-deductive form when measured against the strict standards of formal deductive logic. This is not to say, as the futilitarian seems to maintain, that such assertions are unwarranted. We have perfectly good reasons for asserting the existence of tables, other persons, social and political systems, historic events, "issue clusters," and all the objects of the universe. What we do not have are *necessary* truths concerning them. *This is to say no more than that any synthetic or empirical statement is nonanalytic.* It is a restatement of the difference that distinguishes the truth of a logico-mathematical, from an empirical, assertion. To provide a proof of the assertion "The square root of sixteen is four" is possible in a way that a proof of the assertion "There is a table" is not.

With the *possible* exception of the class of statements sometimes called "basic propositions," such as "I feel hot now," or "I am angry now" (provided the speaker is not subject to linguistic handicap), no empirical assertion is ever indefeasibly true. Certainly there are senses of "certainty" that we will, in ordinary language, apply to assertions about the empirical world. When we affirm a strong belief in the truth of an assertion and give every evidence of a readiness to act upon it, we say that we are "certain" of its truth. Commonplaces like, "If you jump from the Empire State Building, you will surely be injured," and "Eating eggs provides nourishment to human beings," are convictions of that kind. But it is evident that the conviction we justly accord such propositions rests on our commitment to the unproblematic truth of a variety of auxiliary lawlike statements, among others, about free fall, human susceptibility to injury, the laws governing the ingestion, digestion and assimilation of protein. Whatever evidence we have for such auxiliary assumptions is always instantial, that is, of such kind that while we would be mightily surprised if, in fact, jumping from the Empire State Building caused someone no injury and ingesting eggs caused someone to suffer deleterious consequences, such occurrences would not *logically* contradict the premises which led us to believe otherwise. The possibility of such unexpected occurrences is not logically precluded by the truth of the premises on which our present certainty is based. To say "On the evidence that x has jumped from the Empire State Building, one can say that x will be injured" is to say that most, perhaps all, individuals satisfying the first condition also (to date) have satisfied the second. Even when the finite class of instances which provide evidence for such an inference enjoy a truth-frequency equal to unity (it has, in the past, always been true that individuals satisfying the first condition have satisfied the second), counterinstances still remain *logically* possible. Thus inferential truths which share with necessary truths maximum truth-frequency remain marked by a significant difference. One would not utter a logical contradiction by asserting, "It is possible that some time in the future someone, under standard conditions, might jump off the Empire State Building and not be injured." Thus, while in ordinary language we do not distinguish between empirical claims having maximum truth-frequency and necessary truths, the difference between them is of real significance in the analysis of knowledge claims, for the difference exemplifies the difference between logical and factual truth claims.

There is another sense in which we employ "certainty" in characterizing empirical assertions. In making ordinary judgments about matters of fact, that is, in deciding if Richard Nixon won the Presidential election of 1968 we utter the proposition, "Nixon won the election in 1968" when we have calculated the election results. We say that the proposition is conclusively or definitively verified. But as a matter of fact such "complete verification" assumes the truth of a number of contextually unproblematic contingent truths: that one is not suffering hallucination either momentary or protracted; that one has not erred in calculation; that something unexpected will not be revealed by subsequent recount or inspection. Clearly one has no reason to entertain such doubts, but since every empirical affirmation of the simplest sort involves such auxiliary assumptions, the fact that such commonplace claims are not incorrigible is apparent. Again, one is simply saying that all empirical knowledge claims (with some few possible exceptions) are in principle subject to possible future refutation, that is, they are nonanalytic.[12] What we are dealing with in cases of this kind are perfectly respectable inferential truths based on inductive evidence.

If the premises of a deductive argument are incorrigibly true and the argument instantiates a valid argument form, the conclusion must *necessarily* be true. As a consequence, while deductive arguments make explicit whatever is already contained in the truth of the constituent premises, they can never add to the sum of knowledge already possessed. If the conclusion of an argument provides us with knowledge not implicit in its premises, the argument could not be *logically* conclusive. Thus whatever synthetic conclusions we accept, we accept because the premises are true, in the sense that they are supported by compelling evidence, and the reasoning is *responsible,* rather than necessary in the strict logical sense. What results is a conclusion that is *probably* true or which could be *reasonably affirmed.* As had been indicated, we may entertain beliefs of the kind, "The sun will rise tomorrow," with sure conviction, but while it would be legitimate to say we are certain, in practice, of the truth of such a proposition, it is necessary for an adequate analysis of the enterprise we call science to bear in mind that such a claim remains a *reasonable inductive inference* or a *high-order probability statement* rather than a necessary truth.

While formal deductive logic provides for truth ascriptions in the light of given premises once one has the requisite knowledge of the specific uses of logical connectives and the substitution rules governing signs employed in the language, most ordinary reasoning concerns itself with the truth status of the descriptive content of the propositions which serve as premises in any argument. The formal logician, in order to more adequately inspect the validity of argument forms, will employ a symbol or uninterpreted sign system devoid of descriptive reference. He is *not* concerned with how the sentential symbols and predicate and individual variables are rendered meaningful in any descriptive sense. But formal validity is only *one* aspect of argument. When the political scientist defines his terms and we are told, for example, that "By [personality characteristic] we refer to some inner predisposition of the individual" and "the term 'characteristic' applies to the state of the organism" conjointly with the commitment that "'personality' and 'psychological' are treated as synonymous,"[13] we can determine the permissible permutations of such terms as "personality characteristic" and "psychological state of the organism" employing the formal transformation rules governing synonymy. We are dealing with definitions and we can, independently of any experience, determine whether the author has violated any of the established rules governing the substitutability of equivalent terms. But when the same author maintains that "social 'characteristics' can *cause* psychological 'characteristics' . . . ," his claim is synthetic, empirical. And the techniques for certifying such a knowledge claim involve procedures other than those involved in correctly employing some subset of transformation rules.

In other words definitions can be deemed consistent or inconsistent, appropriate or inappropriate, convenient or inconvenient by indicating what one can or cannot do with them. But once a definition is advanced, the rules by virtue of which one term can serve as a substitution instance for another are specific. What makes sentences advancing knowledge claims interesting and important in the knowledge enterprise is their descriptive or synthetic content. In other words when one tenders a knowledge claim of the sort that one entity or process (suitably defined) "causes" another (independently defined), the truth claim has to be warranted by techniques other than formal logic. While we cannot violate any of the rules of formal logic in moving from one proposition to another or generating conclusions from arguments and expect our conclusions to be deductively valid, the conclusions of arguments that add to the sum of knowledge we have about the material world must necessarily invoke other criteria to establish their credibility.

The purpose of argument, deductive or inductive, is to establish true conclusions on the basis of true premises. To satisfy such an intention maximally, deductive logic abstracts its subject matter from any factual reference and occupies itself with the formal characteristics of language. Thus its conclusions never exceed the content of the premises which constitute its antecedents.

The proposition, "Every society has a social stratification system,"[14] permits us to validly deduce that if the United States of America constitutes a society, it possesses a social stratification system. No one minimally possessed of right reason will resist the conclusion to the syllogistic argument: "Every society has a social stratification system; America is a society; therefore, America has a social stratification system." We do not resist such an argument because it is invalid; we dismiss it because it is, in a real sense, trivial. In order to establish the unimpeachable material truth of the major premise, "Every society has a social stratification system," a complete inductive enumeration of all members of the class "societies" would have to be made and each and every member of the class be found possessed of a social stratification system. The general statement which serves as a major premis is equivalent to a finite and exhaustive conjunction of particular statements. It is obvious that if the enumeration is exhaustive, among those particular statements will be one which reads, "America is a society that has a social stratification system."

In effect what has presumably been done has been to employ meaning or semantic rules, rules which identify what is to serve as the designatum of the term "society," and the one makes a similar and independent specification of the designatum of "social stratification system." If the semantic rules are specific enough each member of the class of entities called "societies" can be investigated and the generalization, "for all x, if x is F then x is G" (or in ordinary language, "for all the entities in our universe of discourse, if that entity is a society then that entity has a social stratification system"), can be tendered. But as we have suggested, such a complete enumeration has established by direct evidence that the United States is a society and possesses a social stratification system. The deductive argument would not be ampliative, adding anything we did not know already, and would serve no purpose in such an instance.

One would probably have had to learn that the conclusion to the deductive argument was true before one could have learned that the major premiss was true.

Assumptions, Analogical Argument, and Speculative Hyphotheses

If generalizations of the sort "Every society has a social stratification system," are to have a non-trivial function in the knowledge enterprise, they must be something other than perfect inductions from instantial cases. We do not, in fact, normally employ generalizations covering a finite class of entities or processes. Rather, generalizations are usually employed to support conditionals of the following sort: "If any aggregate of men constitutes a society, then whatever other attributes it displays, it would have a social stratification system." This permits the generalization to be deployed over an *unrestricted* class of entities, past, present and future. Such a generalization can be effectively employed to generate verification studies in empirical science and to afford explanations of individual cases. It is obvious that such generalizations are more significant than complete inductions in which inferences are made from an examined population to a sample of it. But it is equally obvious that they require more than deductive logic to warrant their putative truth.

If we consider the plausibility of the generalization "Every society has a social stratification system," and we construe it not as an instance of perfect induction, but as an inductive generalization which supports subjunctive conditionals so that we expect any organized aggregate which satisfies the first condition "is a society" to satisfy the second "has a social stratification system," then it is obvious that the plausibility of the generalization will depend upon an unspecified number of assumptions, analogical arguments and auxiliary causal hypotheses. For example, stratification theorists might unpack the generalization attributing social stratification to every society into an assumption concerning the potentially *infinite* wants which characterize men and the *limited* disposable material or non-material resources that are available to satisfy them. As long as there are wants which exceed the availability of satisfaction, given certain auxiliary assumptions about individual and/or group egoistic disposition, social stratification, with some enjoying more and some enjoying less satisfactions, seems a plausible and predictable consequence. Thus Hitler, as a "stratificationist," argued:

> If for every creature on this earth the instinct of self-preservation, in its twin goals of self-maintenance and continuance, exhibits the most elementary power, nevertheless the possibility of satisfaction is limited, so the logical consequence of this is a struggle in all its forms. . . .[15]

What results is a conception of society, given certain assumptions, which exemplifies the consequence of struggle: stratification, which is the consequence of the causal interaction of an unlimited demand for "self-maintenance and continuance" and the limited possibilities of their satisfaction.

"Causal" inferences, even of this simplistic sort, constitute a proper subset of inductive inferences. Such inferences, as we shall see, require an elaborate justification. They must minimally satisfy a number of necessary conditions for their credibility. At this point it is only necessary to recognize that the truth status to which such accounts aspire is credibility, confirmability or acceptability. Such an account, because of its ampliative character, can never be logically or formally demonstrative. We can say that it is *established, confirmed,* or *supported* by evidence, meaning by this that the evidence makes its acceptance reasonable. Its establishment never attains demonstrative certainty. Moreover, at this point, something of the logic (in the extended meaning of the term) of "causal" inference becomes obvious.

The connection between stratification in society and the potentially unlimited demands made by the "instinct" of self-preservation and self-maintenance (Hitler speaks of the "unlimited . . . instinct for self-preservation . . .") and the limitations of conceivable satisfactions requires that an inverse inference be made from some discrete sample of creatures who have been characterized by such an "instinct" (once the term has been adequately defined and substantive studies have established that each creature gives evidence of its possession) to an entire population (". . . every creature on this earth . . ." and presumably creatures as yet unborn— a potentially infinite class). Conceivably the generalization involved in such an account might be established by arguing from observations made on non-human population samples and then attributed, by extension, to human populations conceived as sufficiently similar to warrant the ascription. Such an inference is called an "extensional predictive inference" and, in general, rests on a *similarity* between the respective classes conceived as sufficiently pervasive to warrant the attribution. Such an argument is essentially *analogical,* and exploits conceived similarities.

In the informal language of politics, analogies have, since antiquity, done yeoman service. Plato's "parable of the ship" in the *Republic* is an elaborate political analogy in which it is implied that the statesman must possess a body of knowledge comparable in scope, complexity and exactitude to the body of knowledge of "the seasons of the year, sky, stars and wind" indispensable to the navigator (it is a theoretical inference).[16] Plato is arguing that the activities of the navigator are sufficiently similar to the activities incumbent upon a statesman that any conclusions drawn from a study of the one class are applicable, in some sense, to the other. Similarly, John Stuart Mill argued that "like all things, therefore, which are made by men, they [governments] may be either well or ill made . . ."[17] The use of the metaphorical "like" indicates that Mill conceives a significant (theoretical inferential) analogy, i.e., from one class of objects to another, to hold between the production of artifacts and the contrivance of government. He is arguing that any conclusions applicable to the first class are, in some sense, applicable to the other.

Whether convincing or not, analogical reasoning (conceived as supporting extensional or theoretical inference) is regularly employed in the tendering of knowledge claims and in the subsequent discussion it will become increasingly apparent that the concept of "real similarity" is intrinsic to the knowledge enterprise. No two events in experience are ever exactly alike, nor does an object or organism remain identical from one instant of time to the next (the very fact that they occupy a different temporal and/or spatial locus would be sufficient to establish that). Nonetheless, our language employs generic terms, class terms whose extensions cover an indeterminate number of things to which the word can be correctly applied. Unless such simple processes as "perceiving similarities" are admitted, there is no possibility of generalizing beyond the unique occurrence and the single event.

The intuitive grasp of similarities and differences seems to be not only fundamental to the inductive process, but to language itself. Only proper nouns refer to specific cases. Most of the nouns in our language are generic, they have an extension that usually includes an indeterminate reference class. Inverse inference (making inferences from a sample of the population to the entire population) and predictive inference (making inferences from one sample to another sample) employ generalizations of a simple, categoric, extensional and/or theoretical sort in order to permit us to orient ourselves in our environment, venture on predictions, and tender explanations. Such generalizations rest on putative similarities between a reference sample and a population or between one reference sample and another.

Thus one of Hitler's arguments in support of racial purity turns on a calculated piece of analogical and extensional reasoning in which he argued that each animal "race" had a specifically defined genetic patrimony—"The fox is always a fox, the goose a goose, the tiger a tiger, etc., and the difference can lie at most in the varying measure of force, strength, intelligence, dexterity, endurance, etc., of the individual specimens"—and then proceeded to argue that specific human races (however defined) have similar specific biological endowments.[18] He negotiated the distance between reference samples (animal "races" and human races) via an extensional predictive inference whose warrant was a putative real similarity between them. The positive analogy suggested by the argument is defeated by an indication of the significant disanalogy, the negative analogy, that obviously obtains. Fox, geese and tigers constitute *species,* not *races.* Whatever can be argued about species cannot be applied, without supplementary premises, to races. The analogy is seen to be grossly defective; it is faulted by its failure to meet the requirement of *total evidence*. It is a well-established fact that species differ in substantive ways from races. The argument, nonetheless, moves artlessly from species to races as though such evidence were not available. The *minimal* requirement for the use of analogy in inductive reasoning is that *no* significant and relevant *disanalogy* obtain between the samples on which the inference is based and to which predicate ascriptions are made.

The critical and fundamental role of induction in any cognitive undertaking, the indispensable function and pervasiveness of analogical reasoning that subtends much of it, its intrinsic entanglement in semantic and pragmatic issues of staggering complexity have made induction the focus of critical concern for generations of thinking men.[19] Nonetheless, there are no "canons of induction" governing inductive procedures comparable in kind to the canons of logic that regulate the deductive formal sciences. We will have occasion to consider some of the special problems which beset induction in later chapters. For the time being it is sufficient to indicate that the absence of unequivocal procedures for drawing generalizations from any collection of evidence, while it imposes an onerous responsibility on our critical and analytic faculties, has not had stultifying effects.

The fact is that inductive inference operates within the context of funded evidence. In order to examine the rational warrant for a particular inductive generalization, one brings under examination, as a necessary condition, an entire history of the use of a stable core of relevant and unproblematic instances and generalizations, the vast and intricate array of *total evidence*. Inductive generalizations must find their place among a host of instrumentally well-entrenched generalizations, generalizations that employ an established vocabulary having an impressive historic "biography." Certain words have been applied to relationships which have afforded successful generalization in the past—and the referents of those terms have been observed in confirmed relationships shared by samples and populations or other samples to which they have been generalized. Generalizations operate within an environment structured by widely held general principles and evidence statements. The plausibility of an inductive inference depends in large measure upon its congruence with the corpus of well-entrenched rational beliefs. In scientific confirmation we speak of an inductive projection as being "in accord with prior probabilities," as compatible with essentially unproblematic "funded knowledge."

As we shall see, the generation of complex knowledge claims involves the employment of semantic and syntactical precision as well as the exploitation of inductive and deductive strategies. In 1952 it was found that a public opinion poll (the Purdue Opinion Panel, Poll No. 33 of October, 1952) taken among senior high school students, in which students from grades 9 to 12 were asked to choose from among the Presidential candidates available in that year, anticipated within one half of one percent error the actual subsequent Eisenhower popular vote. The collection of such evidence requires that the generalization concerning student preferences employ a specific categoric reference, that is to say that the category "student" be given a specific reference, stipulatively defined by the researcher—further, that if a sample of the population be employed, that sample be representative of the total population—and finally, that responses be sufficiently precise to avoid vagueness and ambiguity. Certain assumptions clearly subtend such an inquiry. Previous attitude and opinion studies, for example, provide funded evidence that questionnaires anonymously executed reflect, although with a certain degree of error, the actual attitudes and opinions held by respondents.

This particular empirical result must, in turn, find a place within the body of funded information. One of the best entrenched findings in empirical political research, to cite one instance of such funded knowledge, indicates that families tend to be homogeneous in their political loyalties—and there is evidence that these loyalties represent subtending attitudes. The degree of confirmed homogeneity in families permits the assignment of a probability estimate to attitude and performance variables of adults when the attitudes and performances of the young are suitably assessed. Conversely, it permits the assignment of a probability estimate to attitude and performance variables of the young when the attitudes and performances of adults are suitably assessed. The inductive findings are, in effect, logically related to funded information.

Because adults can be assumed to possess attitudes and loyalties before they are manifested among the young, it can be reasonably assumed that adults convey attitudes and loyalties to the young. Because we know something of the processes of attitude formation—the disposition of the young to identify with those adults who satisfy their basic nurturance needs and thus to reflect their attitudes and opinions—we begin to generate a complex and logically related linguistic artifact in which our empirical findings are accorded a place in a mutually supportive credibility structure. The empirical findings in the Purdue Opinion Panel support, and find support in, a host of independently established empirical generalizations about the attitudes and opinions of the young and their shared relationship with the attitudes and opinions of adults. These are housed among a set of systematically related propositions concerning attitude formation. The generalizations are the result of inductive procedures—the compatibility of findings is certified by logical scrutiny of their mutual implications. Neither empirical generalizations nor the mutual compatibility enjoyed by any determinate set of propositions could be established without semantic and syntactic precision. Loosely framed generalizations are insulated from inductive disconfirmation simply because of their vagueness and ambiguity. So framed, they offer little, if any, occasion for logical elaboration or the exposure of logical inconsistency.

Domain Variant Truth Conditions

What is important to recognize is that any analysis of the nature and the reliability of knowledge requires a reasonably sophisticated distinction between the domain variant rules governing language use. Every complex linguistic product involves linguistic entities which derive from the analytically distinct domains. Every knowledge claim having inferential character involves either deductive or inductive logic. Deductive logic, in reconstructed language, concerns itself with syntactical rules, and its truth claims are warranted by specific rules of validity. Inductive arguments involve the conjoint concern with semantic meaning and inductive principles, and truth ascription is licensed by appeals to direct or indirect observations (undertaken in unproblematic contexts).

Synthetic knowledge claims, including inductive inference, are governed by evidence conditions which seek to provide maximally reliable knowledge. The determination of the truth or falsity of complex epistemic products, characteristic of inquiries like that of political science, involve a characterization of the truth conditions applicable to the various linguistic domains. The subsequent chapters will attempt to exhibit something of the truth conditions appropriate to each domain—and how an assessment of the various and varying conditions applicable in each domain produce the truth warrants which make the knowledge claims of political inquiry maximally reliable.

Notes

[1] The term "pragmatics" is here used very loosely to cover at least two distinct ranges of concern: 1) the *utility* served by language and 2) the idiosyncratic psychological "connotations" of signs and sign complexes. Charles Morris refers obliquely and primarily to the first when he speaks of "pragmatics" as "the aspect of signs." (C. W. Morris, *Signification and Significance* [Cambridge, Mass.: MIT, 1964], p. 44.) Elsewhere, alluding to the same dimension of meaning, Morris refers to "pragmatics" as, "The study of the relation of signs to scientists. . . . Here belong the problems as to how the scientist operates, the connection of science as a social institution with other social institutions, and the relation of scientific activity to other activities." (C. W. Morris, "Scientific Empiricism," in *International Encyclopedia of Unified Science*, eds. O. Neurath, R. Carnap, and C. W. Morris [Chicago: University of Chicago, 1955], I, part 1, 70). Harold Lasswell and Nathan Leites allude to the same considerations. (Cf. H. D. Lasswell, N. Leites, et. al., *Language of Politics* [Cambridge, Mass.: MIT, 1965], p. 9, n.). We have used the term "pragmatics" to cover a subset of considerations that Morris refers to as the "significance" of signs and sign complexes, i.e., the private psychological meanings such signs may hold for individuals. "Significance" refers to "origin, uses and effects of signs" in so far as private meanings have an origin, a use and an effect. But their origin, uses and effects can be publicly studied and can then be the subject of *public* truth claims. Nonetheless, the private meanings of signs and sign-complexes should be distinguished from standardized public meanings—if only for the sake of analysis.

[2] Cf. F. Waismann, *Principles of Linguistic Philosophy* (New York: St. Martin's, 1965), chap. xvi; L. Wittgenstein, *Philosophic Investigations* (New York: Macmillan, 1953), pp. 30, 43, 353, and *Blue and Brown Books* (Oxford: Blackwell, 1958), p. 23.

[3] H. Morgenthau, "The Impact of the Cold War on Theories of International Law and Organization," in *Theory of International Relations*, ed. A. A. Said (Engle-

115

wood Cliffs, N.J.: Prentice-Hall, 1968), p. 177.

4 For a more comprehensive discussion of this thesis, see A. Pap, *Elements of Analytic Philosophy* (New York: Macmillan, 1949), chap. 8, and P. Alexander, *Sensationalism and Scientific Explanation* (New York: Humanities, 1963).

5 This is not to be understood in the strict sense. To maintain that logical truths are strictly syntactical would commit one to the defense of a thesis that is subject to expert reservation. Charles Morris early suggested such an analysis (C. W. Morris, "Foundations of the Theory of Signs," in *International Encyclopedia of Unified Science,* ed. O. Neurath, R. Carnap, and C. W. Morris [Chicago, University of Chicago, 1955], 1, part 1, 79–137). R. Carnap attempted a formal defense in his early *Logical Syntax of Language* (New York: Humanities, 1951; originally published in 1937), but was forced to revise his position by the time he wrote his *Introduction to Semantics* (Cambridge, Mass.: Harvard, 1948). G. J. Warnock's *English Philosophy Since 1900* (New York: Oxford, 1966), chap. 10, contains a brief but informative discussion of some of these issues.

6 For an introduction to these techniques, cf. S. Gorowitz, R. G. Williams, *Philosophical Analysis* (New York: Random House, 1963).

7 See C. G. Hempel, "On the Nature of Mathematical Truth," in *Readings in the Philosophy of Science,* ed. M. Brodbeck and H. Feigl (New York: Appleton-Century-Crofts, 1953), pp. 149–162; J. Hospers, *An Introduction to Philosophical Analysis* (New York: Prentice-Hall, 1953), pp. 109–123. The difficulty in making sharp distinctions between logical and empirical truths is, as has been already suggested, that in any actual language any attempt to explicitly formulate general rules or conventions that would limit the sphere of syntactical rules as distinct from semantic meanings is misleading and often arbitrary. See J. L. Austin, "The Meaning of a Word," in *Philosophy and Ordinary Language,* ed. C. E. Caton (Urbana: University of Illinois, 1963), pp. 1–21.

8 It is interesting to note that contemporary philosophers in the Soviet Union are prepared to grant the merit of such an account. Cf. L. O. Resnikow, *Erkenntnistheoretische Fragen der Semiotik* (Berlin: VEB, 1968), chap. 9. For those who insist that validity and truth are irredeemably ideological, the gradual admission by the purveyors of "dialectical logic" that formal logic cannot entertain literal contradictions, and that formal sign

systems are synthetically empty and require semantic rules of reference for their material truth, is salutary counterevidence.

9 H. L. Zetterberg, *On Theory and Verification in Sociology* (a much revised edition. Totowa, N.J.: Bedminster, 1963), pp. 31ff.

10 Cf. D. A. Strickland, L. L. Wade, and R. E. Johnston, *A Primer of Political Analysis* (Chicago: Markham, 1968).

11 I. de Sola Pool and R. Abelson, "The Simulmatics Project," in H. Guetzkow, *Simulation in Social Science* (Englewood Cliffs, N.J.: Prentice-Hall, 1962), pp. 70–81.

12 For an interesting and insightful discussion of some of these issues, see M. Black, *Problems of Analysis: Philosophical Essays* (Ithaca: Cornell University Press, 1954), pp. 58–79, and Pap, *Elements of Analytic Philosophy,* chap. 8.

13 F. Greenstein, "The Impact of Personality on Politics: An Attempt to Clear Away Underbrush," *American Political Science Review 61,* 3 (September, 1967), 631 and n. 5.

14 D. Apter, "A Comparative Method for the Study of Politics," in *Comparative Politics,* ed. H. Eckstein and D. Apter (New York: The Free Press, 1963), p. 82.

15 A. Hitler, *Hitler's Secret Book,* trans. S. Attanasio (New York: Grove, 1961), p. 6.

16 Plato, *Republic,* VI, 488a–489a.

17 J. S. Mill, *Considerations on Representative Government* (Chicago: Regnery, 1961), p. 4.

18 A. Hitler, *Mein Kampf,* trans. R. Manheim (Boston: Houghton Mifflin, 1943), p. 285.

19 For an interesting discussion of the general problem of induction, see N. Goodman, *Fact, Fiction and Forecast* (New York: Bobbs-Merrill, 1965); I. Scheffler, *The Anatomy of Inquiry* (New York: Knopf, 1963), pp. 227–326; C. G. Hempel, "Inductive Inconsistencies," in *Aspects of Scientific Explanation* (New York: Free Press, 1965), pp. 53–79; M. Black, "Induction," in *Problems of Analysis,* pp. 157–228.

Suggested Readings

Barker, Stephen F. *The Elements of Logic.* New York: McGraw-Hill, 1965.

Coplin, William D. *Simulation in the Study of Politics.* Chicago: Markham, 1968.

Hospers, John. *An Introduction to Philosophical Analysis.* New York: Prentice-Hall, 1954. Chaps. 1, 2, 3.

Messick, David M., ed. *Mathematical Thinking in Behavioral Sciences.* San Francisco: Freeman, 1968. Part 1.

Rescher, Nicholas. *Introduction to Logic.* New York: St. Martin's, 1964.

Skyrms, Brian. *Choice and Chance: An Introduction to Inductive Logic.* Belmont, Calif.: Dickenson, 1966.

Smart, J. J. C. *Between Science and Philosophy.* New York: Random House, 1964. Chap. 2.

5

On Concept Formation, Conceptual Schemata, and Generalizing Knowledge Claims

At any age, a concept embodied in a word represents an act of generalization . . . . There is every reason to suppose that the qualitative distinction between sensation and thought is the presence in the latter of a *generalized* reflection of reality, which is also the essence of word meaning . . . .

Lev Vygotsky

Concepts. . . mark out the paths by which we may move more freely in logical space. They identify modes or junctions in the network of relationships, termini at which we can halt while preserving the maximum range of choice as to where to go next. . . . Every taxonomy is a provisional or implicit theory (or family of theories).

Abraham Kaplan

It is little more than a truism to assert that there is a dialectical interaction and communality between verbal and conceptual processes and knowledge claims. The "object world," the source of the recognitors which constitute the raw materials out of which knowledge claims are fashioned, remains—without the sorting criteria provid-

119

ed by systematic language use—opaque and unintelligible. The "world," in and of itself, is unintelligible. Nothing about it can be significantly characterized as true or false, meaningful or meaningless. It is our *talk* about the world to which such ascriptions can be made. But to have said as much is not to commit ourselves to the notion that truth and falsity, meaningfulness and meaninglessness, are exclusively ideational artifacts, that they are the products of thought itself or speech itself. The world *presents* itself to us as a temporal flow of experience composed of *discriminable* constituents. The world, even opaque and unintelligible as it is before enformed by language, is not a seamless, homogeneous whole. The mystic's conviction that "All things are one," is not the product of immediate experience unmediated by language—it is the bizarre product of linguistic oversophistication. It is the fevered consequence of verbal gymnastics.

What we encounter in experience are discriminable recognitors, stimuli—the basis of generalizations—identifiable indices of enduring or recurrent sets and subsets of experience. We note similarity and differences in the flow of experience. The similarities and differences are *imposed* upon us. Their involuntary and insistent appearance—their indifference to our indisposition to attend them—is the operational distinction which, in fact, marks out "reality" from daydream. The fact that we can discriminate indices of enduring and recurrent elements in experience, that similarities and differences *do* obtain, provides us with leverage on the future. We can begin to anticipate experience. We order experience to make it intelligible to us—if it is intelligible to us we can begin to operate effectively within it. We are no longer so much subject to experience. We begin to master it.

It is now a commonplace among developmental and comparative psychologists that the ordering of experience can take many forms. The child, for example, faced with the flow of impressions, collects discriminable recognitors together in what appear to us as curious congeries. When he begins to speak, he might use a term to denote nothing more than a vague conglomeration of discriminable impressions that somehow or other came to be associated in his mind. This heaping together of (to us) seemingly disparate elements is the result of the child's attempts to organize experience on the basis of temporary and subjective *relations* that he experiences as obtaining between those elements. The relationships, by virtue of which he groups impressions, may be simple contiguity in space and time or the consequence of the possession of some attribute which, for all practical purposes, we see as idiosyncratic or nonessential.[1] Such congeries are manifestly unserviceable in providing reliable anticipations of the future insofar as their recurrence is at best episodic and accidental. The child uses a sign to identify a collection of impressions that as that *specific* collection will not (or will rarely) recur. Such linguistically primitive conceptual schemata afford no anticipations of future experience—they have no adaptive utility. Furthermore they are by and large unintelligible. The child has, in effect, a partially private, and a manifestly privative, language.

The child, constrained by pragmatic considerations and by the rules governing interpersonal communication, very quickly learns to identify maximally similar, functionally significant and systematically recurrent environmental recognitors—stimuli that can be unproblematically identified by his community of language users and which recur with sufficient frequency to provide him with predictive advantage. He identifies the "real" attributes of things, and deploys signs over them. Adults positively reinforce this disposition. We applaud his success in meaningfully categorizing aspects of his environment, i.e., aspects which will be maximally serviceable in anticipating future experience and which permit him to communicate effectively with the other language users in his community. In reality, we standardize, to an appreciable extent, his sign uses. Such standardization is the prerequisite for the use of words, and language in general, as generalizing instruments.

General Terms

The words in our language have, most characteristically, *general* employments. They do not characteristically have idiographic use. Even proper names can be used, under appropriate conditions, to identify a variable number of referents. They can, under alternate appropriate conditions, be made to have specific reference, but then almost any substantive can be given specific determinate use by the use of indexical or pointer words.

It is obvious that everything in experience is different in *some* sense. The fact that each separate thing (however conceived) occupies, as has been suggested, a different temporal or spatial locus is enough to establish that. Therefore language must be adaptable enough to be used to refer to unique instances. But it is more obvious still that any language that had only the capacity to uniquely refer would not be a language at all. If we entertained a different sign to identify each thing that was different in *any* sense, our language would be as complex as experience itself and would cease to serve the purpose of bringing order to, and orientating us in, that experience. Such a language would be a duplication of experience—and would, consequently, be manifestly futile. Not only would we not be able to order, and orient ourselves in, experience, we would find communication impossible. Each of us would have "different" experiences, each experience couched in appropriately distinctive and specific signs, unfathomable to our interlocutor. Even monologue would be impossible, for in order to recall the simplest past experience we would have to engage a potentially limitless collection of discrete memory elements.

Language, of course, is not calculated to duplicate experience. There would be little point to that. Language is a generalizing instrument. It permits us to organize whole ranges of experience and effectively and intersubjectively talk about shared experience. It accomplishes these tasks because we have the capacity to isolate *recognitors,* those recurrent symptomatic elements in experience that serve as sorting criteria for the effective intersubjective employment of general signs—*concepts.* [2] Concepts are public signs that refer to groups, categories or collections of things, events, impressions or the relations between them; their felicitous use is characterized by the presence of specific symptomatic stimuli (recognitors) which constitute the evidence conditions for their correct employment. Knowledge of a concept implies an ability to identify its recognitors. The behavior exemplified in concept use is perhaps best characterized as an identification or a selection. At the most primitive level the necessary distinctions among attributes are for the most part not dependent on training—they are the immediate response to discriminable stimuli.[3] The stimuli are identified ostensively—"that is red," "that is hard," and their analogues, constitute the "primitives" of ordinary language use. They provide the unproblematic basis of the most elementary concept formation—easy and confident confirmation.

Conceptual Schemata

In effect, as children of whatever language community, we all inherited this elementary, ordinary, and essentially spontaneous conceptualizing faculty. There are spontaneous and relatively unself-conscious ordinary conceptual schemata to which we adapt—which are the patrimony left us by our antecedents—which they spontaneously evolved in order to adapt to the relatively circumscribed demands made in a particular ecological and cultural niche under general historic conditions. We (just as they did) employ language to guide ourselves through everyday activities, and in that essentially untroubled context we (just as they did) talk of external things known to us through their action on our bodies. The primitive terms of such an elementary language refer to essentially unproblematic sensory experience. As we mature and expand the range of our experience, we find ourselves outside the untroubled range of elementary ordinary language. We find ourselves in situations which make different demands upon us—in situations in which elementary common schemata are no longer effective guides. There is insistent reason for undertaking more deliberate inquiry into our untroubled and unself-conscious talk. Such inquiry is none the worse for being undertaken initially within the spontaneous and entrenched framework of the elementary funded language. No inquiry is possible unless *some* conceptual scheme is initially available.[4]

The spontaneous, more complex conceptual language of adults in our society, on the other hand, is couched in terms of macrophysical "thing" objects enjoying multiple predicative and relational properties. We begin with a complicated but unsophisticated language structured by unself-conscious, ordinary conceptual categories. Our use of concepts is undeliberative. Jean Piaget indicates, for example, that seven and eight year olds adequately employ complex conceptual words like "because." Yet their use is unreflective—outside the range of familar employments (probably the consequence of simple mimicry), the use of the concept becomes bizarre. What knowledge the child has of the use of such concepts is, at best, *procedural*. He knows, within a familiar range of uses, *how* to use the concept in commonplace contexts. And such knowledge is, by and large, adequate. He has little, if any, occasion to invoke the term except in familiar circumstances. The conscious and reflective use of the term is the result of using it in new and more complex problem situations. We begin to specify its "grammar" in the measure that the linguistic operation is no longer undertaken in familiar and unproblematic contexts. To become conscious of the grammar of a term, to exhibit its function, is to transfer its use from the ordinary and familiar to the extraordinary and unfamiliar. "Because" is a complex relational concept; its use varies with its context. To understand its implications is to become reflective and deliberate in its use, to be conscious of its varying and various functions.

Spontaneous and unreflective common conceptual schemata are predictably informal. We have procedural knowledge of the use of their constituent concepts. In operating with such concepts attention is focused on the business at hand, the communication or the organizing of experience in fruitful fashion, never on the act of concept use itself. Such concepts, and the schemata in which they unself-consciously appear, are simply "given."

Actually the term "because" invokes a complex concept, a concept similarly invoked by its analogues: "therefore," "since," "if . . . then," "gives rise to," and "produces," among others. In ordinary language, even as adults, we use such signs with the ease of familiarity. We exchange assertions containing such signs and a variety of analogues as though they were all equivalent and equally transparent. It is only when assertions are challenged, and truth warrants are requested, that we begin to realize that the uses of "*a* gives rise to *b*," "*b* because *a*," and "if *a* then *b*" are not at all luminous. We begin to appreciate that the relationship between a and b cannot be adequately characterized in terms of "gives rise to," "produces," or "therefore." Such employments conceal a host of difficulties.

The deliberative use of a complex concept like "because" begins with an effort to characterize its employment. A "because" response is a reply to a "why" question. A "why" question is the result of having observed some variation in human or natural events that occupies our attention. A reasonably discrete class of variable behavior, in the partially formalized sciences, is identified in terms of a "dependent variable." Some variable behavior is identified as "dependent," the consequence of the impact of some one or several operant factors. One asks why individual, collective or natural behavior varies as it does. The response to such questions is made in terms of an "independent" variable or variables effecting changes in a "dependent" variable or variables—ideally a testable hypothesis is framed to account for the perceived variation. The variable behavior of the individual voter, for example, is conceived as influenced by an indeterminate, but finite, number of factors— his intelligence, political socialization and the sum of funded information and motivation among others. One conjures up a schema in which there is a multiplicity of operative influences. One further attempts to isolate specific influences and one speaks of "intervening" variables, and "operative" variables.

Intrinsic to such efforts is a systematic and relatively rigorous effort to specify what is to count as a variable. Concepts are defined in terms of observable recognitors and, if possible, quantified to insure precision and reliability. "Growth rates," and "frequency rates" are assigned to variable behaviors. Crime statistics, voting behavior and the prevalence and salience of attitudes are entertained in order to permit knowledge claims to be formulated with confirmable precision. The relationships between identifiable variables, dependent and independent, are characterized as reversible or irreversible, necessary or substitutable, sufficient or contingent, deterministic or stochastic, sequential or coextensive, or conceived in a complex interdependency relationship.[5]

When the use of constituent concepts, understood to stand in some kind of correlative connection to each other as dependent and independent variables, becomes deliberative, a preliminary or quasi-systematic conceptual schema becomes partially formalized. A concept is given (among others) lexical, criterial or contextual definition. Its use is self-consciously specified. Any systematic knowledge enterprise soon finds itself preoccupied with partial standardization of semantic meaning and partial formalization of the putative relationships that obtain between variables. The unself-conscious ordinary language schema inherited from common discourse becomes gradually transformed. In disciplines like history and political science the process has been less evident than it has been in the maximally formalized sciences, but it is apparent none-theless. The process is manifest in the work of individual authors.

In his youthful works, for example, Karl Marx regularly charac-terized the relationship between variables in terms of metaphors. "Political ideas," for instance, were spoken of as the "efflux" or the "sublimates" of "material life activity." The "economic base" was spoken of as "determining," and sometimes as "conditioning," or "altering" "social consciousness." By the time *Das Kapital* was written, twenty years later, the assertions concerning "effluxes," "sublimating," "giving rise to," "determining," and "conditioning," had become more sophisticated "tendency statements," qualified by contingencies, and countertrends. An effort had been made, by Marx himself, to reduce the exploitation of metaphor and advance testable propositions specifying the relationships conceived to obtain between reasonably well defined variables.

The development of more sophisticated, deliberative conceptual schemata, characterizes the progressive evolution of significant inquiry. Concepts begin to be self-consciously employed. The initial move in the direction of deliberative use generally takes the form of more adequate *definition*. Scholars and research personnel lament the "semantic confusions," the "obscurity, vagueness and ambigui-ty" which markedly interfere "with fruitful research," competent storage, retrieval, and interpretation of information.[6] The claims made via spontaneous and unreflective quasi-scientific conceptual schemata are fugitive—insulated from counterinstances and dis-confirming evidence by virtue of their vagueness and ambiguity.

Such rudimentary preliminary schemata share these traits with the undeliberative schemata of ordinary language. Commonsense admonitions like "look before you leap," and "he who hesitates is lost," are both advanced and defended as true largely because they are couched in the vague and ambiguous language of ordinary discourse which insulates them from both confirmation and disconfirmation. Similarly, Marxist claims like "material life conditions *determine* consciousness," and "material life conditions *alter* "consciousness" are both tendered and conceived true in the same unreflective manner. Maintaining that "material life conditions" *determine* "consciousness," however, means something quite different, and requires a different truth warrant, than saying that such conditions *alter* "consciousness." Nor can we say with any confidence that we understand what the complex sign "material life conditions" unambiguously refers to. Marxist enthusiasts will similarly employ the term "consciousness" as though its signification were self-evident. Ordinary language and rudimentary scientific language harbor such obscure knowledge claims because both are, in variable degree, nondeliberative and imprecise.

It is the search for reliability in assigning truth status to such claims that compels serious efforts at a more systematic exhibition of the logic of concept formation and the "grammar" of their respective uses. Generally these efforts involve a more careful characterization of the semantics and syntactics of concept employment. Signs which refer to properties or relations are accorded explicit, recursive, implicit, criterial, contextual or stipulative definition.

Definition

A definition is a way of teaching someone how to employ the *definiendum,* the sign to be defined. Logicians and mathematicians speak of *explicit* definitions, an enumeration of those attributes conceived as necessary and sufficient to license entry into a class. Thus the explicit definition of a "square" in formal language is: "a quadrilateral figure all of whose sides are equal in length and all of whose angles are equal." Such definitions are characteristic of formal, reconstructed, or artificial languages. They provide the necessary and sufficient condition for entry into a class.[7] The *definiens* is the logical equivalent of the *definiendum*. *Recursive* definitions share essentially the same traits. They are most common in artificial languages where the *definiendum* is defined in terms of a finite series of transformations. They have maximum serviceability in the formalization and mathematization of theory—providing specific meaning for concepts such as "optimum," "equilibrium," "differential," "integral," and the like. Outside the confines of formal or reconstructed languages, however, explicit and recursive definitions appear with remarkable infrequency.

What we generally find in partially formalized disciplines are implicit, criterial, contextual or stipulative definitions. A concept is said to be *implicitly* defined when the principal characteristics of the class of objects it is understood to denote are exhibited in a systematically related set of descriptive propositions which host it.

Any propositions which are statemental constituents of an empirical theory are composed of a logical and a nonlogical (or descriptive) vocabulary. The logical vocabulary can be carefully codified and the structural relations exhibited by the collection of propositions made explicit. Such a collection of systematized propositions (system defined in terms of the *relationships* which obtain between the concepts and statemental constituents) becomes an *analytic* conceptual schema. *Syntactical variance* is partially or maximally reduced in order to reveal the implicit semantic meaning of its constituent nonlogical concepts.

Anthony Downs' *An Economic Theory of Democracy* provides instances of implicit definition. The two major hypotheses which subtend the work are 1) that political parties in a democracy share certain analogous characteristics with entrepreneurs in that they attempt to maximize the number of votes they receive in any election (entrepreneurs attempting to maximize profit) and 2) that citizens behave rationally in politics. These two hypotheses are housed in a partially formalized set of subsumptive propositions. Within the set, "party motivation" is accorded meaning in a subset of "derived" propositions about the "implications" of the primary "postulates," or "axioms." Downs conveniently summarized the derived propositions at the end of his treatise and provided an indication where the interstitial propositions are to be found which make the "deriva-tion" reasonably precise. The complex concept "party motivation" is implicitly (and incompletely) defined in the following set of propositions:

Proposition 1
Party members have as their chief motivation the desire to obtain the intrinsic rewards of holding office; therefore they formulate policies as means to holding office rather than seeking office in order to carry out preconceived policies.

Proposition 2
Both parties in a two-party system agree on any issues that a majority of citizens strongly favor.

Proposition 3
In a two-party system, party policies are (*a*) more vague, (*b*) more similar to those of other parties, and (*c*) less directly linked to an ideology than in a multiparty system.

Proposition 4
In a multiparty system governed by a coalition, the government takes less effective action to solve basic social problems, and its policies are less integrated and consistent, than in a two-party system.

Proposition 5
New parties arise when either (*a*) a change in suffrage laws sharply alters the distribution of citizens along the political scale, (*b*) there is a sudden change in the electorate's social outlook because of some upheaval such as war, revolution, inflation, depression, or (*c*) in a two-party system, one of the parties takes a moderate stand on an issue and its radical members organize a splinter-party to force it back towards a more extreme position.

Proposition 6
Democratic governments tend to redistribute income from the rich to the poor.

Proposition 7
Democratic governments tend to favor producers more than consumers in their actions.[8]

A term so defined is defined via the meaning exhibited in the collection of propositions it "entails." To appreciate the cognitive content of propositions one through seven is to know what "party motivation" means in the context of Downs' discussion. The expression "party motivation" obviously has variable meaning in ordinary language. Downs has implicitly and partially standardized its meaning by lodging it in a logically articulated set of propositions. By doing that, Downs has provided a collection of potentially testable propositions which together provide for public meaning and set some of the principal evidence conditions governing the terms so defined.

Talcott Parsons' treatment of "power" illustrates, similarly, the strategy of establishing and conveying meaning via the "entailments" of "implicit definition."[9] The discussion begins (as is the case with Downs) with an analogy: "Power is comparable to wealth, which, as a generalized societal resource, is allocated to many different social subsystems for 'consumption' or for 'capital' use." From that point on, "power" is implicitly defined in the collection of propositions Parsons argues are "entailed" by the expression. "Entailment" suggests logical interrelatedness, but the logic of such definitions (particularly as they are found in political inquiry) is singularly informal and implicit definitions are, as a result, characteristically porous. Nonetheless, the strategy is that of implicit definition—essentially *analytic* efforts at the public characterization of meaning.

That such is the case is indicated by the fact that authors like Parsons regularly inform political scientists that their schemata "in no way" purport to be empirical contributions. Such efforts, they say, are subject to "logical, not empirical proof"—precisely what one would expect from nontheoretical, analytic formulations.

An implicit definition conveys the public meaning of a sign by housing that sign in a logically articulated set of propositions. Since the logic of such sets, particularly as they are articulated by political scientists in the areas of comparative politics, international relations and general theory construction, is not rigorous, the conceptual terms are therefore only incompletely defined.

An alternate definitional strategy regularly invoked by political scientists is that which attempts to specify public meaning via *criterial* or *range* definitions. These are definitions provided in terms of a system of overlapping and interacting criteria. No one of the criteria is in itself necessary, nor is any one of them sufficient, to provide entry into the class. The set of attributes which license entry into a class are conceived, severally, as relevant (sometimes referred to as "essential") and, given the pragmatic intent of the enterprise in which the concept is to be employed, a judgment of "weight" can be accorded any one or any number of them. Specifying relevant attributes provides the tests which can be employed in establishing whether or not the concept is being correctly deployed over given specimens. In order, for example, to determine if a bit of behavior is to count as a "crime," or as evidence of a "prefascist" disposition, some reference must be made to some symptomatic observable evidence that the specimen is required to display if entry into the requisite class is to be warranted.

By way of illustration one can consider the criterial definition offered by Carl Friedrich and Z. K. Brezezinski characterizing "totalitarian dictatorships." The authors offered, synoptically, four criteria governing entry into the class: 1) an official ideology; 2) a single mass party led typically by one man; 3) a system of terroristic police control; and 4) a technologically conditioned nearcomplete monopoly control of the media of information, the means of coercion and the national economy. Any system of government that evinces all such characteristics is spoken of, properly, as a totalitarian dictatorship. The collection of symptomatic traits constitutes a criterial definition of a special class of objects.

Such a criterial definition can be conceived as providing a dual set of mutually exclusive and exhaustive categories: i.e., totalitarian and nontotalitarian. Such a binary system is obviously inadequate to represent political reality, and authors like Dante Germino have argued that although Fascist Italy "fell short of the totalitarian mark" with respect to the extent and degree of police control employed, the regime, nonetheless, qualified as "totalitarian."[10]

The strategy tacitly employed is to conceive the concept "totalitarian" in terms of criterial, rather than explicit, definition. As defined by Friedrich and Brzezinski, "totalitarian" is an "extreme" type with a graded series of intermediate types occupying attribute space between the two extremes, "nontotalitarian," and "totalitarian." A precise division of the two, Germino implicitly maintains, is "artificial," theoretically sterile, "untrue" to the political reality. The property traits of totalitarianism can, by implication, be exhibited in varying degrees, degrees measured *quantitatively* (e.g., what determinate degree of police control would qualify as "terroristic," what specific measure of formal support must an ideology be given to count as "official"?) or *qualitatively*.

Similarly, should there be no "unitary party," but a "popular front," while the remaining symptomatic traits were in evidence, would the political system still count as "totalitarian" or not? That is, if any *one* of the criterial traits were totally absent would the system *still* be characterized as a member of the class "totalitarian"?

In effect, such criterial definitions in political science are more frequently than not merely programmatic suggestions, a heuristic propaedeutic to systematic inquiry. Such formulations generally constitute suggestive programmatic characterizations— mnemonic summaries of intuitive assessments of a wide variety of descriptive materials. Once the programmatic characterization is given specific reference, what results is usually a typology, an ordering of concepts of a purely comparative sort representing a continuum of complex attribute spaces.

Because of such considerations, and the frequency with which they are not appreciated, political scientists will often differ in their characterizations of systems. Germino counts Fascist Italy as "totalitarian"—Hannah Arendt, H. Stuart Hughes, and Sigmund Neumann refuse to do so. Many political scientists count the Soviet Union as "totalitarian"—Allen Kassof has suggested an alternate classification, "administered society," to accommodate the Soviet Union as a "totalitarian" system without police terror.[11]

Criterial definitions can be effectively employed only if the criteria marking entry into the class is specified with all the precision the subject matter allows. What is, for example, "near monopoly" or "bureaucratic" control of the economy, and how is it measured? If the "unitary party" is spoken of as "hierarchically, oligarchically organized," how is the degree of such organization identified? Each of the criterial attributes has variable manifestations. Moreover, one must decide if a "significant" or "essential" similarity obtains even if one or more criterial attributes are effectively absent. Criterial definitions, to be employed, require judicious "weighing" and specific characterization. The ultimate justification of their use will turn, minimally, on at least the following considerations: 1) are the criteria delivered with sufficient precision to render their employment unequivocal? 2) are the attributes "weighted," that is, are some of the attributes conceived more essential to the generation of more economical and more fruitful schemata in terms of didactic, heuristic, mnemonic, or theoretical yield? The use of criterial definitions is warranted by their power, their ability to more effectively serve as instructional or recall conveniences and/or their capacity to generate more testable propositions involving a wider range of phenomena than any alternative characterization. Ideally, the most suitable characterization would achieve maximal yield in all these respects.

The talk about "essential attributes" of the phenomena under political investigation and "real definitions" which have significant theoretical import, generally alludes to criterial definitions of the sort indicated above.[12] Such definitions are proffered as a consequence of a search for an empirical explanation of some phenomenon or set of phenomena. The inquiry generally begins with concepts borrowed from ordinary language. Their employments in ordinary usage are, however, so vague and ambiguous that their serviceability in any rigorous inquiry is, for all intents and purposes, precluded. In the effort to render their meanings more precise, the investigator undertakes an *explication,* an enterprise involving judicious synthesis and rational reassessment, employing criterial or implicit, rather than explicit or recursive, definition.

Such an explication must permit us to reformulate, in propositions systematically related in relatively precise form, at least a large part of what is customarily expressed by means of the concepts under scrutiny. Moreover, such concepts permit the development of a comprehensive and rigorous theoretical system. Explication attempts to reduce the semantic limitations, vagueness and ambiguities of expressions like "near monopoly control," "bureaucratic," and "hierarchically organized," for the purpose of generating hypotheses that can be syntactically integrated into a theory having explanatory and predictive character.[13]

Such concepts, even when they are housed in a reasonably well articulated theoretical system, are open-textured. As the theory itself finds increasing application, its constituent concepts will take on extended meaning. These meanings are by-products of the theory's application and are exhibited in the findings that the theory itself was instrumental in revealing. The porosity of criterially and implicitly explicated concepts (what Hempel and Kaplan refer to as the "openness of meaning") refers to the fact that such concepts employed for empirical purposes have their meaning progressively elaborated in practice—and that closure is never definitive. The explication approximates, asymptotically, specific meaning. The fact is that in employing a concept in political science we are often faced with the reality that we do not know where to draw the line, for example, between "totalitarian" and "nontotalitarian" political systems (to use only one illustration). A point can be arbitrarily stipulated, but it remains true that for theoretical purposes we may find it advisable to treat the distinction as problematic, the kind of issue that cannot, in principle, be settled beforehand, once and for all.

Premature closure in the explication of meaning can, in fact, impair empirical inquiry. What generally happens is that a stable core meaning is provided for concepts having high yield potential. As inquiry progresses, meaning becomes increasingly specific. Intrinsically vague concepts, having unpredictable use variance, can have little substantive yield in inquiry. But concepts whose meanings are arbitrarily and unalterably fixed can be stultifying. Much of the research in contemporary political science is exploratory. As a consequence concepts are, at best and most frequently, formulated in some preliminary fashion which permits data to be collected, classified, processed, interpreted, stored, and communicated in responsible fashion. One attempts to characterize (i.e., "operationalize") concrete processes and activities implied by the phenomena under observation. The process by virtue of which such "operationalization" proceeds cannot be fully characterized. It involves conscious and unconscious appeal to funded knowledge, familiarity with the specialized and general literature devoted to the domain of discourse. It involves informal logical treatment and an imaginative qualitative analysis of observational data.[14] One formulates a preliminary conceptual scheme in which the criterially or implicitly defined concepts (generally originally borrowed from ordinary speech) occupy a place. Each concept is accorded a criterial or implicit, but open-textured, definition (on the one hand, indicating a relatively stable collection of observable attributes at least one of which must obtain if the concept is to be used felicitously, or on the other, generating one or more testable attributes that would tie the concept down to the empirical world) in order to organize experience effectively. This schema, and the criterially or implicitly defined concepts which inhabit it, is then applied to the complex world of political phenomena. In finding vagueness or ambiguity in them which reveals itself in slackness of fit, redefinition of the concepts and rearticulation of the schema takes place. Since experience is ongoing, redefinition and rearticulations are potentially infinite undertakings, there are no terminal contexts of inquiry in empirical science.

This cannot be understood to suggest that the concepts employed in political inquiry should remain vague and ambiguous. All that is intended is a recognition that while all concepts in empirical inquiry must be possessed of determinate or determinable semantic meaning—that meaning remains, in a real sense, porous. Further inquiry will add unforeseen qualifications to the employment of criterially or implicitly defined concepts. This is as true for *dispositional* concepts, defined via observational evidence sentences (i.e., "autocratic" is a dispositional attribute when ascribed to "government" and is defined in terms of the behaviors of individuals occupying strategic or key roles in the system; but *what* behaviors are to be construed as symptomatic of autocratic government, or what will constitute strategic or key roles, may subtly vary in diverse contexts), as it is for *descriptive* concepts like "democracy" or "fascism" defined in terms of an open, but defining, set of attributes.

Contextual definitions share some of the species traits of criterial definitions. A contextual definition is one "which introduces a symbol *s* by providing synonyms for certain expressions containing *s*, but not for *s* itself. . . ."[15] Thus Nelson Polsby defines "power" in the following way "Power is the capacity of one actor to do something affecting another actor, which changes the probable pattern of future events."[16] The propositional form of such an elliptical contextual definition might be adequately represented as, "*x* stands in relationship *R* to *y* = D_f, *x* changes the *Q* of *y*, but *y* does not change the *Q* of *x*."

One possible instantiation of this construed propositional form might be rendered in something like the following contextual definition: "Power is the capacity of one actor (or group of actors) to do something affecting another actor (or group of actors), which changes the probable patterns of specified future events in circumstances in which the latter actor's (or actors') capacity to so affect the former, in the same sense or manner, is relatively more restricted, minimal or null." Thus R. H. Tawney defines "power" as "the capacity of an individual, or group of individuals, to modify the conduct of other individuals or groups in the manner which he desires. . . ."[17] Lasswell and Kaplan define "power" as "participation in the making of decisions: *G* has power over *H* with respect to the values *K*, if *G* participates in the making of decisions affecting the *K*-policies of H." "Power" can then be defined in terms of the relative frequency of success an individual or a group enjoys in attempting to have his or its purposes achieved. The frequency of success can be measured quantitatively and a "power index" provided—as has been attempted by various game theorists—in a relatively formal manner. Alternately, authors like Robert Dahl can provide signal illustrations of the interplay of interest groups to display the sharing of power or the relative predominance of power.

Contextual definitions are given in relational terms rather than in terms of properties or attributes possessed by an individual or group of individuals. "Power" itself is a nonobservable entity.

It is defined contextually—in terms of relations—in a special form of dispositional analysis. "Power" manifests itself in terms of observable success in influencing outcomes. In its absolute form it is an irreversible relation between two terms. In its nonabsolute form it can be measured in a ratio of success to failure. The concept "power" is not, in and of itself, defined. What is provided are expressions which can be substituted for expressions containing the term "power"—but the concept itself is not assigned properties. Criterial definitions require appeal to at least one of an open, but finite, set of dispositional attributes manifested in observable behaviors. Contextual definitions refer to dyadic, triadic or *n*-adic relations—they do not appeal to possessed attributes.

Such definitions abound in political science literature. "Government" is defined as "the exercise of imperative control within a definite territory, and within that territory it successfully claims a monopoly of the use of force." "Political elite" is defined in terms of that collection of individuals which "comprises the power holders of a body politic."

Like criterial definitions, such contextual definitions support empirical inquiry in that they *suggest* testable hypotheses which warrant their application to any specific case. Since they do tend to support empirical inquiry they are, like criterial definitions, porous, open-textured, in the same sense and to the same degree. Because they support empirical inquiry they are "real" rather than nominal definitions. To know the *meaning* of such concepts suggests how one might determine the *truth* of any assertion in which they appear.

A *stipulative* definition, in turn, is a definition which arbitrarily restricts the meaning of a sign to that meaning assigned to it by the author. Thus Harold Lasswell and Abraham Kaplan stipulatively define "interest" as a "pattern of demands and its supporting expectations," a meaning sufficiently distinct from ordinary usage to indicate its stipulative character.[18] Such a strategy is undertaken as a significant cognitive assist. It can either constitute a mnemonic *convenience*—providing a meaning suitable to ready storage and retrieval—or it might be undertaken out of reasons of *economy*— such usage might be conceived as reducing redundancy or duplication, or alternatively, it might provide simpler logical derivations. It might be advanced because it is understood to generate an *increased number of testable propositions*. Or it might be understood to possess special heuristic significance, as being capable of suggesting a number of directly or indirectly testable propositions that might not have been generated as long as the sign or sign complex remained confined to ordinary usage. In effect, a stipulative definition is introduced because of its potential theoretical yield. That is the motive which prompts such a strategy and that constitutes its ultimate justification. Such stipulations may, in fact, outrage ordinary employments and may be counterintuitive. They, nonetheless, have ample justification and political scientists use stipulations with regularity.

The strategies we have considered are those which are primarily research oriented. They are most frequently employed by practitioners concerned with producing truth warrants for complex empirical claims. The distinction frequently made between "real" and "nominal" definitions refers to the distinction between efforts at serious empirical employments and those which represent notational conveniences. *Nominal* (or lexical) definitions can best be, for our purposes, conceived as conventions which merely introduce an alternative notation for a given linguistic expression. A specified expression, the *definiendum,* is construed to be more or less synonymous with a simple or complex expression, the *definiens.* Nominal definitions are conveniences; they are normally abbreviatory, providing for more parsimonious speech acts. Thus H. V. Wiseman identifies "the common orientation of two or more people" as "culture," and "that organized sector of an actor's orientation which constitutes and defines his participation in an interactive process" as a "role."[19] Such definitions constitute primarily notational conveniences. They facilitate communication by rendering speech stenographic and more economical. Instead of repeating the complex phrase, "that organized sector . . . and so forth," one simply employs the conventional term, "role."

Such terms are, for the purposes of verbal "theory," eliminable by substituting the *definiens* for the *definiendum* throughout. Signs introduced via nominal or lexical definition can be dispensed with, by substitution, from any context in which they appear. Everything said in the abbreviatory notation can be said, presumably, in terms of the (characteristically) longer expression which is its lexical *definiens* and vice versa.

As distinct from "real" definition, "nominal" definitions can be conceived as those definitions which serve, primarily, as conveniences. They are conveniences in that they attempt to make more explicit the thought of their author. They do not, in and of themselves (and this distinguishes them from stipulative definitions), suggest empirical inquiry that would license their use. They are, at best, efforts to employ terms with a relatively specific meaning in the interests of economy and consistency. Thus, when Lasswell defined "the environment of an act" as "the events other than the act itself within which the act is included," he indicated that such a definition was "not intended to be fully precise and rigorous from a strict logical viewpoint, but only to make more explicit than is usually done the framework relating the various concepts employed."[20]

George Homans characterizes such definitions as "nonoperating definitions"—"nonoperating" because the concepts they identify are not defined in such a manner as to generate testable propositions in social science.[21] Such definitions are linguistic conveniences. A "role" is "the behavior expected of a man occupying a particular social position." "Culture" is "the funded pattern of interpersonal expectations and belief systems transmitted by a society." What behavior constitutes instantiation of "role behavior" is *unspecified*. What expectations and what ideational elements are to be admitted as instances of "culture" is equally unclear. One need but compare Bertrand Russell's lexical definition of "power" as "the production of intended effects"[22] to realize its nonoperative character. Knowing that power is the production of intended effects, we know nothing other than a verbal convention. There is no way in which "power" so defined could, in itself, be made the subject of empirical inquiry. Thus we find Karl Deutsch moving from a lexical definition of power: "By the power of an individual or organization, we ... mean the extent to which they can continue successfully to act out their character," a nonoperating definition, to a partially operationalized contextual definition: "Power ... is conceived on the analogy of the hardness scale of minerals, of the scratching of glass by a diamond or of the 'pecking order' in a chicken yard," and finally to an elaborate real definition that permits of substantial specification and quantification of related, directly or indirectly observed, variables. [23]

The shift from "nominal" or lexical definition to "real" definition generally marks the transition from verbal "theory" to verificational strategies, that is to say, the generation and confirmation of testable theories and empirical explanation. The difference is intuitively obvious when one recognizes the nonoperative character of a definition of "power" that characterizes it as the "production of intended effects" as compared with its assessment in terms of a measurable ratio of success to failure in situations of competitive negotiation. "Nominal" definitions can appear in the guise of verbal synonymies, criterial or contextual definitions. Characterizing them as "nominal" simply means, in the context of our discussion, that they are nonoperative, nontestable, because of the lack of specificity or behavioral reference that characterizes them.

Preliminary and Partially Axiomatized Conceptual Schemata

In the effort to produce more substantial theoretical yield, greater predictive and explanatory leverage, natural language gives way to increased standardization and formalization. Ordinary language conceptual schemata are transformed into preliminary conceptual schemata in which critical concepts are afforded, generally, lexical definition. The language style is *academic* and *literary*. Often what is produced are definitional schemata: classificatory schemata, typologies, and taxonomies. Such linguistic artifacts are characteristic of descriptive sciences and are commonplace in comparative politics. Practitioners in this subdomain of political inquiry devote a considerable portion of their scholarly and research time to the generation of definitional and analytic conceptual schemata. One finds, for example, practitioners concerned with "identifying" "open" as distinguished from "closed" political systems, "utopian," as distinguished from "main-stem" and "consensual" political regimes, and "revolutionary," as distinguished from "nonrevolutionary" or "reactionary" political movements.

Where a series of lexical definitions are offered, we possess only pretheoretical formulations. Rarely, however, among political scientists does one find an exclusive preoccupation with definition for the sake of definition. What most frequently is found is what G. Lowell Field has called "experimental naming." One offers a definition, initially in lexical terms, of an intuitively critical concept. Attempts to identify instances of the class term force reformulation of the definition in terms of intersubjective recognitors—that is to say, an open-textured contextual or criterial definition is generated. The language style becomes *eristic;* the practitioner becomes concerned with "fit," with his ability to apply the general term to features of the object world. The concern becomes one of evidence and of the putative relationship between propositions conceived of as credible. As concepts are empirically defined, in terms of recognitors, and the relationship between propositions in which the concepts are housed is increasingly well specified, the preliminary conceptual schemata give way to partially axiomatized and, in some cases, fully axiomatized conceptual schemata. Fully axiomatized conceptual schemata are calculated to fully reveal the semantic and syntactic properties of the linguistic products with which they deal.

As a matter of fact most political scientists remain at the eristic language level, and partially axiomatized conceptual schemata are their characteristic products.

In general, political scientists do not isolate the nonlogical from the logical vocabulary of their formulation—and as a consequence rarely generate specifically analytic conceptual schemata (schemata which seek to reveal the syntactic structure that relates any set or subset of propositions). Political scientists are rarely concerned exclusively with defining the concepts with which they are preoccupied—and as a consequence only rarely generate specifically definitional conceptual schemata. Generally, political scientists simultaneously involve themselves in a number of definitional, analytic and experimental pursuits and what they produce are partially axiomatized conceptual schemata. The properties such artifacts display are 1) at least some of the critical concepts (which frequently serve as "independent" and "dependent" variables) are reasonably well defined in terms of experimental or observational expectations; 2) some subset of propositions are conceived as "basic" from which "theorems" can be derived by logical operations.

What results are the partially formalized "theories" with which the students of politics have become familiar. An instructive instance (because of its familiarity) of a macro "theory" having to do with political systems and political behavior is the "Marxist" schema. Originally, Marx's own formulations were couched in academic and literary language. Concepts like "material productive forces" and "material activity" were loosely defined—at best rendered in terms of incomplete nominal definitions (for example, in the *German Ideology,* Marx speaks of "mental production" as "expressed" in "the language of politics, laws, morality, religion, metaphysics, etc. . . ."), and the relationship between propositions expressed metaphorically (mental life is understood to be "interwoven" with material activity). By the time Marx was producing his mature work, critical concepts were either more precisely defined or in the process of more adequate definition (Marx was in the process of a more careful formulation of the concept "class" when death overtook him). In that work certain propositions are clearly more basic than others. For example, the proposition of the "increasing emiseration of the proletariat" provides the logical basis for a number of derivative propositions, among them: 1) the size of an industrial "reserve army" would increase with the progressive maturation of capitalism; 2) the downward mobility of entire sections of the bourgeoisie would follow that maturation; 3) with the downward mobility of the interstitial and peripheral bourgeoisie, utopian socialism will disappear and proletarian socialism will assume its place; 4) the class consciousness of the proletariat would thus develop directly with the maturation of the capitalist system.

The logic of the derivation is never precise because the entire artifact is delivered in what is essentially eristic language. The nonlogical elements are never fully standardized and the logical relations never fully formalized. Nevertheless, it is intuitively obvious that the formulations found in *Das Kapital* gravitate toward a different linguistic level than those found in the early writings.

The early writings offer, at best, heuristic possibilities, suggesting the cognitive yield inherent in a "broad perspective" on a complex subject matter. Partially axiomatized schemata, delivered in eristic language, are concerned with experimental and observational confirmation of at least critical propositions. This requires "real" definition of central concepts. If the credibility of a collection of propositions is to be enhanced, some attention must be accorded deductive relations, logical derivations from truth claims previously established or assumed. Generally evidence conditions are, at best, minimally satisfied and proofs sketched rather than rigorously formulated. What results is a cognitive product enjoying one or another degree of plausibility—and there are frequently a number of candidate formulations that share something of the same truth status. These are conditions met in most areas of political inquiry as well as history, macrosociology, and clinical psychology.

In one sense or another the partially formalized sciences proceed from ordinary language schemata to partially axiomatized schemata. What passes for "theory" in political science is most frequently just such a partially axiomatized schema. The construction of such a schema requires, minimally, a fairly rigorous definition of critical concepts and an exhibition of the logic that subtends a reasonably discrete collection of propositions. The construction of a partially axiomatized schema requires, furthermore, the identification of a subset of those propositions as basic to the set. Conjointly employed with such a subset of propositions are a group of reasonably well specified rules of transformation that permit transition from one proposition to another (the transformation rules of logic constitute a case in point). These characterize the relationships that can obtain between propositions. Transformation rules can be conveniently described as syntactical rules. Given the basic descriptive propositions of the system and the transformation rules which govern admissable derivation, one can generate entailed propositions called *theorems*. The basic propositions are underived (assumed or the patrimony of funded knowledge). Theorems are derived by operating on the basic propositions via transformation rules (with definitions constituting a subset of transformation rules).

Such a system makes at least partially evident what is implicitly contained in the basic propositions. It reveals the "grammar" of the commitments made when one makes knowledge claims of that sort. It makes meaning maximally clear by revealing what is entailed in each material judgment. David Braybrooke has partially axiomatized the collection of propositions generated by research on electoral arrangements and the number of political parties. He has selected a subset of those propositions having maximal yield and then has attempted to rigorously deduce the remaining propositions as theorems. The purpose of the exercise is to maximally reduce semantic and syntactical indeterminacy and thus draw out implications.[24] Robert Axelrod has published a brief account of a specialized axiomatization of conflict of interest.[25]

Preliminary conceptual schemata (what Homans calls "orientating statements," and which David Willer indicates can yield neither testable propositions nor predictions since they do not allow "definitive relational statements"),[26] which are employed to orient oneself in a universe of discourse, at times give way, in the effort to reduce semantic and syntactical indeterminacy, to what are essentially analytic conceptual schemata (exemplified in the work of Talcott Parsons and a variety of "systems theorists") and rudimentary or sophisticated axiomatic systems, depending on whether primary (but not exclusive) attention is devoted to semantic or syntactical variance.

Throughout the process, concept formation proceeds apace. There is a constant interchange between conceptual schemata and viable concepts. Presumably what ultimately results are maximally testable propositions whose truth warrants can be produced upon challenge. The fact is that if one is attempting to generate defensible knowledge claims, it is impossible to avoid something like the procedure that has been informally described in the preceeding pages. We harbor, at the commencement of a systematic inquiry into political understanding, a nondeliberative ordinary language conceptual schema, or schemata, which provide rudimentary taxonomies or typologies which permit the identification of classes of discriminable stimuli. Having identified such classes, we proceed to discover what relationships might obtain between them. We, more often than not, find ourselves confused and unable to fully anticipate futures. As a consequence we proffer more specific definitions which affect the rudimentary or nondeliberative schemata we commence with. We produce more sophisticated and deliberative linguistic entities which characterize putative relationships and define independent and dependent variables more precisely. Concepts are transformed from vague classifications of discriminable types into empirical indices, and symptomatic evidence statements establish their intersubjective employment. Paul Lazarsfeld and Morris Rosenberg outline the process in the following summary fashion:

> The first step (in empirical concept formation) seems to be the creation of a rather vague image or construct that results from the author's immersion in all the detail of a theoretical problem. The creative act may begin with the perception of many disparate phenomena as having some underlying characteristic in common. Or the author may have observed certain regularities and is trying to account for them. In any case, the concept, when first created, is some vaguely conceived entity that makes the observed relations meaningful. Next comes a stage in which the concept is specified by elaborate discussion of the phenomena out of which it emerged. We develop "aspects," "components," "dimensions," or similar specifications. They are sometimes derived logically from the overall concept, or one aspect is deduced from another, or empirically observed correlations between them are reported. The concept is shown to consist of a complex combination of phenomena, rather than a simple and directly observable item. In order to incorporate the concept into a research design, observable indicators of it must be selected.[27]

Antecedent to the formulation of generalizing knowledge claims one must entertain a preliminary conceptual schema or "framework of inquiry," which permits the identification of reasonably discrete classes of entities which we have spoken of as *variables*. The term "variable" is loosely employed in political science inquiry to designate any *concept* used in empirical investigation. Thus Robert Merton speaks of "concepts ... [which] constitute the definitions

. . . of what is to be observed; they are the variables between which empirical relationships are to be sought," and proceeds to speak of such concepts as "status," "role," "social distance," and so forth.[28] In this broad sense a variable is any qualitative or quantitative concept used in empirical inquiry. When a relationship is to be established between variables, *dependent* variables signify those variables that are functions of the activity of an *independent* variable. The independent variable is the variable whose changes or differences are regularly associated with changes or differences in the dependent variable. In ordinary language we informally speak of the independent variable or variables being the "cause" or "causes" of the dependent variables.

The Canons of Induction

In order to establish the relationships between variables we employ rough procedural guides long since (in 1841) conveniently summarized in "Mill's Canons of Induction." As procedural guides Mill's methods of inductive investigation constitute a convenient, if simplistic, introduction to inductive argument. They are employed to discover invariant relationships among events—but events must first be characterized typologically, criterially, or contextually so that any event is understood to be an instance of a reasonably specific *class* of events. The first step in inductive inquiry is the development of a classificatory or typological schema. To discover regularities in experience one must have some initial assessment of what constitutes discrete aspects of the whole of complex and confusing experience. Mill's canons are applicable only after some classificatory schema is deployed over experience. Then one can begin to talk meaningfully in terms of the presence or absence of variables and the relationships understood to obtain between them.

Mill's methods are known respectively as 1) the method of agreement, 2) the method of difference, 3) the joint method of agreement and difference, 4) the method of concomitant variation, and 5) the method of residues.[29]

The first method, *the method of agreement,* very briefly, contends that "that variable (or variable complex) which is always present in the circumstances in which the dependent variable is present is causally connected with that variable." It simply means that whenever *a* (say a heat source of at least 212°F obtains) is present in specifiable circumstances (the border conditions specify that the heat source must be "contiguous" and the water must be "at sea level"), *b* (water) will boil.

The second method, *the method of difference,* summarily put, maintains that "that variable (or variable complex) which is always absent in each instance when the dependent variable is absent is causally connected with that variable." More schematically, whenever *a* is absent, *b* will be absent. If there is no suitable heat source attaining 212°F (at sea level) attending a container of water, that water will not boil.

The third method, *the joint method of agreement and difference,* is a conjoint employment of both the method of agreement and the method of difference. In order to more firmly establish an invariance, an empirical regularity, circumstances are sought in which the dependent variable is present and the independent variable identified—as well as other circumstances in which the dependent variable is absent and the independent variable is absent as well. In experimental inquiry this joint method is exemplified in the use of *control groups.* In order to test the causal efficacy of *a,* two identical groups are selected. One group is subjected to *a* (experimental exposure) and the other is not. If the group subject to experimental exposure to *a* manifests *b* and the control group, innocent of exposure to *a,* does not, we hold *a* to be the empirical antecedent of *b*. Political scientists employ such techniques to identify the impact of information on voting subjects, psychiatrists to assess the efficacy of therapy, sociologists to measure the influence of education on racial attitudes, educators to measure the influence of new teaching techniques on performance. Such techniques can become very sophisticated in the effort to control for the influence of extrinsic or unidentified variables. *Randomization* is employed to ensure the substantial identity of the samples under test. A complicated four-group research design may be exploited to diminish threats to internal test validity, but the basic conceptions remain those suggested by Mill's third canon.[30]

The fourth method, *the method of concomitant variation*, suggests that "where one variable (or variable complex) always varies in specified circumstances in a positive, or negative, relationship with the degree to which another variable (or variable complex) varies, that variable (or variable complex) is causally connected with that variable (or variable complex)." Which simply means that where the circumstantial variable *a* varies directly or inversely with *b*, the method of concomitant variation permits us to argue that *a* is (probably) connected with *b*. The contemporary techniques in political inquiry which exploit correlations between variables trafficks on Mill's method of concomitant variation. Wherever there is a constant or significant and recurrent negative or positive correlation between variables, we conceive of this as a necessary constituent of what we refer to in ordinary language as a "causal connection."

The fifth method, *the method of residues,* maintains that "when one variable (or variable complex) of a compound phenomenon is always associated with discrete variables constituting the circumstances, then the remaining variables of the circumstances are causally connected with the remaining (or residual) variables of the total phenomenon." This simply means that if one can account for some aspects of experience by identifying some discrete variables as their antecedents, whatever remains of the experience can be assumed to be the product of the remaining independent variables. The residual elements of experience can (probably) be regularly associated with those residual variables that have not already been identified as their antecedents.

Such canons are, of course, no more than procedural guides to inductive reasoning. They must be employed with sustained vigilance —and claims generated by their use can only, at best, constitute guarded knowledge claims. Recently, in Toledo, the passage of a strict gun control law was followed by a statistically impressive decline in criminal homicides. The methods of agreement and correlative variation suggested that a connection obtained between the reduced availability of firearms and the reduced incidence of homicides. It was only after the general category "criminal homicides" was further analyzed, and it was found that the incidence of criminal homicides in which weapons other than guns were employed fell to the same degree as those in which guns were used, that the putative connection between the reduction of the number of guns available and the decline in the number of criminal homicides was revealed as counterintuitive. The use of the canons of inquiry require not only procedural skills that the research social scientist develops by being familiar with the funded knowledge of his discipline, but a sensitive awareness of ordinary logic, and a considerable degree of analytic and linguistic sophistication.

The entire process could not begin without a preliminary conceptual schema that permits one to identify discrete and recurrent aspects of experience—to employ concepts felicitously. But the application of concepts inherited from nondeliberative schemata very rapidly reveals their vagueness and ambiguity and hinders their function in the service of anticipating experience. Concepts are redefined, similarities and differences are noted that had been hitherto unassessed. Conceptual schemata undergo partial standardization and partial formalization. Different regularities are identified. Relationships are more systematically characterized. One seeks more reliable recognitors as indicators of concept use. One scrutinizes the *internal validity* which governs concept employment—to determine whether, in fact, the experience to which one appeals for evidences of truth adequately and consistently unpacks the implicit meaning of the concept. One assesses the *external validity* of concept use—to determine whether, in fact, the semantic rules governing its use permit one to reliably apply the concept over directly or indirectly observable phenomena.

The application of Mill's canons is a first step in the complex process of discovering and confirming generalizations. The summary characterization given here conceals the taxing procedures employed in empirical inquiry to confidently warrant generalizing knowledge claims. When empirical inquiry reveals what is taken to be an invariance, a finding, the discovery of a regular relationship between dependent and independent variables, the investigator is faced with the responsibility of establishing the *reliability* of the symptomatic recognitors by which he identifies classes of observables as well as identifying them as dependent or independent variables. That is to say, do his recognitors provide for *congruent* findings (can a finite variety of recognitors be employed in a number of instances to identify the same invariance)? Are his recognitors sufficiently *precise* (that is, do his recognitors register consistently for the same observer)? Are his recognitors *objective* (can they be used by any observer similarly circumstanced for the same determinations)? A measure of congruence would be given in terms of the degree of referential variance or invariance between recognitors. The measure of precision would be given in terms of the degree of variance or invariance between readings. Finally, the measure of objectivity would be given in terms of the degree of variance or invariance between observation reports provided by different observers.

The effort to establish the reliability of a truth claim would involve some or all of such efforts at reducing indeterminacy. Each of them involve a systematic concern with language employment. Only when the concepts provided by ordinary language and preliminary conceptual schemata are shaped into the relatively standardized and relatively formalized concepts of a higher level of speech employments can anything like confirmation be forthcoming. To establish an invariance, a "fact," involves specification of meaning (the observance of semantic rules), as well as a relatively precise specification of relationship understood to obtain between concepts thus reasonably well defined (the observance of syntactical or structural relations).

Induction and Empirical Knowledge Claims

The exploitation of constant conjunctions, either instantial or correlational, has now become a standard source of empirical hypotheses for political scientists. The now venerable finding that the party identification of children is highly correlated with that of their parents was only one of the first generalizations entertained by empirically orientated political scientists. The degree of correlation has been found to be contingent upon the degree of parental politicization, the salience of issues, and differences in chronological maturity (among other things), but the regularity of the correlation is no longer seriously doubted by anyone. Even the most recent studies indicate a high degree of intergenerational agreement persists—in spite of the "rebellion" of our youth. Studies of parent-youth samples indicate that a relatively high degree of correspondence obtains between the party identification of respondents and that of their parents. Such consistent replications constitute the warrant for an inductive generalization.

Such generalizations are characteristic of empirical work in political science. Correlations have been identified, among others, between political participation and position on socioeconomic status scales, between political participation and group identity, between political participation and sex, between political participation and religion. The studies identifying such correlations are often very sophisticated, employing careful research designs to attempt to insure randomization and reduce threats to internal and external validity. That is to say, care is taken to reduce or identify contamination of the experimental result by extraneous variables and to attempt to insure that whatever experimental results obtained can be projected from the experimental sample to the population—an inverse inference.

At times such intercorrelations are products of a special piece of research. Recently, for example, M. Kent Jennings and Richard G. Niemi discovered, in the course of their research, that while a high intergenerational correlation obtains between attitude objects in the concrete, salient and reinforced domain of party loyalty, far less is found with respect to a range of other attitude objects varying from a moderate correlation to no correlation whatsoever.[31]

At other times such intercorrelations are sought to confirm or disconfirm a generalization that has been a possession of popular wisdom or traditional political science for some considerable time. Herbert McClosky's "Consensus and Ideology in American Politics,"[32] was undertaken with the specific intention of examining the thesis that "consensus" is "necessary" for a viable "free society." In effect, the thesis under inspection was one that argued a necessary relationship of some sort between "consensus" and the maintenance of a particular kind of political order. Is it, in fact, the case that viable "free societies" always evidence some measurable degree of "consensus"—are the two, in some sense, intercorrelated?

McClosky's study attempted to assess such truth claims by framing testable propositions employing some determinate meaning for "consensus" and "ideology." Responses on survey questionnaires were conceived as complex recognitors for attitudes held (in effect, the responses counted as *evidence* of attitudes held—they were obviously not held to be *logically equivalent* to attitudes held). What was found was that "political influentials" (the "articulate minority," the "political elite"), defined in terms of those people who concern themselves with public affairs to an unusual degree (as distinct from the "nonelite majority"), evidence a considerable measure of consensus on ideological matters. In other words, there is a positive correlation between "political involvement" and a disposition to hold consensus views on political matters. The initiating common-sense claims were given *qualified support.*

To *confirm* the general claim, it would be necessary, minimally, to show that consensus, even if such consensus is construed as a characteristic of political influentials alone, is the necessary condition of a viable "free society." Wherever a "free society" (suitably defined) obtains, "consensus" (again, suitably defined) invariably obtains. Where there is no consensus, there could be no "free society." If a "free society" were found to obtain where no consensus could be identified, the original claim might be suitably modified so that "consensus" could be treated as a substitutable variable, with some determinate number of "functionally equivalent" variables providing for the same effect. The process of confirming generalizations entertained in ordinary language, or traditionally funded schemata, is no simple task. It often taxes the creative imagination of the research political scientists far more than is popularly imagined. There is, in effect, nothing "mechanical" about applying inductive canons to empirical research.

The very process of pursuing an inductive study compels researchers to attempt adequate definition of construed variables, anticipate relations, and identify those recognitors that are to count as evidence for the categoric variables themselves, and the relations conceived as obtaining between them. It is not difficult to identify instances of the application of Mill's canons in political science research. Any research that identifies intercorrelations, any that attempts to assess the effects of the impact of experimental or nonexperimental exposure, that uses control groups, that undertakes pre-test and post-test observations, that uses a four-group design and its more or less sophisticated variants, invokes Mill's methods of agreement and difference, his joint method and his method of concomitant variation and of residues.

Typical of the studies conducted by political scientists and political sociologists is that offered by Robert O. Schulze, "The Role of Economic Dominants in Community Power Structure."[33] He begins by reviewing the conceptual schemata entertained by students of community power and suggests that while some communities have been extensively studied, little comparative work has been done and still less has been done that provides evidence of longitudinal changes. After his indication of available schemata, the author discusses what he calls a "rudimentary theory"—a conceptual framework provided in academic language style. The author then proceeds to identify concepts critical to his schema, "economic dominants" and "local involvement" among the most important. "Economic dominants" are "operationally defined" (in this case criterially defined) as those who (*a*) occupied the top formal roles in the largest industries and banks in the community under study; or (*b*) were members of the boards of directors of two or more of such industries and banks. The author then attempted to reconstruct the correlation between being identified as an "economic dominant" and "involvement" in local political activity (by occupying public office). The frequency with which economic dominants held public office was then reconstructed from archival materials from the period 1823 until 1954.

The strategy involved is inductively standard—and the results provide the evidence base for empirical generalizations, the raw material for significant theory construction.

Warranting Empirical Truth Claims

Empirical invariances can never be *definitively* established. They are *warranted*. We have confidence in them. Our confidence in them becomes entrenched when we successfully employ them to predict futures. Such confidence is warranted, but it is not incorrigible. We recognize that new observations may disconfirm our predictions and that alternative formulations might predict observations equally well or better. We try to anticipate such experiences by considering alternative hypotheses before committing ourselves to our generalized truth claim. We try to establish, for example, the truth of a *null-hypothesis* (a hypothesis that contends that the variable we have identified as causally effective has, in fact, no effect). None of these tactics invincibly insulates us against counterevidence and conceptual reformulation. Nonetheless, invariances are discovered and confidence is invested in them.

When such invariances are locked into systematic and subsumptive relations with other invariances and the interstices filled with propositions which may not have been confirmed by observations, but which are the artifacts of logic or speculation, what gradually emerges is a *theoretical system*. All the efforts we have briefly characterized: concept formation, taxonomies, systematic efforts at adequate characterization of concepts, preliminary conceptual schemata, analytic conceptual schemata, rudimentary or formal axiomatization, the employment of deductive and inductive procedures, are all calculated to mature into theories—the distinctive product of science as a knowledge enterprise.

Ordinary Language, Experience, and Sophisticated Knowledge Claims

Theories are the artifacts of deliberative language use. We undertake such use only when we are challenged by demands other than those of ordinary experience. Sophisticated language employment is a consequence of complex and unusual challenge. Ordinary language inhabits a nondeliberative conceptual schema that is serviceable for the orientations of everyday life. We are content with its vaguenesses, ambiguities and tense obscurities as long as we face only ordinary adaptive requirements. At its most primitive levels language reflects the most elementary concern of generic language users. Thus while it is true that the languages of peripheral peoples, those who do not speak what Benjamin Whorf has called Standard Average European, are characteristically incongruent among themselves and significantly different from those of Europeans, there appears to be reasonably good agreement between such languages about the signification of basic words.[34] That such languages are mutually intertranslatable indicates that there obtains, in principle, a commonality in experience. Outside the range of variation traced to conventional and historic determinants, personality, style and dialectal variables, the differences that obtain between languages seem to be a function of pragmatic focus. When languages are extended beyond their pragmatic concerns (for example, when language is extended without sophistication into nonexperienced or inexperienceable domains like life after death or some transempirical supernatural region), it becomes for all intents and purposes unintelligible.

When language develops cognitively, in the effort to anticipate futures, predict outcomes, and reliably explain phenomena, complex, deliberate, and systematic conceptual schemata are produced. In these well-developed areas of inquiry, characterized by the various sciences in the industrially advanced language communities of the world, there is usually a relatively stable collection of linguistic rules which permit substantially unproblematic storage and communication of the circumstances, procedures, and results of research. Each such discipline exploits a protocol language, a basic set of unproblematic knowledge claims on the basis of which the complex linguistic entities of a standardized or partially standardized and formalized or partially formalized science can be erected. As long as specialized languages operate in such contexts utterances are transparent; one sees through them to the complex reality they signify. One characterizes collections of things through the refined and relatively rigorous medium of concept and conceptual structures; one identifies variables and characterizes the relationships that unite them in one of a variety of ways. One successfully predicts and explains.

Generalizations will be made in every language community. Ordinary language generalizations are adequate to the demands of ordinary situations. Within each language community generalizations will be made at different language levels. But they will all be made in terms of concepts employing observable recognitors as symptomatic indicators. Concepts will, in effect, be operationalized. They will refer to directly or indirectly observable referents. All will be warranted by evidence statements which refer to such recognitors. Such evidence statements confirm the felicitous use of concepts. The ultimate purpose of such efforts is to provide the basis for explanation and prediction; it is the efficacy in serving that function that distinguishes warranted generalized knowledge claims from mythopoeic and symbolic language use. It is that efficacy which motivates people from industrially peripheral but "developing" areas to teach their young the partially or maximally standardized and partially or maximally formalized language of science.

Under the goad of developing effective adaptive language in problematic contexts, nondeliberative conceptual schemata develop analytically into a variety of linguistic entities calculated to generate reliable generalizing knowledge claims, which can then be articulated into the systematic and subsumptive relations exemplified in scientific theories. It is to this process that the contemporary "revolution" in political inquiry would inure its students. It is the deliberative use of language that by and large characterizes the "revolution" itself.

Notes

1 Cf. L. S. Vygotsky, *Thought and Language* (Cambridge, Mass.: MIT, 1962), chap. 5.

2 Cf. A. A. Ljublinskaja, *Die psychische Entwicklung des Kindes* (Berlin: Volk und Wissen, 1961), pp. 153–155.

3 For a contemporary discussion of the empirical analysis of concept attainment, which also provides a significant bibliography, see L. E. Bourne, Jr., "Concept Attainment," in T. R. Dixon and D. L. Horton, eds., *Verbal Behavior and General Behavior Theory* (Englewood Cliffs, N.J.: Prentice-Hall, 1968), pp. 230–253. For an account of the metascientific analysis of conceptual language, see R. Carnap, "Psychological Terms Can All Be Reduced to 'Observable Thing-Predicates,'" in L. Krimerman (ed.), *The Nature and Scope of Social Science* (New York: Appleton-Century-Crofts, 1969), pp. 362–373.

4 Cf. W. V. O. Quine, *Word and Object* (New York: Wiley, 1960), pp. 4f.

5 H. Zetterberg, *On Theory and Verification in Sociology* (Totowa, N.J.: Bedminster, 1965), pp. 68–72.

6 Cf. H. D. Lasswell and A. Kaplan, *Power and Society: A Framework for Political Inquiry* (New Haven: Yale, 1965), p. xix.

7 M. Black, "Definition, Presupposition, and Assertion," *Problems of Analysis* (Ithaca: Cornell, 1954), pp. 24–45.

8 A. Downs, *An Economic Theory of Democracy* (New York: Harper and Row, 1957), pp. 295–300.

9 T. Parsons, "On the Concept of Political Power," *Proceedings of the American Philosophical Society,* CVII, 3 (June, 1963). The term "entailment" is used here with qualifications. Works like that of Downs, and that of Talcott Parsons, are not sufficiently rigorous to permit the licit drawing out of implications—consequently their "implicit definitions" are always, in principle, impaired. In order to specify exhaustively the imlications of a term "implicitly defined," a greater degree of formalization would have to be entertained. Nonetheless, such works do attempt to implicitly define critical expressions.

10 D. L. Germino, *The Italian Fascist Party in Power* (Minneapolis: University of Minnesota, 1959),

chap. 8; for Friedrich and Brzezinski's discussion, cf. C. J. Friedrich and Z. K. Brzezinski, *Totalitarian Dictatorship and Autocracy* (New York: Praeger, 1962), chap. 1.

[11] A. Kassof, "The Administered Society: Totalitarianism Without Terror," *World Politics*, XVI, 4 (July, 1964); W. Ebenstein, "The Study of Totalitarianism," *World Politics*, X, 2 (January 1958).

[12] Cf. G. J. DiRenzo, "Conceptual Definition in the Behavioral Sciences," in G. J. DiRenzo, ed., *Concepts, Theory and Explanation in the Behavioral Sciences* (New York: Random House, 1966)

[13] Cf. C. G. Hempel, *Fundamentals of Concept Formation in Empirical Science* (Chicago: University of Chicago, 1967), pp. 11ff.

[14] Cf. P. Lazarsfeld and A. H. Barton, "Qualitative Measurement in the Social Sciences: Classification, Typologies and Indices," in D. Lerner and H. D. Lasswell et. al. (eds.), *The Policy Sciences: Recent Developments in Scope and Method* (Stanford: Stanford University, 1959), chap. 9.

[15] Hempel, *op. cit.*, p. 4.

[16] N. Polsby, *Community Power and Political Theory* (New Haven: Yale, 1966), p. 5.

[17] R. H. Tawney, *Equality* (New York: Harcourt, Brace, 1931), p. 230.

[18] Lasswell and Kaplan, *Power and Society*, p. 75.

[19] H. V. Wiseman, *Political Systems: Some Sociological Approaches* (New York: Praeger, 1966), pp. 4, 21.

[20] Lasswell and Kaplan, *op. cit.*, p. 4, and n. 4.

[21] G. C. Homans, *The Nature of Social Science* (New York: Harcourt, Brace & World, 1967), pp. 10f.

[22] B. Russell, *Power* (New York: Barnes and Noble, 1963), p. 25.

[23] K. Deutsch, *The Nerves of Government* (New York: Free Press, 1966), pp. 111, 112–127. Cf. R. Dahl's comments on the use of the concept "power" in political science, R. Dahl, "Cause and Effect in the Study of Politics," in M. Lerner (ed.), *Cause and Effect* (New York: Free Press, 1965), p. 92.

[24] D. Braybrooke, "An Illustrative Miniature Axiomatic System," in N. W. Polsby, R. A. Dentler, and P. A. Smith, *Politics and Social Life* (Boston: Houghton Mifflin, 1963), pp. 119–130.

[25] R. Axelrod, "Conflict of Interest: An Axiomatic Approach," *Journal of Conflict Resolution*, XI, 1 (March, 1967), 87–99.

[26] D. Willer, *Scientific Sociology: Theory and Method* (Englewood Cliffs, N.J.: Prentice-Hall, 1967), p. 67.

[27] P. F. Lazarsfeld and M. Rosenberg (eds.), *The Language of*

Social Research (New York: Free Press, 1955), p. 15.

28 R. K. Merton, *Social Theory and Social Structure* (New York: Free Press, 1957), p. 89.

29 This account is taken from N. Rescher, *Introduction to Logic* (New York: St. Martin's, 1964), chap. 18. For a summary and convenient account of Mill's methods, cf. S. F. Barker, *The Elements of Logic* (New York: McGraw-Hill, 1965), chap. 6, pp. 212–238.

30 Cf. D. T. Campbell and J. C. Stanley, *Experimental and Quasi-Experimental Designs for Research* (Chicago: Rand McNally, 1963).

31 M. Kent Jennings and R. Niemi, "The Transmission of Political Values from Parent to Child," *American Political Science Review,* LXVII (1968).

32 H. McClosky, "Consensus and Ideology in American Politics," *American Political Science Review,* LVIII (1964).

33 R. O. Schulze, "The Role of Economic Dominants in Community Power Structure," in L. A. Coser (ed.), *Political Sociology* (New York: Harper, 1966), pp. 167–180.

34 C. E. Osgood, "The Cross-Cultural Generality of Visual-Verbal Synesthetic Tendencies," *Behavioral Science,* V (1960), 146–149; cf. R. Brown, *Words and Things* (New York: Free Press, 1958), chap. 7. For an interesting and competent discussion of the "Whorf-Sapier hypothesis," see M. Black, *Models and Metaphors* (Ithaca: Cornell University, (1962), chap. 17.

Suggested Readings

Angell, Richard B. *Reasoning and Logic.* New York: Appleton-Century-Crofts, 1964.

Hempel, Carl G. *Fundamentals of Concept Formation in Empirical Science.* Chicago: University of Chicago, 1967.

Homans, George C. *The Nature of Social Science.* New York: Harcourt, Brace & World, 1967.

Kaplan, Abraham. *The Conduct of Inquiry: Methodology for Behavioral Science.* San Francisco: Chandler, 1964. Chap. 2.

6

On Laws, Theories, and Models

Perhaps every science must start with metaphor and end with algebra; and perhaps without the metaphor there would never have been any algebra.

Max Black

The purpose of systematic inquiry is to discover novel facts about the attributes of things experienced, and to discover among such attributes, invariant relations which begin to bring order into the flow of experience, and which, in the final analysis, serve to explain and anticipate that experience. Rationality is itself predicated on the assumption that we can learn from experience and that acts undertaken in accordance with that experience are more conducive to successful adaptation than acts randomly undertaken.

When we talk of intelligent conduct, and attribute intelligence to animals, we generally mean no more than that some discriminable environmental stimuli serve the animal as cues invoking a generalized pattern of response that satisfies some goal requirement in his life space. When we attribute rationality to men we generally mean that men display evidences of intelligent behavior different only in measure and not in kind from that displayed by animals. But more than that we generally imply that men can undertake a critical course of imaginary trial and error that involves the giving of reasons and the complex and conscious weighing of evidence. The weighing of evidence entails an awareness of the norms of evidence, the criteria by virtue of which we identify instances of warranted claims and rebut those which are faulted. The giving of reasons and the weighing of evidence instantiates *rational* as distinct from *intelligent* rule-following behavior.[1] Where rule following is nondeliberative and unself-conscious we may have intelligent behavior (in this sense the activity of computers or the reflex or stimulus-response activity of animals may be spoken of as "intelligent").[2] Where rule following is deliberative and critically self-conscious we can legitimately speak of rational conduct.

Necessary for rationality is a natural *or* constructed language; necessary and sufficient for rationality would be that linguistic capacity capable of asserting time specified, and unrestricted or probabilistic material judgments and the identification of the evidence conditions that warrant them.[3] Rationality implies *ratio*, the giving of reasons, the evidencing of *propositional* rather than *procedural* knowledge (the knowing *that*, rather than the knowing *how*)—the issuance of dated, lawlike assertions and the specification of the evidence that is their support.[4] The ascription of rationality implies the possession of a true language which uniquely characterizes man. When we metaphorically extend the meaning of "language" to "computer languages," to the "language" of the bees, or speak of the gestural "language" of primates, we at least tacitly recognize that such "languages" cannot accommodate the giving of reasons, the minting of truth claims and the identification of evidence conditions which render them negotiable.

To act rationally, men employ generalized knowledge claims in the governance of their conduct—but more than that they consciously and deliberately assess the weight of evidence understood to support such claims. Within the context of ordinary language conceptual schemata, the descriptive lawlike statements which obtain are generally loosely formulated tendency statements which do not specify the range or scope of their application. Nor do they fully characterize the conditions in which such generalizations are understood to hold. Thus "absence" is said to "make the heart grow fonder," while "out of sight" conduces to "out of mind." *Both* commonsense tendency statements are entertained as true within the same commonsense framework of generalized expectations simply because the generalizations are so loosely framed that it is impossible to specify the cases over which either is to be deployed, characterize the relationships each exhibits, or indicate the conditions under which either is understood to be applicable. What such generalizations express is elliptical, incomplete and/or vague knowledge of a limited and ill-defined range of instances. Such knowledge is capable, at best, of giving a rough guide to expectations in the broadest ordinary circumstances. Similarly generalizations like "all power corrupts," which were popular for a long time in the study of politics, are vaguely suggestive and are understood, at best, as inductive generalizations having *some* application in *some* commonsense circumstances.

Such generalizations, which constitute loose reasons for undertaking or refusing to undertake courses of action, are inductions. They are predicated on observations of a loose and accidental sort and in the absence of more adequate evidence provide the grounds of choice between one behavior or set of behaviors and another. But such reasoning has obvious limitations. A reasonable belief, the grounds for a course of action, would be a warranted belief, in that it was not clearly incompatible with other held beliefs and was supported by the best available descriptive evidence. This first condition could be met only if some assessment of logical consistency or compatibility of propositional knowledge were possible. Consistency can obtain only where the terms used are not so vague and ambiguous as to make a measure of logical compatibility impossible. Conceptual obscurity (vagueness and ambiguity) is the hallmark of commonsense generalizations. Consequently one has no measure of the internal consistency of any set of such claims. The effort to produce warranted beliefs drives rational men to produce more rigorously formulated conceptual schemata, peopled by concepts in which semantic and syntactical indeterminacy is maximally reduced. Only then can some judgment be made concerning the internal consistency of a system of beliefs.

The effort to provide the best available descriptive evidence in support of a generalization requires not only that the *terms* employed to characterize experience be maximally precise, but that the *relationship* obtaining between them be specified with sufficient precision to permit us to discriminate between instances of confirmation and disconfirmation of the putative invariance.

Moreover, since generalizations serve to anticipate futures or explain aspects of complex experience as well as provide the constituents of giving reasons for the choice of one rather than an alternative course, it is incumbent upon one that he have at least a rudimentary appreciation of what constitutes a genuine inductive, as distinct from counterfeit or seeming inductive, generalization. In ordinary language, we speak of inductive generalizations as *laws,* empirical propositions which assert some invariance between properties or events—the invariance construed as accounting for variable behavior.

Lawlike Assertions

To assert and defend a lawlike invariance requires that that invariance be characterized with sufficient clarity to permit it detection, with specificity sufficient to permit instances to be identified which will count as its confirmations or disconfirmation as well as identify occasions when such an invariance can be employed to anticipate futures. In order to minimally accomplish such tasks both the *descriptive content* of putative lawlike propositions, as well as the conceived *relations* understood to obtain between its constituent variables must be characterized.

As a guide to the characterization of the latter, Hans Zetterberg has conveniently schematized five disjunctive sets of conceivable relations between variables that have been employed in social science investigation.[5] He identifies the possible relationships between variables (or variable clusters) in the following fashion: 1) as *deterministic* or *stochastic* (in the former case, if x, then invariably y, and in the latter, if x, then probably y); 2) as *reversible* or *irreversible* (in the former case, if x, then y, and if y, then x as well, while in the latter, if x, then y, but if y, then no conclusion about x); 3) as *sequential* or *coextensive* (in the former case, if x, then later y and in the latter, if x, then also y); 4) as *necessary or substitutable* (in the former case, if x, and only if x, then y, while in the latter,

if x, then y, but if z or any functional equivalent, then also y);
5) as *sufficient* or *contingent* (in the former, if x, then y, irrespective
of anything else, while in the latter, if x, then y, but only if z).

If we consider a reasonably well-known account of putative social
and political invariances—that advanced by Marx and Engels in
the *Communist Manifesto*—it is obvious that their talk of "inevitable" social events stems from a conviction that they posses knowledge of social laws construed as 1) deterministic, 2) irreversible, 3)
sequential, 4) necessary, and 5) sufficient. Only such a construal could
make talk of "inevitabilities" responsible (if such talk is employed
for cognitive purposes). Such claims are, in fact, rarely found in
social science literature, since they constitute the strongest possible
knowledge claims and the evidence conditions which warrant them
are the most demanding. As we have suggested, Marx withdrew
these claims when he undertook to meet the evidence conditions
which might certify their truth. There is little talk of "inevitabilities"
in *Das Kapital*. In his most responsible work Marx made regular
recourse to "tendencies," or "tendency statements," a recharacter-
ization of the "inevitable" invariances he had claimed to have discovered in his youth. The invariances he spoke of in *Das Kapital* are
almost all stochastic and contingent, rather than deterministic and
sufficient.

One can trace such recharacterizations or reformulations of claims
throughout the work of Marx and Engels. In his youth Marx spoke
of the "multitude of productive forces accessible to men" which
determined the "nature of society. . . ." "Life is not *determined*
by consciousness, but consciousness by life." Marx spoke metaphorically about this relationship:

> The phantoms formed in the human brain are also, *necessarily,*
> *sublimates* of their material life process. . . . Morality, religion,
> metaphysics, all the rest of ideology and their corresponding forms
> of consciousness, thus no longer retain the *semblance* of indepen-
> dence. . . .[6]

Fourteen years later Marx wrote: "It is not the consciousness
of men that *determines* their existence, but, on the contrary, their
social existence *determines* their consciousness." He apparently

conceived the relationship between the complex variables, "material powers of production," "relations of production," and "social consciousness," to be deterministic, irreversible, sequential, necessary and sufficient interconnections.[7] Thirty-five years later, in a letter to H. Starkenburg, Engels recharacterized these relationships, in part, in the following way: "Political, juridical, philosophical, religious, literary, artistic, etc., development is *based* on economic development. But all these *react upon one another* and also upon the economic base."[8] In a letter to C. Schmidt, addressed to the same subject, Engels spoke of "the whole vast process" as going on "in the form of *interaction*—though of very unequal forces, the economic movement being by far the strongest, most primeval, most decisive— that here everything is *relative* and *nothing absolute*. . . ."[9]

The relationship between the "material life processes" or the "material powers of production," "social relations" and the "forms of consciousness" was by that time, apparently, construed as stochastic, reversible, sequential, substitutable, and contingent, in what Zetterberg calls an "interdependency" relationship. Truth claims which exemplify such relations are significantly different from claims embodying "inevitabilities." They are considerably easier to defend. They constitute different claims and must satisfy different (and considerably weaker) evidence conditions.

It is fruitless to attempt the assessment of any generalizing knowledge claim unless one can determine with some precision what *kind* of claim is being made. Much ink has been spilled, for example, in the effort to determine the credibility of Marxist truth claims. The fact is that Marx and Engels tendered different truth claims at different times and under different circumstances and for different purposes. There is good internal evidence that they were considerably confused about the kinds of claims they wished to make. Marx, for example, in the same paragraph where he speaks about life "determining" consciousness, tells us that men "alter" their thinking and the products of their thinking along with their material production and their material intercourse. To say that the conditions governing material processes "alter" consciousness is to claim considerably less than that such conditions "determine" consciousness. Ideas, furthermore, are variously spoken of (metaphorically) as "echoes," "phantoms," "reflexes," "effluxes," and "sublimates"—but echoes and reflexes do not influence their causes—and yet Engels speaks of ideas as influencing the course of events.

The fact is that these propositions, while meaningful in a significant sense, are not serious generalizing knowledge claims. They do not assert lawlike invariances. Concepts like "productive forces," "material life processes," "consciousness," "social relations," and their analogues, are simply too vague and ambiguous to unequivocally refer to any specific class of referents. We cannot unequivocally identify their presence or absence. Therefore we cannot unequivocally confirm any putative relations between them. Furthermore, the relationships which are construed as relating such loosely framed variables are themselves so loosely framed that they can be characterized as deterministic on some occasions and stochastic on others, irreversible on some occasions and reversible on others—and so on.

Engels, for example, in 1847 made a revolutionary political party a *substitutable variable* in the putative invariances that account for revolutions (revolution would take place *with* or *without* a revolutionary party), while Lenin was to make the political party a *necessary condition* of revolution (in order to make a revolution it was necessary to have a revolutionary party). And yet we persist in talking about *a* "Marxist theory" of society, consciousness, and revolution exemplified in the disparate works of such people as Luxemburg, Kautsky, Lenin, Stalin, Mao Tse-tung, Castro, Guevara, and Debray. Strictly speaking, there is, outside of some portions of *Das Kapital,* no Marxist *theory*. There *are* theoretical propositions in *Das Kapital*, but most of Marx's own work on society, consciousness and revolution is *pretheoretical*—involving taxonomic sketches, preliminary conceptual schemata, incomplete criterial definitions and fugitive hypotheses—all of which constitute moves in the direction of theory construction insofar as they provide for competent description and tender *suggestions* for research. The principal function of the bulk of Marx's work is *heuristic*, rather than explanatory. It orients us with respect to empirical inquiry. In itself, it explains little and predicts still less. Where Marx or Engels did venture on reasonably specific prediction, such predictions, little more than informed guesses, were almost always unfortunate.

Generalizing knowledge claims that are to function as invariances in explanation and prediction have certain *prima facie* identifying species traits which permit one to sort them out from their heuristic or counterfeit counterparts. To serve in predictions and explanations, generalizing knowledge claims must evidence a significant degree of semantic and syntactical invariance. Variables and the relationship obtaining between them must be characterized with testable precision. This generally involves the extensive use of measurement and the transformation of qualitative concepts into their quantitative counterparts. That mathematics has become the language of empirical inquiry is not a consequence of the perversity of men. Systems of measurement provide for the ordering of qualities by degrees in some ordinal scheme, quantitative measurement in terms of unit magnitude and in terms of ratio variances and invariances—which provide the measures of *precision, congruence,* and *objectivity* that are required for significant and reliable inductive generalization.

Generalizing knowledge claims that are to serve as laws must, first of all, constitute genuine generalizations, that is, they must formulate an invariance that covers a class having indefinitely more members than those inspected. A generalization, limited to those members of a class all of which have been observed, is a *descriptive* generalization. One inspects a class or a subset of a class and formulates a generalization that applies only to the class or the subset inspected; for example, "All Presidents of the United States have been male." Such a generalization does not afford predictive leverage. Knowing such a generalization one could not anticipate the sex of the next president of the United States without introducing a number of auxiliary assumptions of a truly lawlike character.

A genuine generalization, on the other hand, permits an *inductive inference* from the class on which the generalization is based to an open and indefinite class. Such a generalization would be one which claimed that "All societies have a stratification system." Such a generalization is not descriptive if it can be used to support a subjunctive conditional of the sort: "If anything were a society, it would have a stratification system."[10] If such a generalization, "All societies have a stratification system," is empirical and not simply a definition (i.e., if one could indicate what would count as empirical counterevidence against the claim that all societies possess stratification systems), such claims are lawlike generalizations. They support subjunctive conditionals and counterfactuals ("if that had been a society, which we know is not the case, it would have had a stratification system").

Given this analysis, it is clear, for example, that Engels believed that Marxism provided genuine lawlike assertions. In the letter to Starkenburg, referred to above, Engels insisted that if Napoleon had not existed (a counterfactual, since Napoleon had existed), someone else would have served in the same capacity and to the same effect. Similarly, Engels claimed that if Marx had not existed (a counterfactual, since Marx did exist), someone else would have provided mankind with the "Marxist theory." Only genuine lawlike assertions could possibly provide the warrant for such claims. Engels was apparently convinced that Marxism possessed insight into the lawlike invariances governing the relations between men in society.

Besides referring to a nonfinite class and thereby supporting subjunctive and counterfactual conditionals, generalizations that are to qualify as lawlike propositions are unrestricted as to time and place. Thus an assertion that anything that satisfied the criterial attributes of society would invariably possess an independently defined stratification system is lawlike because it is unrestricted. If generalizations are tendered which have a restricted range of application (for example, generalizations that apply only to Euro-American political or social systems), those generalizations are lawlike if they can be shown to be the deductive consequence of more comprehensive lawlike assertions which themselves contain only terms of unlimited or nonfinite application. Thus an invariance is considered lawlike if it applies to a nonfinite class, or if it is an invariance that applies to a finite class but is deductively derivative from other invariances which themselves enjoy unrestricted application.

George Homans, for example, has argued that most of the lawlike statements of restricted range that one finds in the social sciences implicitly refer to invariances of human psychology that have nonfinite and nontemporal (i.e., unrestricted) application. In most instances such invariances are little more sophisticated than commonsense generalizations. One need but consider Robert Dahl's comments on the invariances governing the exercise of power in political circumstances to discover the interred lawlike generalizations which subtend it:

> [Power] is a central notion in the study of politics; and certainly it is essentially . . . a causal notion. . . . When we say that A is powerful . . . we mean that A can induce other people to respond to something in some way. This is clearly a causal notion. When one says that the President has more power to influence foreign policy than I have, then I think one means that the President can cause behavior in the State Department or Congress or in Germany or elsewhere that I cannot cause.[11]

Clearly, an invariance which trafficks on such notions would involve appeal to certain regularities of unrestricted generality governing human behavior, generic responses to the anticipation of reward and fear of punishment, as well as a variety of common-sense generalizations about human psychology. Any invariances involving "power relations" would be the deductive or quasideductive consequence of appeal to such higher-order (and perhaps commonsensical) generalizations. This is, at least in part, what Michael Scriven calls attention to when he refers to the regularities to which historians (and one might add in extension, political scientists) make appeal as "truisms," common-sense generalizations of unrestricted range. Thus a historian, questioning Dahl on his conception of causal notions, suggested that in exploiting an invariance in order to account for an event (the advent of the Civil War in this case), he would ultimately have to make appeal to what he called "a generalization approaching almost a law of behavior," to which Dahl replied that he "enthusiastically" agreed that that constituted the manner in which one might proceed.[12]

As the preceeding discussion suggests, generalizations that function as laws inhabit systems of deductively related propositions. Generalizations remain "essentially" descriptive if they find no place in a deductively articulated schema. A law is normatively characterized as 1) an invariance that can be deployed over a nonfinite class, and which consequently supports subjunctive and counterfactual conditionals, 2) which is unrestricted as to time and place, 3) which finds its place in deductive schema, and finally, 4) which is directly or indirectly testable.

Classificatory Schemata

Such an explication would exclude from the class of lawlike propositions those generalizations which are syndromatic, coextensive. A syndromatic generalization is one which constitutes an assertion of coexisting attributes of the form: "If x is present, then other specifiable elements y and z are coextensive with x." Such generalizations are generic propositions ascribing traits to discriminated classes. Such propositions function as definitions and constitute the basis of typologies or taxonomies. The fact is, as has been suggested with respect to the conceptual schemata employed by children, experience can be ordered in a nonfinite number of ways. Thus G. Lowell Field, in his discussion of comparative politics, indicates that a "practically infinite number of schemes" could be devised for the classification of political regimes.[13]

There is, in effect, no right or wrong way of ordering experience, political or otherwise. The taxonomic categories used for descriptive purposes recommend themselves not because they make any claim upon "reality" (whatever that might be), but because they prove capable of employment in the process of formulating genuine generalizations. Thus David Apter suggests a set of "analytic and descriptive categories" which permit the classification of political systems in terms of "social stratification," "government" and "political groups"—subsequently characterized on other dimensions— the purpose of which is "to make possible some generalization about how the presence, absence, or clustering of certain combinations of variables affect politics."[14]

But unless variables are defined with some precision their presence, absence or clustering cannot be asserted with any confidence. For that reason analytic conceptual schemata, essentially taxonomies, are developed which, in and of themselves, do not constitute genuine generalizing knowledge claims. Names are assigned to discriminable constellations of elements in the domain of inquiry, and the investigator is encouraged to venture into the world to discover them.

Talcott Parsons has called the enterprise of providing such analytic schemata, "theorizing in the strict sense." Strictly speaking, it is not "theorizing"—it is "taxonomizing," "classifying" or "typologizing." Parsons' *Toward a General Theory of Action* is best characterized as providing a system of definitions, a "sociological taxonomy." For the political scientist the analogue activity produces an orderly and convenient schema for the classification and description of things political. Classificatory schemata (one type of linguistic artifact produced by analytic conceptualization) are predicated on syndromatic generalizations. Such schemata become productive of descriptive generalizations when the political scientist undertakes research within his universe of inquiry and finds that the syndromatic invariances identified in his schemata have discriminable counterparts in the object world. One finds that one can describe elements in the domain of inquiry using the concepts of the taxonomic schema. Such schemata inspire descriptive studies. The universe of discourse is segmented in terms of the schema. But to label discriminable and recurrent aspects of the domain and to specify their distribution is not to explain them. What results is a sorting out of things, a systematization by classification. The sets of characteristics, the syndromatic generalizations, which determine what is to fall into each class constitute sorting criteria.

There is nothing "real," "natural," or "definite" about such systematization, for its particular form depends upon the *pragmatic* purpose the systematizer has in mind. In biology the classification of creatures into kingdoms, phyla, classes, orders, families, genera, and species have varied in time not only with the quantitative change in available information, but with the qualitative difference in the purpose of classifying. In political science the classificatory schema of Aristotle has given way to the almost infinite variety of schemata that abound in political science texts today. No one is "more real," more "natural," or "truer" than its alternative. Some simply have *logical* properties which recommend them. They are internally *consistent,* provide categories which are *mutually exclusive* and *exhaustive* of elements in the universe of inquiry, are more *powerful* insofar as they include more aspects of experience and, in satisfying such considerations, do so with greater *elegance* or *parsimony* than any alternative formulation. Such schemata are developed because they are understood, ultimately, to assist in the discovery of genuine invariances. Those that have greater *theoretical yield* have research consequences which recommend them, but such schemata do not themselves establish invariances. Lawlike invariances are established by *observations* on the object world. Logical schemata provide the necessary antecedents—the categories and their range of application—which make such research activities possible.

The use of the expression "logical schemata" suggests "systematization"—and a fully articulated schema is one in which there is an orderly progression from the simplest to the most complex syndromatic generalization or vice versa. (For our purposes, we need not here distinguish between "logical schemata," "definitional schemata," "typologies," "classificational schemata," and "analytic conceptual schemata.") Zetterberg cites the taxonomy provided by Max Weber as a signal instance of such a schema. In such a schema "social order" implies "body politic" or "political relations," which, in turn, implies "interpersonal relations," which, in turn, imply the analytically primitive notion of the action of an individual actor. It is relatively common practice for political scientists to employ such schemata in orientating themselves to their subject.

Syndromatic generalizations provide the logically necessary basis of classificatory systems. Such generalizations are *pretheoretical* insofar as the schemata they subtend make, in themselves, no knowledge claims. They are *analytic* schemata and are used, logically speaking, as a preliminary to theorizing. The qualifier, "logically speaking," is introduced to indicate that, in practice, classificatory schemata are often (if not universally) the by-product of long familiarity with a particular research domain and consequently imply, in fact, a *theoretical* orientation. The distinction made between the pretheoretical and theoretical character of various linguistic entities is insisted upon only for analytic purposes. Thus Lowell Field, in speaking of his analytic conceptual schema for the classification of political regimes, indicates that his schema was arrived at "by specifying, testing and revising concepts over a period of ten years"—

which means that the schema was applied (hence was construed as having extralinguistic reference), and their utility tested within the confines of some theory of political development.[15]

The distinction between syndromatic generalization and genuine generalizing knowledge claims is often obscured in practice and the two processes telescope into a single complex activity. Nonetheless, the distinction is clear. Syndromatic characterizations are not, in themselves, genuine generalizing claims. Nothing in nature or experience may satisfy the criteria for entrance into an analytically defined class (i.e., the class may be a "null class," having no members). There are, furthermore, many different kinds of properties that the objects under scrutiny may exhibit, and a choice among them for those which are to serve as syndromatic traits depends, ultimately, on the service such an ordering can perform in theory construction. Some properties or attributes will be selected, for example, because they are easily observable and/or easily quantifiable. The reason for this is that under such circumstances system properties and the state of the system can be conveniently characterized over time. Such characterizations assist in discovering lawlike generalizations that may become the process laws which give systematically ordered sets of propositions their explanatory and predictive force.

Systematic and Historic Process Laws

If we can adequately characterize the properties and state of a system (assume our universe of inquiry is the political system) at time t, we are, after successive investigations at times t_1, $t_2 \ldots t_n$, in an optimum position, using the canons of inductive investigation, to suggest the functional relations between constituent variables, identifying some as dependent, and others as independent. Adequate analytic schemata, generally introduced via lexical definitions, provide the initial leverage for the determination of lawlike, functional relationships between constituent variables.[16] In the process, as has already been suggested, lexical definitions give way to substantive and more sensitive contextual, implicit and criterial definitions. Syndromatic relations, expressed in analytic conceptual schemata, provide the sorting criteria necessary for the provision of *systematic process* and *historic process laws*.[17] Systematic and historic process laws constitute the principal types of tested inter-dependence between variables employed for explanatory and predictive purposes. When such interdependences are genuine generalizations of unrestricted range (or are derivative of assertions of unrestricted generality) capable of supporting subjunctive and counterfactual conditionals and prove capable of inhabiting a deductive set of propositions, which is itself subject to direct or indirect confirmation, they constitute laws in the domain of inquiry.

Systematic process laws are lawlike statements of predictive or retrodictive relationships between variables which can be determined via knowledge of the present state of the system. In physics, for example, given the present state of a system of *n* bodies at a specified time, and the relevant laws of mechanics, one could predict or retrodict the state of the system at any subsequent or past time without any supplementary historic information about the system. Such laws are characteristic of the maximally formalized natural sciences. The minimally or partially formalized social or behavioral sciences are characterized by the abundance of *historic process laws* which require information about the antecedent history of the system if current response or any past or subsequent state of the system is to be anticipated.

The work of Chalmers Johnson provides illustrative instances of how theory construction in contemporary political science proceeds employing process laws. Johnson begins his account of revolutions by identifying the two ranges of discourse requisite to any "conceptual rigor": the analytic and the synthetic.[18] He employs analytic classificatory schemata to provide categories necessary for talking about the object world. What results are variously called "typologies" or "conceptual schemata" which do not, in themselves, deliver genuine lawlike generalizations. Johnson speaks of "using the ideas of role, norm, and status," for "conceptualizing" the "system of social action," an activity which provides the categories that subserve the identification of discriminable, enduring and/or recurring elements in the political environment under scrutiny.[19]

Such conceptualizing, commencing with what we have called a preliminary conceptual schema, can become a rigorous analytic conceptual schema or taxonomy. Even when it attains the rigor of an axiomatized system it does not, in itself, reveal (as Johnson himself insists) "what causes a revolution in a concrete case." To accomplish such purpose we need operational indices, semantic rules, which will identify some constellation of symptomatic recognitors as instances of "role," "status," "equilibrium," "dysfunction" and so on. The analytic conceptual schema must be bound to the world with the ligaments of semantic meaning rules. The process of binding such concepts to the object world is often loosely spoken of as "operationalizing." In a chapter entitled, "Measuring Disequilibrium," for example, Johnson suggests such operationalization by identifying the empirical indices that are to serve as indicators of key concepts such as "equilibrium." As indicators of "equilibrium" or "disequilibrium," he suggests, among others, suicide rates, the military participation ratio, heightened ideological activity and the possible correlation between general and particular crime rates.[20] The definitions offered via such indicators are criterial and afford an indeterminate, if finite, set of intersecting and overlapping attributes a society is to have if the ascription "equilibrium" or "disequilibrium" is to have empirical import.

The use of criterial definition is evident throughout his work. In his effort to specify the causes of revolution he provides the characterization: "Multiple dysfunction plus elite intransigence plus X equals revolution."[21] When the operational rules for the application of such a formula are provided, what results looks like a systematic process law. Whenever multiple dysfunction plus elite intransigence plus X obtain (and whether they obtain would be empirically determined by the provision of semantic rules for the felicitous application of the constituent concepts), revolution results. This kind of account permits Johnson to maintain that "revolution is endemic and, *ceteris paribus*, an insurrection is inevitable" in South Africa.[22] As a matter of fact it would seem that the lawlike generalizations that Johnson formulates are historic rather than systematic process laws because the *"X"* alluded to above refers to "accelerators," in some cases the appearance of a charismatic (or pseudocharismatic) leader who mobilizes masses for revolutionary struggle. In that cose it would, on one construal, be plausible to assume that some appeal is made to the biographical history of the revolutionary leader and the full account of the lawlike generalizations covering revolutions would have irreducible historic dimensions (this is also strongly suggested by Johnson's use of the *ceteris paribus,* "all things being equal," clause). Johnson seems to opt for an analysis which, in general, would minimize the influence of personalities on revolution —but there are cases where he specifically mentions the necessity of "biographical and historical information" to complete the account. [23]

In this regard it seems intuitively clear that personality variables, essentially historic in character, will have greater predictive significance in some situations rather than others. And, as Robert Tucker has argued, there are cases where generalizations covering political events cannot be tendered unless the developmental history of some particular individual is disinterred; a consideration which would make the generalizations entertained by political scientists *historical* rather than *systematic process laws.* [24]

However one construes the efforts of political scientists, it seems clear that their preoccupation is with generating generalizing knowledge claims, lawlike assertions, calculated to assist us in understanding complex political phenomena. Thus Johnson characterizes his efforts as an attempt to formulate "the necessary and sufficient causes of a revolution. . . ." He speaks of "two clusters of mutually-influencing necessary, or remote, causes of . . . revolution," and then proceeds to attempt an account of its sufficient cause. [25]

To speak of *necessary* conditions of an event (as has been already suggested) is to say that whenever y is present, x is its invariable antecedent; whenever y is present, x is present, or y is never present unless x obtains, although y may be absent when x is present. If we speak of some x as a *sufficient* condition of y, what we intend is that whenever x is present, y is present, or x is never present without the incidence of y, though y may be present when x is absent. If we assert that x (or, in Johnson's account, some cluster of variables) is the *necessary* and *sufficient* condition of y, we assert the strongest sense of invariance. We hold that y is never present unless x (or the requisite cluster of variables) is present and x never obtains without y obtaining as well. This is clearly a case of a genuine generalization supporting predictions. Since, in the case of Johnson's account, the unrestricted generalization supports conditionals and counterfactuals, refers to a nonfinite class, and inhabits a systematically integrated collection of propositions—we have a confidently asserted lawlike knowledge claim.

One might legitimately raise a number of substantive questions about the formulation of such a lawlike assertion, but it seems clear that we have an instance of a candidate generalizing lawlike knowledge claim, the product of analytic treatment of a preliminary conceptual schema, parastic upon lexical definitions which gradually transform themselves into contextual and criterial definitions which identify recognitors that characterize constituent concepts— which in their turn permit the application of the canons of inductive inquiry.

The account provided here for the generation and identification of lawlike assertions is necessarily schematic and stenographic. There are any number of more extended, detailed and competent accounts.[26] We have been concerned, by and large, with suggesting something of the "logic" (understood in the informal sense) of such procedures as well as affording some specifics for the identification of various linguistic entities to be found in political science literature as well as criteria that might subserve responsible assessment of their truth status.

Theories and Models

At least implicit in the preceeding discussion has been a recognition that the ultimate purpose of the aggregate activities in political science research is the production of viable *theories* which provide the most competent explanation of complex phenomena. Implicit as well has been a suggestion of what "theory" can most meaningfully be understood to be. Minimally, "a theory is a systematically related set of statements, including some lawlike generalizations, that is empirically testable."[27] Observations of discriminable and recurrent aspects of experience mature into concepts (or significantly modify funded or ordinary language conceptualizations), which in turn develop into preliminary and/or partially axiomatized conceptual schemata which may, in turn, themselves develop into fully axiomatic systems. When axiomatic systems are bound to the object world through operational definitions (which give relatively specific meaning to the relations between their conceptual constituents and those constituents themselves), they produce *theories*.

In the natural sciences, theories have a reasonably well standardized form. In a maximally formalized science, a theory is understood to include: (1) a *calculus* (an uninterpreted axiomatic system) which provides maximal syntactical determinacy; (2) a set of *semantic rules* of interpretation which assign determinate empirical meanings to the primitive terms of the calculus thereby relating it to an evidential or empirical base; and (3) a *model* for the calculus, in terms of more or less familar conceptual or visualizable materials, which illustrates the relationships between variables in structural form, one of several interpretations of the calculus itself.[28]

The process through which formal theories are produced in natural science is essentially that of the social sciences. The differences are the consequence of maximal standardization of concepts and formalization of syntactical relations that have become characteristic of maximally formalized sciences like physics. Fully axiomatized systems which are uninterpreted become purely syntactical structures (calculi). They maximally exhibit the fully determinate relations understood to obtain between uninterpreted primitives. Such formal structures are devoid of descriptive content, but they afford maximal syntactical precision. In order to restore empirical content to the logical calculus, a set of meaning or semantic rules or coordinating definitions are provided which specify the empirical meaning that is to be accorded the primitive and explicitly and implicitly defined terms of the calculus. In empirical sciences, the calculus alone, without a systematic specification of the intended empirical referents, is not considered a theory; it is a piece of pure mathematics; it is a strictly formal linguistic entity. Its sole test is consistency. A *model* would be a mapping of the calculus over some non-linguistic entity, visualizable or mechanical, in which all valid sentences of the calculus are satisfied.[29] In long established sciences there is a tendency for scientists well socialized to the discipline to make ready transfer from the calculus to the model. If the model satisfies all the valid sentences of the calculus, and the word "theory" is employed to mean interpreted calculus, then "model" and "theory" become, for all intents and purposes, synonymous. This can happen in the maximally formalized, but is precluded from happening in the minimally or partially formalized, sciences. In some of the maximally formalized sciences models of *parts* of the calculus are employed for convenience, the model radically simplifying the calculus and serving as a convenience to thought and communication. It is understood by practitioners of such sciences that the model serves as a stenographic reference to part of the calculus. Since social scientists have few such calculi, their use of models is significantly different.

In the formalized sciences models are parasitic on calculi. The implications of the model are contained in maximally explicit form in the calculus. The model is a highly simplified, easily visualized or conceptualized, schema.

The situation is significantly different in the social sciences. The terms "theory" and "model" are deployed over a variety of linguistic and non-linguistic entities. Terms like "theory," "conceptual schemata," "theoretical framework," "conceptual devices," "models," and "approaches," are used interchangeably.[30] Actually the confusion that attends such vague and ambiguous use can be appreciably reduced if the standard interpretation of theory is maintained as a prescriptive guide. This linguistic recommendation is suggested as a device for reducing the variance in the use of such terms.

An organized and systematic knowledge enterprise that has transcended the level of description and has generated testable generalizations about directly or indirectly observable entities attempts to explain those generalizations by exhibiting them in a subsumptive set of propositions that make the confirmed generalizations the deductive consequence of more general propositions. The deductive validity of the system is maximally exposed by expressing it in a formal axiomatic system or (if uninterpreted) a calculus in which a subset of propositions are identified as *axioms* and the propositions which are deductive artifacts of the axiom set and the *transformation rules* for operating on the set are identified as *theorems.* If such a collection is articulated in the form of a calculus, the primitives, rules for the formation of formulas, and the basic logic (or transformation rules) of the set are fully specified. A theory which finds expression in such a calculus is given standard formalization. A partially formalized theory exhibits not a whole calculus but parts of a calculus which exhibit the deductive steps involved in the treatment of some select area of concern. Such linguistic entities are partial theories insofar as they do apply to a restricted range of phenomena. Nothing is gained by calling them anything else than partially formalized theories. Calling them "models" generates some confusion. A model for theory T is one (of a nonfinite number) of alternate interpretations of the calculus of T.[31] To call a partial theory or a partial calculus a "mathematical model," introduces a measure of vagueness and ambiguity that serves no cognitive purpose.

The principal role of models in extensively formalized disciplines is to serve as a representation of the calculus which is intuitively more familiar. Such models serve illustrative purpose; they are heuristic and pedagogical aids. We may use spatial diagrams to illustrate the features of a deductive system, and such diagrams are helpful in the consideration of the logical relationships between classes. A model, then, is a visualizable, a stenographic schematization, or a more easily conceptualizable representation of a theory.

In minimally formalized disciplines the distinction between theories and models is maximally reduced and their roles frequently confused. The distinctions do appear in some political science literature, specifically in some cases[32] and implicitly in others. Thus Lowell Field maintains that a model is a "way of thinking about the subject" and a theory is a "set of formal assumptions"[33]— which makes the distinction we have suggested in an informal fashion. But in most cases in political science a wide variety of linguistic entities are identified as "models" to the utter confusion of everyone.

Political scientists tend, in general, to talk of models as "intermediate steps along the road to theory,"[34] and in a significant descriptive sense this is true. Vernon Van Dyke speaks of models as linguistic entities "advanced in connection with searches for explanation."[35] The question immediately arises: when models constitute explanations, how are they to be distinguished from theories? Thus Herbert Simon, in at least one place, simply makes the terms model and theory synonymous.[36] In effect, should such a view of "models" be entertained, the function of a model would be to explain and predict—precisely the function of a theory.[37] More than occasionally in political science literature *any* linguistic entity that, *in any sense,* assists in generating explanations and predictions becomes a theory. Thus David Easton, referring to the variety of "theoretical frameworks," "conceptual devices," "models," "approaches," and "strategies," calls them all "theories," but cautions us that in political science "theory in any ideal sense is as yet little known" and that "strategies," "models," and "approaches" might, as a matter of fact, be more coherently conceived as "programs for analysis that *under appropriate conditions* could develop into theories more rigorously defined."[38]

If we are to preserve the necessary distinction between pretheoretical linguistic entities and theoretical entities, some preliminary distinguishing features have to be identified. The antecedent discussion suggests that research requires some conceptual apparatus as necessary before work can be undertaken. In informal disciplines like political science we generally commence with *ordinary language conceptual schemata*, a conceptualization of classes of phenomena, subtended by a rudimentary rationale, whose purpose is to furnish the descriptive terms and relations that putatively characterize the objects of inquiry. Where such schemata are partially standardized and partially formalized (i.e., where at least one indigenous concept is explicitly, implicitly, contextually, or criterially defined and one deductive connection between their constituent propositions is specified), we can legitimately speak of *preliminary* and at least partially *analytic conceptual schemata* (what are sometimes referred to in political science literature as "analytic models"). The introduction of standardization and formalization is the necessary consequence of attempting to search out and warrant truth claims. Ordinary language concepts are, in general, too vague and ambiguous to support significant research and verification studies. *Axiomatized* or *partially axiomatized systems* reduce semantic and syntactical variance and when operational procedures (which identify symptomatic recognitors or provide for direct verification for the descriptive and contingent content of such systems) are afforded, we can speak of *theories*.

The distinction between the various linguistic entities, while it cannot be made rigorous, is established by the primary purpose served by such entities. If their purpose is heuristic, to orientate and to suggest testable hypotheses— to provide a "point of view" or a "perspective"—they can be characterized as ordinary language, preliminary or analytic conceptual schemata. If they are uniquely descriptive, they are applied definitional or classificatory schemata or typologies. Their function is didactic and heuristic. When such linguistic products generate testable propositions, they can be characterized as theories, or if one wishes to preserve the distinction between general theories and theories of restricted range, partial theories—the distinction being the range and scope of the explanatory and predictive propositions in the articulated set.

The elementary test of whether we are in fact dealing with conceptual schemata or theories is whether the collection of propositions with which we are occupied contains directly or indirectly testable propositions. Thus when Talcott Parsons insists that his effort is not concerned with "empirical generalization as such nor with methodology," this can be reasonably interpreted as meaning he is generating pretheoretical, partially formalized and standardized, analytic conceptual schemata the merit of which will be determined *ultimately* by its usefulness in empirical research.[39] Such schemata *could* mature into theory if, as Richard Sheldon suggests, "one can give factual meaning to the categories in terms of operations and provided one can derive from these categories relationships subject to empirical test."[40] Without the provision of such elements the schemata remain essentially pretheoretical, and serve basically a didactic and heuristic pupose. They provide a convenient vehicle for characterizing a range of inquiry and, should any empirical regularities be identified through their use, for their convenient storage and recall. Since every taxonomy suggests relations, they can, in a vague but essential sense, suggest exploratory hypotheses. But a conceptual schema, no matter how intricate, is not, in itself, a theory. Such a schema, characterized by conceptual clarity, allows an investigator to identify the significant and recurrent features of the object world, but until such schemata are capable of generating verificational studies (i.e., until an indication of how they can, in fact, be applied is given), they remain pretheoretical.[41]

Most of the "models" employed in contemporary political science are *propaedeutic* to theory construction; they are its antecedents. They perform the functions characterized above. They are didactic insofar as they generate taxonomies, "conceptual boxes" for the identification, storage and recall of discriminable aspects of political reality. They are heuristic insofar as the features of reality so conceptualized *suggest* something of the relationships understood to obtain between reasonably discrete classes of phenomena. Mutually exclusive and exhaustive sets of categories can be conceptualized and these sets can be conceived as intersecting and overlapping in complex and intricate fashion. One can call such linguistic entities "models" or "paradigms" if one chooses—but they are basically taxonomic and nontheoretic and their uses are didactic, heuristic and, at best, descriptive. They are not, in any literal sense, theories. Their ultimate merit can be judged only when they subserve effective theory construction. Thus David Apter suggests that the test of a set of "categories" is its ability to produce "useful results."[42] "Useful results" seems to imply explanatory and predictive yield. Lowell Field accordingly suggests a new set of conceptual categories in the hope that they will help to disinter "causal relations" and "significant generalization" in the field in comparative politics—that is to say that such a schema will assist, *ultimately,* in the generation of testable propositions.[43] Until they are capable of generating verificational studies, they remain pretheoretical conceptual schemata.

To suggest that *all* the linguistic contrivances employed in the production of testable propositions are "models" is unprofitable and obscures their relatively distinctive attributes—and if no distinction is drawn between models and theories as a consequence of the indisposition to search out distinctions, the confusion is compounded. Most linguistic entities that are identified as "models" in political science are analytic or descriptive nontheoretical schemata, either definitional, classificational or typological (the "ideal types" frequently referred to in comparative politics texts constitute a case in point), which, at best and in themselves, make descriptive empirical claims.[44] The measure of their initial admissibility is their internal consistency and that can be determined only in the measure of their *logical properties*, clarity and precision. The measure of the worth of an empirical theory is empirical *confirmation*. In theoretically rich disciplines nontheoretic formulations would make their appearance as a part of viable theories. Accordingly the assessment made of such nontheoretical formulations would be predicated on the assessment of the theories of which they constituted a part. Since political science, like most of the social sciences, is embarrassed by the paucity of viable theories, the sole measure of the worth of nontheoretic formulations depends largely on their logical properties, clarity and precision, range of application, and relative logical simplicity. Their heuristic merit can be judged only if such schemata ever come to subtend a theory.

Anatol Rapoport conveniently summarizes the above distinction:

> The stuff from which human relations and social structure are made is not evident intuitively. It must somehow be distilled, or abstracted from innumerable "events," and the selection of these events depends to a great extent on one's experiences, cultural background, and biases.
>
> Nevertheless, the social scientist does try to select the fundamental entities of his field of interest. This process of selection, however, is so laborious and involved that it often constitutes the bulk of the social scientist's efforts, and so he hardly ever gets around to stating "postulates." He must first relate his terms to referents. These referents cannot be simply exhibited; they must themselves be abstracted from a rich variety of events, generalizations, and relations. By the time a number of these referents have been so abstracted and christened, one already

has a bulky "system" before the work of seeking out "laws" has ever begun. Such "system," particularly in sociology, is sometimes taken to be "theories."

.... For the mathematician, as for the physical scientist, a "theory" is a collection of theorems, that is, statements in the form of implications, which, if applied to the physical world, become predictions as to what will be observed if certain conditions obtain. For a social scientist, a "theory" is often (in effect) a system of reference, that is, a multitude of definitions. . . . That is to say, the theoretician of social science invites the reader to categorize his observations in a certain way. . . . This effort constitutes a considerable part of the social scientist's preoccupation with "theory."[45]

Only *some* of the conceptual schemata of political science mature into theories. In order to so evolve, the constituent concepts must be defined with testable precision (a specification of recognitors that constitute symptomatic indices for the use of concepts) and the relationships understood to obtain between such operationally defined variables be specified (generally in quantified terms as deterministic or stochastic, necessary or substitutable and so forth). Until that occurs, what we are dealing with are conceptual schemata of various types, articulated at various levels of sophistication. Among those schemata only some could reasonably be identified as "models."

Models as Replicas, Analogues, and Analogies

If we take our cue from ordinary language, an analysis results that remains substantially true to the use of the term "model" suggested by our characterization of a model as an alternate and admissible interpretation of a calculus. If we exclude cases where the term "model" is used for normative purposes (as in the case of "model" boy and fashion "model"), the term model is generally used for cognitive purposes to cover instances where some *relationships of substantive similarity* obtain between two (linguistic or nonlinguitic) entities. To say that entities share some substantive similarities is to say that they are *structurally similar* in some respect. Thus the most familar kind of descriptive model is the scale model, a *micromorph* (or *macromorph*) or *replica* of some natural or constructed entity. The model is related to its original in a fashion that could be reduced to precise rules according to which the dimensions of the one could be turned into the dimensions of another. A model airplane which is 1/72 the size of the original shares structural properties with its original. The similarity shared is expressed in terms of scale, and a simple scaling up would fully restore some features of the original. (A macromorph would require a scaling down—as, for example, with a model of an amoeba.)

The relationships between parts of the model can be expressed in mathematical terms. The models are replicas of the original; there is a one to one correspondence between some elements of the model and some elements of the original of which it is the model. Certain relations are preserved, but the similarities that relate models to their originals are not exhaustive. The degree of similarity is expressed in the mathematical formulae employed to restore features of the replica to its original dimensions. The model is never identical in all respects with its original. But since both the original and the model are fully known, the differences between them can be made explicit. We neglect certain aspects in which there are positive dissimilarities and concentrate for illustrative or didactic purposes on the similarities (in their rule-governed reduction or enlargement). Such models are similar to their originals in a specific sense or senses and they serve essentially didactic purposes or as conveniences in testing (as in the case of using scale models in wind tunnels) when the originals are too unwieldy or too small for direct test. Such models have not found their way into political science research.

An *analogue* or *formal* model exemplifies something of the same features. An analogue model is substantively similar to its original. The analogue or formal model is one of an unspecified number of permissible interpretations of a calculus. As we have indicated, an analogue model, in a formalized science, is an object world interpretation of a formal linguistic entity. The object world is understood to share structural properties with its original formal language analogue. The sharing of formally defined structural properties is spoken of, in formal disciplines, as *isomorphism*.

In empirical science, when an interpretation of a calculus is made, the interpretation is mapped over a nonlinguistic domain, i.e., the object world. A calculus, because it can be interpreted in a nonfinite number of ways, can be mapped, potentially, over an indeterminate range of objects. When such a mapping takes place it is held that the calculus and the nonlinguistic range over which it is mapped are isomorphic, the structural properties attributed to the calculus can be attributed to the range of the object world over which it is mapped.

If a calculus is given a descriptive interpretation, we refer to it as an empirical theory. If the laws of one empirical theory are applied to an alternate range, and the structural properties of the laws (but not their content) are retained in the analogous range, the first theory can be spoken of as the model of the other. The theories are isomorphic. If part of the calculus is given a nonlinguistic interpretation (for example, the formula identified as Ohm's law, which applies to the conductivity of a metallic conductor) and the formal features of the law are preserved in another (as is the case of Poisuelle's law governing water flow through a fairly narrow pipe with a circular cross section), then the laws (not their content of reference) are isomorphic and the conduction of electricity "models" water flow and vice versa. *Precisely what is modelled is explicated in the calculus that subtends both.* In such a manner the modelling of one range by another avoids the fundamental problem which afflicts all analogical reasoning: to what extent is one range "similar" to another; to what extent does the positive analogy apply and at what point does disanalogy begin?

When the scientist entertains a hydraulic model for electric current flow, we are able to determine precisely in what sense and to what measure "similarity" applies—"similarity" is explicitly characterized in the calculus. We know a great deal more about water than Poisuelle's law governing its flow properties. Similarly we know a great deal more about electricity than Ohm's law. But as long as we are concerned with the features of the one which model the other, the knowledge of the formal properties of the calculus that subtends both eliminates any temptation we might suffer to translate any information not actually derivable from the calculus from one range to the other. The guarantee of "similarity" that obtains between the two is contained in the calculus and the guarantee extends only over the implications of the calculus. Thus when the physical scientist speaks of water waves modelling electromagnetic waves, the similarity that obtains between the one and the other is guaranteed by the calculus of which both are interpretations. The viability of models in formalized science is provided by the availability of a calculus that guarantees their isomorphism. Unless such a calculus obtains, the use of the term "model" is *metaphorical*. Models in physical science perform a variety of functions, among them to give a physical interpretation of a calculus. Where two ranges provide alternate interpretations of the same calculus, one models the other. The ranges share isomorphic features. Where no calculus obtains, the use of the term model may be seriously misleading.

In physical science a model of a calculus is primarily a conceptual convenience. It often serves little purpose beyond providing a mechanical or more familiar visualization of abstract formulae. If the nonlogical or descriptive concepts occurring in the basic generalizations of a theory (interpretations of the uninterpreted axiomatic system) are all observable properties or relations, there is little purpose in generating a model for the theory. This suggests that the model in formalized sciences is eliminable. In fact the actual predictive and explanatory work of the theory is unimpaired by the absence of a model. The actual predictive and explanatory work is performed by the calculus. The functions of models, even in the formalized sciences, are *didactic* and *heuristic*.

If a calculus is given a physical interpretation via semantic rules for the interpretation of uninterpreted symbols in the calculus, and every valid sentence of the calculus is given interpretation, we can talk of the interpretation of a model or an empirical theory. At this level of formalization one is employing the formal definition of a model ("a possible realization in which all valid sentences of a calculus are satisfied") and a characterization of a fully formalized descriptive theory. Only at such a level could "models" and "theories" be equivalent terms. In most physical sciences (not to speak of the social sciences), a model is usually a partial interpretation of the calculus, a convenience in conceptualization.

Both replicas and analogue models have defenses against the indiscriminate exploitation of putative similarities. There are defenses, in both cases, against the extension of the range of similarities beyond a guaranteed and specifiable range, or if such illicit extensions are undertaken they are readily identified. Such safeguards are not readily available in many instances when models are employed in the minimally or partially formalized sciences, and particularly in political science.

In the social sciences the term model is employed primarily when some *suggestion* of substantive similarity between two entities is tendered. Such suggestions can be conveniently referred to as *analogical models* and have characteristics significantly different from those of replicas and analogue models.

An analogical model is a didactic and heuristic device—like all models employed for cognitive purposes. It is employed in minimally formalized sciences to suggest *something* about the properties and relations understood to obtain within the domain of inquiry. Some objects of inquiry are tolerably well known, like animal cells ar the homeostatic properties of organisms, while others, like societies or political systems, are not. An investigator may suggest a transfer of information from one range to another via analogy. Thus James Miller identified the central thesis of general systems "theory" as one which seeks "formal identities between various physical systems, the cell, the organ, the individual, the small group or species, and the society."[46]

The suggestion that "formal identities" obtain between such disparate entities attempts to conflate analogical and analogue models. Ludwig von Bertalanffy, one of the founders of general systems "theory" (which has had significant influence in political science), counselled his followers that we may begin to characterize the phenomena under inquiry via analogies, but that "analogies are scientifically worthless." What is required is the determination of "logical homologies" (what we have termed isomorphisms) if explanation in the literal sense is to be forthcoming. "Homologies," he insisted, "provide very useful models and are widely used in this way in physics." To say that "homologies" obtain between different empirical ranges is to maintain that the phenomena in both are "governed by structurally identical laws."[47]

In effect, the founders of general systems theory conceived their models as analogue models. The fact is that the general systems theory now popular in political science does not deploy *analogue* models but *analogical* models. While such analogies are not scientifically worthless (performing very valuable didactic and heuristic functions), they are *not* analogue models. They do not exploit a calculus ("identical laws") which guarantees the isomorphic character of the disparate ranges over which they are mapped. When David Easton speaks of "systems" as disparate as the "smallest cell in the human body," "organisms," "human personality," "societies," and "political systems" as sharing some features, he is clearly talking analogically. No known calculus can be mapped over all such nonlinguistic entities. Consequently the laws of one range cannot be transferred to another. Such analogies are invoked to suggest *something* about disparate phenomena. What such analogies do suggest is impossible to determine with any precision. Political systems can be conceived as in *some* ways like cells and organisms. But, unlike replicas, such substantive or analogical models are not mutually governed by rules for transforming the model into its original. Unlike analogue models, such models are not alternate interpretations of some uninterpreted axiomatic system. Analogical models are analogies and, unconstrained by any clear rules governing their use, suffer all the limitations of analogical reasoning. One is never quite certain how far the analogy is to be pursued.

The human body has well-confirmed homeostatic properties. The political system *may* have some homeostatic properties. Some of the properties governing heat balance in the body may be, in some sense, analogous to those restoring equilibrium in the political system—but in what sense and in what measure is impossible, at this time, to specify. Were such analogical models replica or analogue models, we would know, at least in principle, how to characterize the extent of positive and negative analogy which covers them.

But analogical or substantive models are neither of these, and as a consequence and at best, they serve the same didactic and heuristic function as preliminary conceptual schemata. They suggest categories for the classification of sets of discriminable phenomena and they posit, with no more than intuitive specificity, the relationships between them.

The difference between the preliminary conceptual schemata and the analogical models employed by political scientists is a consequence of the fact that analogical models are predicated upon *putative similarities* between political events or event complexes and some better known area of inquiry. Thus system theorists and structural functionalists exploit knowledge of, and employ the vocabulary of, better known physiological or cybernetic systems. But until the range of the similarities are specified and the analogues of laws obtaining in the better known area are confirmed as obtaining in the political range, such models have no more merit than the exploratory (preliminary and partially analytic) conceptual schemata with which inquiry must commence in any case. The conviction that analogical models have, in themselves, greater scientific merit is illusory. The impression of greater significance is purchased by the fictive (and in large part illegitimate) transfer of knowledge from some well researched area, to the political range. We know a great deal about the processes maintaining homeostasis in organisms. But such knowledge is not transferrable to some other research range by fiat. The presence of homeostatic or re-equilibrizing processes may be *suggested* by analogical models, but until such processes are confirmed as system-specific mechanisms in the primary universe of inquiry such models are no more than analogical.

Analogical models are preliminary conceptual schemata of a distinct type—those that offer the suggestion—predicated upon putative similarities between one range of phenomena and another— that one universe of inquiry is *somehow* like another. Armed with such heuristic insights, the political scientist is disposed to structure the discriminable elements in his research environment in a special fashion. How serviceable such structuring is can only be determined when lawlike generalizations covering the primary universe of inquiry are forthcoming and made subject to test—or when such generalizations are lodged in the deductive schema that constitutes a theory and the entire linguistic entity measured directly or indirectly against the object world.

There are a variety of analogical or substantive models employed in political science literature. Some make their appearance as "mathematical models," highly schematized and elliptical mathematical formulas which pretend to tell us something about putative relations in the object world. These traffic on analogical relations between some mathematical relations and the relations between discrete aspects of political reality. Generally such formulas are advanced as being highly "idealized," with an unspecific number of qualifications understood as bearing on them. Such formulas are analogical models and not analogues because one cannot specify in what sense and in what measure and under what circumstances they are understood to hold. At times the expression "mathematical model" simply refers to any quantified theory. In such cases we are concerned with a theory which has predictive and explanatory function. Much of game theory is given in terms of mathematical representation. Game theory, at its best, provides a mathematical representation of an empirical theory of behavior (a subset of utility theory in economics) in "game" situations. The theory may entertain "idealizations" of "rational participants" which qualify its applicability to any specific case, but it is intended to predict how people will behave, or explain their behavior in the past, in "gaming" situations.

Some analogical models appear in the form of diagrams suggesting, for example, the putative "structure" of "power relations." They may be called something like the "pyramidal model of power distribution," and make their appearance as a figure representing intersecting pyramids. Or they may be spoken of as a "model of the political system," and appear as diagrams showing the "exchange of flow" properties in terms of arrows and boxes. Such diagrams and schematizations may suggest that power is "distributed" in some way or another or that "inputs" react with institutions in some fashion. They are construed as providing some kind of "understanding of complex phenomena."[48] But the only conceivable kind of understanding they can provide is analogical.

It is the kind of "understanding" afforded by metaphor and parable. If the "understanding" desired is to have a more specific cognitive character, it will involve the generation of specific and testable knowledge claims, the by-product of more rigorous linguistic entities: analytic schemata, axiomatic systems, calculi perhaps, and a deliberative explication of appropriate semantic rules of correspondence. "Understanding" would become "theoretical understanding," and analogy and metaphor would work toward their own exclusion.

This is what, in effect, happens whenever models are employed in cognitive inquiry. Models are never, in themselves, explanatory. If a model predicts or explains, it is either a complete or partial interpretation of a calculus and then it is the calculus which performs the actual work. The model is parasitic upon the calculus. It may be very suggestive insofar as it recommends the extension of knowledge to untried ranges, but in and of itself it cannot guarantee the extension. A promising model is not one that explains or predicts, for that is not its function. It is one rich with implications that suggest novel hypotheses which must themselves be articulated in a systematic fashion and subject to test independent of the model which suggested them. A good model neither predicts, explains nor confirms. It suggests a manner of passing from one aspect of the model to another or an extension of properties or relations from some better known area of inquiry to another. But the price of employing models, whether those models be replicas, analogue or analogical models, is "eternal vigilance."[49]

An analogical model is a sustained metaphor. The implications and suggestions generated by the use of such analogical models can be drawn out only via standardization of their descriptive terms and a characterization of their structure. With micro- or macromorphic models (replicas) we recognize where dissimilarities begin and similarities leave off because we know their originals in detail. With analogue models the subtending calculus specifies the range of appropriate similarity. With substantive or analogical models we have only a promissory note on such specifications. Payment is forthcoming only after considerable semantic and syntactical effort. If payment is forthcoming there will be objective ground for the analogical transfer of knowledge from one universe of inquiry to another. But once the regularities governing the primary universe are established, continued reference to the model is, for explanatory or predictive purposes, unnecessary. Models are promissory notes on theories. The availability of viable theories is the cognitive reserve that makes them negotiable intellectual currency.

Notes

1 Cf. P. Winch, *The Idea of a Social Science* (London: Routledge & Kegan Paul, 1960), chap. 1; L. L. Thurstone, *The Nature of Intelligence* (Paterson, N.J.: Littlefield, Adams, 1960), chap. 12.

2 Cf. S. Hook (ed.), *Dimension of Mind* (New York: Collier, 1961), Part II: "The Brain and the Machine."

3 Cf. J. Bennett, *Rationality* (London: Routledge & Kegan Paul, 1964), particularly pp. 94ff.

4 Cf. R. J. Fogelin, *Evidence and Meaning: Studies in Analytic Philosophy* (New York: Humanities, 1967).

5 H. L. Zetterberg, *On Theory and Verification in Sociology* (Totowa, N.J.: Bedminster, 1965), pp. 69ff.

6 K. Marx and F. Engels, *The German Ideology* (Moscow: Progress, 1964), pp. 37f.

7 Cf. K. Marx, *A Contribution to the Critique of Political Economy* (Chicago: Kerr, 1918), pp. 11f.

8 Engels to Starkenburg, January 25, 1894, in K. Marx and F. Engels, *Selected Works* (Moscow: Foreign Languages, 1955), 11, 504.

9 Engels to C. Schmidt, October 27, 1890, in *ibid.*, p. 496.

10 Cf. D. Easton, "Categories for the Systems Analysis of Politics," in D. Easton (ed.), *Varieties of Political Theory* (Englewood Cliffs, N.J.: Prentice-Hall, 1966), p. 148; D. E. Apter, "A Comparative Method For the Study of Politics," in H. Ekstein and D. E. Apter, *Comparative Politics* (New York: Free Press, 1963), p. 82.

11 R. Dahl, "Cause and Effect in the Study of Politics," in M. Lerner (ed.), *Cause and Effect* (New York: Free Press, 1965), p. 93.

12 *Ibid.*, p. 97; cf. M. Scriven, "Truisms as the Grounds for Historical Explanation," in P. Gardiner (ed.), *Theories of History* (New York: Free Press, 1959).

13 G. Lowell Field, *Comparative Political Development* (London: Routledge & Kegan Paul, 1967), p. 15.

14 Apter, "A Comparative Method . . . ," *op. cit.*, p. 82.

15 Lowell Field, *op. cit.*, p. 16, n. 6.

16 Cf. R. Harré, *An Introduction to the Logic of the Sciences* (New York: St. Martin's, 1967), chap. 3.

17 For these distinctions, see R.

Rudner, *Philosophy of Social Science* (Englewood Cliffs, N.J.: Prentice-Hall, 1966), pp. 29–40.

[18] C. Johnson, *Revolution and the Social System* (Stanford: Stanford University, 1964), p. 3.

[19] C. Johnson, *Revolutionary Change* (Boston: Little, Brown, 1966), p. 45.

[20] *Ibid.*, chapter 6.

[21] Johnson, *Revolution and the Social System*, p. 12.

[22] Johnson, *Revolutionary Change*, p. 32.

[23] *Ibid.*, p. 70.

[24] R. Tucker, *The Soviet Political Mind* (New York: Praeger, 1963), chap. 5.

[25] Johnson, *Revolutionary Change*, pp. 90f.

[26] P. Lazarsfeld, "Evidence and Inference in Social Research," in D. Lerner (ed.), *Evidence and Inference* (New York: Free Press, 1958), pp. 107–138, affords a brief but more useful account. Cf. R. Dubin, *Theory Building* (New York: Free Press, 1969), for a more extended account of the subject.

[27] Rudner, *op. cit.*, p. 10.

[28] E. Nagel, *The Structure of Science* (New York: Harcourt, Brace & World, 1961), p. 90; for a more systematic treatment of the structure of theories, cf. P. Suppes, "What is a Scientific Theory?" in S. Morgenbesser, *Philosophy of Science Today* (New York: Basic Books, 1967), pp. 55-67.

[29] P. Suppes, "A Comparison of the Meaning and Uses of Models in Mathematics and the Empirical Sciences," in H. Freudenthal (ed.), *The Concept and the Role of the Model in Mathematics and Natural and Social Sciences* (New York: Gordon and Breach, 1961), pp. 165f.

[30] Cf. G. Sjoberg and R. Nett, *A Methodology for Social Research* (New York: Harper & Row, 1968), pp. 28ff.

[31] R. B. Braithwaite, "Models in the Empirical Sciences," in E. Nagel, P. Suppes, and A. Tarski (eds.), *Logic, Methodology and Philosophy of Science* (Stanford: Stanford University, 1962), pp. 224–231.

[32] Cf. E. J. Meehan, *The Theory and Method of Political Analysis* (Homewood, Ill.: Dorsey, 1965), pp. 149f.

[33] Lowell Field, *op. cit.*, p. 171.

[34] R. T. Golembiewski, W. A. Welsh, and W. J. Crotty, *A Methodological Primer for Political Scientists* (Chicago: Rand McNally, 1969), p. 430.

[35] V. Van Dyke, *Political Science: A Philosophical Analysis* (Stanford: Stanford University, 1960), p. 106.

[36] H. Simon, and A. Newell, "Models: Their Uses and Limitations," in L. White, *The State of the Social Sciences* (Chicago: University of Chicago, 1956), p. 66.

[37] Golembiewski et. al., *op. cit.*, p. 431.

[38] D. Easton, "Alternative Strategies in Theoretical Research," in D. Easton (ed.), *Varieties of Political Theory,* p. 9.

[39] T. Parsons, *The Social System* (New York: Free Press, 1951), p. 3.

[40] R. C. Sheldon, "Some Observations on Theory in Social Science," in T. Parsons and E. Shils (eds.), *Toward a General Theory of Action* (New York: Harper and Row, 1951), p. 43.

[41] Cf. G. C. Homans, "Contemporary Theory in Sociology," in R. E. L. Faris (ed.), *Handbook of Modern Sociology* (Chicago: Rand McNally, 1964), p. 957.

[42] D. E. Apter, *Some Conceptual Approaches to the Study of Modernization* (Englewood Cliffs, N.J.: Prentice-Hall, 1968), p. 356.

[43] Lowell Field, *op. cit.,* pp. vif.

[44] Cf. D. Martindale, "Sociological Theory and the Ideal Type," in L. Gross, *Symposium on Sociological Theory* (New York: Harper & Row, 1959), pp. 57–91.

[45] A. Rapoport, "Uses and Limitations of Mathematical Models in Social Science," in *ibid.,* pp. 351f.

[46] J. G. Miller, "General Behavior Systems Theory," in *Chicago Behavioral Sciences Publication, No. 1* (Chicago: University of Chicago, n.d.), p. 5.

[47] L. von Bertalanffy, *Problems of Life* (London: Watts, 1952), p. 200.

[48] Cf. C. Roseman, C. G. Mayo, and F. B. Collinge, *Dimensions of Political Analysis* (Englewood Cliffs, N.J.: Prentice-Hall, 1966), p. 198, and D. Easton, *A Framework for Political Analysis* (Englewood Cliffs, N.J.: Prentice-Hall, 1965), p. 75.

[49] R. B. Braithwaite, *Scientific Explanation* (Cambridge: Cambridge University, 1955), p. 93.

Suggested Reading

Braithwaite, R. B. "Models in Empirical Science," in E. Nagel, P. Suppes, and A. Tarski (eds.), *Logic, Methodology and Philosophy of Science.* Stanford: Stanford University, 1962.

Brodbeck, M. "Models, Meaning, and Theories," in M. Brodbeck (ed.), *Readings in the Philosophy of the Social Sciences.* New York: Macmillan, 1968.

Kaplan, A. *The Conduct of Inquiry.* San Francisco: Chandler, 1964. Chapter 3.

Rudner, R. R. *Philosophy of Social Science.* Englewood Cliffs, N.J.: Prentice-Hall, 1966. Chapter 2.

Suppes, P. "What is a Scientific Theory," in S. Morgenbesser (ed.), *Philosophy of Science Today.* New York: Basic Books, 1967.

7

On
Explanation

... There are clearly two factions within the social disciplines. One of them exuberantly embraces the scientific ideal; the other exalts its own intuitive understanding as being superior in logic and in principle to scientific explanation of the ways of man. Insofar as the division falls between those who count and measure what is not worth counting or measuring and those who speak shrewdly though imprecisely about more interesting matters, the issue is one of strategy rather than one of logic or principle. Whatever is accessible to insight and intuitive understanding is also, in principle, accessible to scientific explanation. Until they are so explained, insights however shrewd remain precarious as knowledge. Less name calling and more cooperation is wanted.

May Brodbeck

Of all the products of cognitive effort it is explanation which enjoys most signal honors. Explanation is spoken of as the "chief objective" of science, the "principal preoccupation" of rational man, the goal of all cognitive enterprise. Throughout our lives, in our ordinary pursuits and our specialized concerns, we encounter explanations with compelling regularity. And yet, for all that, irrespective of the fact that we coin, tender, welcome, rebut and dismiss linguistic artifacts that are identified as explanations, we generally find ourselves at a loss when we are asked to characterize explanations. In effect, we credit ourselves with procedural skills in recognizing explanations and yet we find ourselves incapable of formulating any discursive knowledge that might assist in identifying them—a competence which would provide us advantage in our efforts to distinguish spurious explanations from their genuine counterparts. We find ourselves lamentably ill-equipped to discuss and analyze "explanation," to offer anything like an assessment of what might pass for criteria of adequacy that would admit one and dismiss another.

The Meanings of "Explanation"

The fact is that the term "explanation" is a word in common use and shares in the vagueness and ambiguity of ordinary language. The term is used variously and vaguely in ordinary language, but generally is found to refer to four major types of cognitive activity: 1) coming to know the *meaning* of S; 2) coming to *know how* to do Z; 3) exhibiting the *grounds* of p; and 4) coming to *know why p*. Max Black provides an instance of 1) when he indicates that "Whenever I speak of 'definition' in this essay I shall mean an explanation of the uses of some word or phrase."[1] We provide explanations of type 2) when we direct others in the making of an apple pie or in the programming of a digital computer. Type 3) is instantiated when we exhibit the reasons for saying that every equilateral triangle is equiangular, or why the sum of its angles must be 180 degrees. What is required in such cases is a demonstrative argument whose conclusion is the necessary consequence of premises which include general geometrical statements held jointly with rules governing their transformation.

Explanations of type 1) are meant to provide the meaning of a word, phrase, complex sign, literary product, or nonlinguistic symbol or symbols. They find expression in lexical, contextual, criterial, recursive, or explicit definition, explications or literary "interpretations," or in adjunctive conveyances of meaning (ostensive "definitions," gestures and signals). They are offered in response to requests like, "Explain the meaning of 'probability,' " or questions like "Explain what Jesus meant by 'turning the other cheek.' " Explanations of type 2) involve providing complex directions that serve as guides to successful performance and are tendered in response to requests like, "Explain how you organize a flow chart," or questions like "Explain how one lubricates an automobile." Explanations of type 3) are formal demonstrations and inhabit the formal or constructed language domain; they are offered to satisfy the request for an explanation of the type, "Explain why the sum of the angles of any triangle equal 180°." Explanations of type 4) are accounts which pretend to satisfy inquiries of the following sort: "Explain why Hitler came to power in Germany," or "Explain why America became involved in the Vietnam War."

It is explanations of type 4) that tend to constitute the principal focus of concern when men speak of explanations in general.[2] It is this kind of explanation, explanations which pretend to account for why the descriptive event x happened, or why descriptive events of class X happen, that Alan Donagan conceives to be definitive of science.[3] Ernest Nagel, in turn, maintains that the "distinctive aim of the scientific enterprise is to provide systematic and responsibly supported explanations," expanded elsewhere in the characterization of science "as directed to the attainment of systematic but reliable knowledge, so that its products are taken to be warranted conclusions about more or less extensive uniform conditions under which various kinds of events take place."[4] In other words, science is concerned with reliably answering "why" questions.

Scientific Explanation

The explanations to which science characteristically addresses itself (those characterized as type 4 above) are "why questions," questions at various levels of sophistication: "Why is the sky dark at night?" "Why does forcing hot gases out of the rear end of a jet engine make an aircraft accelerate forward?" "Why did Mussolini come to power in post-World War I Italy?" "Why does lysozyme dissolve mucopolysaccarides?" Such questions can be addressed to concerns of various degrees of generality. They can attempt an explanation of *unique* occurrences, e.g., "Why did Mussolini accede to power in post-World War I Italy?"—or they can attempt an explanation of a *class* of occurrences, e.g., "Why does forcing hot gases out of the rear end of a jet engine make an aircraft (*any* aircraft) accelerate forward?"

As a science, political science is no less concerned with such questions than is any other. Political inquiry shares, along with the related social and natural sciences, a number of common strategies and produces a variety of common explanatory linguistic artifacts. Roger Brown has provided a convenient inventory of explanation types which permits the classification of explanations tendered and entertained by social scientists in general, and political scientists in particular.

He distinguishes six types of answers to "why questions": 1) those that are *genetic* in character, that provide a temporally ordered sequence of events that make the occurrence of the *explanandum* event (the event to be explained) intelligible;[5] 2) those that invoke the actor's or actors' *intention* in order to render some human action or actions comprehensible; 3) those that advance an actor or actors' *reasons* for undertaking some action or actions in order to exhibit "the point of it"; 4) those that employ *dispositional* terms, which permit comprehension of an action in terms of instantiating a tendency to behave in a certain way; 5) those that refer to the *function* of the explanandum event, illuminating its systemic purpose in a given context; and 6) those that appeal to *empirical generalizations* in order to subsume the explanandum event under a class of regular occurrences.[6]

Genetic Explanation

Genetic explanations are common strategies in political science. Historical accounts, like that of Barrington Moore's *Social Origins of Dictatorship and Democracy,* for example, are replete with genetic accounts. What such accounts provide is a "significant narrative," a "continuous series" or "colligation" of occurrences in which the explanandum is the conclusion of a tandem sequence of events that evidence a "general movement." The individual occurrences recited in the narrative enable us to locate the explanandum event in the context of an "overall pattern," in what has been called "a specialized habit of understanding which converts congeries of events into concatenations. . . ." The suggestion is that "the distinctive characteristic" of a genetic account provides for an "understanding" which "consists of comprehending a complex event by 'seeing things together' in a total and synoptic judgment which cannot be replaced by any analytic technique." [7]

Genetic explanations, however synoptic, can be characterized as "linear." This is suggested by their identification as "colligations" and "concatenations," and in terms of "ordered" and "continuous" series. More specifically, their linearity is the consequence of the fact that each constituent proposition which makes up the explanatory account (the *explanans*) is of the same logical type, that is to say, that the response to the query as to why a particular event (the *explanandum*) took place is made by advancing a statement of one or another or a series of particular events (the explanans) as its explanations. No generalizations are explicitly referred to. Even if a class of individuals constitute the subject of an explanandum, or the subjects of the propositions that together constitute the explanans, the propositions themselves refer to each class at some *particular* spatiotemporal locus.

A simple illustration of such an account is that of Samuel Lubell's genetic explanation of why Senator Joseph McCarthy received support from the German-American ethnic community. That community was opposed, so the account proceeds, to American involvement in the Second World War because of that community's pro-German sentiment, but the war itself destroyed "the ethnic base" of pro-German isolationism. But if the events which followed the war destroyed the possibility of pro-Germanism and its related isolationism, it left the German-American community an advocate of a "strong policy" against Russia and the "Communists," for

Russia was one of the principal anti-German forces during the War. The late Senator Joseph McCarthy, a spokesman for an insistent anti-Communist and anti-Soviet policy, tapped this recruitment source.[8]

This is, of course, a fragment of a more extensive narrative, but the features it exhibits are sufficiently like those of more complex accounts to illustrate the points to be developed. The account is linear in that each of the constituent propositions refers to a specific spatiotemporal event. As such, it harbors no explicit restricted or unrestricted generalizations. And yet such a narrative does afford "insight" or "understanding," and as such it constitutes a candidate explanation. It would be an answer to the question, "Why did McCarthy do better in those Wisconsin townships with a high incidence of German-Americans than he did in the rest of the state?"[9] The answer to the question takes the form of relating it in a "significant" fashion to a particular antecedent event or particular antecedent events, in this case to the pro-German sentiments of the ethnic minority and world circumstances in the post-World War II period. In some sense these events constitute constituent elements in a complex and interrelated whole. The explanandum event is somehow explained by "relating" it to its antecedents.

But to suggest that events are "related" or "linked" in a "synoptic judgment" tells us very little about the character of the "relating" or "linking" such events enjoy or the adequacy of the explanation the entire account delivers. Some explications of genetic explanations explicitly commit themselves to a criterion of adequacy in terms of "acceptability" to "some person, investigator, craft, audience, etc." The audience, the account continues, must "raise no further demand for explanation in that particular context." The audience, individual or collective, "doffs its hat"—psychic puzzlement is abated. The measure of adequacy is, in effect, the ability of a candidate explanation to meet an "acceptance criterion."[10]

To assume such a posture has considerable merit. The "abatement of puzzlement" or "acceptance" criterion is obviously a commensense criterion that we all regularly employ—and it serves as an intuitive indicator of when efforts at explanation have been *psychologically* successful. Furthermore, it finds application in almost every conceivable instance in which explanations, of whatever kind, are requested and tendered. An explanation *can* be understood to be generically characterized as any exchange in which psychic puzzlement is resolved. The verb "explain," in ordinary language, is employed synonymously with locutions like "making matters plain or comprehensible," the kind of activity that could conveniently be conceived as productive of hat-doffing and avowals of comprehension. Authors like Michael Scriven and William Dray tend to so measure the adequacy of explanatory exchange.

Such a construal of explanatory adequacy implies that hat-doffing, acceptance and avowals of comprehension, are the consequence of the abatement of specific psychic puzzlement. The individual, investigator, craft, or audience is beset by a *specific* puzzle. They have a *particular* question in mind. It is *that* particular question which requires treatment. Only the individual, investigator, craft, or audience knows when its own puzzlement has subsided. In this sense explanations are certainly adequate when puzzlement has subsided. Our history books and political science texts are filled with members of the species. Their test of adequacy would be an avowal of comprehension or an assertion that their puzzlement has abated on the part of those to whom explanation was addressed.

The question is whether such "synoptic judgments" or "specialized habits of understanding" are amenable to any alternate and perhaps more penetrating analysis and more objective criteria of adequacy. It would seem that one could subject such judgments to critical assessment and perhaps explicitly reveal features which their treatment as "colligations," or "continuous series" obscures. Is it possible, in effect, to search out an explication of what it means to "link" the collection of antecedent propositions which are conceived as affording the grounds for explanation and the explanandum that might provide the analyst with prescriptive advantage—criteria of adequacy which would permit one to distinguish the knowledge claim that explanation actually obtains from mere believing, opining, guessing, surmising, and feeling sure that one has an explanation?

Objective Criteria for Explanatory Adequacy

There has been a long philosophical tradition, at least as old as Plato, which conceives that knowledge must be construed as logically independent of the particular state of mind of anyone who claims to possess it—independent, as well, of the society and culture of which its possessor is a member and of the psychic states of mind of any audience exposed to it—independent of anything other than the relationship between the proposition or proposition set conceived as embodying what is known and what is, in fact, the case. This is a tradition which understands the distinguishing feature of reliable knowledge to be its *objectivity*. This seems to be the principal thrust of Carl Hempel's analysis of explanation.

For a long time mathematicians were disposed to rest content with formal truths which were *intuitively* appreciated. Only with the rigorous development of metamathematics were formal tests of adequacy established by virtue of which the concept of mathematical "proof" could be explicated. While significant problems still beset formal proof theory in metamathematics, the discussion has been elevated to an incomparably more sophisticated level. Formal proof theory has reduced the variances attributable to individual psychological idiosyncracy and specialized, and perhaps arcane, "intuiting." Analogously, Hempel has argued, a theory of explanation, like proof theory in metamathematics, must be explicative, an effort to develop prescriptive criteria of adequacy that would reduce the indeterminacy that attends the ordinary use of explanation. As a consequence, the effort to characterize adequacy criteria for explanation occupies itself maximally with syntactic and semantic concerns and consequently maximally reduces contextual and "acceptance" concerns.[11]

In the last analysis, it is probably trivially true that an adequate appreciation of explanation will involve a detailed comprehension of its syntax, semantics, *and* pragmatics in general, but for the sake of clarity and analysis the unpacking of suitcase terms like "connected series," "colligations," "seeing the overall pattern," and "linking" in terms of syntactics and semantics recommends itself. This seems to be particularly urgent in the case of genetic explanations—since such accounts are so prominent in political science, their acceptance all but universal, and their rationale so obscure.

In the case we have cited, the fragment of a connected series which is advanced as a partial explanation of the political support given to Senator Joseph McCarthy, it is intuitively obvious that there is a "connection" between ethnicity, pro-Germanism, the circumstances following the Second World War and the tendency for German-Americans to support, with greater frequency, an anti-Soviet program of a man like McCarthy than would be the case with Americans of diverse ethnic provenience. These events are all intuitively "linked"; the question is *how* are they linked. How are propositions of the same logical type, even if they follow each other in temporal succession, "linked" in a manner which permits them to serve as the explanans of an explanandum event? There is clearly no one lawlike statement of the sort: "After any international war (of some specified dimension) members of any determinate ethnic community (however characterized) will support a specific kind of politician (however he be characterized)" that would "link" singular propositions in a fashion that would explain the occurrence of the explanandum event. Genetic accounts generally take the form of narratives. The relations between antecedent events and the event or events they are marshalled to explain are generally tacitly *assumed*. Events are selected because of the "significance" they possess with respect to the "total pattern" of events under scrutiny. The events so selected fall into an "ordered sequence" and the explanandum event is their "natural" outcome.

Thus the German-American minority is intuitively understood to have been pro-German before the advent of the Second World War. Such a fact is "brute" insofar as it is simply asserted. It constitutes a given factual premise in the narration. It, itself, is in fact obviously predicated upon a number of *generalizations,* either universal or probabilistic, concerning the relation of the individual and the preferences and attitudes of his primary reference group. The assertion that the German-Americans as an ethnic community tended to be pro-German rests on generalizations (which are testable in principle) concerning the prepotent psychological predispositions toward ethnocentricity shared by all human beings, the shaping of those dispositions through primary and secondary socialization within various reference communities, and the ultimate outcome in terms of self-identification with the attitudes and political preferences of regional, political, national, religious, ethnic, and racial confraternities.[12]

Whether or not such lawlike generalizations are warranted is a matter of complete indifference for analysis. They are what make the initial premise of the "colligation" "intuitively" comprehensible. They are the "truisms" which make such assertions transparent. We expect German-Americans to be pro-German because we tend to uncritically accept such generalizations.

The remaining constituents of the explicans, the references to the Second World War and its outcome, are introduced *ad hoc.* They are not themselves explained (although we know what strategy such explanation might take). They are brute, contingent facts. There is no generalization that links the premiss concerned with the attitudes of German-Americans and the character and outcome of the Second World War. They are conjoined in the narrative because together they prepare for the subsequent step in the sequence. If German-Americans had a tendency to be pro-German prior to, and perhaps during the Second World War, there are common-sense generalizations which would lead us to accept the contention that they would tend to be opposed (in varying degrees and contingent upon their varying circumstances) to Germany's enemies and specifically the Soviet Union (since such opposition would not be mitigated by any naturalized loyalties—as would be the case with respect to the United States). There are minimal intra-psychic tensions in maintaining such hostility against Russia (rather than their adopted homeland) even after the total defeat of Germany and the prevalence of circumstances which made Germany's resurgence most improbable. That is to say there are some well-founded or generally accepted generalizations concerning human behavior, cognitive consistency and attitude formation and persistence that render the genetic account plausible—and that account would not be plausible unless those generalizations were at least *tacitly* entertained.

Under these circumstances, and given the conviction that such generalizations hold, one would expect that a political figure like that of the late Senator from Wisconsin could anticipate support from substantial elements of an ethnic community so composed and so disposed. This would be true even though such a community was undergoing regular change in terms of membership. The pre-World War II German-American community had regularly lost membership through natural attrition, but given the reasonably well-known generalizations concerning primary socialization and the intergenerational transmission of political loyalties, we expect some features of that community's preferences and political attitudes to remain constant even though there is successive substitution of its constituent members.

What the genetic account provides, given the analysis, is an *explanation sketch, a partial and incomplete explanation,* when assessed against the prescriptive model of explanation that recommends criteria of adequacy which make explanation rest upon a full statement of the constituent generalizations and statements of initial and contingent conditions, which together, as the explanans, provide for the deductive generation of the explanandum.

Genetic accounts are *partial* because they do not explain why one particular politician, Senator Joseph McCarthy, and no other, fulfilled the specific historic and political role he did. That would require supplementary explanation. Such accounts are *incomplete* because they do not explicitly indicate the general lawlike propositions which provide the logical potential to make the transition from some collection of propositions to the explanandum event. Only when the tacitly assumed generalizations are disinterred can one fully assess the grounds for such an account. The events that are marshalled to fill in the temporal sequence of a genetic account are selected because some lawlike generalizations are tacitly held. Until such generalizations are exposed, one cannot assess the significance of the selection, nor assess its evidence base. The lawlike generalizations that provide the selective criteria for "significant" events in the explanans are most frequently tendency statements characterized by terms like "tend to be," "are likely to," "more or less," or their analogues. In short, genetic explanations of particular events are analyzable into a sequence of probability or tendency explanations whose instantial premises refer to particular events selected on the basis of tacitly held lawlike generalizations and which occur in tandem rather than concurrently. The explanandum event is a deductive consequence of holding the instantial premisses and the lawlike generalizations together.[13] This seems to be implied in Walsh's recognition that "colligation needs to be supplemented by further processes if historical explanation is to be complete."[14]

Gustav Bergmann has suggested that explanation in history, specifically genetic explanations, exemplify what he calls "imperfect knowledge," knowledge about an "open" process, one in which not all the relevant variables of any interactive process are known and in which not all of their interrelationships can be exhaustively specified. In such cases the process under scrutiny can only be described at various times, and at each time a catalogue of contingent variables ("brute facts") introduced, the interactions of which will provide for the "state description" of the "system" at that point in time. Such accounts are imperfect insofar as they produce only partial and incomplete explanations. They afford "historical explanations," and are subtended by historic process laws, laws which have explanatory and predictive capacity only when some antecedent conditions are known and specified and which hold only under certain conditions. The employment of such laws is characterized by the presence of the *ceteris paribus* clause, the "all things being equal" stipulation. Such explanations and predictions are characteristic of political science accounts. Often the "all things being equal" stipulation cannot be fully characterized, and the best available explanation is a plausible judgment, or a probable outcome.[15]

This is not to say that such accounts do not abate puzzlement. They frequently do so satisfy. The prescriptive analysis of explanation is not to exhibit how political scientists in fact go about satisfying questions put to them by their audiences; it is rather an effort to reduce the subjectivity of such accounts. The *merits* of such analysis derive from the consequent precision and clarity that attends them. The *hazards* run are those which create a disposition to cavalier treatment of all accounts that do not self-evidently and exhaustively meet analytic adequacy criteria.

That progress in the analysis of explanation has nonetheless been made cannot be gainsaid, even if only to make those committed to subjective criteria of adequacy state their criteria with some precision and without seeking refuge in metaphor and circumlocution.

Explanation via Intentions, Reasons, and Dispositions

If genetic explanations lend themselves to explicative analysis, objective in character, *explanations via intentions, reasons and dispositions* are, in principle, no less amenable. In fact, in any significant genetic account of human action intentions, reasons and dispositions are regularly invoked as explanatory. At various stages in ordinary genetic accounts, as they are found in political science, references are made to the intentions of participants, their reasons for acting, and their dispositions to so behave.

Our treatment of such candidate explanations can obviously be only schematic at best. Its sole purpose, at this point, is to indicate that the sometimes extravagant claims made for such explanations cannot be unproblematically supported. There is good evidence that explanation via intentions, reasons, and dispositions follows very much the prescriptive pattern of explanation suitable for the analysis of explanation in the natural sciences. In effect, explanations via intentions, reasons, and dispositions cannot unequivocally be construed as intrinsically different from explanation via lawlike regularities conjoined with propositions which specify relevant initial or antecedent conditions.

There has been nonetheless, at least since the turn of the twentieth century, a persistent effort to draw a significant methodological distinction between the social and the natural sciences. The arguments have turned on a variety of putative distinctions. Wilhelm Windelband, Heinrich Rickert, and Wilhelm Dilthey were among the foremost proponents of the view that the "human" sciences are irreducibly distinct from the "natural" sciences and that the explanations of the one are methodologically distinct from those

of the other.[16] The aspect of the social sciences on which they tended
to fix their attention was that which they understood to definitively
characterize it: the fact that human history was an artifact of human
intention (a notion at least as old as Giambattista Vico's *New
Science*).

Conceived in such fashion, "intentions" can be treated for our
purposes as roughly equivalent to "reasons," and Alan Donagan,
who has taken up Windleband's and Dilthey's argument, so construes them.[17] Now it seems that such a construal stems from a
concept of human "rationality" which itself involves an implicit
notion of man being possessed of what R. S. Peters has called a
"directive disposition," in that men "will take means which lead
to ends if they have the information and want the ends."[18]

The notion of "directive disposition" involves, in ordinary
language, the element of "purposiveness." We are all so familiar
from our own general experience with purposive or "intelligent"
behavior that, in seeking the explanation of the behavior of others,
the general notion of purpose or directive disposition, the pursuit
of ends through appropriate means, immediately suggests itself
as a possible explanatory schema. We "intuitively" understand the
behavior of others because we analogically project on their behaviors
the familiar features of our own directive disposition. We have
privileged experience with reasoning and intending. We also
frequently know what our motives are or were—and we talk loosely
about all of this as our or others' purposes in acting.

Robert Butow has provided, by way of illustration, the following
account of the behavior of Japanese officials involved in the conduct
of the Second World War and the deliberations concerning Japan's
surrender at its termination:

Although imperial Headquarters continued to enjoy success in de-
ceiving the masses, the propagandists failed to confuse the
more informed of the ruling elite—men whose understanding
of the actual situation was now so well founded that they could
not be fooled any longer, if, indeed, they ever had been. The difficulty was that those who held official positions were fighting not only
the battle of the homeland but also the battle of their individual

destinies. To save the nation they would very likely bring ruin
to their own doorsteps, for at least a few of the key figures at
this time were the same men who had been in power prior to and
at the time of Pearl Harbor. Although they may have been opposed
to the war from the very beginning and may have been clandestinely
planning to terminate the conflict at the earliest opportunity,
not one of them ever resigned his position of responsibility in
protest over the actions of his government to which he supposedly
inwardly took exception.[19]

Butow went on to indicate that Shigenori Togo was one such individual, and that his decision not to resign during October or Novem-
ber of 1941 was the consequence of a decision that he "could not
save the situation then by resigning."

Such an account, which is by no means unusual in the literature
of political history, is a convincing, if highly condensed, explanation
of why some Japanese officials acted as they did during the critical
closing months of Japanese-American hostility. What is most significant for our analysis is the fact that such an account involves
implicit recourse to *intentions, reasons, motives,* and *purposes.*
On the pages immediately preceding the above quoted fragment
Butow specifically refers to the "reasoning" and "intentions"
of Kantaro Suzuki, and to the "promotion of their purpose" by
the Japanese "peace party." Butow characterizes his entire account
(overt behaviors and implied intentions, reasoning and purposes)
as an effort to produce "the one explanation" that fits the complex
and confused circumstances.

In the course of the pages immediately antecedent to the above
fragment Butow provides a catalogue of contextually relevant
facts, the condition of the Japanese and the disposition of Allied
armed forces, the state of Japan's population and economy, logistics
problems which beset the conduct of the struggle and the character
and reasoning of participants. The personal character of the major
participants is broadly sketched in by reference to the training and
traditions characteristic of the Japanese strategic elites. Specific
constraining social norms are detailed with commendable precision.
The function of the culturally induced constraints of *haragei,*

for example, and the behavior pattern it fostered is indicated. The deliberations undertaken by the major participants are made comprehensible by an appeal to intuitive understanding of what would be considered significant by *any* rational person who, given certain welfare aspirations, finds himself in such a *situation* possessed of knowledge of the *alternatives* open to him, given the *prevailing training* and *social constraints* to which he was subject.

The whole account traffiks on certain tacit, but commonly understood, convictions about *generic* human rationality. Psychologists, who have a systematic concern with such generic properties, characteristically refer to "rationality" as a dispositional property of human beings. [20] Leon Festinger speaks of a "positive motivation to know one's environment" which is endemic to a variety of sentient creatures, a disposition to "find out what they can and cannot do in the environment in which they live," and which among human beings manifests itself as a "motivation" to "hold *correct* opinions, beliefs and ideas about the world in which they live and to know *precisely* what their abilities enable them to do in this world."[21]

There are, in fact, precious few contemporary psychologists who would recognize themselves in Robert Strausz-Hupé's recent characterization of a "scientist." He tells us that the "scientist," "confronted by the data of experience, prescinds from a problem those aspects which are not susceptible to measurement and to causal explanation. His purpose is to explain the phenomenon in terms of causation, not of purpose, intention, and values." He then goes on to indicate that there are social scientists who are "behaviorists" and who "banish consciousness" from any account of human action and abandon any effort at explanation via intentions and purposes.[22] There are few "behaviorists" of this sort. Rarer still are psychologists or social scientists who conceive human behavior reducible—"via a behavioristic psychology—to a purely physiochemical complexus of interrelated processes amenable to a complete explanation in terms of value-free concepts and categories of the natural sciences."[23]

Should there be any such psychologists or social scientists, they are hardly to be found among those pursuing their researches today.

The scientific treatment of conscious human action involves recourse to speculative or confirmed *generalizations* governing human consciousness and behavior drawn from protracted and systematic studies concerned with behavior genetics (the heritability ratios for the transmission of various mental factors, for example), perceptual psychology, personality formation (the influence of primary and secondary socialization, the role of reference communities), developmental individual psychology (the processes of concept formation, learning, language behavior and the deliberative faculties), social psychology, attitude formation and motivation, cognitive congruity and dissonance, selective perception conjoined with a panoply of special research in specific problem areas. The results of this kind of generalizing research surfaces in political science in any number of ways. The influence of personality research is evident in the work of Milton Rokeach, Harold Lasswell, Gordon DiRenzo, to mention only those that readily come to mind. That generalizations produced by special research in psychology subtend explanations of human behavior has become so much of a commonplace that one hardly need argue that accounts like that of Butow are parasitic on what we know of human conduct in general—and that what we know is framed in low-order or high-order, confirmed or speculative generalizations, tendency statements, and/or probability estimates. Nor is such strategy restricted to contemporary political scientists. One can find the purveyance of generalizations concerning human action undertaken, for example, in the work of standard and traditional political "theorists." Jeremy Bentham, to cite one example, insisted that

> nature has placed mankind under the governance of two sovereign masters, pain and pleasure. . . . They govern us in all we do, in all we say, in all we think; every effort we can make to throw off our subjection will serve but to demonstrate or confirm it. In words a man may pretend to abjure their empire; but in reality he will remain subject to it all the while.[24]

We resist such traditional accounts explaining human behavior involving such unrestricted generalizations about motives and intentions *not* because they involve empirical generalizations, but because they frequently collapse into empty tautologies having little, if any, explanatory and predictive yield. This also suggests why we are suspicious about "intuitive" explanations of human action. When Windelband, Rickert, or Dilthey (or their modern counterparts) suggests that we competently "understand" individual or collective human behavior because we "indwell" in human reason—that human purpose is intuitively understood because we have privileged access to the processes which manifest themselves in act—one can only suggest that while it is true that we frequently impute motives, intentions, reasons, and purposes analogically to actors in any given situation because we see in them conscious agents like ourselves, we frequently do so incorrectly. Only in the measure that we can *confirm* such imputations, such similarities, can such accounts be *warranted*.

Our "intuitions," the products of our own introspections into our own personal behaviors, reasonings, intentions, and motivations, provide us with common-sense and common-language explanatory *hypotheses*. But they await *confirmation*— and confirmation can only be the result of appeal to some public and testable generalizations concerning individual or aggregate human psychology. Christian Bay's recent criticism of "behavioral literature" in political science turns, in part, on the contention that such literature has not concerned itself with problems of "substantive rationality" and "human needs." In fact he insists that what is required for adequate explanation in political science is a "satisfactory *theory* of human needs" encompassing both "latent need-behavior and manifest want-behavior." His charge is that the explanation of human activity is faulted, at least in part, because of the inadequacy of the *generalizations* employed in explaining human behavior.[25] What we require are *more,* and *better confirmed, empirical* generalizations to explain conscious behavior. Which suggests, in effect, that explanation via intentions, reasons and dispositions can be reasonably construed as predicated on the availability of empirical generalizations of lawlike character.

The fact that we "indwell" in human reason can hardly be conceived as providing us, in itself, defensible insight into human action. We frequently are confused about our own reasons, intentions, and motives for behaving. It makes perfectly good sense to say that I *thought* my behavior was motivated by a specific intention or motive, but that my psychoanalyst convinced me that I was in fact acting out an "unconscious" motive or intention. My reasons are often revealed, in fact, to be rationalizations. To say that I understand Hitler's treatment of the Jews because I can appreciate his reasons, intentions, or motives, is merely a foothold on an explanation of his conduct. Hitler's activity may have been the result of pathological disorder. To give an account of his "reasoning" may simply be totally inadequate and/or inappropriate, unless I have some *evidence* that he can be correctly classified as a specific personality type whose members instantiate particular syndromatic behaviors; i.e., I can subsume his behavior under a lawlike generalization. Without some reasonably specific notion of generic rationality and some general account of departures from such trait specific general concept, it would be, in principle, impossible to satisfy the evidence conditions for any responsible explanation of aggregate or individual acts in terms of "intentions," "motives," and "purposes."

Narratives like that of Robert Butow, which account for specific or aggregate human behaviors in terms of intentions, dispositions, or reasons, depend for their plausibility on warranted or unproblematically entertained general assertions concerning rationality. The latter is treated as a dispositional term operative in an environment in which specific goals are entertained by human agents, relevant and contextually determinate facts about the situation are known to those agents, and the social constraints under which those agents act out their behavior are specified. The account as it finds expression in Butow's text is *elliptical*. Once again it constitutes an explanation sketch. Once filled in, it would reveal itself as an argument in which lawlike propositions are conjoined with statements of initial conditions which together entail the explanandum or explananda as a consequence or as consequences.

Needless to say, contemporary psychology does not possess an adequate account of rationality, nor do we have a comprehensive theory of learning behavior and socialization. What we do possess, more often than not, are vague generalizations that are entertained as "truisms." But the paucity of confirmed generalizations governing human behavior is no argument that more precise and better confirmed generalizations should not be sought. Until such generalizations are available, explanations which rest upon commonsense generalizations will remain, at best, plausible—with an all but infinite number of alternate, and perhaps equally plausible, candidate explanations in contention. Under such circumstances political historians will tender various and varying explanations—and each will jostle and contend for place. Until we possess a viable theory or viable theories of individual and aggregate behavior, we must be satisfied with plausibilities.

To argue that plausible explanations are more than that would be stultifying. As we learn more about the intricacies of human behavior, our "intuitive" insights and the "synoptic judgments" which make explanations now plausible will be modified significantly, and our explanations will become more credible. Until insights, analogical reasoning, and "indwelling" find confirmation in specific lawlike generalizations, they remain heuristic—suggestive and imaginative sources of speculative hypotheses productive of plausible explanation. We intuitively understand something of human motivation, human reasoning, and human intention, but the advent of systematic psychological inquiry has indicated that our most insistent and irrepressible intuitions can be outrageously mistaken. Confident explanation in such areas would be the result of the availability of confirmed restricted or unrestricted generalizations concerning human rationality, intention, and motivation held in conjunction with a complex statement of initial conditions.

The Explanatory "Uniqueness" of Social Science

The suggestion that we do not possess confident explanations of human conduct generates considerable resistance among political historians and those who have committed themselves to the thesis of a distinct methodology in the pursuit of understanding in the social sciences.

The objections such persons raise generally invoke references to genetic and "reason analysis" explanations as methodologically distinct social science products. As objections they explicitly turn on the conviction that explanations are forthcoming in social science without recourse to "covering" laws. A recent article by K. W. Kim illustrates the strategy involved.[26] He concerns himself with genetic explanation in general and "reason analysis" explanation in particular in order to marshall his case. The treatment of Kim's arguments will be necessarily schematic and summary, but suggests the kind of analysis to which such objections can be made subject.

Kim has objected to the effort to analyze explanation in terms of "covering" or general laws because he feels that political historians do, in fact, provide perfectly adequate explanations without explicit *or* implicit reference to generalizations. He suggests that political inquiry frequently concerns itself with 1) "unique" events, 2) nonevents, and 3) the "reasons" human participants offer for acting rather than the "causes" of historic events—concerns which do not lend themselves to analysis in terms of lawlike generalizations conjoined with initial conditions.

Kim suggests that the political historian's preoccupation with "unique" events, events that are "of interest to us because of their peculiar characteristics"—such as the Russian Revolution—simply cannot be treated in terms of generalizations. They are in some sense intrinsically and irreducibly idiographic. Unfortunately for the credibility of his objection, he admits that such events do, in fact, admit "significant generalizations" to be deployed over them. He insists, however, that such generalizations as are invoked are "insufficient" to *explain* the occurrence of such events.

As a matter of fact, what he seems to be pursuing is a "complete explanation," the product of what Bergmann has called "perfect knowledge," explanation in terms of systematic process laws by virtue of which any state description of a system at time t_1 is explained as the necessary consequence of some antecedent state description of the system—given those systematic process laws. From Newton's law of gravity, for example, held in conjunction with knowledge of the position of the sun and the planets at any particular time, their position at any subsequent or antecedent time could be predicted or retrodicted. All that we know of the social sciences indicates that we do not have such laws available to us. History, political science, and social science in general have only historic process laws at their disposal—tendency statements and probabilistic assertions deployed over open systems in which "brute facts" are entertained as antecedent and contingent conditions in accounting for any explanandum event.

The explanation of the Russian Revolution involves generalizations concerning the aggregate behavior of whole classes, generalizations concerning latent and manifest dispositions, status threats, the consequence of ignorance, political apathy, impaired communication, as well as generalizations concerning the lives of various historically significant personalities, such as Lenin, Nicholas, and Rasputin. That Lenin was born at the time he was is a "brute fact." It *could* be explained if one were concerned with Lenin's genealogy, but in the context of the Russian Revolution Lenin's existence simply functions as an antecedent condition (similar strategies are employed in any "natural science" explanation of special occurrences). The Russian Revolution as a "unique" event is explained in terms of a complex intersection of generalizations which will, because of brute contingencies, never be repeated—but each constituent generalization in the complex intersection is a regularity. The peculiar configuration at that particular time is unique; the probabilistic generalizations or tendency statements that constitute the substance of explanation are not.

To argue from analogy: each day experiences weather that is in some sense unique, but every day's weather is the result of the intersection of a number of recurrent regularities that constitute the explanation base of the science of meteorology. When Kim grants that "some events are better explained by contextually limited generalizations than by purely universal propositions," he seems to be saying little more than that history and political science explanations involve historic process laws rather than the systematic process laws of physics and that historians and political scientists tend to exploit *restricted* generalizations. A conclusion everyone will grant, but which does nothing to establish the case that explanations in political science do not stem from generalizations or that they are methodologically distinct from those in the natural sciences.

Similarly his treatment of nonevents simply exemplifies the character of genuine lawlike generalizations. Lawlike generaliza-

tions, as we have suggested in the preceding chapter, support subjunctive conditionals and counterfactuals. That something did *not*
take place is as amenable to explanation via generalizations as is
the fact that something *did* take place. In insisting that every historical work contains "judgments of possibilities," Max Weber clearly
indicated that such possibilities were to be construed within the
framework of "a positive knowledge of the 'laws' of events."[27]
Kim admits as much in saying that "Admittedly there is no use in
pretending that all such negative factors which one may find it
necessary to posit will always defy the use of appropriate general
laws," but then goes on to insist, that "it seems, however, equally
foolish to assume that all such negative factors will necessarily
fall within the legitimate claim of the regularity principle." One can
only indicate that to make *any a priori* claims in social science would
be hazardous. But if any "nonevent" were conceived to be
inexplicable by appeal to regularities, would we not then be left
with a *mystery* rather than a scientific question?

Finally, the suggestion that explanation via "reasons" (or intentions or motives) avoids appeal to generalizations appears to be,
on its face, false. (Whether "reasons" can be successfully construed
as "causes" is a problem that cannot be treated here—it remains
a vexed problem in philosophical psychology and linguistic analysis.)
Kim admits that "general laws and 'relative explanations' do certainly have an important role to play," but goes on to say that the
"understanding" of reasons is not explaining in the sense of providing
predictive leverage. If we know an agent's reasons for acting, we
may understand it, but we would not be in a position to predict it.

There are obviously many issues involved in such a discussion.
It seems clear, however, that whatever understanding is the result
of the appreciation of reasons, intentions, or motives is parasitic
upon generalizations about human rationality and motivation
operating within contextual and initial conditions and operative
sociocultural constraints (the "brute facts" of a situation). Moreover,
adequate understanding in such instances *does* provide predictive
leverage. We constantly make low-order predictions about the
individual and aggregate political behavior of human beings—only
because we have warranted statistical generalizations or tendency

statements about individual and collective human behavior and an appreciation of the contexts in which they act out that behavior. When we "understand" human behavior, we have more than a foothold on predicting it.

Explanations of reasons, intentions, and motives seems to implicitly appeal to generalizations of a broadly dispositional kind. Psychology, as we have suggested, has devoted considerable attention to the adequate formulation of criteria for the assessment of "rational behavior," and the factors which influence its exercise. Most of the generalizations that such inquiry produces are probabilistic so that predictions employing them are themselves probabilistic and most suitably refer to aggregate behavior. Most frequently historians or political scientists are not concerned with the precision and evidential adequacy of such statistical generalizations or tendency statements, but their explanations (even in terms of "reason analysis") will depend on such regularities, and the credibility of their accounts depends upon them. The explanans proffered to account for individual or aggregate behavior include statistical generalizations or tendency statements about dispositional properties generic to human beings—motives and intentions entertained by specific subgroups of human beings, and the putative motives, intentions, and reasons active in the deliberations and actions of individual actors. The regularities employed to generate explanations in these circumstances are context dependent insofar as expectations are governed by the initial and contingent conditions (the subjective and objective information base upon which the action of individuals and collectivities is based, the social constraints under which means are characterized as appropriate to the selected ends) which make dispositional ascriptions applicable.

To fully characterize the regularities as well as the social and individual circumstances which condition the application of relevant generalizations in any particular case involves more work than the historian or political scientist is disposed to apply. Generally such accounts are given only in terms of the indispensable or necessary conditions that attend such occurrences. We say we know why Hitler invaded Poland when we know his overall intentions or his specific reasons. Certainly any adequate explanation of his behavior would include a statement of such necessary conditions. But any explanatory account which pretended to reasonable adequacy would admit reference to generic concepts like "rationality," "directive disposition," the regularities governing "normal" and "abnormal" personality traits, the function of specific instances of information, and limiting conditions within such operative and dispositional regularities. Since historians deal with events that have, in fact, transpired, they are content to indicate only some of the necessary conditions or only part of the sufficient conditions determining an occurrence. They *know* that sufficient conditions for the occurrence did obtain—for the event did, in fact, take place. But the necessary and sufficient conditions for the occurrence of the explanandum are not explicitly stated. In most cases they know they obtained, but they simply do not know what they might be. They do know that such conditions *must* have obtained, for the event *did* take place.

As a consequence the historian, or the political historian, can offer a convincing account of the past, but has little leverage on the future. He doesn't really know why some past event took place—he can *assume,* however, with confidence, that each event was the result of the intersection of necessary and sufficient conditions. Sufficient understanding is conveyed by his simple statement of some of the necessary conditions or part of the sufficient conditions in terms of the "underlying," "initiating," or "immediate" causes governing the explanandum event. But if one wishes to undertake a maximally responsible appraisal of contending explanations, one is driven to an assessment of the credibility of its subtending generalizations and auxiliary assumptions—as full a statement of the implicitly assumed necessary and sufficient conditions as possible.

The historian or political scientist is concerned with understanding the action of individuals or groups in terms of some indispensable necessary conditions, and this concern is frequently, if not regularly, satisfied by recounting the reasons, intentions or motives of the actors. All explanations are answers to problems and therefore can be assessed against acceptance criteria. Does the individual, craft, or audience recognize the adequacy of the tendered account? But the acceptance criterion can hardly serve as the *sole* criterion of adequacy.

Explanation via Functions

The fact that historical or political science explanations respond to specific kinds of questions makes reasons, motives, and intentions explanatory. Something much the same can be said for *functional* explanations when they manifest themselves as something other than an alternate expression of "purposive" explanation in terms of motives, reasons, and intentions. There is at least one kind of "functional explanation" that can be subsumed under the analysis of explanations via motives, reasons, and intentions. That is the kind of account given for institutions in terms of their manifest "purposes" or "functions."

Thus Ernst Hass' treatment of "functionalism" is a concern with the "tasks" assumed by institutions in terms of the "needs and desires" of individuals or aggregates.[28] He cites a passage from David Mitrany which commits the "functional approach" in political science to seeking out a "common index of need" among political agents and political clientele. Such an approach can be unpacked in an analysis of individual or collective motive, reason and intention construed as operative within some reasonably specific context and governed by some specific and relevant constraining norms.

Functional explanations constitute a distinct type of explanation when appeal is made to "purposes" manifest in situations which are *not* artifacts of conscious human activity. Thus in Robert Merton's familiar discussion of the "functions" of the "political machine,"[29] "manifest functions" can often be analyzed in terms of the explicit desires and conscious motives, intentions and reasons of participant actors in any specific institutional context. But "latent functions" are consequences which attend manifest functions but which are often unintended and unmotivated and clearly *not* the result of the reasoned, goal-oriented acts of any individual or group. We say that the political machine "welds" ordinary men and women together in an "elaborate network of personal relations" even though such an effect was not intended by the men who created the political machine. The precinct captain becomes a "friend in need," in a society which has become increasingly impersonal not because he chose to become one, but because of the "logic of the situation."

People are "alienated" in a complex and impersonal situation and, in order to pursue his own interests and realize his ends, the precinct captain fulfills unintended functions that help to sustain the "system" of which he is a part.

The political machine, through its local agents, thus fulfills an important but unintended social function by humanizing and personalizing all manner of assistance to those in need. Such a function may not have been planned, intended, or humanly or humanely motivated. But we come to understand these latent functions of the political machine by seeing them in the context of generalizations concerning the viability of organizations and the conditions which sustain them—generic "human needs," "status deprivations," "anomie," "atomicity," and "depersonalized situations." If knowledge of generic human needs were not available as funded information, if tendency laws concerning collective human behavior were unknown, if we knew nothing of interpersonal response patterns, such accounts would be unintelligible.

This should not be surprising. Functional explanations were consciously borrowed from biology and physiology where they are used to explain the "purpose" of a structure or organ within an integrated organism. Biologists know that in order for an organism to remain viable its structures and organs must function in a manner that permits the vital activities of the organism to continue. Thus they know that the function of the kidneys is to maintain a specific chemical balance in the blood, a balance that is necessary to the viability of the organism. But to have said that is to say nothing more than that the absence of kidneys in the normal human body would produce a system threatening chemical imbalance in the organism— a lawlike generalization concerning kidneys, the condition of the blood and the system requisites of organisms that is the consequence of regularity analyses. We know the functions of the various parts of the body because we entertain a well-confirmed catalogue of lawlike generalizations concerning their activities. None of the functions is "intentional" or "motivated." Functions are characterized in propositions that could, without information loss, be translated into lawlike generalizations about the consequences for the organism of the presence or absence of some structure or organ.

When functionalism was adopted by the social sciences, it was originally heralded as a methodologically distinct explanatory strategy. But such claims were clearly exaggerated. Functional explanations are employed not only in biology but to account for the activity of constituent elements of servomechanical and cybernetic systems as well. In effect, such explanations are not unique to the social or biological sciences. They have found their way into the physical sciences as well. They are neither more nor less "mechanical" or "organic" than any explanation. They are explanations in terms of warranted statistical or unrestricted generalizations applied in circumstances in which specific initial conditions can be characterized. To maintain that the function of x is y is, in the majority of instances, to claim no more than usually x (but not only x for there are functional equivalents of x) produces or aids in producing y which functions essentially in system S. Such propositions can tell us no more, and frequently tell us considerably less than their corresponding lawlike assertions. Where there are no well-confirmed lawlike generalizations to which recourse can be made, functionalist accounts can provide, at their very best, only heuristic insights—i.e., "useful ways of thinking"— not explanations.

Like historical explanation, and explanation via reasons, intentions and motives, functional explanations are offered in response to specific queries. Thus they do not concern themselves with a full statement of subtending generalizations; they allude to them and invoke a commonsense appreciation of them. As a result such explanations tend to be elliptically formulated—many of the tacit generalizations which "link" variables in the account are interred and the limiting conditions and contingencies which make them applicable are at best stenographically characterized. Functional explanations tend to be partial, that is, they do not offer anything like an exhaustive explanation for the presence of any number of "brute facts" which are relevant as antecedent or contingent factors in the explanation itself nor do they explain why one institution or agency (in the case of functional explanation in political science) rather than any of its functional equivalents satisfies the "purpose" or serves the viability of the system under investigation.

Functional explanations are *historical* in character, *elliptical* and *partial,* and in general focus themselves on the regular recurrence of individual, collective, or system needs that can be satisfied by a variety of functionally equivalent activities or structures. The accounts are generally very complex, but there is no evidence that they are predicated on anything less than putative generalizations, either unrestricted, statistical or probabilistic—conjoined with a statement of antecedent or initial conditions. Functional explanations can be understood to account for the effect or effects of some activity or the presence of some social structure upon some complex whole. But the content of such explanations can be reasonably construed as equivalent to a conjunction of lawlike propositions conjoined with a statement of initial conditions in terms of which, given x under such and such conditions, one would expect y with such and such a degree of probability. The fact that functional explanations refer to effects rather than consequences should not obscure the analysis.[30] In general, functional explanations, like historical explanations, indicate the presence of some condition which suggests the presence of some subtending lawlike generalizations. Robert Brown suggests as much in saying that "the search for knowledge of functions presupposes a belief in some laws or lawlike statements. . . . We can only predict and explain in terms of functions when [they] contain lawlike generalizations . . . ."[31]

Some function explanations are heuristic in the sense that they characterize the object of inquiry in certain ways—suggestive of the influence of putative variables and to refer obliquely to subtending lawlike generalizations. The degree of understanding they impart is equivalent in extent and quality to the degree of understanding imparted by any preliminary conceptual schemata. They are, in effect, promissory on more adequate accounts, explanations which account for the working of the object of scrutiny in terms of explicit lawlike formulations and an adequate characterization of initial conditions.

Explanation via Empirical Generalization

If genetic, intentional, reason analytic, dispositional, and functional explanations can be dealt with by such an analysis, so can explanations which employ empirical generalizations. Empirical generalizations of the sort employed by political scientists are not lawlike in the manner we have characterized. Empirical generalizations are not unrestricted in their range of applicability, but may, as a matter of fact, be derivative of laws of unrestricted range. Categoric generalizations like, "A tolerant and easy-going Dad does not build up in the son the head of steam which creates a political rebel,"[32] can be construed as derivative of genuinely lawlike generalizations.

The political scientist may not be concerned with such derivations in his search for the explanation of political behavior in any specific context. His appeal in explanation may be to simple empirical generalization—and his recourse may produce the hat-doffing in his audience that signifies a surcease from puzzlement. A more formal treatment of his account may very well produce the explicit derivation and in the face of persistent questioning such an account may or may not be forthcoming. In order to assess precisely what one is committing oneself to in accepting an explanation via empirical generalizations (qualitative or statistical), it may be necessary to persist in such questions. The response would reveal the theoretical commitments embedded in the explanation. The understanding which results would be qualitatively different from the understanding which is the product of being provided an empirical generalization of which the explanandum event is an instance.

We may have good inductive evidence that an empirical generalization holds, that tolerant and easy-going fathers do not, in fact, produce sons who are political rebels, and we would be licensed to affirm such a proposition with confidence. We can affirm the constant conjunction of one variable cluster and another and we intuitively link them. Such generalizations assert that there is a (relatively) invariant association of variable clusters, but they do not assert that the generalization holds over an unrestricted range. In order to specify their range of applicability a far more elaborate undertaking would be required and what would result would be the articulation of a *theory* in which the restricted generalization would be lodged. To deliver such a theory would be to impart theoretical understanding, the delivery of a subsumptive set of propositions from which generalizations of restricted range are the deductive implicants of generalizations of unrestricted range within specifiable or specified initial conditions. To have delivered such a linguistic entity would be to deliver a maximally adequate explanation of any explanandum in the domain of inquiry. That political scientists attempt to do just that is indicated by the publications that have inundated the market in the past generation.

The Prescriptive Model of Explanation

As a cognitive device used to account for the occurrence of an empirical event or a class of such events, explanation could be conceived in any number of ways. What has been suggested here has been a recommendation that explanation should be analyzed in terms of an explanans—a set of assertions composed of two subsets of logically distinct propositions, the first subset specifying relevant laws and the second the particular antecedent or initial conditions which identify the circumstances as among those covered by the law or laws invoked in the first subset. This constitutes the substance of an argument of deductive form, the conclusion of which is the explanandum, the event to be explained. The explanans, composed of relevant laws of strictly universal or probabilistic form, is adduced to account for the explanandum, the phenomenon to be explained. The schema of such an explanation takes the following form:

$$
\begin{array}{ll}
L_1, L_2 \ldots, L_n & \text{(General laws)} \\
\underline{C_1, C_2 \ldots, C_n} & \text{(Initial conditions)} \\
\therefore \quad E & \text{(Event to be explained)}
\end{array}
\left.\phantom{\begin{array}{l} L \\ C \end{array}}\right\} \text{Explanans}
\quad \text{Explanandum}
$$

In such an interpretation $L_1, L_2 \ldots, L_n$ represent general laws (either unrestricted or probabilistic or their derivatives) and $C_1, C_2 \ldots, C_n$ represent statements of particular fact which characterize the circumstances or the conditions to which the law or laws are applicable. The horizontal line separates the argument from its deductive conclusion. The explanandum is the deductive consequence of conjointly holding the general laws and the initial conditions. It is *logic* which "links" or "relates" the constituents of the explanation. If we consider some commonplace explanatory strategies familiar to students of political inquiry, the role of "covering laws" becomes apparent.

Sociologists and political scientists concerned with differential collective behavior frequently entertain a relatively high-order empirical generalization, couched in academic language, which maintains that one of the necessary conditions antecedent to episodes of collective "deviance" is the relaxation of stable patterns of inter-personal expectation, i.e., "role-governed" behavior. Riots tend to erupt, by way of illustration, on hot summer days at beaches, recreational resorts, taverns and public places where individuals are most likely to be removed from their familial and occupational role attachments. Mob violence is more probable where role obligations are reduced to a minimum by the relative assurance of individual anonymity. Students and adolescents who find themselves occupying the transitional interstices between childhood and adult roles are more disposed to participate in collective deviance, riots, and "senseless acts." Recent immigrants to urban centers, having vacated traditional roles and as yet uninitiated into trade unions, voluntary associations or neighborhood groups, provide the recruitment base for bizarre religious cults.

Such considerations constitute the beginnings of an explanation. A generalization is invoked and a set of conditions described which characterize some subject instance falling under the scope and range of the generalization. Together such propositions constitute an informal and incomplete explanans. The explanandum event, the riot, the high recruitment potential of bizarre cults, the "senseless acts," would be the deductive consequence of the antecedent general and specific truth claims.

A competent explanation of any specific occurrence not only would require a maximal reduction of the semantic and syntactical variance that afflicts the invoked generalization, but would seek to establish the covering generalization as a derived consequence of lawlike assertions. One would begin to articulate a *theory* of collective behavior. A more complete explanation would invoke, for example, a psychological theory adequate to characterize the personality determinants operative in the subject situation as well as to identify the influence of extraneous variables affecting predicted responses. In effect, most explanations in the social sciences remain partial, elliptical and historical in character, but can be supplemented. That they are not is a consequence, in large part, of the fact that such explanatory accounts are sought, invoked and entertained because we seek to *control* behaviors and in controlling behaviors we are most concerned with those aspects of behavior *most amenable to our influence*. We are rarely concerned, for example, with the biological determinants of individual and collective human behavior, although behavior geneticists are fully aware of the influence of genetic factors on individual and collective behavior. Thus we tend to be content with partial and elliptical accounts.

The strategy of explanation, for all that, is fairly obvious. Explanation, for maximal reliability, requires warranted lawlike assertions, or their putative derivatives, held in conjunction with a characterization of initial conditions which certifies the applicability of the lawlike assertions or their derivatives. Explanations will enjoy various degrees of completeness and ahistoricity. Only their rational reconstruction can reveal the degree of competence and reliability that can be legitimately accorded them.[33]

Such an analysis attempts to exhibit the structure of a *reasoned* explanation, showing how an account is maximally defensible. It is *not* a *description* of what social scientists *do;* it is an attempt to reveal the logical structure of a *maximally reliable* explanation. It is concerned with the logic of justification—not the logic of discovery.

It is only necessary to rehearse our elementary understanding of formal truth to recognize that certainty accompanies logical truth. The revelation of an argument as a logical truth establishes, conclusively, its truth status. When an explanation is revealed as a deductive argument, its conclusion entailed by its antecedent premisses, no more conclusive warrant can be offered for its truth status. Entailment "links" or "connects" the constituent propositions, the lawlike generalizations "cover" the initial conditions and both sets of propositions—the lawlike assertions and the statements of initial conditions—jointly held, *logically* generate the conclusion. If the premises are true, the conclusion *must* be true, which means that an explanation, to be cognitively compelling, must be logically valid and empirically true, i.e., an explanation must be *sound*. There are public criteria (satisfied via argument and empirical evidence) certifying the empirical truth of the premises and the logical structure of the account. Entertaining such an analysis of explanation permits one to judge explanatory adequacy by public and neutral criteria. No amount of hat-doffing, acceptance, avowals of psychological satisfaction, or enthusiasm can provide a reasonable substitute for such reliability. The task of analysis is to show why certain statements held to be true are understood to afford justification for holding some other statements as true. That justification must rest on the truth of the statements themselves and in the logical relations which obtain between statements, rather than in the mind or emotion of an individual, craft, or audience.

It is obvious that explanation in social science, particularly political science, will frequently be elliptical and partial for a variety of reasons. These include the lack of well-confirmed lawlike regularities, the complexity of the subject matter, the open character of the subjects under investigation, the special pragmatic concerns of investigators, the appeal to commonsense assumptions that one's audience can intuitively and unproblematically supply, ignorance of what might constitute the elements of the *ceteris paribus* (all things being equal) clause which materially influence the argument, as well as the disposition to make recourse to "tendency statements" which do not allow the assignment of any specific quantitative probability to the conclusion.

Like all recommendations the proposed analysis is vindicated by its putative cognitive yield. It is recommended not because such an account adequately *describes* what social scientists in general, or political scientists in particular, actually *do* in advancing explanations, but rather because it suggests what an adequate explanation *should be*. In effect it challenges proffered explanation—and requires that each be scrutinized against specific public norms of adequacy. Should there be adequate explanations that cannot meet such criteria, we should ultimately be in a position to know *why*—either our proffered criteria are too restrictive or are imprecise. Contending alternate "adequate" explanations would have to exhibit the *criteria* (public or private) which *license* their adequacy. Such criteria would, minimally, have to enjoy greater range of application (including more instances of ordinary language explanation than does the proposed schema) as reliable (permitting as much cognitive confidence in the account as does the proposed schema), and be at least as compatible with what we know about language and logic. Should any such alternate adequacy criteria be formulated, the above proposed deductive schema for explanatory adequacy would be abandoned.

Until that time the schema proposed above can serve to goad social scientists into making their cognitive commitments explicit. Its employment makes taking refuge in metaphor and simile suspect. If one insists that events are "linked" and "ordered" in a "significant" account, one becomes obliged to specify how such "linking" and "ordering" are accomplished and what constitutes a measure of "significance."

The explication of scientific explanation offered here is advanced in order to goad political scientists to more carefully consider those products they have, and will, entertain as explanatory. The account is offered with no pretension of adequacy. A significant body of literature has grown up around the issue of adequate explanation and there is no doubt that the analysis will continue. Those philosophers of science who originally advanced the "covering law model" of explanation have, since it was first formulated, considerably modified the original explication. There is little doubt that refinements and revisions will continue.[34] Nonetheless, the analysis has produced a measurable increase in sophistication on the part of political scientists. The analysis compels practitioners of political inquiry to publicly state, with precision, the grounds they conceive as supporting explanation.

That the "covering law model" is productive of positive results is evidenced by the fact that even those who have a vested interest in opposing such "positivistic" and "analytic" devices have, after considerable resistance, simply surrendered to them. East Germans, for example, long vociferously opposed to what they understood to be "anti-Marxist positivism," have simply adopted the covering law model of explanation in their most recent publications devoted to the philosophy of science. In 1968 an "editorial collective" at the Institute for Philosophy at the Karl Marx University of Leipzig published their *Die Wissenschaft von der Wissenschaft,* which duly contained a section devoted to "The Explanatory and Predictive Function of Theories."[35] The schema of explanatory adequacy they offered differed, from the schema given above only insofar as the initial conditions were identified as B_1, B_2 ... B_n with B_1, B_2, ... B_n representing "Bedingungen" ("conditions") and G_1, G_2 ... G_n representing "Gesetzesaussagen" ("lawlike propositions"). The explanandum was conceived as "logically deducible" from the explanans. The only thing missing was reference to the non-Marxist source of the prescriptive explication. The source is, of course, the philosophy of science as it has developed in the West. As early as 1934 Karl Popper maintained that "To give a causal explanation of an event means to deduce a statement which describes it, using as premises of the deduction one or more universal laws, together with certain singular statements, the initial conditions."[36]

Such a construal provides an account of explanation in terms of "covering laws" of unrestricted or probabilistic form jointly held with statements of initial conditions. It is obvious that such an explication renders explanation equivalent to "theory" as "theory" is minimally understood. If a theory is understood to be "a systematically related set of statements, including some lawlike generalizations, that is empirically testable," then an adequate explanation would be a minimal theory. In general, however, we use the term "theory" to cover those linguistic entities in which some lawlike propositions are themselves the deductive consequences of more general lawlike assertions. A competent and maximally reliable explanation is the result of entertaining a theory in which lower-order generalizations are the deductive consequences of the higher-order generalizations held. To say that we can adequately explain events within a universe of inquiry is to say that we have a viable theory of, or viable theories in, that universe of inquiry.

Notes

1. M. Black, *Problems of Analysis: Philosophical Essays* (Ithaca: Cornell University, 1954), p. 24.
2. Cf. J. Hospers, "What is Explanation?" in A. Flew, *Essays in Conceptual Analysis* (New York: Macmillan, 1956), p. 94.
3. A. Donagan, "Are the Social Sciences Really Historical?" in B. Baumrin (ed.), *Philosophy of Science* (New York: John Wiley, 1963), p. 278.
4. E. Nagel, *The Structure of Science* (New York: Harcourt, Brace & World, 1961), p. 15, "The Nature and Aim of Science," in S. Morgenbesser (ed.), *The Philosophy of Science Today* (New York: Basic Books, 1967), p. 4.
5. Cf. A. Kaplan, *The Conduct of Inquiry* (San Francisco: Chandler, 1964), pp. 332f.; W. H. Walsh, *An Introduction to Philosophy of History* (New York: Hutchinson's University Library, 1951), p. 59; W. Dray, *Laws and Explanation in History* (London: Oxford University, 1957), pp. 66–72.
6. For Brown's account, see R. Brown, *Explanation in Social Science* (Chicago: Aldine, 1963), pp. 42–44, *passim*.
7. L. O. Mink, "The Autonomy of Historical Understanding," in W. Dray (ed.), *Philosophical Analysis and History* (New York: Harper and Row, 1966), pp. 184, 191.
8. S. Lubell, *The Future of American Politics* (2d ed., revised. Garden City, N.Y.: Doubleday, 1956), p. 164.
9. S. Lubell, *Revolt of the Moderates* (New York: Harper, 1956), p. 268; cf. also H. Hodges, Jr., C. Graham, and P. Anderson, "A Sociological Analysis of McCarthy Supporters," a paper delivered at the 52nd Annual Meeting of the American Sociological Society, Washington, D.C., August, 1957.
10. W. Dray, *op. cit.*, pp. 68f.
11. Cf. C. Hempel, *Aspects of Scientific Explanation* (New York: Free Press, 1965), pp. 425–428; R. H. Weingartner, "The Quarrel About Historical Explanation," in M. Brodbeck (ed.), *Readings in the Philosophy of the Social Sciences* (New York: Macmillan, 1968), pp. 349–362; J. J. C. Smart, *Between Science and Philosophy* (New York: Random House, 1968), p. 57.
12. Cf. H. Cantril, *The Psychology of Social Movements* (New York:

John Wiley, 1963), chaps. 1 and 2.

[13] E. Nagel, *The Structure of Science,* pp. 564–68; cf. C. Hempel, "Explanatory Incompleteness," in Brodbeck (ed.), *op. cit.,* pp. 398–415.

[14] Walsh, *op. cit.,* p. 63.

[15] G. Bergmann, *Philosophy of Science* (Madison: University of Wisconsin, 1957), pp. 115–119.

[16] Cf. W. Windelband, " Geschichte und Naturwissenschaft," in *Praeludien* (5th ed., Tuebingen, 1915), 11, 136–160; H. Rickert, *Grundprobleme der Philosophie* (Tuebingen: Mohr, 1934), *Die Grenzen der Naturwissenschaftlichen Begriffsbildung* (2d ed. Tuebingen: Mohr, 1913). Selections from the writings of W. Dilthey are available in English in H. P. Rickman (ed.), *Wilhelm Dilthey: Pattern and Meaning in History* (New York: Harper, 1961), and W. Dilthey, "A non-Positivist Conception of History," in A. Donagan and B. Donagan, *Philosophy of History* (New York: Macmillan, 1965), pp. 90–98.

[17] A. Donagan, "The Popper-Hempel Theory Reconsidered," in Dray (ed.), *op. cit.,* pp. 127–159, and "Are the Social Sciences Really Historical?" in Baumrin (ed.), *op. cit.,* pp. 261–282. The distinctions between reasons, intentions and motivation cannot be pursued here. The literature devoted to their analysis is vast, but some of the more important

accounts include P. Gardiner, *The Nature of Historical Explanation* (London: Oxford, 1955), part IV; G. Ryle, *The Concept of Mind* (New York: Barnes & Noble, 1949), pp. 113f., chap. 5; R. S. Peters, *The Concept of Motivation* (New York: Humanities, 1960); G. E. M. Anscombe, "Intention," in D. F. Gustafson (ed.), *Essays in Philosophical Psychology* (Garden City, N.Y.: Doubleday, 1964), pp. 30–40; A. R. White, *The Philosophy of Mind* (New York: Random House, 1967), chap. 6; A. I. Melden, *Free Action* (New York: Humanities, 1964), chaps. 9–12; C. Taylor, *The Explanation of Behavior* (New York: Humanities, 1964), chaps. 2, 3, 10; A. R. Louch, *Explanation and Human Action* (Oxford: Blackwell, 1966), chaps. 2, 6; F. V. Smith, *Explanation of Human Behavior* (2d ed., London: Constable, 1960), chaps. 2, 3; "Part Four" in L. I. Krimerman (ed.), *The Nature and Scope of Social Science: A Critical Anthology* (New York: Appleton-Century-Crofts, 1969).

[18] Peters, *op. cit.,* p. 4.

[19] R. J. C. Butow, *Japan's Decision to Surrender* (Stanford: Stanford University, 1967), p. 73.

[20] Cf., for example, R. B. Zajonc, "Balance, Congruity and Dissonance," in M. Jahoda and N. Warren (eds.), *Attitudes* (Baltimore: Penguin, 1966), p. 261.

[21] L. Festinger, "Motivations Lead-

ing to Social Behavior," in R. C. Teevan and R. C. Birney (eds.), *Theories of Motivation in Personality and Social Psychology* (Princeton: Van Nostrand, 1964), p. 140.

[22] R. Strausz-Hupé, "Social Science Versus the Obsession of 'Scientism,'" in H. Schoeck and J. W. Wiggins (eds.), *Scientism and Values* (Princeton: Van Nostrand, 1960), pp. 223, 224f.

[23] W. H. Werkmeister, "Social Science and the Problem of Value," in *ibid.,* p. 20 Compare any account of behavioral analysis, e.g., J. R. Millenson, *Principles of Behavior Analysis* (New York: Macmillan, 1967).

[24] As cited in D. Butler, *The Study of Political Behavior* (London: Hutchinson University, 1966), p. 28; cf. J. Bentham, "The Philosophy of Economic Science," *Jeremy Bentham's Economic Writings,* ed. W. Stark (London: George Allen & Unwin, 1952), pp. 79–119.

[25] C. Bay, "Politics and Pseudopolitics: A Critical Evaluation of Some Behavioral Literature," *American Political Science Review,* LIX (March, 1965), pp. 39–51.

[26] K. W. Kim, "The Limits of Behavioral Explanation in Politics," *The Canadian Journal of Economics and Political Science,* XXXI (August, 1965), 315–327.

[27] M. Weber, *Methodology of the Social Sciences* (New York: Free Press, 1949), pp. 173f.

[28] Cf. E. Haas, *Beyond the Nation-State* (Stanford: Stanford University, 1964), chap. 1. Haas renders a number of sophisticated distinctions that cannot be pursued here, but it is clear that much of the understanding obtained in the functional accounts he provides stems from what he calls the "observer's capacity to identify himself with human motives that all of us accept as 'real' and relevant to the study of politics," a capacity "capable of replication" and which could not be called "intuitive in any rigorous sense of the term." Cf. *ibid.,* p. ix.

[29] R. K. Merton, *Social Theory and Social Structure* (Revised and enlarged edition. New York: Free Press, 1963), pp. 72–82.

[30] Cf. E. Nagel, "A Formalization of Functionalism," *Logic Without Metaphysics* (New York: Free Press, 1957), pp. 247–283.

[31] Brown, *op. cit.,* pp. 129f.

[32] R. E. Lane, *Political Life* (New York: Free Press, 1965), p. 207.

[33] Cf. N. J. Smelser, *Essays in Sociological Explanation* (Englewood Cliffs, N.J.: Prentice-Hall, 1968), pp. 110–115; C. G. Hempel, "The Function of General Laws in History," in *Aspects of Scientific Explanation* (New York: Free Press, 1965), pp. 231–243. The latter volume contains Hempel's most complete statement of his position.

[34] Cf. C. G. Hempel, "Explanation and Prediction by Covering Laws," in Baumrin, *op. cit.,* 1; and N. Rescher, "Fundamental Problems in the Theory of Scientific Explanation," in *ibid.,* volume II. A restatement of the "covering law model" appears in A. C. Isaak, *Scope and Methods of Political Science* (Homewood, Ill.: Dorsey, 1959), chap. 7; an attempt to formulate an alternate explication is found in E. J. Meehan, *Explanation in Social Science* (Homewood, Ill.: Dorsey, 1968).

[35] *Die Wissenschaft von der Wissenschaft* (Collective authorship. Berlin: Dietz, 1968), pp. 212–217.

[36] K. Popper, *The Logic of Scientific Discovery* (New York: Basic Books, 1959), p. 59.

Suggested Readings

Brodbeck, M. "Explanation, Prediction and 'Imperfect' Knowledge," in M. Brodbeck (ed.), *Readings in the Philosophy of the Social Sciences*. New York: Macmillan, 1968. Chapter 21.

Carnap, R. *Philosophical Foundations of Physics*. New York: Basic Books, 1966. Chapter I.

Hempel, C. G. "Scientific Explanation," in S. Morgenbesser (ed.), *Philosophy of Science Today*. New York: Basic Books, 1967. Chapter 8.

Nagel, E. *The Structure of Science*. New York: Harcourt, Brace & World, 1961. Chapters 2 and 14.

Wartofsky, M. W. *Conceptual Foundations of Scientific Thought*. New York: Macmillan, 1968. Chapter 10.

8

On Understanding and Knowing

... It is not by looking at things, but by dwelling in them, that we understand their joint meaning. We can see how an unbridled lucidity can destroy our understanding of complex matters. Scrutinize closely the particulars of a comprehensive entity and their meaning is effaced, our conception of the entity is destroyed.

Michael Polanyi

A person who cannot play chess can still watch games of chess. He sees the moves being made as clearly as does his neighbor who knows the game. But the spectator who does not know the game cannot do what his neighbor does—appreciate the stupidity or cleverness of the players. [This is the] difference between merely witnessing a performance and understanding what is witnessed.

Gilbert Ryle

Cognitive disciplines, those that pretend to contribute to our knowledge about ourselves or our environment, occupy loci on a continuum ranging from those minimally, to those maximally, standardized and formalized. If one conceives "standardization" as referring to the degree of semantic invariance that obtains in a discipline, one intuitively appreciates the qualitative distinction that separates the language style of "existential philosophy" from that of organic chemistry or nuclear physics. Similarly, if "formalization" refers to the explicitness of the syntactical relations that obtain between propositions entertained by a cognitive enterprise, the differences between aesthetics and geometry become equally transparent. Abraham Kaplan has recently suggested the typology of language styles that we have used to characterize the linear continuum one finds connecting ordinary and reconstructed language.

Kaplan identifies the language style of literature, clinical accounts and general history as essentially *literary*. The development of an *academic* style is at least in part the consequence of stipulative standardization of semantic meaning and the development of a technical vocabulary. *Eristic* language style, in turn, is the consequence of a sustained and relatively systematic, but informal, effort to exhibit the syntax and semantics of linguistic artifacts—in order to begin to meet the adequacy criteria of formal (i.e., logical), and the evidence conditions of substantive, discourse. More formal and rigorous efforts at producing specifically syntactical invariance generate *symbolic, postulational* and *formal* language artifacts—in which semantic *and* syntactical variances are maximally reduced.[1]

The transition from literary to formal language styles is initially characterized by systematic efforts to establish semantic invariance. Eristic language concerns itself with empirical evidence warrants for truth ascriptions as well as logical consistency—and is consequently concerned with 1) logical relations and implications that obtain between propositions couched in 2) relatively standardized language. One begins to understand what is to count as evidence for any cognitive assertion only when one knows, with considerable specificity, what is being asserted. In order to know what such assertions entail, at least some logical derivations must be explicitly characterized. All of which requires, as a necessary condition, internal consistency. Symbolic language style begins to reveal, as transparently as possible, the syntactical structure of argument in order to certify internal consistency. Symbols are employed rather than terms

having substantive referents, for one technique for exhibiting syntactical relations is to divest assertions of their semantic meaning.
The elimination of semantic referents via the use of special notational devices helps make syntactical relations increasingly apparent.
Symbolic language style is characterized by the use of reconstructed
language, artificial language systems, special notational devices
calculated to reduce semantic and syntactical variance of ordinary
language. Postulational language focuses specifically on the logical
relations that obtain within such a collection of propositions.
Its principal concern is syntactic rigor. When postulational
language matures into uninterpreted calculi, axiomatic and empirically "empty" collections of systematically related sentential forms,
discourse is conducted in the formal style.

Political inquiry, in itself, operates at various linguistic levels.
Empirical studies are conducted most responsibly in the eristic
style, supplemented by frequent efforts at more extensive formalization which invoke symbolic, postulational and formal techniques.
A not inconsiderable part of the work in political inquiry, however,
is conducted in literary and academic language. The bulk of political
theory, for example, is conducted at this level, and thus shares the
species traits of performances conducted at the same linguistic
level in history, clinical psychology and comparative literature.
Many, if not most, of the issues which occupy participants in these
domains turn on the vagueness and ambiguity that attends terms
employed in the very discussion of issues. Claims are made and
counterclaims are lodged in language borrowed from ordinary and
literary language. While such language has the advantage of common
currency, it does obscure the literal meaning of any specific claim
being advanced and of any counterclaim offered in rebuttal. Very
often the merits of *either* claim cannot be assessed—simply because
one cannot unequivocally characterize what is, in fact, being asserted.
Such discussions almost invariably succeed only in generating heat
rather than light and can, on critical occasions, be simply counter-
productive. One receives the decided impression that a great deal
of conceptual machinery has been put into motion, but that precious
few gears have meshed.

The advent of what has been loosely called "linguistic or analytic philosophy" was at least in part the consequence of a pervasive recognition of the critical role language plays in the knowledge enterprise. One of the immediate by-products of increased sensitivity with respect to language employments was a recognition that discussions conducted exclusively at literary and academic linguistic levels were rarely productive of cognitive significance. They often seemed to serve cathartic or expressive, sometimes ritual or ceremonial, but rarely cognitive, purpose. It was felt, by a number of practitioners, that some preliminary efforts at relatively rigorous standardization and formalization in language use might serve some therapeutic purpose. Such efforts might not resolve disputes, but they might assist participants in determining what, in fact, the dispute was about. The intentions of what might be called, with some pretension, "conceptual" or "linguistic" analysis, are therapeutic or homeopathic—such analyses are efforts calculated to dispel linguistic confusion and expose substantive as distinct from fictive problems by distinguishing between them. [2]

Such efforts are characteristic of twentieth-century philosophy. Philosophers have spoken of our century as the century of "analysis," but the identification of the main current of critical philosophical thought as "analytic" or "linguistic" obscures a diversity of trends and a multiplicity of foci. "Analytic or linguistic philosophy" is a generic reference to a *variety* of analytic efforts and for the purposes of this discussion a distinction can be made between analytic practitioners in terms of the language level on which they operate. In general it can be said that analysts like Ludwig Wittgenstein, J. L. Austin, Gilbert Ryle, and A. J. Ayer focus their analyses on the literary, academic and eristic language levels, while specialists like Rudolf Carnap, Arthur Pap, Arthur Tarski, Patrick Suppes, and R. M. Martin deploy their skills over symbolic, postulational, and formal language concerns. Others like Charles Morris and Jerrold Katz have occupied themselves with a systematic and synoptic account of language itself, a general theory of signs and symbols. [3]

The list of participants in the developments of contemporary analytic philosophy could be extended to considerable length. Their work can be characterized, in general, by only the vaguest criterial definition. They can all be said to concern themselves with the nature and function of symbol and sign systems in the accumulation, processing and exchange of information and the criteria governing truth ascription in the various analytic and substantive language domains.

The degree of sophistication that has become characteristic of analytic philosophy imposes impressive burdens on those who attempt to remain minimally abreast of developments. Therefore analytic philosophers have tended to organize themselves into guilds of severely restricted membership. Communication becomes increasingly specialized and whatever benefits might accrue from more sophisticated and perceptive linguistic analyses are restricted to a constituency of specialists. This has had unfortunate results for minimally formalized disciplines like political science. Those political scientists, traditionally identified as "theorists," who might be expected to have either affinity with, or cognizance of, developments in analytic philosophy have shown themselves to be either indisposed to interact with representatives of contemporary philosophy or to have remained uninformed with respect to its character and utility. That such appears to be the case is unfortunate because much of what passes as substantive dispute in some areas of political science, particularly political theory, might very well be an artifact of the informal, literary, or academic language in which practitioners carry on their discussions.

Ordinary, informal, and literary language is characteristically beset by vagueness, ambiguity and tense obscurity. Ordinary, informal, and literary language is eminently suitable for ordinary, informal and literary purposes. One obviously runs considerable risk, however, when one employs such language styles to address academic or formal issues. We tend to intuit meanings in informal discourse—and such intuitions may be perfectly adequate for ordinary purposes—but they may well harbor ambiguities and vaguenesses that fault intelligibility, produce fictive dispute and license equivocations in anything other than ordinary language contexts.

One could, in fact, compose a catalogue of vague and ambiguous terms employed in the informal discussions commonplace in the discursive treatments characteristic of political science, but one term, "understanding," recommends itself for preliminary treatment

1) because of its regular appearance in the literature, 2) because it is made to shoulder an inordinate burden when it is invoked, and 3) because of its intrinsic vagueness and ambiguity.

The aim of this chapter is to illustrate the obscurity that attends the ordinary and literary use of such terms—and to suggest that at least a considerable part of the disagreement that separates "schools" of "political thought" is fictive, the product of imprecision and ambiguity in the nondeliberative use of ordinary language concepts.

"Understanding" and Political Science

Recently Mulford Sibley urged those who would systematically study politics to seek "understanding." ". . . To understand politics," he went on in clarification, "implies the kind of insight characteristic of the artist as well as the precision which we usually associate with science—the comprehension of interrelations of parts to whole in addition to the analysis of parts themselves." He went on to suggest that only a "postscientific" knowledge could produce the "understanding" to which he exhorted us. This knowledge somehow "transcends scientifically verifiable propositions." It is a "vision" which while it might rely in part on the results of scientific inquiry "always goes beyond them," just as the poet, the artist and the religious mystic go beyond them. In effect, Professor Sibley insists pradoxically that the *"science* of politics" is a science only if we have attained understanding and knowledge which intrinsically involve imaginative and specifically *"unscientific"* procedures and judgments.[4]

Professor Sibley's account resonates ideas found in a variety of places. Russell Kirk, for example, has insisted that the social scientist (and by implication the student of politics) has "deprived himself of the principal instruments for understanding human behavior," by neglecting "intuitive sources of wisdom," by failing to understand that it is "imagination, in the long run, [that] rules the world, not scientific research. . . ."[5] At almost the same time Glenn Tinder maintained that since "the totality of social and political reality cannot be scientifically comprehended," we are "obliged to found our conception of it on faith," and thereby attain social and political understanding.[6]

In a variety of places, in a variety of circumstances, one finds muted or more strident echoes and reformulations of such convictions. In some sense they are all injunctions to seek a more comprehensive "understanding" of man's political life, a "knowing" more synoptic than that which could be obtained through "science." Unfortunately all these terms, "understanding," "knowing" and "science," are mercurial. None of them are simply transparent. One does not simply see through them to their meaning. The term "science" is opaque enough—at this point the term "understanding" (and subsequently, "knowing") recommends itself to us for explication.

The Uses of "Understanding"

Like "meaning" and "truth," the term "understanding" is widely used in ordinary and discursive professional literature as an honorific, an appraisive, and a cognitive ascription, and yet its use in all cases is singularly obscure. At times, in ordinary language, the term "understanding" is used in gratitude, as when one says, "You are so understanding," and it seems to mean little more than that one has been sympathetic—one has appropriately empathized. Such tributes are important in interpersonal exchange, but they do not constitute the focus of our concern (nor can they be construed as "mystic" or "postscientific"). We are concerned here with the cognitive uses of "understanding" because so many claims are made in its name in a great deal of literary and academic political science literature.

Because ascriptions of "understanding" have such high emotional salience, and because the use of "understanding" and its cognates is imprecise, what is required is a sustained analysis, only the beginnings of which can be undertaken here. Since the expression finds its origin in ordinary language it is there that analysis must commence, for the uses, in the available political science literature, of "understanding" as a cognitive ascription rarely transcend those of ordinary language employments.

In ordinary language the expression "understanding" is, at times, simply used as a synonym for "knowing," as in the case of "Nixon *understands* how to politically manage various interest groups," or alternately, "Nixon *knows* how to politically manage various interest groups." The evidence conditions which would warrant a knowledge claim with respect to the former would warrant such a claim with respect to the latter as well. Furthermore, we are said, in ordinary speech, to *understand* a word when we *know* its meaning. We understand what our interlocutor meant to say when we are prepared to assert that we know what he means. In such cases "understanding" once again telescopes into "knowing," and the truth ascription made to putative understandings is warranted by the same evidence that warrants any empirical knowledge claim. We might rephrase what our interlocutor has said (provide a lexical definition) and then solicit his explicit approval of our rendering. In such cases we initially rely on the most elementary of human gestures, the nod or the assent, as satisfying the evidence conditions for both the understanding and the knowing. We may, of course, find ourselves to have been in error, or alternately our interlocutor may invoke a sometimes tedious exchange between us to attempt to tease out the meaning of a word, expression or sentence before we can confidently assert that we understand or know. At its conclusion, hopefully, both of us will understand or know what was intended. At its commencement neither one of us might be able to assert, confidently, what that was. For all that the understanding is no more than a warranted knowing—meeting the same evidence conditions as any other empirical knowledge claim.

In other cases in ordinary usage we seem to distinguish between "understanding" and "knowing," as when we say, "I understand German, but I don't know how to speak it." In such cases we seem to employ the two expressions "understand" and "know" to distinguish between different *performatory skills*. In making the above claim I claim that I generally know the meaning of German words and sentences, but my skill in spontaneously recalling German vocabulary and formulating German sentences is minimal or, for all intents and purposes, nonexistent. Understanding and knowing, nonetheless, seem to conflate. The distinction is entertained in order to conveniently refer to two different performatory skills.

There seem to be instances in ordinary usage where something like the same distinction between performatory skills is intended, as when we employ locutions like, "I know the doctrines of existentialism, but I don't understand them." "Knowing" in such cases seems to involve skill in rephrasing, reiterating by rote, formulating, and recognition of, the substantive doctrines. "Understanding," in such a context, would seem to involve skill in finding applications for, or appreciation of, such doctrines. One seems to be suggesting a distinction between knowing how to correctly reiterate such doctrines, and knowing how to apply them to any determinate circumstance or knowing what might constitute evidence of their truth or falsity. "Understandings" of such kinds seem to be special kinds of *knowing how* and *knowing what*. They constitute special instances of procedural and/or propositional knowledge—warranted by nothing other than standard "empiriological" techniques.

In many instances of its use in ordinary language "understanding" simply conflates with "knowing," or alternately is used to distinguish different kinds of knowing how and/or knowing that. Such uses are relatively easy to analyze and determination of the truth status of any claims made employing the term "understanding" is relatively simple. Whatever is understood to confirm true instances of knowing how or knowing that would confirm true instances of such understanding. None of which requires anything other than standard verification procedures common to empirical inquiry.

But there are particularly fugitive uses of "understanding" that are more difficult to analyze. There are clearly cases of such uses in claims like, "He really understands art," or "He really understands politics." It is difficult to specify with any precision what is meant by such omnibus ascriptions. In order to distinguish some kind of intelligible meaning in such expressions, one would have to attend their employments in a variety of specific instances—and their use may very well be completely idiosyncratic or simply expressive. The burden of proof in such cases is on the claimant.

Sometimes, however, in cases where a claim is made that one "understands" *a* work of art—what seems to be implied is that one claims to have correctly "interpreted" it. Here "understanding" seems to involve "interpretation" or alternately "appreciation."

The "appreciation" of a work of art can best be left to the aesthetician to analyze (for "appreciation" as it is used in this context is an aesthetic term). For our purposes the "understanding" of a work of art, via "interpretation," has enough analogues in social (and, by implication, political) science to warrant a summary and hopefully catalytic discussion in the effort to understand what kind of claim is being made when one insists one possesses some *special* "understanding" that is "postscientific," "mystic," "intuitive" or the product of "faith."

"Understanding," Interpretation, and Theory

Psychoanalysts and clinicians regularly speak of "understanding" dreams. Alternately they speak of "interpreting" dreams. This is a more interesting use of "understanding" than that ordinarily found in common speech, for it involves more than *simple* procedural or propositional knowings. It has academic and eristic employments. What is invoked in pretending to such understandings, is, in fact, an elaborate *theoretical infrastructure*. This is elliptically expressed by saying that one knows how to interpret dreams and such interpretation produces understanding where no understanding hitherto obtained.

In order to interpret dreams one must *know* a variety of simple *generalizations*. One must "know," for example, that the manifest dream content is a disguised, symbolically represented, dramatized, and condensed rendering of the latent dream content. One must "know" that the male genital organ might, in dreams, be represented by swords, rifles, torches, lances, lanterns, umbrellas, dirigibles, ships, trains, sticks, flag poles, fingers, arms, legs, pipes, torpedoes, sausages, loaves of bread, as well as any elongated object. But propositional knowings of this sort are, in and of themselves, inadequate to understanding or interpreting dreams. One must also know the *generic purpose* of dreaming. "Freud," Angel Garma insists, "has *demonstrated* that unfulfilled wishes are at the bottom of *all* dreams" (emphasis supplied).[7] One has particular knowings about regularities, generalizations concerning the dream processes of disguise, representation, dramatization, and condensation as well as knowledge of the overall strategy of dreaming. An "understanding" or an "interpretation" is a result of operating with both *particular* and *systemic* knowing. One knows particular generalized response patterns as well as the generic (and apparently unrestricted) "function" of the dream. Both the particular and systemic knowing which together constitute such understanding are, nonetheless in principle, subject to direct or indirect empirical test.

Such "understanding" seems to be predicated upon a systematic knowledge of confirmable *theory,* as well as the particular confirmable *generalizations* governing particular instances that are the objects of specific interpretation. The fact that it is a rare occurrence for two clinicians or psychoanalysts to tender the same interpretation of any given dream (or have the same understanding of a dream) strongly suggests, among other things, that Freudian (or neo-Freudian) theory is incomplete and/or imprecise, and consequently beset by syntactical and semantic indeterminacy that make confirmation of its "understandings" or "interpretations" suspect.[8] Under such circumstances there seems to be little real possibility of confirming one interpretation or understanding as opposed to another. For any *one* understanding *any number* of alternate and equally plausible interpretations can be forthcoming (and usually are). The suspect character of such understanding is a consequence of the relative absence of semantic rules for unambiguously tying down at least some of the critical Freudian concepts to observations, as well as the very slackness and incompleteness of the syntactical structure such concepts inhabit.[9] Understanding fails because there is serious theoretical disability. Understanding fails because one lacks a viable theory of the universe of inquiry, not because one lacks "vision" or "artistic insight."

If it is difficult to confirm such understanding, one can appreciate how little confidence one can have in claims that one "understands" politics or art or a particular work of art. Such understandings seem to require not only simple knowings of the sort that can be relatively easily established, like knowings concerned with art or political history, or skills in the execution of works of art or political acts, or recognition of techniques employed in such performances. They seem to require something like a defensible "theory" of art, or a "theory" of whatever universe of inquiry of which one is said to have an understanding. Since there is no recognizable "theory" for art, much less for politics in general, omnibus claims that one "understands" art or politics seem to be manifestly indefensible. One seems to be able to render some plausible case or another for ascriptions of such understandings, but there seems to be scant opportunity to choose between alternative understandings. To take refuge in locutions like "seeing the point of it," of "having artistic insight," does not enhance our confidence. Metaphors, similes and parables do not constitute warrants for truth claims, particularly when one claims some synoptic and omnibus understanding.

It seems clear that "understanding" has more diversified uses than "knowing."[10] In some cases the terms are used as substitution instances of each other; in others they are used to distinguish between different kinds of knowing. In the most interesting cases "understanding" subsumes procedural (or performatory) and/or propositional (or discursive) knowledge, but specifically refers to a more "global or synoptic vision." We would hardly be prepared to maintain that someone understood something, a sentence, a proof, a concept, complex sign or theory, or any of their uses or referents, unless we were also prepared to assert that he knew something specific about it or them. If someone were to insist that he understood dogs and yet could not tell breeds apart, could not anticipate typical canine behavior, nor train a dog adequately, or demanded that dogs learn and satisfactorily execute logical proofs, we would legitimately identify his claim as spurious or a signal instance of conscious or unconscious humor.

The *necessary* condition for the legitimate claim to understanding is evidence of *some* relevant and specific procedural and/or propositional knowledge. And all such knowledge claims must meet appropriate "empiriological" evidence conditions. There are clearly techniques, skills and discursive knowledge embedded in any synoptic understanding. To understand quantum physics one would at least have to know some confirmed truths about physics, how to undertake mathematical operations, and understand something of experimental procedures, but it seems equally obvious that understanding is not exhaustively reducible to such simple knowings. [11] What seems to be required is a complex (and ideally systemic) knowing: a recognition of the "framework" or "schema" in which such knowings find a place.

Henri Poincaré seems to be suggesting something of the same thing in a passage that has been widely exploited by contemporary neo-obscurantists:

> If you are present at a game of chess, it will not suffice, for the understanding of the game, to know the rules for moving the pieces. That will only enable you to recognize that each move has been made conformably to these rules, and this knowledge will truly have very little value. . . . To understand the game is wholly another matter; it is to know why the player moves this piece rather than that other which he could have moved without breaking the rules of the game. It is to perceive the inward reason which makes of this series of successive moves a sort of organized whole. [12]

Now it seems fairly obvious that Poincaré is *not* suggesting that "understanding" requires some mystic insight. The "inward reason" he refers to does not refer to an arcane knowing. Knowing the rules governing the movement of chessmen obviously does not constitute understanding the game of chess. To understand the game one must at least also appreciate the strategy which subtends the moves. One knows that the purpose of the game is to defeat one's opponent and one knows how that can be accomplished. One comes to understand a dream by knowing, in part, that its strategic and overall purpose (presumably) is wish fulfillment and the reduction of psychic tension. That is the "point" of it. Knowing the point of it means, in such instances, that one understands the purpose or function of the subject activity. All the subsidiary knowings partake of increased "significance" because they are housed in an activity that has an avowed and acknowledged purpose. Thus Michael Polanyi, illustrating "understanding," cites the case exemplified by the engineer "grasping how the parts of a machine fit together and function jointly." [13] Elsewhere he speaks of understanding as "*comprehending*: a grasping of disjointed parts into a comprehensive whole." [14]

Understanding chess involves no mystery, no "transcientific insight" (whatever that might be). It involves knowledge of the rules governing the permissible movements of the individual pieces and it involves recognition of the determinate purpose of the game, which in turn entails the ability to effectively anticipate and appreciate the moves of one's opponents (ideally a viable theory of game behavior). Such anticipations and appreciations require considerable procedural and propositional background knowledge, at least implicit knowledge about the probabilities governing alternate choice and ideally the personality characteristics of the players. That none of this is arcane or mysterious is evidenced by the fact that programmers can program a computer to play a respectable game of chess. There is no technological restriction on the chess-playing capacity of machines. It is now almost within the range of technological possibility to construct a chess-playing machine that would be superior to most human chess players. Which simply means that there are not only rules governing the moves of the pieces in the game, but rules governing the game itself. We understand the game and the computer that plays it. Furthermore the rules governing the permissible moves of individual pieces and the rules governing the strategy of probabilities in anticipating an opponent's moves can be specified. These latter rules are generally implicitly known by human players and are evidenced by their performances—they are explicitly programmed into the computer. The computer "knows" how to play chess, that is to say, the behavior of the computer instantiates what we mean by "machine intelligence," just as the dog "understands" our commands. The evidence condition for affirming that the computer or the dog knows or understands is the same in both cases: successful public performance. The dog's performatory skill exemplifies what we mean by "animal intelligence," just as the computer's performance exemplifies what we mean by "machine intelligence."

Both animals and machines can be said to manifest intelligent behavior, and possess that measure of intelligent "understanding." Our "understanding," on the other hand, of both animal and machine behavior is procedural, propositional *and* systemic (we can do [perhaps more slowly or not as well] what certain animals or machines might do, we know particular knowings about their doings and we know something of the laws governing animal learning, computer logic, and what has been loosely called "machine psychology"). Our "understanding" is not only *intelligent* (exemplified in the performatory skills that characterize "tacit knowing"), but *rational* as well (exemplified in propositional and systemic knowing). Animal and machine "understanding" can be adequately characterized as intelligent—our "understanding" (when it is linguistic and systemic) is rational. We possess (at our best) *theoretical* understanding. We are capable of advancing claims and meeting the evidence conditions which warrant their truth status. Such claims are the products of formal or empirical theory, i.e., the consequences of systematically related propositions that equip us to retrodict, predict and explain linguistic or nonlinguistic events, or constellations of such events, that occur in formal or empirical domains.

Neo-obscurantists and romantics frequently take umbrage at this kind of analysis and suggest that "understanding" is really some sort of ineffable appreciation that could never be codified or subjected to formulae. Thus Polanyi provides instances of "understanding" which he conceives as instantiating occurrences of unspecifiable and nonformulable "understanding." One unfortunate instance he selects is the procedural skill of the diagnostician.[15] This is a kind of "understanding" which is "gestalted," for which no rules *are* given and for which no rules *can* be given. It is the last clause which merits attention. The diagnostician rarely is equipped, in fact, to exhibit the rules governing his efforts. The same is frequently true for those who felicitously employ the language of or who "do" politics. But to say that such "tacit knowledge" of rules does not require that they be formulated, does not entail that such rules *cannot* be formulated. Thus there have been, in fact, efforts to standardize and specifically formulate diagnostic procedures. In the 27 empirical studies which have resulted, 17 have shown that the statistical and standardized techniques (which could and have been programmed into computers) were clearly superior to diagnosis offered by any one skilled diagnostician possessed of "intuitive understanding." Meanwhile, 10 of them showed no appreciable difference between formalized and "intuitive" diagnoses, and in no case was the individual diagnostician's "intuitive" efforts superior to those of the statistician employing formulae.[16] The skilled diagnostician or gifted politician ultimately warrants his claim to understand by successful performance. But his performance is predicated on (in principle) publicly formulable systemic (or theoretically organized) propositional knowledge.

"Understanding" as "Synoptic Vision"

The use of "understanding" as referring to some "synoptic vision," or "comprehending the whole," refers, in fact, to a variety of performances. It can refer to the "understanding" of a clinician or diagnostician who "understands" how to diagnose diseases and teaches pupils by examples how to proceed. But there seems to be no compelling reason to imagine that such understanding of the "whole" cannot be equally well unpacked into formulas. The "understanding" of a "whole" might, on the other hand, refer to understanding the purpose or function of a machine or of a psychic or physiological process. This understanding seems clearly capable of being subjected to determinate and forthright analysis and public test. Purposes and functions of this sort can be exhibited. The purposes of machines can be determined by inquiring into the intention of their inventors (propositional knowledge). The function of psychic or physiological processes can be established by confirming lawlike relations, for example, between psychic energy states (unfulfilled gratification, in the case of the Freudian interpretation of dreams) and latent dream content— and equilibrium states of the system under scrutiny and the operation of glands and organs in the case of organisms. *These latter understandings are predicated on the availability of comprehensive theory.* Their purpose is to *explain.* This latter kind of understanding is a consequence of having a viable theory of a universe of inquiry at one's disposal. The appeal to "synoptic vision" in such cases is an obscure reference to the availability of a viable theory, and whatever understanding obtains is dependent upon it.[17]

In all the cases of understanding we have considered there seems to be no room for ineffable, transcendent, transempirical or "postscientific" understandings. When we say that our dog understands us, we are prepared to say that we know he understands us because he *performs* appropriately upon visual, olfactory, tactile or auditory cue. We muster the same evidence statements for the ascription of his understanding and the claim that we know that he understands. When we say that Nixon understands how to politically manage interest groups, we provide evidence for his understanding, and for our claim that we know he understands, by citing the empirical evidence conditions he has satisfied and our awareness of such confirmed instances. We accredit our claim that we understand German by publicly performing suitably. When we say that we don't understand a doctrine although we know its tenets, what we seem to be saying is that we have failed to grasp any purpose or utility to which it can be put. We do not know *how* to apply the doctrine in any determinable circumstance. What we require for such understanding are clear and confirming instances of functional employment, that such doctrines have some determinate yield. When someone says he understands dreams, or politics, or history, he seems to be saying that he possesses a great deal of background knowledge (both procedural and propositional) as well as knowing something of its purposes either in terms of some theoretical system or some intended utility. The clearest cases of understanding are predicated on the availability of an articulated and viable theory and some determinate and specifiable purpose. We have such understanding when we have an adequate theory and recognize a publicly specifiable and intersubjectively testable purpose.

The distinction between the various uses of "understanding" is at least as old as Aristotle. He distinguished between that understanding which is the understanding of synoptic or global causes and principles (propositional and systemic knowing), and that kind of understanding which instantiates applied skill in particular instances (procedural knowing). The former is best characterized as theoretical understanding, while the latter finds its exemplifications in learning and teaching by example. A skilled craftsman, a diagnostician, a psychoanalyst, or a politician may exhibit model performances for the instruction of his apprentices. But model instances of understanding seem to require something more than understanding *how* to perform. Observations of paradigmatic performances can ultimately reveal the rules or laws governing those instances, and those rules and laws inhabit theories. If the performances are invariant, subtending laws and criteria may ultimately be revealed by a careful and sustained regularity analysis. One performs successfully because such performances reveal invariances that can be expressed in propositions organized in some systematically related set, characterized by relative semantic and syntactic specificity, which we call theories.

In order to understand mathematics or logic what more would be required than to know and successfully execute the permissible permutations entertained by logic or mathematics, to know their rationale in metamathematics and metalogic, as well as recognize the purposes they effectively serve? Similarly, to understand politics what more would be required than to successfully evidence truth claims, to possess effective theory, to successfully undertake theory construction, and possess an awareness of the purposes of politics? Obviously the appeal to the "purposes" of mathematics, logic or politics requires an appreciation of ethics and metaethics—for purposes thus understood frequently exemplify interests and it is interests that provide the initial substance of values. But understanding remains the product of a public and corrigible enterprise for all that. To insist that one knows *the* purpose of politics implies that one has a single and synoptic normative theory of life or politics that is *publicly* defensible. If that "theory" is semantically obscure, if its syntax is slack, if it can appeal to no simple or complex constituent knowings, if it rests on "faith" alone, it can only impart the illusion of understanding. It constitutes a fictive understanding.

Normative theory, whether synoptic or partial, requires special treatment that falls outside the confines of this analysis and will be dealt with subsequently. At this point all that requires our insistence is the fact that legitimate understanding implies systematic cognitive techniques that are broadly and characteristically described as "intersubjective." There is mathematical and logical theory that is subject to public and neutral criteria for its assessment and understanding is predicated upon it. There is empirical theory, systematic and cognitive, requiring public and neutral criteria for its assessment—and there is normative theory, equally systematic and cognitive, requiring public and neutral criteria for *its* assessment—and understanding is dependent on it. Whether or not one chooses to call all such cognitive activities "science" is a matter of stipulative and prescriptive language use. Certainly there is a long tradition of employing the word "science" to cover them all. More recently the word has been reserved for specifically empirical theory and there is some merit in so construing it—if one does not neglect the recognition that in collecting, processing, interpreting and employing synthetic information, analytic and normative constituents perform (as we shall suggest) intrinsic and essential functions.

Whether this legitimate recognition implies that cognitive performances must be supplemented by "mystic" and "intuitive" adjuncts is quite another matter and seems to be the product of a narrow and implausible analysis of normative language. Such a conjecture is generally the result of conceiving some aspects of the cognitive enterprise as irreducibly and irredeemably "personal," "subjective," or "transrational." Such a conjecture merits separate analysis, for it threatens the knowledge enterprise with an invasion of "faith" that can only succeed in defeating understanding— *however* understanding is to be interpreted.

The Nature of Understanding

Understanding implies explaining, and explaining entails the giving of reasons, and judgments concerning the adequacy of reasons given involve appeal to intersubjective criteria to warrant them. The adequacy of justificatory argument will be intersubjectively determined by domain variant and domain invariant criteria: the analytic domain requires different evidence conditions than the synthetic, and the normative requires different evidence conditions from both. Synoptic understanding, when it involves human purposes and values, invokes elements of all three language domains integrated into a systematic and publicly defensible linguistic structure. Such understanding is the most comprehensive of understandings. Few men can legitimately pretend to the competence required for such integrative comprehension. Most of us are graced with fragmentary understanding, corrigible and relative to our circumstances, capacities and irrepressible disabilities. Most understanding is partial and fragmentary at best. The most effective and comprehensive understandings have, in fact, been provided by natural science. Corrigible knowledge claims are tendered as a consequence of systematic observation governed by syntactically and semantically invariant, or systematically variant, conceptual schemata, subject to reasonably specific evidence conditions (semantic and syntactical concerns), all calculated to increase effective control over ourselves and our environment (an essentially normative concern).

In our impatience with partial understanding and corrigible knowledge we frequently escape into the exalted reaches of a special "understanding" which pretends to reveal to us the "hidden nature of things," or the "inner being of things."[18] Such understanding seeks to transcend "empiriological" techniques and requires something called "analogical intellection" or the "dialectic"—or abandons "empiricism" for "dwelling within the unspecifiable particulars of the external manifestations" of the world, or in order to "pour ourselves into new forms of existence...."[19] Such understandings are apparently sought through procedures which are neither logical, empirical nor normative or any intelligible combination of the three. No specification of how one is to proceed is ever tendered nor are the confirmation techniques governing them even vaguely characterized. The semblance of understanding is purchased by the indiscriminate exploitation of simile and metaphor. We are counselled to "pour ourselves" into "new forms of existence" by "indwelling," in order to attain some precious understanding, or we are advised to "generalize" from our own experience in order to understand, for example, the "sentience" of rats and homing pigeons. Students of politics are similarly counselled to "relive" the "workings of the mind" of a politician in order to "understand" him.[20] How we are to proceed, with such "indwellings," "pourings," and "relivings" is never specified—still less are we told how we can distinguish *successful* "indwellings," "pourings," and "relivings" from those that are *unsuccessful*. The insistent question is how are we to know we understand if we don't *know* that we have successfully dwelt within, poured ourselves in, or relived new forms of existence?

The fact is that the term "understanding" is variously deployed by men over a variety of performances ranging from identifiable instances of appropriate animal responses, to our spontaneous recognitions of sounds, faces and complex things, to our intuitions about and theoretical appraisals of the world, to analogical reasoning and mathematical insights, as though all these processes and the determination of their truth were all of the same logical kind. What is minimally required, in fact, in all such instances is the most elementary distinction between the processes through which such putative *understanding is attained,* the *character of the putative understanding itself,* and the process by virtue of which the *truth status of such understanding is determined.*

Social scientists (and political scientists by implication) will frequently suggest that researchers obtain some special "understanding" by "participating" in a culture or in a "life style." What they are obviously alluding to is the real possibility that direct experience often *suggests* generalizations and regularities of potentially high theoretical yield. Interacting with persons of different social or cultural provenience provides occasion for the discovery of intentions, dispositions, aspirations, idiosyncracies, and obscure regularities that might otherwise escape detection. Such "indwelling," or "participation" can have heuristic merit. But whatever comes to be "appreciated" by such participations must be formulated in *propositions* that are, in principle, subject to *public* test. If not, the "understanding" obtained is but little removed from the empathy, familiar to all of us, that is so psychologically satisfying, but cognitively hazardous. By "participating" we develop *feelings* that we "know" a people, a subculture, or some alien political system. But feelings, although eminently satisfying, never provide the evidence warrant for a defensible "understanding."

To obtain the most comprehensive understanding of criminals, for example, one need not be a criminal, nor need one have "indwelt" among them. Learning about them might be much easier if one can effectively undertake participant observation. There is pedagogical merit to such a strategy—and there may very well be heuristic advantage—but in the last analysis whatever "understanding" is obtained must meet the adequacy criteria of systemic and/or propositional knowing, the public test to which all simple and complex knowledge claims must, in the final analysis, be subject.

All claims to "understanding," whatever the character of the "understanding," must meet public tests of accreditation. We say a dog "understands" what we say when he publicly *performs* appropriately. We know something of *how* he comes to understand. Learning theory is a respectable cognitive enterprise. We know a great deal about primary and secondary conditioning. The dog knows nothing of all this. He simply "understands"—which means that he can *perform*. We "understand" his understanding in a more comprehensive way and "indwelling" with him is neither necessary nor sufficient to its attainment. We have at least a partial *theory* of animal learning. The truth status of the theory is determined by the standard and formulable procedures of empirical science. Similarly, we ourselves come to recognize faces and sounds in an unself-conscious way. We have "tacit knowledge" of *how* to recognize familiar faces and sounds—but the test of such knowledge is public performance, for we have all too frequently and all too painfully been led astray by such "tacit" processes. We also have comprehensive systemic understanding of such processes.

Psychologists have been occupied with such things for years—and whatever theories they have generated stand or fall before public test and provide whatever understanding we have of the processes involved. Similarly we have "intuitions," "imaginative insights," we proceed frequently by "analogical leaps." But such "intuitions," "insights," and "analogical leaps" can be, and frequently have been, woefully in error. They can be, and have frequently been, enormously helpful. But such intuitions and insights cannot warrant *themselves* as true, do not themselves constitute unimpeachable understandings. They do not, in and of themselves, inform us whether they are productive of error or truth. They are, at best, preliminary (and sometimes essential) to understanding. Like substantive or heuristic models or preliminary frameworks, such "hunches" or "intuitions," like "participating" or "indwelling," do not constitute understanding. In and of themselves they are heuristic—promissory notes on understanding. They may function in a critical way as part of the "logic of discovery," but are not themselves knowledge. They can only be spoken of as providing "understanding" if "understanding" is given the vaguest and broadest possible construction. Under such circumstances they would constitute "understandings" which could never be characterized as true or false, as leading or not leading to any determinate consequence. So broad a construal of "understanding" would sacrifice our ability to judge between inept and competent performance, between truth and falsity, between stupidity and genius.

Nor is it necessary in evaluating such "intuitions" to specify how such "hunches" are come upon. There is no "logic of discovery" as such. *What we do possess is a public logic of evaluation, a public process of truth ascription.* When we say we understand we can mean no more than that our understanding can suffer public test. Any understanding that pretends to transcend that scrutiny is a mystic understanding, a secret "wisdom" which, like the currency which we mint ourselves, may give us enormous personal gratification, but is, for all that, nonnegotiable.

Putative understanding which is not subject to public test inevitably reduces itself to a claim that one *feels* one understands or one *feels* one knows. But the internal act of feeling or believing, no matter how insistent and irrepressible, is not competent evidence of a genuine understanding or a complex knowing. *Feeling* or *believing* something to be the case can but rarely do the work of *knowing* something to be the case. In asserting that one knows or understands x, one may or may not describe something about the knower (that he feels or believes x), but one does assert something held to be true about the world.[21] Outside of philosophy classrooms attributions of knowledge are not understood to reflect what is going on in the consciousness of anyone. Rather they purport to exhibit something about language or the object world, based on evidence obtained through maximally reliable methods, methods which present us with the fewest occasions for being forced to retract our claim than any alternate candidate methods.

This distinction is evident in our ordinary use of words like "feel" and "believe." It makes perfectly good sense to say "I felt I knew or understood quantum physics," and then append the clause, "but I was wrong," while it makes no sense to say, "I knew or understood quantum physics, but I was wrong." To say that "I feel that I understand politics," does not entail that I do, in fact, understand politics. There are perhaps some limiting cases in which "feeling" may, in a significant sense, be equated with simple *knowing,* but it appears never to be the case that *feelings* ever credit a claim that one possesses *understandings.* Even when understanding and knowing are conflated, the understanding and the knowing are never simple knowings that could be equated with feelings. When we say we understand or know the meaning of a term or sign complex, the feeling or believing that we understand or know and the understanding and knowing are still distinguishable. When we deal with cases like Nixon's understanding or knowing how to politically manage interest groups, the understanding or knowing is obviously a complex knowing. *We* may *feel* that he understands or knows, and *he* may *feel* that he understands or knows, but we and he might well be mistaken. In effect, one can never be said to have privileged access to understanding. It is never personal. While there is a sense in which we can be said to have self-certifying "personal knowledge" (of tweaks, itches, pinches and pains), there seems to be no case in which we can talk intelligibly and intelligently of "personal understanding."

When students or colleagues, in moments of stress, insist that they "understand" something but cannot evidence it or give expression to it in performances of any kind, such a self-attribution has all the earmarks of a counterfeit claim. Such a claim reduces itself to assertions about their inner feelings and *inner feelings never satisfy the evidence conditions for understanding.* Inner feelings have purely psychic reference; understanding implies something about language, the world and the individual in it. Understanding reveals itself in complex locutionary acts or in manifest public performance. The feeling that one possesses understanding may or may not accompany that possession. *Feeling* that one understands is clearly neither the necessary nor sufficient evidence condition for certifying that one understands.

Understanding is the product of simple and complex knowing, procedural, propositional and systemic knowings, the possession of publicly demonstrable skills, intersubjectively warranted propositional knowledge and the possession of a viable partial or comprehensive theory of a universe of inquiry. Knowing in all these senses is intrinsic to understanding—and to say we understand is to say we have such knowings at our disposal. To claim to know is obviously central to the claim that we understand. To appreciate how one warrants understanding is to appreciate, minimally, how knowing is warranted. To claim to understand is clearly distinct from the *belief* that one understands. To assert that one understands is to assert, minimally, that one is prepared to make knowledge claims. To make legitimate knowledge claims is to assert something other than one feels or believes; one knows.

Knowing

Knowing, like understanding but unlike believing or feeling, has, for all significant purposes, objective reference. This distinction is the distinction between epistemological objectivity and epistemological subjectivity. When we speak of knowledge as warranted belief, the emphasis should be on *"warranted"* and *not* "belief." While knowledge assertions may generally be taken to imply belief states, knowledge ascriptions are *warranted* via logically autonomous criteria. In all empirical truth claims, for instance, that come under effective scrutiny, if one cannot be said to know by virtue of some discriminable properties or relations in the object world, and has no excuse for his inability to so warrant his claims to knowledge, then he can be legitimately expected to withdraw them (although he may not, in obvious fact, do so). No *belief* that he knows, no matter how firmly held, can serve as their evidence warrant.

There are times, in ordinary speech, when "believe" acts "parenthetically," as in cases when verbs like opine, guess, suppose, suspect and estimate are arranged in a scale which alludes to the reliability of available evidence. When we assert that "I believe that Nixon will win the next election," the parenthetical "I believe" signals a paucity of evidence. In such cases believing is, like opining, guessing, supposing, suspecting and estimating, a limiting case of knowing. It constitutes a guarded knowledge claim. This is to be distinguished from the cases in which a psychological state is appealed to as evidence of material truth.[22] Having granted the treatment of believing as a guarded knowledge claim, it would be a mistake to fall into the natural error of construing knowing as a particular or exalted state of mind. It is impossible to make sense of the notion that there are truth-certifying states of mind for material knowledge claims.[23] In such cases to say that one believes or feels something to be the case cannot be conceived as referring to psychological states. It elliptically refers to the quality and/or the measure of available intersubjective *evidence*.

Robert Fogelin has persuasively argued that on the best construal of belief and knowledge, their connection could best be considered contingent. There are cases in which it makes perfectly good sense to say that someone knew something to be the case and yet could not bring himself to believe it. Granted these are peripheral, and that normally we like to think that when an individual commands adequate warrant in behalf of some truth this will engender a corresponding belief on his part in its truth, there is no *necessary* connection between them. One may refuse to believe that his nation is the aggressor even after all the conceivable confirming evidence is in. An individual may have all the confirming evidence conceivable that he is suffering terminal cancer and yet, for a variety of reasons, refuse to believe it.

Such considerations provide us with a foothold for a preliminary, and necessarily incomplete, analysis of what it can mean to say that we know anything. Our initial suggestion could be framed in something like the following formulation: Whenever we claim to know, we must understand that we have put ourselves under the obligation of providing upon request, the *intersubjective domain variant and domain invariant evidence* that would warrant the claim. This is understood to be an ordinary language rendering of Fogelin's schema for interpreting any knowledge claim. Fogelin argues that a knowledge claim can be interpreted as instantiating the schema: "X commands adequate grounds for *p*." Both the ordinary language rendering of the schema and the schema itself

are sufficiently different from alternate formulations and schemata
to require some justification.

John Austin interprets knowledge claims in the following manner:
"Whenever I say I know, I am always liable to be taken to claim
that, in a certain sense appropriate to the kind of statement (and
to present intents and purposes), I am able to prove it."[24] A. J.
Ayer interprets knowledge claims thusly: "I conclude then that
the necessary and sufficient conditions for knowing that something
is the case are first what one is said to know be true, and secondly
that one be sure of it, and thirdly that one should have the right to
be sure."[25] Roderick Chisholm, in turn, has suggested: "'S
knows that h is true' means: (i) S accepts h; (ii) S has adequate
evidence for h; and (iii) h is true." Israel Scheffler offers the following
schema: "X knows that Q if and only if (i) X believes that Q, (ii)
X has the right to be sure that Q, and (iii) Q."[26]

It appears obvious that only Austin's rendering is substantially
similar to that offered here. Ayer, Chisholm and Scheffler all 1)
include assertions of *belief* or *acceptance* as well as the condition
that 2) what is held to be true, *is* true, beyond the evidence available
for its truth. But if we accept the suggestion that the relationship
between believing and knowing is contingent and neither necessary
nor sufficient for knowing, the inclusion of "believing" and "accepting" as necessary for maintaining that someone knows is inappropriate. This is qualified by the recognition that if one were oneself to tender such a claim it would be expected that one believed
what one claimed. Dropping "believing" or "accepting" would be
appropriate in cases where we wanted to maintain that someone
knew something but didn't (in the psychological sense) believe it.
If we accept the contingency relationship between believing and
knowing, it would seem unnecessary to insist upon belief states
as necessary to epistemic *states,* although they might necessarily
attend epistemic *assertions* (a person who knows, and says he
knows, can be expected to believe he knows). Should such qualifications be accepted there would be no need to require "accepting,"
"being sure of," or "believing" to attend knowledge ascriptions
and the public and neutral character of truth ascription would
become more patent. Knowledge would be understood to be knowledge whether anyone accepted, was sure of, or believed, it.

This suggests something concerning the further requirement that to know something to be the case necessitates that what is held to be the case actually *be* the case. This has been a common requirement placed on knowledge claims since the time of Aristotle. It has generated an enormous body of literature that is both profound and interesting. It cannot be our purpose here (and it is outside our competence) to enter into the discussion concerned with a truth that is conceived to exist independent of our evidence for it. A reasonable interpretation of this requirement might be that if a truth can be understood to be a truth even if no one accepts it (since acceptance of a truth is only contingent upon the evidence competent to warrant it), truth has an analytically detached character which seems to suggest its independence of truth-certifying procedures. What such an analysis, in fact, suggests is that there are truths which are truths irrespective of the fact that no one has collected the evidence available for their support. If one wishes to occupy himself with such logically possible truths, one can be charged with little other than being preoccupied with materially empty but logically possible eventualities.

Truth ascription becomes, in fact, a living and momentous issue when someone has collected and/or commands *evidence* in its support. Men advance, defend or rebut truths only when some domain variant or domain invariant *evidence* is available with which they can contend. Until the adequacy of such evidence is in contention, h or Q (or what-have-you) may well be true, but they will engage no human resources. Truths become objects of serious human concern only when they engage men in the process of determining their truth, when they become the objects of applied cognitive scrutiny, when they are asserted, evidenced and assessed. The processes involved in evidencing and assessing will make appeal to domain variant or invariant evidence and invoke domain variant or invariant standards and are productive of understanding and knowing. The evidence conditions governing matters of fact differ from those appropriate to mathematics and logic, language, law, appraisals, prescriptions, art-criticism and philosophy. The standards appropriate to one will not be those appropriate to the others. But all require a characterization of evidence conditions and appeal to standards of adequacy.

A student can be said to *know* that the area of a triangle equals

$\frac{1}{2}bh$ if he knows the proof of the theorem and can reproduce it upon demand. He *understands* geometry if he understands how axiomatic systems are generated and how they are given empirical interpretation. If a student can successfully undertake sums in simple mathematics, he can be said to know how to do sums. He can be said to understand mathematics if he knows how to do addition, subtraction, multiplication and division, knows how number systems are generated, and how they come to be applied to the material world.

The processes are in some respects similar and in some respects different in the case of factual knowledge. There are, for example, material assertions which can be construed as epistemically primitive. When I assert, as a case in point, that I feel a pain, the evidence condition certifying the assertion is that I do, in fact, feel a pain. (I have privileged access to the evidence for the assertion.) It is odd to ask me what the evidence conditions for my asserting that I have a pain might be. The evidence for my pain is my feeling it and unless I am simulating or suffering linguistic handicap in asserting it, I implicitly provide the evidence for the assertion. I know that I have a pain in an unself-conscious way. But I could not be said to understand my pain. In ordinary language we can be said to understand pain when we have suffered it, but that simply means that we can successfully empathize, analogically project our feelings on others in appropriate circumstances. Simply to suffer pain is not to be in a position to say we cognitively understand it. Similarly, a man may suffer cancer and not understand it. The kind of primitive knowing which is reducible to feeling is important to human sympathy—it may have pedagogical utility and heuristic merit—but it does not constitute substantive understanding. The doctor who says he does not understand my pain is not lamenting his incapacity to empathize—he may know full well how to do that—he is elliptically referring to his inability to judge the origin, course and implication of my pain. He doesn't understand it in the sense of being able to subsume it under the theoretical generalizations that constitute his "synoptic understanding" of disease processes.

The analogue of this distinction can be pursued throughout the knowledge enterprise. We have a variety of epistemically primitive truths at our disposal—simple knowings whose truth conditions involve simple "seeings" and "feelings." We often say we see that something is the case and yet we might be told that we really didn't understand what we saw. The fact is that understanding in such cases refers to a more inclusive set of simple and complex knowings in which our primitive knowing must contend for place. This in turn suggests that the distinction between knowing and understanding can be unpacked in terms of the notion of "total evidence."

Evidence and Truth

Even the simplest material assertion involves a complex array of background information, a "theory load," which renders such claims problematic and, in principle, corrigible. Any constituent proposition of that complex array of background assumptions and auxiliary hypotheses may have to be surrendered in the face of conflicting evidence. Even the simplest truth claim is lodged in a network of claims all of which are subject, in principle, to reassessment. Each is compelled to find a place within the body of total evidence. It is this consideration which fosters the analytic distinction between evidence and truth. No matter what evidence we have for an assertion, it is still possible to maintain that truth has, in fact, eluded us.

We say that someone has a right to assert that he knows x when he commands the evidence adequate to x. And yet we might very well wish to maintain that the truth of x still eludes him. Thus we say that the best minds of the early Middle Ages had every right to hold that they knew the earth to be the center of the heavens, and yet the "truth" was that the earth was only one of many bodies gravitating around the sun. Their claim at time t was defeated by the evidence available at time t_1. At time t their claim would have passed for a warranted knowledge claim—at time t_1 we deflate their claim into a "belief." Their knowledge claim that the earth was the center of the heavens, against the body of total evidence available at t_1, is adjudged a faulted belief. From the advantaged perspective of time t_1 we can distinguish between the circumstances governing the evidence conditions for *h* (that the earth is the center of the heavens) and the truth of *h*. The distinction between the evidence for *h*, and the truth of *h*, however, breaks down when one is confined to a specific temporal period. Within the confines of that period the evidence conditions for *h* are the only legitimate grounds for asserting the truth of *h*. We only preserve the distinction *analytically* by referring to evidence conditions and truth separately.

The concept of total evidence is obviously time conditioned. Since such is the case, an analytic distinction between total evidence and truth must be entertained for clarity's sake. But this simply constitutes another way of alluding to the fact that *all* material knowledge claims are intrinsically corrigible. It is a restatement of the probabilistic character of our knowledge of the material world. The only material knowledge claims that have ever been proffered as candidates for infallible or incorrigible knowing have been pinches, tweaks, aches and itches: self-referrals to which we each have privileged access. And such occurrences never qualify as understandings. Understandings, no matter how simple, require all the machinery of responsible cognitive assessment. In their paradigmatic instances they require the availability of systematic theoretical knowledge that is the product of the confluence of analytic, synthetic and normative procedures that separately and together meet appropriate evidence conditions for the characterization of their truth status.

Once these elementary considerations are appreciated, one can recognize the merit of Fogelin's suggestion that knowledge claims can be interpreted as instantiations of the schema: "X commands adequate grounds for *p*." To say that X knows *p* is to assert that X can satisfy the evidence conditions for *p*. What the evidence conditions are will vary from claim to claim and from time to time. The concept of total evidence is time and circumstance conditioned. The task of the student is not to attempt to provide for *infallible truth,* but to estimate the truth *responsibly.*

If this account holds for knowledge claims in general, the claim that one specifically *understands* is supported by still more demanding requirements. To hold that one understands, except in the case of the most trivial ordinary language locutions, implies that one commands a viable theory and further that one can identify at least the most critical background assumptions and auxiliary hypotheses that subtend the claim and which are themselves antecedent to the formal theory. To suggest that such understanding is the product of "artistic insight" or "mystic intuition" is bizarre. To suggest that understanding is the product of "imagination" is seriously misleading. Imagination, the intuitive perception of "wholes," the "synoptic vision" are all, as has already been suggested, immensely important as propaedeutic to understanding, but do not themselves constitute understanding. To say that understanding is "postscientific" is in part true if "science" is conceived as applicable only to analytic and synthetic concerns—since normative considerations are intrinsic constituents of cognitive activity. But it can be misleading if such a claim is combined with the insistence upon the employment of "prescientific" or "unscientific" methods of truth determination.

To claim that one understands complex phenomena is to claim, minimally, that one possesses procedural knowledge (skills of a variety of sorts) and propositional knowledge (discursive and theoretical truths warranted by evidence) of simple and complex kinds. To measure the evidential adequacy of all such claims involves analytic, descriptive and pragmatic considerations. To adequately characterize what will count as evidence of the truth of such claims requires recourse to analytically precise conceptual schemata— schemata that permit the unambiguous categorization of discriminable elements of experience. Only under such conditions can it be said that one competently describes. Conceptualization is, of course and in considerable measure, determined by one's purpose. Ordinary language schemata are adequate to the needs of ordinary life. One's purpose can be unproblematically assumed. One wishes to survive and one wishes to understand the enduring and recurrent features of his environment in order to meet the elementary demands of his social and natural circumstances. For this primitive and all but universal purpose we exploit funded generalizations and unproblematic predicative and relational categories which permit us to successfully negotiate within our macrophysical universe.

Most of the language of political science is language in the service of this unproblematic dimension. Political scientists have little difficulty producing the warrant for claims like "There are nine men on the Supreme Court," or "Richard Nixon won the 1968 Presidential election." When such claims are challenged, the unproblematic response to them is, "count them yourself," or "tabulate the results yourself." Such questions can be reasonably characterized as "factual." General signs like "nine," "men," and "Presidential election," and proper nouns like "1968" and "Richard Nixon" can be unpacked into unproblematically perceived recognitors, recurrent and discriminable features of experience that serve as indicators for the successful use of ordinary language signs. Primitives, children and the uninitiated can be taught to recognize the warrants for such assertions without difficulty. "Factual questions," so conceived, can be understood to be those questions for which it is always in principle possible for there to be or to have been an observer who would be in a position to answer the question by direct observation.[27]

For this reason a distinction is generally made between "easily decided" observations, what used to be called "protocol statements," and "theoretical propositions"—the distinction being between the unproblematic auxiliary assumptions and funded generalizations which attend the confirmation of ordinary language claims and the complex and problematic assumptions and hypotheses which attend theoretical claims. That there is no absolute or infallible distinction between "factual" and "theoretical" assertions was obvious even to the earliest positivists. The fact is that even an "observation statement" may, itself, in the course of our attempting to more adequately understand the world, be sacrificed. The difference between "observation statements" and "theoretical statements" is that the former are threatened with abandonment with only minimal frequency, while the latter are regularly open to challenge and more frequently rejected or revised.[28] The former are the products of common experience and are tested daily in our efforts to get on in the world and are consequently well entrenched. None of us has difficulty in our daily circumstances in confirming that we do, in fact, see a man before us. We enjoy no such confidence when asked to determine the manhood and humanity of creatures like *Pithecanthropus erectus* or the *Australopithecines.* Distinctions of that order require the machinery of analytic conceptual schemata that are not the possession of ordinary men, nor the products of ordinary language. We confirm or infirm such identifications only if we can invoke the formalized and standardized language of specialized conceptual schemata.

The "factual questions" to which systematic knowledge makes recourse are the unproblematic and warranted assertions which ordinary language equips us to tender and confirm. "Here yellow borders on blue," "Here two black points coincide," "There is a table," "Nixon won the Presidential election of 1968," are just such uninspiring candidate assertions. Their distinctiveness lies in their immediacy. They are not instances of "pure" experience— since "pure experience" (whatever that might be) permits of *no* distinctions. They are assertions about the macrophysical world made in the ordinary language in which distinctions are made on the basis of recurrent and discriminable recognitors—distinctions which are confirmed and reconfirmed daily in unproblematic practice. Certain observation statements have sufficient stability (even though all remain, in principle, corrigible and variable over time) to permit, at any particular time, tests of the credibility of any complex or theoretical claim. As Nelson Goodman has expressed it:

Credibility may be transmitted from one statement to another through deductive or probability connections; but credibility does not spring from these connections by spontaneous generation. Somewhere along the line some statements, whether atomic sense reports or the entire system or something in between must have initial credibility. So far the argument is sound. . . . Yet all that is indicated is credibility to some degree, not certainty. To say that some statements must be initially credible if any statement is ever to be credible at all is not to say that any statement is immune to withdrawal. For indeed, . . . no matter how strong its initial claim to preservation may be, a statement will be dropped if its retention—along with consequent adjustments in the interest of coherence—results in a system that does not satisfy as well as possible the totality of claims presented by all relevant statements. In the "search for truth" we deal with the clamoring demands of conflicting statements by trying, so to speak, to realize the greatest happiness of the greatest number of them .... That we have probable knowledge, then, implies no certainty but only initial credibility.[29]

It is the initial and unproblematic credibility of factual or observation reports which make them basic to the production of warrants for knowledge claims.

The fact that direct or indirect appeal is made to observation statements to certify instances of knowing indicates why internal consistency, standardized categorization and axiomatization are necessary for the development of complex understandings and explanations.

Consistency is a domain invariant requirement for the simple reason that contradiction renders any collection of formal or material propositions truth functionally sterile. A logic that entertains contradictions could never distinguish between truth and falsity—and would be useless.

Consistency is no less a requirement in the articulation of material truth claims. Unless the propositions in which knowledge claims find expression are internally consistent, we would never be in a position to directly or indirectly confirm or infirm a knowledge claim. Mutually contradictory unproblematic observations could both be taken as confirming and infirming an inconsistent descriptive claim. We would never be in a position to discover anomalies. We would never be surprised by experience, for *any* experience would be compatible with an intrinsically contradictory system. Such a system would be sterile; it could not identify instances where anticipations were falsified by experience. It could neither support truth nor characterize falsity. It would be vacuous. We would know all things because we knew nothing.

Observation statements, while not themselves isolated certainties, are basic to the process of confirming knowledge claims. They themselves, individually and collectively, must be accommodated in systems which host other initially credible or subsequently established assertions and in the process may themselves be sacrificed. But there are no circumstances in which *all* such initial credibilities are sacrificed at one and the same time. Such statements, the products of ordinary language and ordinary public experience, provide relatively stable and relatively independent direct or indirect measures of referential, predictive and explanatory reliability for standardized and formalized languages. Such languages may, in turn, come to partially displace or modify the initially credible assertions of ordinary "thing" language in a complex dialectical process, but at no one time is one language simply and in its entirety displaced by another.

The control exercised by initially credible observations does not depend on their certainty. All that is necessary for establishing evidence conditions is that the credibility enjoyed by observation statements permits us at particular times, and under specifiable circumstances, to challenge the expectations which serve as evidence for the truth and falsity of other and perhaps more complex knowledge claims. When an expectation is not fulfilled, we can choose between rejecting the entrenched or initially credible observation statement which disconfirmed it or rejecting totally, or in part, the claim from which it flowed. The problem in such a situation is to determine which loss would more seriously reduce the aggregate sum of reliable knowledge claims. The rejection of a well-entrenched knowledge claim has impact on the entire system of unproblematic claims. It is for that reason that they are sacrificed with relative rarity. To drop the expectation which flows from the hypothesis advanced by an exploratory inquiry and undertake internal systematic revision of the analytic or quasi-analytic conceptual system or theory which was its source involves less threat to funded knowledge. In most instances the choice is relatively easy. Unproblematic observation statements provide the basic evidential support for complex material knowledge claims. In other cases it may become exceedingly complex to make decisions as to which to jettison—as when we speak of "crises in science." But in all cases, ultimately, what we mean by saying we know something to be the case is to say that we can "describe reality," "state the facts," and "satisfy our expectations," and these are condensed references to recurrent and discriminable aspects of essentially unproblematic public experience.

The fact is that the conceptual schemata and theoretical systems of the standardized and formalized knowledge enterprises we call science are ultimately rejected or accepted on the basis of relatively unproblematic observations. No theoretical system is forever insulated from them. No theoretical system which pretends to apply to the material world can produce a language system capable, in principle, of fully insulating itself against falsification. Anomalies appear in all such systems—observed "facts" which cannot be assimilated without generating inconsistency. Such anomalies can be (and have frequently been) neglected for extended periods of time. But ultimately one must contend with them. The historical result has been the production of an alternate system internally consistent but more powerful. One which can encompass the essentials of the antecedent system, yet extend the range beyond its periphery and which permits more inclusive prediction and greater control over our natural and social environment.[30]

The knowledge claims made by political scientists are not simply the artifacts of their various language styles or conceptual schemata. Initial conceptual schemata may direct the political scientist's attention to particular aspects of his social and political environment. But the assertion that, "The activists within political parties are likely to come from ethnic groups that sanction gregarious activities and/or seek political advancement; from occupations free of regular work schedules and directly benefiting from political activity; and from the dominant social group within the locality being represented," is a complex knowledge claim whose warrant derives from observations made with relative independence from the system of thought which assisted in its formulation. The formulation of such categoric empirical generalizations as "The higher the socioeconomic status, the greater the conservative vote," is a knowledge claim warranted by relatively autonomous observations. Finally, to say that confirming observations require referential precision in order to provide for the congruence, precision and objectivity is a requirement made essential by the warranting process which certifies reliable truth rather than a by-product of the process of discovery.

That discovery should be distinguished from confirmation is evident by the requirements imposed on knowledge claims: such claims must be consistent and have as reference at least some facts which are, in principle, discriminably independent of the system of thought which serves in the process of discovering them. Logical consistency, predictive power, factual reference, descriptive simplicity, and parsimony (elegance or logical simplicity) have traditionally been, and with some variation are, criteria administered to warrant individual truth claims and the theoretical systems they inhabit irrespective of the methods employed in their formulation. Without such tests of adequacy every system of thought would be the equal of any other. Knowledge would have no foothold outside the language in which its claims are made. We would know no more today than our ancestors knew in antiquity—we would only have a different language.

Modern physics not only employs a different language than did Aristotle; it is more competent and more inclusive. It not only represents a change in vocabulary, it permits us to better *understand* and more adequately control our environment. It permits us to explain more adequately and predict with greater precision. Nor has this cumulative growth in understanding been restricted to the natural sciences. We know more about politics than Plato could ever conceive. We know more about politics, in fact, than did our teachers. It seems equally evident that our students will know more about politics than we.

Understanding, Knowledge, and "Insight" in Political Inquiry

That our students will know more about politics than we is essential if they are to better understand it. Understanding implies knowledge and the knowledge implied by understanding is the knowledge obtained by the reasonably well-understood processes of science employing logical and experimental contrivances that can be adequately characterized. That normative elements function in a critical way in the process is equally evident and will be accorded subsequent treatment. None of this is "mystic" nor is any of it predicated on "faith." To make understanding and knowing rest on such dubious adjuncts is to attempt to resolve problems of analysis by conjuring up mysteries.

It is impossible to make much sense out of admonitions that the student of politics must seek out an "understanding" that is similar to the "insight" of the artist or the mystic. Anyone who has ever undertaken a piece of scholarly or experimental research knows that in commencing his work he entertains vague hunches, common-language conceptual schemata, speculative hypotheses, intuitions, and heuristic "frameworks." One inevitably approaches the world with a conceptual patrimony funded in the literature devoted to one's universe of inquiry.

Such hunches and schemata provide some leverage on the subject under scrutiny, but none of them constitute "understanding" of a substantive area of concern. "Hunches" might reduce intrapsychic tension, "frameworks" conceivably provide a foothold on comprehension of a complex environment, and "faith" might well afford one irrepressible conviction. But none of these, in and of themselves, could constitute a truth warrant that would recommend itself to other than the intellectually indigent or the invincibly ignorant. "Hunches," "insights," "intuitions," "imaginings," and acts of "faith" are all strategies employed when one *commences* inquiry or has no substantive or probative evidence that could warrant a confident knowledge claim—they are perhaps necessary preliminaries to systematic inquiry.[31] To imagine that they constitute anything other than the first effort to orientate oneself in a complex and perhaps recalcitrant environment, a first effort to begin to sort out and systematize the constellation of factors that enter into individual and collective human behavior and the institutions through which that behavior finds manifest expression, is to grievously fault one's cognitive obligations.

Certainly the "vision" which the research scientist shares with the mystic, the poet and the artist, the "intuitions" that "indwelling" produces, the "imagination" which he uses in generating speculative hypotheses, does not qualify as "understanding" or "knowing" in any intelligible sense. If there is some putative sense of "understanding" or "knowing" to which such strategies appeal, it is incumbent on those who pretend to exploit it to make clear how they achieve such "extrascientific understanding," what its nature might be, and how they certify its truth. Until that time we will continue to recommend that "understanding" and "knowing" in political science be purchased at the cost of standard techniques of public, neutral and corrigible inquiry characteristic of science broadly conceived, invoking the formal reliabilities of logic, the maximal reliabilities of empirical inquiry, and the plausible judgments characteristic of normative discourse. To conduct such efforts with minimal responsibility requires that inquiry be conducted with language that does not take refuge in semantic vagueness, feckess logic, bootless parable and empty metaphor.

Notes

1. A. Kaplan, *The Conduct of Inquiry* (San Francisco: Chandler, 1964), pp. 259–262.

2. Cf. F. Waismann, *How I See Philosophy* (New York: Macmillan, 1968), pp. 1–38.

3. The primary literature in this area is abundant and no more than basic works could be included in a bibliographical footnote. Those works would include: L. Wittgenstein, *The Blue and Brown Books* (New York: Harper, 1958), *Philosophical Investigations* (New York: Macmillan, 1953), *Remarks on the Foundations of Mathematics* (Cambridge, Mass.: MIT, 1967); J. L. Austin, *Sense and Sensibilia* (New York: Oxford, 1964), *How to Do Things with Words* (New York: Oxford, 1965), *Philosophical Papers* (Oxford: Clarendon, 1964); G. Ryle, *The Concept of Mind* (New York: Barnes and Noble, 1949), *Dilemmas* (Cambridge: Cambridge University, 1960); A. J. Ayer, *The Problem of Knowledge* (New York: St. Martin's, 1956), *Language, Truth and Logic* (New York: Dover, n.d.), *The Foundations of Empirical Knowledge* (London: Macmillan, 1958); R. Carnap, *Logical Syntax of Language* (New York: Humanities, 1951), *Introduction to Semantics* (Cambridge, Mass.: Harvard, 1948), *Meaning and Necessity* (Chicago: University of Chicago, 1956); A Pap, *Semantics and Necessary Truth* (New Haven: Yale, 1958); A. Tarski (with A. Mostowki and R. M. Robinson), *Undecidable Theories* (Amsterdam: North Holland, 1953), "Der Wahrheitsbegriff in den formalisierten Sprachen," *Studia Philosophica,* I (1936), 261–405; P. Suppes, *Introduction to Logic* (Princeton: Van Nostrand, 1957); R. M. Martin, *The Notion of Analytic Truth* (Philadelphia: University of Pennsylvania, 1959); C. S. Morris, "Foundations of the Theory of Signs," in *International Encyclopedia of Unified Science,* ed. O. Neurath, R. Carnap, and C. W. Morris (Chicago: University of Chicago, 1958), pp. 77–138, *Significance and Signification* (Cambridge, Mass.: MIT, 1964); J. J. Katz, *The Philosophy of Language* (New York: Harper, 1966).

4. M. Q. Sibley, "The Limitations of Behavioralism," in J. C. Charlesworth (ed.), *Contemporary Political Analysis* (New

York: Free Press, 1967), pp. 51–71, particularly pp. 52, 56ff., 66f.

5 R. Kirk, "Is Social Science Scientific?" in N. W. Polsby, R. A. Dentler, and P. A. Smith (eds.), *Politics and Social Life* (Boston: Houghton Mifflin, 1963), pp. 60–64.

6 G. Tinder, "The Necessity of Historicism," *American Political Science Review,* LV (1961), pp. 560–565.

7 A. Garma, *The Psychoanalysis of Dreams* (New York: Delta, 1966), p. 21.

8 Cf. E. Nagel, "Methodological Issues in Psychoanalytic Theory," in S. Hook (ed.), *Psychoanalysis, Scientific Method and Philosophy* (New York: New York University, 1959), chap. 2.

9 Some efforts have been made in these directions, but to date not much of Freudian "theory" can support serious inquiry. Cf. R. R. Sears, *Survey of Objective Studies of Psychoanalytic Concepts* (New York: Social Science Research Council, n.d.); P. Madison, *Freud's Concept of Repression and Defense: Its Theoretical and Observational Language* (Minneapolis: University of Minnesota, 1961); J. A. Arlow and C. Brenner, *Psychoanalytic Concepts and the Structural Theory* (New York: International Universities, 1964). For discursive criticisms based on the semantic and syntactical indeterminacy of Freudian "theory," cf. A. Salter,

The Case Against Psychoanalysis (New York: Citadel, 1963); H. K. Wells, *Sigmund Freud: A Pavlovian Critique* (New York: International, 1960); E. R. Pinckney and C. Pinckney, *The Fallacy of Freud and Psychoanalysis* (Englewood Cliffs, N.J.: Prentice-Hall, 1965).

10 F. Waismann, *The Principles of Linguistic Philosophy* (New York: Macmillan, 1965), pp. 348f.

11 I. Scheffler, *Conditions of Knowledge* (Chicago: Scott, Foresman, 1965), pp. 18ff.

12 H. Poincaré, *The Value of Science* (New York: Dover, n.d.), p. 22.

13 M. Polanyi, *Personal Knowledge: Towards a Post-Critical Philosophy* (New York: Harper and Row, 1964), p. 184.

14 M. Polanyi, *The Study of Man* (Chicago: University of Chicago, 1965), p. 28.

15 Polanyi, *Personal Knowledge,* pp. 54f.

16 P. Meehl, "When Shall We Use Our Heads Instead of the Formula," in H. Feigl, M. Scriven and G. Maxwell (eds.), *Minnesota Studies in the Philosophy of Science* (Minneapolis: University of Minnesota, 1958), II, pp. 498–506.

17 Cf. *Parts and Wholes,* ed. D. Lerner (New York: Free Press, 1963).

18 Polanyi, *The Study of Man,* p. 20; J. Maritain, *The Range of Reason* (New York: Scribner's, 1952), p. 8.

[19] Polanyi, *Study of Man,* pp. 33, 34, 57f., 62 79.

[20] Polanyi, *The Tacit Dimension* (Garden City, N.Y.: Doubleday, 1967), p. 16.

[21] Cf. A. P. Griffiths, "Introduction," in A. P. Griffiths (ed.), *Knowledge and Belief* (London: Oxford University, 1967), pp. 8f.

[22] Cf. J. O. Urmson, "Parenthetical Verbs," in A. Flew (ed.), *Essays in Conceptual Analysis* (New York: Macmillan, 1956), chap. 9; R. M. Chisholm, *Perceiving: A Philosophical Study* (Ithaca: Cornell, 1957), pp. 17f.

[23] R. J. Fogelin, *Evidence and Meaning* (New York: Humanities, 1967), pp. 74ff.

[24] J. Austin, "Other Minds," *Philosophical Papers* (Oxford: Oxford University, 1961), p. 53.

[25] A. J. Ayer, *The Problem of Knowledge* (Harmondsworth: Pelican, 1956), p. 35.

[26] Chisholm, *op. cit.,* p. 16; Scheffler, *op. cit.,* p. 65.

[27] Cf. P. Herbst, "The Nature of Facts," in A. Flew (ed.), *Essays in Conceptual Analysis,* chap. 7.

[28] No attempt can be made here to pursue the discussion of "protocol statements" in the literature of the philosophy of science. A. J. Ayer has collected some of the most significant discussions in his *Logical Positivism* (New York: Free Press, 1959). In his connection see the articles by Moritz Schlick and Otto Neurath.

[29] N. Goodman, "Sense and Certainty," *Philosophical Review,* LXI (1952), 160–167.

[30] This touches on a complex and sensitive issue in the philosophy of science and obviously cannot be exhaustively treated here. The reader is referred to the discussion of P. K. Feyerabend's views, which argues a counterthesis to the account suggested here, in R. S. Cohen and M. W. Wartofsky (eds.), *Boston Studies in the Philosophy of Science* (New York: Humanities, 1965), II, pp. 157–261, and D. Shapere, "Meaning and Scientific Change," in R. G. Colodny (ed.), *Mind and Cosmos* (Pittsburgh, University of Pittsburgh, 1966), pp. 41–85. On this issue, cf. H. Feigl, "Philosophical Tangents of Science," in H. Feigl and G. Maxwell (eds.), *Current Issues in the Philosophy of Science* (New York: Holt, Rinehart and Winston, 1961), pp. 1–17.

[31] On the relationship of "intuition" and "imagination" to knowledge claims, cf. M. Bunge, *Intuition and Science* (Englewood Cliffs, N.J.: Prentice-Hall, 1962).

Suggested Readings

Capaldi, Nicholas. *Human Knowledge: A Philosophical Analysis of Its Meaning and Scope.* New York: Pegasus, 1969.

Scheffler, I. *Conditions of Knowledge.* Chicago: Scott, Foresman, 1965.

Stephens, W. N. *Hypotheses and Evidence.* New York: Crowell, 1968.

Wartofsky, M. W. *Conceptual Foundations of Scientific Thought.* New York: Macmillan, 1968. Chapter 10.

9

On Normative Discourse

... I submit that all political problems are in the end ethical problems. And by political problems I mean here both the day to day problems faced by the legislator, and the problems of political theory, of how government itself is to be organized or justified. Politics in both these senses depends, I suggest, on ethics.
Brand Blanshard

Ultimate political goals are most often stated in terms which are so general that hardly anyone—at least among those who are on speaking terms—would deny being committed to them.
Felix Oppenheim

I contend that there are no serious moral problems that cannot in principle be resolved by the practice of rationality.
Robert Olson

"Normative discourse" involves all locutionary acts in and through which we express evaluation, prescribe and proscribe acts and tender reasons for or against evaluations and prescriptions. Its function is appraisive, prescriptive and justificatory. We employ normative language to express shock and indignation, to admit responsibility, to express guilt or remorse, to praise and blame, to appraise or evaluate, to enjoin or to prescribe, to admonish or reprove, to deliberate about and to raise and resolve moral issues. Normative language specifically involves characteristically expressive, appraisive and justificatory constituents.

One of the principal features of normative discourse is its peculiarly "perlocutionary" function. Normative discourse employs locutionary acts calculated (implicitly or explicitly) to exercise some influence and/or to produce some effect; when one evaluates or prescribes, and offers reasons for so appraising or prescribing one can be said, generally, to have intended to exercise some influence over himself or his audience and over his own or their subsequent behavior.[1] This seems to be the reason why meta-ethicists have consistently conceived normative terms to have not only "expressive," but "dynamic" or "persuasive" function as well.

It would seem plausible to maintain that the simple expressive function of language is not, in a significant sense, perlocutionary. That is, if one simply wishes to express his outrage or hurt, it is a matter of complete indifference whether one has an audience or not, or whether they are or are not in any sense influenced by his outrage or hurt. The function of such language is essentially cathartic. Simple expressive language is spontaneous and whatever effects or influence it invokes is unintentional, nondeliberative and non-cognitive. But we rarely, if ever, use *moral* language for such *simple* expressive and cathartic purposes. Generally, we employ normative locutions in a complex deliberate or unconscious attempt to influence our audience (or ourselves)—to prompt them (or ourselves) to reevaluate, to reassess, and to resolve to do better. We *may* remonstrate simply to relieve psychic tension (and in that sense produce some effect), but when we seriously engage in such efforts it is for the purpose of influencing or persuading others or ourselves in a more or less rational and deliberate manner.

Perlocutionary Discourse

In his early analysis of ethical terms and ethical locutions, A. J. Ayer characterized them on the one hand as "*simply* expressions of emotion," as *"simply* evincing . . . moral disapproval," and "*merely* expressing certain moral sentiments," and yet on the other that "they are calculated also to arouse feeling and so to stimulate action."[2] Normative utterances are, in effect, locutionary performances that have, characteristically, perlocutionary intention. We embark upon such performances not *merely* to give expression to attitudes, but to influence the moral sentiments, reasonings and behavior of ourselves and/or our audience.

C. L. Stevenson has similarly suggested that the major function of normative locutions is "to create an influence. Instead of merely describing people's interests they change or intensify them. They recommend an interest in an object, rather than state that the interest already exists." The language user is not describing any particular state of affairs, except insofar as he is "trying to change it by his influence. . . . Thus ethical terms are instruments used in the complicated interplay and readjustment of human interests."[3]

This seems to mark *a* (if not *the*) significant distinction between normative and descriptive (or empirical) discourse. Descriptive discourse is not *essentially* perlocutionary; it is *constative* or simply or essentially cognitive. That is to say while it is true that declaring, asserting, opining, affirming, reporting, describing and explaining are generally undertaken, for example, to effect communication and in principle all such undertakings are implicitly intersubjective, successful communication is not *essential* to such locutionary performances—they are as successful, *cognitively,* when we rehearse our knowledge in privacy as when we communicate to a constituency. Furthermore constative utterances, utterances which make truth claims, may or may not influence our or anyone else's attitudes or behavior nor is its essential purpose to do so. We have already suggested that we may know that certain claims are fully warranted—true—and yet not act on them. They are nonetheless true.

Such a distinction strikes us, *prima facie,* as odd. If constative utterances need not successfully communicate, and whatever truths they assert need not necessarily influence behavior, why on earth would they be of interest to us?

The key to the solution is contained in the question. Strictly cognitive utterances are of interest to us because they are, in fact, of interest to us. Nor is this simple punning. If it is a tautology, it is an instructive tautology. Like, "Business is business," it conceals an argument—it is, itself, an elliptical argument. We are interested in truth because truth provides us with predictive advantage in the social and natural world—and it is in our interest in terms of welfare benefits to have that leverage. That is to say, we help to satisfy elemental welfare needs by attending to truth. Not a few philosophers have alluded to just such an interest in characterizing the utility, purpose, or function of truth. The allusion is to the satisfaction of primitive and elemental needs—the need for survival, for example. If the individual or group had no interest in survival in any form (natural or supernatural), it would be difficult to conceive of any interest they might have in warranted truth. People concern themselves with truth because truth has proven itself to be one of the most effective tools for enhancing our capacity to survive, as well as effecting our multifold purposes, in the world. In order to satisfy the multiplicity of felt needs, elemental needs, safety needs, love needs, esteem needs, the need for the preconditions of need fulfillments (equity, opportunity, knowledge), among others, truth functions in a critical and irreplaceable fashion.[4]

What this implies is that our concern with constative utterances— our concern with the success of communication and with acting on the basis of warranted truth claims—is predicated upon an irreducible normative assumption. We feel that communication *should* be successful and that courses of action *should* be the consequence of a true assessment of facts, assessed potentials and probabilities. In *feeling* that communication *should* be successful and that men *should* act on the basis of warranted truth, we have added a perlocutionary dimension to a linguistic performance. Men *should* communicate and *should* act on the basis of truth rather than falsehood and conjecture because successful communication and truth serve the interests of need satisfactions of a variety of kinds, ranging from the satisfaction of elemental wants to derived or ideal wants such as justice, goodness and beauty. A value, in effect, is the measure of a satisfaction of an elemental or a derived want[5] and we seek to satisfy wants effectively and expeditiously. Truth serves instrumentally and expeditiously in satisfying individual and collective, elemental or derived, needs.

This is hardly more than was said by David Hume a long time ago. Constative utterances assert truths. Hume went on to say:

> But where the truths . . . are indifferent and beget no desire or aversion, they can have no influence on conduct and behavior . . . . What is intelligible, what is evident, what is probable, what is true procures only the cool assent of the understanding, and, gratifying a speculative curiosity, puts an end to our researches. Extinguish all the warm feelings and prepossessions in favor of virtue, and all disgust and aversion to vice; render men totally indifferent toward these distinctions, and morality is no longer a practical study, nor has any tendency to regulate our lives and actions.[6]

Hume accounted for what has been called the "felt motivational force" of normative discourse[7] by attributing that force to the prevalence of positive or negative *sentiment* generated by felt need. The dynamic quality that makes normative utterances perlocutionary, capable of influencing our behavior and the behavior of our audience, arises out of those "affections" that are constitutive of the "original fabric and formation of the human mind."

It is a rare philosopher (I can think of none offhand) who would argue that truth and communication are *intrinsic* goods, that they are valuable in and of themselves. They are, at best, *instrumental* goods, serving to satisfy some felt want. If men did not choose to survive, did not aspire to the satisfactions that attend the esteem accorded by their reference community, did not glory in acclaim and admiration, did not feel that interaction and interpersonal exchange somehow enhanced their fulfillment of self, it is difficult, if not impossible, to conceive why they would seriously occupy themselves with truth and successful communication. In effect, truth determination is an instrumental good; it serves in the satisfaction of a variety of unproblematic individual and collective human wants.

Men are concerned with normative issues because such issues have immediate or mediate bearing on some real or fictive human need. Since the decline of religion the only defensible set of adequacy criteria for appraisive ascription, the issuance of recommendations and prescriptions, are complex compounds of welfare and satisfaction variables of the population to which normative discourse is addressed. "Values in the extended sense consist in or arise from needs and wants in the narrow sense."[8] Thus Ralph Barton Perry suggests that *"a thing—any thing—has value, or is valuable, in the original and generic sense when it is the object of an interest—any interest. Or, whatever is object of interest is ipso facto valuable."*[9]

The analysis of characteristically ethical terms as they are employed in political science or anywhere else involves ultimate reference to some individual or collective, primary or derived, human interest. All attributions of "goodness," by way of illustration, involve the suggestion that the object or subject to which attribution is made in some way ministers to human want or interest. To suggest that something ministers to human want but is not good can be satisfactorily construed to mean that something may be calculated to satisfy some human interest but at the same time violate some other countervailing human interest—immediate satisfaction, for example, as opposed to long-range or ultimate satisfaction.[10]

Should such preliminary suggestions be convincing one understands why normative discourse is conceived as essentially perlocutionary: interest implies sentiments of attraction and aversion, and private interests overlap and intersect in complex patterns with public interests, short-range interests conflict with long-range interests, interests conflict with each other, and primary interests conflict with derived interests. To engage in normative discourse therefore is to attempt to resolve differences, reduce conflict, make interests congruent, convince or be convinced, persuade or be persuaded. Normative discourse is essentially dynamic, calculated to be persuasive, intentionally and deliberately undertaken to influence judgment and reform behaviors. A constative utterance succeeds in doing something when we have succeeded in *saying* something: we describe, explain and predict. A perlocutionary performance is normally conceived as producing certain consequential effects upon the feelings, judgments or actions of ourselves or our audience by *doing* something: warning, recommending, commending, evaluating, reproving, convincing, prescribing, and commanding.[11]

We would like our constative performances to be successful, to communicate and convince. But that is a consequence of the fact that we *feel* that communicating and convincing serve some human interest. When we are asked why we think communication and truth are significant, we embark on normative considerations—and such an activity is perlocutionary. We tender, rebut or accept, justificatory argument. We enter into normative discourse. Men *should* communicate and they *should* abandon faulted truth claims. Such convictions are clearly normative and require normative vindications to warrant them.

Normative Argument

The vindications that warrant normative utterances include both constative utterances (true descriptions, explanations, probabilities and predictions) and appeals to attitudes or interests. It is the latter which provides the dynamic force of normative language. What this implies is that normative disagreement can mark a difference not only in *factual disagreement,* disagreement concerning the truth of constative or declarative propositions, but *disagreement in sentiment*—and characteristically, in *attitude.* If normative discourse necessarily invokes interest in order to render itself "dynamic," to deploy "felt motivational force," any normative argument must explicitly or implicitly involve other than appeals to warranted analytic or synthetic truth claims in order to function successfully. It is this consideration, a *metaethical* and *pragmatic* consideration, a consideration in the informal logic of normative language, that has forced the abandonment of all forms of naturalism and has opened the gap now identified as the "is/ought dichotomy."

Since the time of Hume normative philosophers have recognized that no recitation of "facts," constative utterances, can in and of themselves generate a normative conclusion. No catalogue of factual or logical assertions, no matter how extensive, is capable of generating a conclusion in which the prescriptive "ought" legitimately figures. There have been any number of attempts to bridge the logical gap between constative and perlocutionary utterances, but none have, to date, been recognized as successful.[1][2] Nonetheless, some political philosophers and many political "theorists" continue to argue as though normative discourse involved no special problems. Thus Herbert Marcuse's attempted vindication of "revolutionary violence" turns on the supposition that the facts of history, the study of past revolutions and their successes and failures, license enjoinments, injunctions, proscriptions, prescriptions, recommendations, and urgings. He argues that "good" and "right" be *defined* in terms of "human freedom" and "happiness." "'Good' and 'right' . . . mean serving to establish, to promote, or to extend human freedom and happiness. . . ." Then he proceeds to indicate that, as a *matter of fact,* "historical revolutions" were "usually advocated and started in the name of freedom . . ." and that they have "demonstrably" served to enhance "freedom." He concludes that we are thereby "justified" in invoking violence (since it is a historic *fact* that established classes never voluntarily surrender their privileges) to further "freedom"—that one "should," if necessary, provoke suffering and turmoil to serve such laudable ends. The "end," he informs us, "justifies the means."[13]

There are any number of difficulties with this kind of argument, only one of which concerns us at the moment. Even if we grant all the premisses of Marcuse's argument—we must accept his *stipulative definition* of "good" and "right," which, conjoined with his pronouncements on revolutions and their effects, would vindicate our undertaking, and justify the claim that we "should" undertake the course of action he recommends. But no set of analytic statements conjoined with descriptive utterances, in and of themselves, ever imposes an obligation or provides a justification, unless the analytic statements *imply,* by definition, normative elements. Thus Marcuse defines anything that enhances "freedom" and "happiness" as "good" and "right." If this is not to be simply a bald pronouncement on his part, *he must present an independent vindication in support of such a definition.* It is clearly *not* self-evident that "good" and "right" mean "serving to establish, to promote, or to extend human freedom and happiness."

Once this is understood, it is obvious that whatever success Marcuse's argument enjoys is obtained by *imposing* a definition on his constituency. Why would anyone be compelled to accept *his* definition of "good" and "right"? If we recognize that definitions are empty in the sense that they do not tell us anything about the world, but rather inform us about *how someone intends to employ the language,* our obvious reprise is to simply dismiss the proffered definition unless *reasons* can be given in its support. There are any number of mutually exclusive ways of defining "good" and "right." Hedonists have defined "good" as "pleasure." Religionists have defined "good" as anything undertaken in accordance with God's will. Lenin defined the "good" in terms of the class interests of the proletariat. Gentile, as the philosopher of Fascism, defined the "good" as that which serves the realization of man's potential humanity. Hitler defined the "good" as that which fulfilled man's evolutionary purpose. Without such antecedent *persuasive definitions* the recitation of whatever facts is to no purpose. Such definitions *proclaim* what they are in effect obliged to *establish*.

We all intuitively grant that once we *know* what is "good" or "right" we *ought* to do it. (What else *ought* we to do—but that which is "good" or "right"?) We use terms like "good" and "right" precisely because their use permits us to mobilize our own energy and the energy of others in the service of some task. In order to effectively accomplish such mobilization we must stipulatively define what we take "good" and "right" to be. The question that should concern us is: how do we vindicate stipulative use? Without vindication such pronouncements would be idio-syncratic—statements of each author's felt preference. A felt pref-erence, unfortunately, can never serve to support a normative argument that involves the interests of others. This is not to say that men cannot be influenced in their behavior by a variety of tech-niques: blandishments, threats, violence, surgical insult, drugs, ritual incantations, spurious arguments, rank falsehoods, and the imposition of arbitrary restrictions on their language use. But the only legitimate technique that can be employed to influence the behavior of rational agents, if we are serious in our normative enterprise, is *the provision of compelling public arguments*. When a scientist recommends that space be defined in terms of a four-dimensional continuum, he is not arbitrarily imposing a definition upon us. He exhibits the purpose of such redefinition. When the anatomist defines a whale as a "mammal" rather than a "fish," his recommendation is predicated on the fact that such a redefinition permits a systematization of zoological classification that efficiently and effectively organizes an array of existing knowledge. Such a redefinition provides more substantive descriptive, predictive and theoretical advantage than any alternative definition. The redefinition in such instances is anything but arbitrary and its vindication is eminently rational.

If we are intent upon redefining the "good," no *arbitrary* stipulation will do. If the redefinition of the "good" is calculated to influence behavior, our fiduciary responsibilities as rational and consequently moral agents, compel us to advance *public reasons* for thinking that some policy, which is the entailed consequence of accepting our stipulative normative definitions, is preferable to any alternate policy. Although normative discourse may commence with feelings, reason is its ultimate arbiter and serves to produce attitudes—and attitudes, unlike sentiments and feelings, are sustained dispositions for which we can be, and are, held responsible.

Such an account is admittedly at once a commonplace and a curiosity. In our more lucid moments we all tend to accept the injunction that normative disagreement should be resolved by reasoned argument. In our moments of desperation (after we have been fruitlessly involved in normative dispute) we hold that since all normative disagreements involve human sentiment and interest in some critical way, those disagreements ultimately involve a recourse to feelings, and since feelings are eminently personal we make recourse to talk about "ultimate values," which are "indefeasible" and "invincible."

One need but review some of the recent literature in political science to discover instances of such desperate strategies. Fairly recently R. C. Pratt insisted that one's normative commitments rest ultimately on "primary values," which are the "core beliefs of one's ethical and political value system" and "for which we feel no justification is required and for which none can be offered." It follows as a consequence that "a disagreement over primary values cannot be resolved by reason"—an argument repeated with approval by Mulford Sibley.[14] Vernon Van Dyke, in turn and in one place, insists that "ultimate values must be regarded as self-justifying; they are simply postulated."[15]

The curious feature about such an account is that it is advanced by representatives of completely divergent points of view. Pratt suggests "faith" as the source of "ultimate values"—Sibley appeals to "prescientific" or "tacit" knowings—and both Pratt and Sibley oppose "positivism" in political science. Van Dyke, on the other hand, identifies his account with the "positivistic" persuasion. Both "positivists," "fideists," and "traditional" political theorists thus consciously or unconsciously conspire to convince us that reason has no leverage over "ultimate values." In effect (some tacitly and some explicitly), all recommend refuge in some form of transrationalism to resolve normative disagreement.

Other than the fact that whatever is true in such an account is trivial and whatever is wrong is outrageously wrong, one is advised to consider its pragmatic implications. If ultimate values are the consequence of commitments made on personal "faith," or are simple "assumptions" or "postulates," forever insulated against reason, how does one undertake to resolve normative disagreement? One can only have recourse to blandishments, threats, violence, surgical insult, drugs, psychotherapy, ritual incantations, specious argument, rank falsehoods, or the imposition of arbitrary definitions.

What is true, but trivial, about such accounts is the suggestion that there are some "primary values" which lend normative force to any collection of factual assertions. These values generally make their appearance in the form of words having high emotive salience, "survival," "freedom," "happiness," "democracy," "fulfillment," "justice," as well as an inordinately long list of similar candidate expressions. All such terms (and they are context and time dependent —some signs will have greater emotive or persuasive force at one time and in one context rather than another) possess the faculty of engaging interest, invoking sentiment. That is, in fact, their function. They are included in the catalogue of normative terms because they possess that faculty. Such terms constitute the *unproblematic values* which engage disputants in normative discourse and provide the dynamic force which sustains the exchange and permits the transit from the "is" to the "ought."

The Nature of "Primary Values"

It makes very little *prima facie* sense to ask why one thinks that "survival," "happiness" or "freedom" is to be pursued. Scholars, philosophers and humanists of all types and persuasions, for all and sundry times, have advanced "survival," "happiness," "freedom," or "pleasure" as "primary or ultimate values"—and we do not, in fact, resist according value to such terms. They do, as a matter of fact, engage our interest. What might one oppose to such "primary values": death, unhappiness, slavery or pain? No thinker in history has ever argued that extinction, unhappiness, slavery and pain are *intrinsically* good.[16] Terms like "existence," "happiness," "freedom," and "pleasure" are terms that invoke *general approbation*—"good" being the most general term of approbation in our language. Terms like "unhappiness," "slavery," "pain," "death," "vice," "bad," are terms that elicit disapprobation. Such terms are invoked because, in and of themselves, they elicit sentiments of *approval* or *disapproval*. Their meaning is all but exhausted in their emotive function. Their principal function is perlocutionary; they are calculated to engage our positive or negative interest, to influence and produce effect. In some cases their use is exhaustively characterized by their very dynamic or persuasive use. Thus Henry Kariel suggests that we can learn a great deal about political values from existential psychology, for it teaches us that men "should be themselves," that their decisions should be "authentic," in order to organize human efforts around "undefined freedom." If we understand such "values," he suggests, we will bend every effort to "enlarge the sphere of freedom."[17]

If one considers such arguments, one finds that no constative affirmations are made or implied. What else should men be if not themselves? How else should they behave except "authentically"? If "freedom" is not defined, how can we be seriously obliged to enlarge upon it? In effect we are all prepared to opt for "existence," "freedom," "fulfillment," "happiness," "authenticity," "being oneself," "pursuing the good life," but in having so opted we know nothing more than before we so opted. Nor would knowledge that one's opponent in normative disagreement opted for such "primary values" be informative in any substantive sense. The rather simpleminded distinction between Communists, Fascists and democrats, for example, that rests on the assumption that they individually or severally entertain different "primary values," is simply false. When Barrington Moore suggests that Fascists "violently" reject "humanitarian ideals, including any notion of potential human equality," he is simply historically wrong.[18] Early in his youth Benito Mussolini insisted that his "primary value," a value that he entertained throughout his political career, was that "man should fulfill himself as man (*sii uomo*)"[19]—clearly a "humanitarian" ideal. Giovanni Gentile, the philosopher of Fascism by Mussolini's choice, invoked the same injunction forty years later. He also added that man is the "end," the goal of all enterprise, things were only means. All men, for Gentile, were equal denizens of Kant's "kingdom of ends." Furthermore, he insisted that Fascism was the culmination of humanism, the fulfillment of complete humanism.[20]

It is simply not true that normative disagreement in the political arena is predicated on different "core," "root" or "ultimate values," Neither Fascists, National Socialists, Marxists nor democrats opt for different values in the privative and primitive sense suggested in the account offered by Pratt and Sibley. Lenin, for example, in offering justificatory argument for his political values, made ultimate appeal to his intention to create a "paradise on earth" for men—an unproblematic value. Hitler argued that his intentions were to satisfy man's deepest aspirations—and every issue of the *Nationalsozialistische Monatshefte* carried the term "Freedom!" on its masthead—again the ultimate appeal was to unproblematic "primary" values.

Such commitments to "ultimate values" are simply too common, if not universal, to suggest that they constitute the source of real differences in serious normative dispute. Such commitments give us no cognitive advantage in discriminating between candidates, they afford no predictive leverage in anticipating outcomes.[21] They are explained by having a rudimentary comprehension of how such terms of positive commendation function in normative discourse *as a technique to engage interest*. They are terms of high emotional salience and their use *psychologically* compels our attention; they engage our interest because they tap affirmative sentiments. In and of themselves they are noncognitive—which is *not* to say that normative dispute is noncognitive. It simply means that in order to engage interest one must tap a sentiment and characteristically normative terms are conjured up to perform just such a perlocutionary function. Such terms function in a critical and irreducible manner in normative discourse—but it does not mean that normative disputes are reducible to such terms. If we are serious about engaging in dispute, we will have to undertake something more than the rehearsal of "ultimate values" or the issuance of bromides.

We will have to assume that our opponent understands the rudimentary and informal logic of normative discourse. We *assume* that he is engaged by terms like "survival," "freedom," "happiness," "fulfillment," "justice," "authenticity," "right," and "good." As a matter of historic fact no political philosopher has ever failed to be engaged by such terms. There has been no thinking Fascist, National Socialist, Marxist, segregationist, democrat, "progressive," or "conservative," who has not been positively engaged by such expressions—which more than suggests that disagreement lies elsewhere. If "primary values" refer to "feelings" and "sentiments," the fact need not particularly distress us. The fact is that we all share common sentiments about "primary or ultimate values." There are perhaps cases where an individual is, in fact, sincerely committed to death, destruction and maximizing pain. But I suspect that we would (with good reason) dismiss such an individual as the proper subject for psychotherapy rather than identifying him as a *bona fide* disputant in normative discourse.

The Resolution of Normative Disagreement

Serious normative discussion commences when we offer *reasoned stipulations* for the suasive terms employed to engage our interests, and when we *argue* that some one or another course of action furthers or diminishes the potential satisfaction of "survival," "freedom," "happiness," "fulfillment" or what-have-you. But such disputes are intelligible and intelligent. We offer reasonably clear argued *definitions* of terms—we offer *reasons* for according oneself with such a definition—and then we collect *evidence* to support our conviction that one rather than another policy, one rather than another list of priorities, furthers our *clear, public* intentions. We ask our opponent what he conceives as prerequisite to "survival," what he means by "freedom" or "fulfillment." If the terms go "undetermined" or "undefined," any further discussion is futile. One test of justificatory argument of any sort is internal consistency. Contradictory systems, as we have seen, are sterile; they are inherently incapable of characterizing either truth or falsity. Whenever a normative theorist pretends to hold that internal contradiction does not destroy a justificatory argument, the search for truth is faulted and a calculated or unconscious deception has begun. Without definition and reasonable specificity no significant discussion is possible.

When we are enjoined to "enlarge the sphere of freedom," and are then informed that freedom is "undefined," we recognize that that injunction is of no account. Freedom, being undefined, could never be identified. We cannot do that which we are, in principle, incapable of doing. If the injunction that we are morally obliged to do something is to be binding, it must entail, minimally, that we are capable of knowing what we are to do and having done it, knowing that we have, in fact, done it. This requires a reasonably specific definition of what is to be done. Only then would we know what counts as successful and faulted performance, when we have satisfied a moral obligation. Only a reasonably clear characterization of what we are enjoined to do begins to put us under the obligation to do it. Thus it is not particularly helpful to define "freedom" by taking refuge in similarly obscure, complex and undefined emotive expressions. Thus when Marcuse defines "freedom" as the "good," and the "right," or as the "possibility of a fulfilled existence worthy of man," or tells us that our "positive" ideal should be a "free and rational future society" which is, in principle, "beyond definition and determination," we are little better off than when we started.[22] We are incapable of identifying what is *not* conducive to the society Marcuse recommends unless we can define "freedom" and "rationality" with some specificity, and unless we tender factual determinations concerning what *is* necessary and/or sufficient for their realization in fact.

If we observe how normative discussion actually proceeds, we will notice that some unproblematic value or values are, at its commencement, invoked: i.e., "freedom," "integrity," "fulfillment," or "survival." Then such terms are defined with some precision in terms of physiological, psychological, and emotional needs—empirical matters. No recourse to argument is made to engage the audience's approval of the unproblematic values initially invoked. Terms like "survival," "freedom," "integrity," and "justice" are, in fact, employed because they possess *unproblematic* positive emotive force. In this sense all contemporary normative theorists implicitly or explicitly accept a rudimentary emotive theory of normative meaning. We assume that our audience will be disposed to approve of survival, freedom and justice. If they opt for death, slavery and injustice, we dismiss them, and rightly so, as not understanding the simple informal logic of moral dispute. If they are serious, they are not opting for death, pain, slavery, and the lack of integrity. What they are attempting to suggest is that they refuse our definitions—and what we hold to be freedom and justice are slavery and injustice. On such occasions we are engaged in a dispute about alternative definitions, for definitions like all analytic assertions, are invoked to serve some purpose—they rest on a rationale. If we wish to vindicate our proffered definition, we must provide that rationale for *public* scrutiny.[23]

Normative discussion either commences with a statement of unproblematic values—or preliminary probes are made until common sentiments are tapped. The "primary values" to which some political theorists resort are general and unproblematic values, so general and so unproblematic that hardly anyone would resist being committed to them. No one seriously resists identification with "freedom," "fulfillment," "justice," "peace," "beauty," "right," and "good." Serious discussion commences, in fact, when one seeks to define such terms of general approbation, when one attempts to establish that one such value should have priority over the realization of another, when one attempts to articulate a logically coherent collection of propositions (including warranted descriptive truth claims, lawlike assertions and probability estimates) which vindicate the prescriptions, proscriptions, recommendations and warnings which constitute the moralist's stock-in-trade. In effect, serious discussion commences when the "primary values" invoked to generate interest are unpacked *cognitively:* one scrutinizes vindications offered for proposed definitions, tests the logical consistency of argument, assesses the evidence mustered to support factual claims and probability statements, and publicly weighs alternatives in terms of projected total outcomes. Once this has been accomplished, one has assumed an *attitude*—a disposition to behave in a reasoned and consistent manner with respect to a reasonably well-defined range of alternatives.

No one, for example, would resist the prescription that human needs (broadly conceived and empirically characterized) be satisfied whenever and wherever possible, and when and where they do not conflict with other individual or collective, immediate or derived needs. But any such prescription is to little account unless some characterization of "human needs" and their "fulfillment" is given in terms of public evidence and argument. Assertions about "human needs" must be supported by reliable evidence. In this respect political theorists, and moralists in general, have learned a great deal from the organized body of information provided by systematic inquiry into human physiology, biology and psychology. Such information is absolutely essential in attempting to indicate what "primary values" like "justice," "equality," "freedom," and "fulfillment" might effectively mean.

That practicing moralists of almost every persuasion have become aware of such considerations is evidenced, for example, by the "secularization" of religious and political morality. It has become increasingly the case that "morality" is unpacked in terms of human welfare needs, individual and collective, immediate or derived. When we resist fulfilling some human need, what is required is a justification of why we resist. To attempt that, we appeal to some other collection of unproblematic values (in terms of alternate human needs) that might conceivably be sacrificed in attempting such satisfaction ("liberty" as opposed, for example, to "equality"). There are, in effect, intersecting "demand curves." Such curves are not, in general, explicitly formulated either for individual or collective wants. Nor do they regularly or even frequently take on the hierarchical form suggested by those theorists who see "life styles" predicated on a single value or a single specific set of "core" or "root" values. Value "systems" are not, in general, hierarchical. They are more like nets, interconnected sets of propositions founded on sentiment and grounded in facts about the world in which human activity and competition between needs take place.

Values arise from needs and wants. These needs and wants can be either elemental (like "survival") or derived (like "justice"). Each manifests itself in a distinct, but mutually interactive, demand disposition. It is clear that in some contexts survival will take priority while in others men will die for justice (however construed). No simple hierarchy of values would satisfy such variations in performance. Secondary, instrumental, or "extrinsic" values are those which maximize the efficiency of our attempts to satisfy primary wants or needs.[24] Here the procedure is decisively rational. We are dealing with means to relatively specific ends and the ultimate arbiter here is evidence, adequately collected, responsibly processed, and competently interpreted. The methods of adjudication in such instances are clearly those developed in standard science.

Thus when Erich Fromm enjoins us to seek out "freedom" and "integrity," he characterizes them as imperative needs—certified by evidence that indicates that if one does not satisfy them one courts "insanity." He further admonishes us that if we are "domineering" or "submissive" rather than possessed of "integrity," we will "never" find "satisfaction."[25] These are all empirical knowledge claims and they are warranted by meeting the evidence conditions that govern normal science. Is it *true,* in fact, that if some specific needs of man ("freedom" and "integrity") are not satisfied, he will become insane? Is it *true* that the effort to dominate or the disposition to be submissive *never* leads to satisfaction? In order to establish the warrant for such unrestricted descriptive claims one must know what kind of analytic distinctions and synthetic evidence are required. We accept or rebut such arguments on their *cognitive* merits. We become involved in such arguments because we sense the approval which attends the concern for fulfilling human needs or wants (avoiding insanity and attaining satisfaction). But the emotive component no more makes such discussion "subjective" or "idiosyncratic" than does the recognition that men undertake the search for truth as a consequence of an "exploratory instinct" (to use Pavlov's unhappy expression) or a dispositional "thirst for knowledge."

We no more *demonstrate* the truth of our moral convictions or the merits of our value priorities than we *demonstrate* the truth of our descriptive utterances. Both rest on analytic *and* descriptive adequacy criteria—and demonstration is appropriate, as we have seen, only in the former domain. Our commitment to descriptive truth, moral judgment, or normative priorities is never licensed by a demonstration—it is a commitment which is both fallible and corrigible. But to have said that is *not* to have said that moral scepticism is any more defensible than scepticism about our knowledge of the object world. We realize that we can never be *logically* certain that our perceptions reveal features of the object world or that inductive procedures are invincibly incorrigible, but that does not mean that we therefore have no reason to affirm that our sensory organs afford knowledge of discriminable features of the object world. In order to affirm that we know a great deal about the world we inhabit, it is *not* necessary to demonstrate that some "observation statements" are indefeasibly or logically true. We, in fact, entertain systems of thought in which certain initial credibilities are funded. Any constituent proposition in that initial deposit of funded empirical credibilities can, in principle, be rejected for good reason. In making new affirmations those entrenched credibilities may be displaced. But we *do* get on in the world—we *do* tender explanations which afford insight into predictions, we *do* anticipate outcomes successfully, and our control over nature and ourselves does expand. We have every reason to believe that we have knowledge about the world of experience—even though we cannot license that knowledge with demonstrations. Demonstrations are appropriate to one restricted domain of discourse; it is a mistake to attempt to impose adequacy criteria appropriate to one domain over the whole universe of discourse.

Similarly, our funded and unproblematic values, that one should fulfill human needs, satisfy human wants, and their cognate imperatives, are eminently credible. Any of them, of course, however they are characterized, and whatever priorities we assign them at any particular time and in any particular situation, might be subsequently modified or rejected for good reason. But that does not mean that we do not have warranted moral convictions any more than the fact that every scientific proposition is, in principle, corrigible means that we have no knowledge about the world. Moral scepticism is no more defensible, and is certainly more pernicious, than epistemological scepticism.[26]

We know, with as much reason as we have for knowing anything, that pain inflicted for no purpose is bad, that war and oppression, in and of themselves, are hateful and wrong. If someone advocates inflicting pain, it can only be because he holds that pain is productive of some ultimate welfare effect. When Hitler opted for the mass immolation of the Jews, it was not because he argued that pain and death were intrinsic goods. Hitler argued that the Jews, as a "race" or "Volk" (he alternated between these two distinct characterizations), were *all* purveyors of destruction and, if permitted to survive, would not only destroy culture, but humanity itself. His appeal was not to the intrinsic goodness of massacring Jews or inflicting pain, but to an unproblematic value, the enhancement of culture, or more fundamentally, survival. The assertion that the Jews were harbingers of death and destruction was a *factual claim,* to be accepted or rejected on the basis of its objective and evidential merit. The immolation of men through specific design is *never* self-recommending and, in fact, Hitler never argued that it was. Hitler never argued that killing was intrinsically good. He argued that war was one of the techniques "Nature" employed to insure "survival of the fittest," those who would support and foster culture and increase man's collective survival potential—and these were cognitive claims. The rationale for war followed the same informal logic as the rationale for the extermination of the Jews.

The informal logic of such arguments is evidenced in the work of professionals. H. L. A. Hart, for example, has argued for a "minimum content of natural law" and means no more by his argument than that there are a number of self-recommending values which are *prima facie* engaging. He mentions, for example, survival.

Given survival as an aim, there are a number of entailed or derivative considerations which themselves rest on contingent knowledge about men and the world: the *fact* that human beings are vulnerable, the *fact* that they enjoy approximate equality (no individual is so much more powerful than others that he is able, without cooperation, to confidently prevail), the *fact* that altruism is a limited dispositional property, that resources are, in *fact*, limited, the *fact* that men's knowledge is imperfect and their will deficient.[27] Survival is an unproblematic and self-recommending value and we all, in general, harbor sentiments approving it. Which does not mean that as an unproblematic value it can never be brought under scrutiny. But the burden of argument is on the opponent of survival. The answer to the question, "Why survive?" is "Why not?" The fact that survival as a value cannot be demonstrated as impeccably true does not mean that it is not as well-entrenched as the principle of induction. No one has successfully demonstrated that inductive arguments are logically impeccable. When the sceptic indicates as much, our reply is "What do you suggest we employ if not induction?" Demonstration, logical impeccability, is a domain specific acceptability criterion. It is appropriate to formal discourse. It is not appropriate to all constative or normative discourse. We make a corrigible and fallible, but reasoned case, for empirical knowledge claims. We make the same sort of case for normative ones.

We face the object world with certain entrenched descriptive and normative credibilities at our disposal. We accept the principle of induction unless we have reason to reject it. We order our experience with considerable success by entertaining it as an antecedent assumption which we have every reason to credit. Similarly, we face the domain of normative discourse possessed of well-entrenched and credible values. We have at our disposal a number of well-entrenched values: survival, happiness, fulfillment, and freedom, among others. Any or all can at one time or another be brought under scrutiny—and our oppenent will have to argue that, in some sense, nonsurvival, unhappiness, debasement and slavery are to be sought or supported. But it is evident that neither nonsurvival, unhappiness, debasement or oppression can be advanced as self-recommending values. A case must be made for suicide, for example, or for the extrinsic or instrumental value of unhappiness, oppression or the loss of freedom. Such arguments would be either idiosyncratic—applying to special instances (as in the case of suicide), or themselves shown to rest on other unproblematic values (when we argue that "unhappiness ennobles," or "imprisonment rehabilitates"). A normative vindication must at some point tap unproblematic values—and such values are *universalizable* in principle. Being universalizable such values are objects of public appraisal. Being objects of public scrutiny, the instrumental value of reason, as an ultimate recourse in normative dispute, becomes obvious. Normative discussion arises from the interaction and competition of *prima facie* and self-recommending wants or needs within historic and contextual objective constraints and resource limitations. There is nothing intrinsically good or evil about any entrenched values, and operating in the world may lead to a subsequent reevaluation of any one of them in terms of which original wants are transformed or abandoned. Nothing outside the object world and the world of human reason is necessary for this process to begin and to proceed apace once men become engaged.

There is nothing intrinsically good in satisfying wants or needs; one simply doesn't know what else to satisfy. One has a good reason for satisfying a need or want because it is a *felt* need or want. One may discover overriding reasons for not satisfying one want or another because wants and needs are lodged in an interactive and complex constellation—serving one need may impair the fulfillment of another. If it is a fact that men have a variety of needs and wants that can only be satisfied in association—the entailed commitments that follow include a host of what used to be called "*prima facie* obligations": promise-keeping, gratitude, integrity, beneficence and so forth.

Each individual has at his disposal an elaborate network of values developed under the impact of special and contextual constraints and circumstances. As long as he can pretend that his decisions are strictly self-regarding, his ultimate appeal may be to *preferences,* wants and needs and satisfactions that are personal. If there are any such self-regarding acts, personal preferences would be their vindication. But most (if not all) normative discussion involves the wants and interests of others as well as oneself, and arguments calculated to resolve them must appeal to more general values and in the last analysis universalizable nonproblematic values. These values tend to be, by the very character of the generality, cognitively empty. This is the merit of the emotive analysis of value terms.

But as a matter of fact we never argue about these "primary values," and they never constitute the grounds for accepting one course of action rather than another. What we do argue about are the definitions to be accorded self-recommending values like "survival," "freedom," "happiness," and "fulfillment." This taps the formal language domain and is governed by its adequacy criteria. Or we may argue about *the* most effective and efficient means of achieving ends once we have agreed on their adequate characterization—or we may argue about what one policy rather than another implies with respect to total outcomes. All this taps the empirical or descriptive, as well as the formal, language domains and is subject to their conjoint domain specific evidence conditions.

Normative argument is difficult to resolve primarily because there are any number of unproblematic values that can be individually and collectively entertained. Most normative priorities, the option for one policy rather than another, involve a host of enormously complex questions concerning possible outcomes, anticipated costs and conceivable implications. In effect, normative arguments are difficult to resolve not because they are normative, but because they are enormously complex. What one requires for their resolution is best evidence, for subtending all but an exiguous number, are universalizable unproblematic values. What one requires is not mystic insight, or "humanity," but *tolerance*, a disposition to enter into involved and detailed inquiry, an indisposition to invoke hasty generalization, exploit hyperbolic and condensed language, and a recognition that the only legitimate recourse in dispute is reasoned judgment.

Normative Argument and Cognitive Activity

Normative argument commences with an appeal to unproblematic values sustained by unreflective sentiment. If one has learned a natural language possessed of general terms of approbation, one's interest is engaged by those terms. The appeal of general terms of approbation provides the common sentimental base from which argument proceeds. Initial agreement is not difficult to obtain simply because such commitment involves no specific cognitive entailments. Serious argument begins when definitions are offered for critical terms and when facts, interpretations, predictions, and judgments are marshalled to vindicate a specific priority, recommendation, injunction, proscription, prescription, or evaluation. But all this proceeds within the confines of rationality. If one finds himself uttering logical inconsistencies, makes appeals to truth claims that are unwarranted, tenders predictions that are vague or unsupported by the best possible evidence, offers explanations that are faulted, such an argument can no longer serve to vindicate a normative posture.

Karl Marx began his enterprise with an appeal to "fulfillment" and "freedom." "Fulfillment" and "freedom" were subsequently explicated (particularly in the period between 1843 and 1845) in terms of "alienation," and "alienation" was, in turn and ultimately, analyzed in terms of the consequences of a particular form of economic activity. Marx spent his mature life explicating what "freedom" and "fulfillment" meant. What this involved was the articulation of a specifically social science *theory*—in the formal sense of theory. In order to vindicate his moral commitments it was necessary for Marx to invoke the entire machinery of rational inquiry. His normative posture is only as defensible as the antecedent premises, both analytic and empirical, of the argument that vindicates them. If the statemental components of his vindication, the analytic, description, explanatory and predictive assertions constituent to his account are impaired, the entire vindication is in such measure impaired. [28]

Once the entire normative argument has been rehearsed, an individual can be said to assume a normative *attitude*. Most sophisticated "emotive theorists" recognize that the original attempt to interpret ethical language in terms of "mere sentiment" was flawed. Contemporary metaethicists speak of ethical assertions as expressing *attitudes* and not *sentiments*. The distinction is relatively clear. One *can* be held responsible for one's *attitudes*. They are the consequence of rational assessments, choice and acts of will. Attitudes, furthermore, frequently will conflict with sentiments—and on occasion attitudes require the suspension of sentiments (when, for example, we are expected to tender judgments of guilt or innocence). One *cannot* be held responsible for one's *sentiments*—they are spontaneous. Sentiments may act as motives, but they can never constitute vindications (except in those instances of purely self-regarding acts). Our attitudes, on the other hand, require justificatory argument—and that argument will invoke constative utterances, warranted truth claims of a formal or descriptive order. Attitudes are, *in principle,* defended by rational argument.

What this implies is that although values are intrinsically and irreducibly the products of felt needs and wants, decisions made to pursue one rather than another effort at satisfying one or another need or want (however defined) can be understood to rest ultimately on public argument and their merits judged by common tests of adequacy. This is not to say that disputants will always and invariably recognize good arguments from bad ones—any more than the scientific method insures that all practitioners of science will be good scientists. What it means is that we have objective standards of evaluation for normative argument. Any normative argument that is the product of impaired logic or faulted factual, explanatory or predictive assessment, is a *bad* argument and fails as a vindication of an attitude, a policy or a course of conduct.

Normative Language and "Value-Free" Science

This analysis suggests something not only about the character of normative dispute, but of science as well. Political scientists are lamentably disposed to involve themselves in discussions about the "value-free" status of their inquiries. Other political scientists will insist with equal emphasis that science cannot be "value free." The argument becomes truly perverse when the claim is made that because science is either value free or not value free *all* objective claims can be warranted or *no* objective claims can be warranted.

There are a host of confusions involved in such discussions. One turns on the notion of "objectivity," a notion that occupied us at some length in Chapter Two. At this point "objectivity" means unimpeachable reliability for truth claims in the formal, and maximal reliability for truth claims in the descriptive, domain. Science is objective, in this sense, irrespective of the personal needs or wants that motivate a man to concern himself with scientific or strictly logical pursuits, because intrinsic to science and logic are standards which guarantee maximal and absolute reliability, respectively. There are no descriptive truth claims that are, in fact, more reliable than those made by science, nor formal truth claims more reliable than those made by logic.

Even if an individual undertook political science inquiry because of the basest motives, the love for money, the desire to dominate and oppress, the lust for personal status, or his Marxist or Fascist persuasion, his work would nonetheless be *judged* on the basis of the *intrinsic norms* of science or logic, norms which prevail because they have shown themselves to be maximally or absolutely reliable. This implies, of course, a recognition that reliability has at least insistent instrumental value for men. Its instrumental value is obviously essential to men who wish to get on in the world, who wish to navigate in time and space and anticipate futures. Any *recommendation, warning* or *prescription* that is indifferent or oblivious to reliable knowledge about the world is no recommendation at all. Any *evaluation* based on vague and ambiguous criteria, that cannot make recourse to confirmed properties of the objects under evaluation is no evaluation at all. In effect, while science and logic are not value free (since they are undertaken by men to satisfy some felt need)—they are objective and their objectivity implies autonomous norms intrinsic to science, independent of the motives which moved the researcher to undertake his pursuits. Conversely, normative judgments, whether they are productive of recommendations, injunctions, prescriptions, or evaluations, are not "fact free" nor "logic free," and therefore are equally, and to that measure, objective. No normative "principle," "ultimate or primary value," innocent of conjunction with fact and logic, is capable of producing a defensible recommendation, injunction, prescription, or evaluation.

Values, logic, and fact are inextricably united in the knowledge enterprise. Logic is pursued because some men see some point in it—its instrumental value in the service of "survival," "fulfillment," "happiness," "freedom," or what-have-you. But once logic is undertaken, it is governed by autonomous public norms for certifying its formal truth claims. Similarly social and natural science is undertaken to provide a more exhaustive catalogue of warranted truth claims which have served eminently well as instrumental to the satisfaction of any number of human wants as well as the assessment of the total outcome of any one rather than another policy. The entire constellation of values, logic and fact we entertain at any one time constitutes a network in which we attempt to maximize internal cognitive strength as well as maximize total value outcomes. Choices at any point in the system can generate asymmetrical normative or cognitive strains that threaten the entire fabric with formal incongruity and cognitive inconsistency and involve the possible rejection of well-entrenched values and facts. Values, logic and fact interact throughout the extended cognitive system in complex fashion. There is constant and responsible readjustment in order to maximize cognitive congruence, constancy, and reliability as well as maximize total value outcomes. We seek order in the descriptive world because our exchanges can thereby be systematized and our expectations confidently entertained. We seek order in our moral universe for the same reason, and in order to responsibly assess how the satisfaction of one value will influence our pursuit of other values.

To accomplish these ends recourse to reasoned argument is our only responsible strategy. Political scientists have often been so confused about the informal logic of normative discourse, about the determinate function of systematically acquired knowledge in the resolution of normative disagreement, that they have argued that "social science [can only make us wise] in all matters of secondary importance, but we have to be resigned to utter ignorance in the most important respect: we cannot have any knowledge regarding their soundness or unsoundness; our ultimate principles have no other support than our arbitrary and hence blind preferences."[29]

This doleful account is misleading in a number of ways, but its fundamental defect is a result of having assumed that the "ultimate principles" to which political theorists make ready recourse have, in and of themselves, cognitive and action implications and must be sought outside of systematic inquiry in "faith," "intuition," or a nonscientific "history." Ultimate political principles, as we have argued here, are essentially devoid of cognitive content and have few, if any, strict implications for behavior. They are conjured up to engage interest and to provide the dynamic force for normative argument. Therefore it is a mistake to imagine that one is obliged to "prove" or "demonstrate" their "truth." They are "self-recommending" only insofar as they recommend nothing specific at all. Their function is to engage sentiment. They begin to function *cognitively* when they are defined, when the proffered definitions are vindicated by exhibiting possible outcomes, when the import of the policies such stipulative definitions entail are characterized in terms of total cost and total outcomes against the multiplicity of values harbored and the cognitive consistency sought—when they provide vindications for attitudes.

Normative disagreement in politics rarely, if ever, involves disagreement in terms of the "grand alternatives" presumably generated by commitment to "ultimate principles." Disagreement arises when such "ultimate principles" are defined and their implications, within the context of prevailing normative, natural and social constraints, are drawn out. We can and do certainly argue *cognitively* about such matters. We show that one self-recommending value, defined in one or another way, has perhaps unforeseen consequences with respect to other self-recommending values. Or we indicate that the evidence that is marshalled to support one program rather than another is inconclusive or that probable outcomes are so obscure that it would not be prudent to sacrifice one self-recommending value in the vague hope that some other might be achieved. What techniques could we better invoke than those of the best available social science in order to accomplish all that? What significant evidence do we have that "faith," "insight," or "intuition" could more responsibly serve our purpose?

Social science has produced ample evidence that most people do not have clearly articulated values, much less any one specific subtending value, or specific set of values, to which all judgments are subject. Most people harbor a collection of vague generalizations they will identify, under challenge, as their values. It is only in public dispute that those "intuitively" held values are explicated, assessed, and accepted or rebutted. Only in public dialogue are sentiments forged into defensible and responsible attitudes.

Value systems are comfortably pluralistic: more than one state of affairs is intrinsically desirable. Goals are pursued rationally only when all the implications of pursuing one value are drawn out—and at any one time we tend to seek a balance between competing value claims. Demand curves for one value will intersect and mutually affect others. Balance is obtained by cataloguing the self-recommending values entertained by each participant in dispute and affording them a preliminary rank order of preference and then drawing out the implications of such an ordering in terms of the total outcome of each alternative. Demand and indifference curves can be mapped (game theory in political science has been aggressively pursuing this kind of enterprise for some time). [30] This requires that values be articulated and defined with reasonable precision, that standards be set that would at least minimally identify fulfillment and default, that argument be undertaken to indicate what factual implications there are in pursuing one or another intrinsic or instrumental value. All of which requires sophisticated philosophical analysis and the best evidence provided by systemic social science inquiry. All of which is complex, unproblematically rational, and, unless one is irredeemably tendentious, scientific.

It is curious that some political theorists believe that the solution to such complex issues as normative dispute can be forthcoming by appeal to some simple "primary values." More curious still is the insistence that such "ultimate principles" are the gift of some "trans-, post-, or extra-scientific insights." Some of the most complex issues facing man are conceived amenable to solution through the employment of strategies at once so simple and so inscrutable.

We are all prepared to admit that making responsible truth ascriptions in the formal domain is a complex and difficult task. We train our students for years to master the rudiments of logic—and we often fail to even suggest the difficulties which accompany metalogic. We are similarly prepared to recognize the difficulties involved in making responsible truth ascription in the empirical domain. And we train students for years in adequate research techniques—without even beginning to broach some of the issues of metascience or the philosophy of science. Yet we tend to think that the resolution of normative disagreement is eminently simple. In political science we make little, if any, effort to indicate the training requisite to responsible truth ascription in the range of normative discourse. We afford little, if any, training in ethics—much less metaethics. We tend to impart the false conviction that normative discourse is transparently simple. All that is required is an appeal to deeply felt values, a hierarchy of values, a hierarchy that rests on some felt preferences which are either "self-evident," the result of an "act of faith," an "utterance of conscience," or more vaguely still, "a product of the human condition." To pretend that normative discourse involves anything less than the most difficult and complex rational procedures, anything less than the exercise of sophisticated analytic skills and rigorous factual appraisal, is to deceive.

Notes

1. W. P. Alston, *Philosophy of Language* (Englewood Cliffs, N.J.: Prentice-Hall, 1964), pp. 35f.
2. A. J. Ayer, *Language, Truth and Logic* (New York: Dover, n.d.), pp. 103, 107, 108. Emphasis supplied.
3. C. L. Stevenson, *Facts and Values* (New Haven: Yale, 1963), pp. 16f.
4. A. Maslow, "Psychological Data and Value Theory," in A. Maslow (ed.), *New Knowledge in Human Values* (New York: Harper and Row, 1959), pp. 119–136; R. G. Olson, *The Morality of Self Interest* (New York: Harcourt, Brace & World, 1965), p. 58.
5. H. Margenau, "The Scientific Basis of Value Theory," in Maslow (ed.), *op. cit.*, pp. 38f.
6. D. Hume, *An Inquiry Concerning the Principles of Morals* (New York: Bobbs-Merrill, 1957), pp. 5f.
7. A. Sesonske, *Value and Obligation* (New York: Oxford, 1964), p. 20.
8. B. Moore, Jr., "Tolerance and the Scientific Outlook," in R. P. Wolff, B. Moore, Jr., and H. Marcuse, *A Critique of Pure Tolerance* (Boston: Beacon Press, 1965), pp. 53–79; E. Meehan, *Theory and Method of Political Analysis* (Homewood, Ill.: Dorsey, 1965), chap. 8; M. Scriven, "Science, Fact and Value," in S. Morgenbesser (ed.), *Philosophy of Science Today* (New York: Basic Books, 1967), p. 176.
9. R. B. Perry, *Realms of Value* (Cambridge, Mass.: Harvard, 1954), pp. 2f.
10. Cf. B. Barry, *Political Argument* (New York: Humanities, 1965), p. 29.
11. J. L. Austin, *How to Do Things with Words*, ed. J. O. Urmson (New York: Oxford, 1965), lecture viii.
12. John Searle has argued that performative activities embodied in descriptive accounts imply an "ought" when the description relates promises made and institutional obligations assumed. Cf. J. Searle, "How to Derive 'Ought' from 'Is,'" in P. Foot (ed.), *Theories of Ethics* (London: Oxford, 1967), pp. 101–114.
13. H. Marcuse, "Ethics and Revolution," in R. T. De George (ed.), *Ethics and Society* (Garden City, N.Y.: Doubleday, 1966), pp. 133–147.
14. R. C. Pratt, "A Note on David Easton's Approach to Political

Philosophy," *Canadian Journal of Economic and Political Science,* XX (1954), p. 373; M. Q. Sibley, "The Limitations of Behavioralism," in J. C. Charlesworth (ed.), *Contemporary Political Analysis* (New York: Free Press, 1967), pp. 53f.

[15] V. Van Dyke, *Political Science: A Philosophical Analysis* (Stanford: Stanford University, 1960), p. 9. Van Dyke provides a more comprehensive and convincing discussion in "Values and Interests," *American Political Science Review,* LVI (1962), 567–576.

[16] Cf. W. G. Runciman, *Social Science and Political Theory* (London: Cambridge University, 1965), pp. 170–173.

[17] H. Kariel, "The Political Relevance of Behavioral and Existential Psychology," *American Political Science Review,* LXI (1967), 339.

[18] B. Moore, Jr., *Social Origins of Dictatorship and Democracy* (Boston: Beacon Press, 1966), p. 447.

[19] B. Mussolini, "L'uomo e la divinità," in *Opera Omnia di Benito Mussolini,* ed. E. and D. Susmel (Florence: La Fenice, 1961), XXXIII, p. 22.

[20] Cf. A. J. Gregor, *Contemporary Radical Ideologies* (New York: Random House, 1968), chap. 4; *The Ideology of Fascism* (New York: Free Press, 1969), chap. 5.

[21] Cf. Barry, *op. cit.,* pp. 34f; C.

Frankel, *The Case for Modern Man* (Boston: Beacon, 1956), chap. 5.

[22] H. Marcuse, *Negations: Essays in Critical Theory* (Boston: Beacon, 1968), p. 39; "Repressive Tolerance," in Wolff, Moore and Marcuse, *op. cit.,* p. 87.

[23] Cf. P. Corbett, *Ideologies* (New York: Harcourt, Brace & World, 1965), pp. 168f., 183f.

[24] Cf. M. Scriven, *Value Claims in the Social Sciences* (Publication no. 123 of the Social Science Education Consortium. Lafayette, Ind.: Purdue University, 1966), pp. 20ff.

[25] E. Fromm, "Values, Psychology and Human Existence," in Maslow, *op. cit.,* pp. 151ff.

[26] Cf. C. L. Stevenson, "Ethical Fallibility," in De George (ed.), *op. cit.,* pp. 197–217.

[27] H. L. A. Hart, *The Concept of Law* (Oxford: Clarendon, 1961), pp. 189–195. This is precisely the rationale offered by Marcuse in his *One Dimensional Man* (Boston: Beacon, 1964), pp. 76f.

[28] Cf. A. J. Gregor, "Marxism and Ethics: A Methodological Inquiry," *Philosophy and Phenomenological Research,* XXVIII (1968), 368–384.

[29] L. Strauss, *Natural Right and History* (Chicago: University of Chicago, 1953), pp. 3f.

[30] Cf. J. Von Neumann and O. Morgenstern, *The Theory of Games and Economic Behavior* (Princeton: Princeton University, 1947); Barry, *op. cit.,* chap. 1.

Suggested Readings

Murphy, Joseph S. *Political Theory: A Conceptual Analysis*. Nobleton, Ontario: Dorsey, 1968. Chap. 1.

Oppenheim, F. *Moral Principles in Political Philosophy*. New York: Random House, 1968.

Parsons, T. "Evaluation and Objectivity in Social Science: An Interpretation of Max Weber's Contribution," *Sociological Theory and Modern Society*. New York: Free Press, 1967.

Scriven, Michael. "Science, Fact and Value," in S. Moregenbesser, *Philosophy of Science Today*. New York: Basic Books, 1967.

10

On Noncognitive Discourse

Every sentence has meaning, not as being the natural means by which a physical faculty is realized, but, as we have said, by convention. Yet every sentence is not a proposition; only such are propositions as have in them either truth or falsity. Thus a prayer is a sentence, but is neither true nor false.

Let us therefore dismiss all other types of sentence but the proposition, for this last concerns our present inquiry, whereas the investigation of the others belongs rather to the study of rhetoric or of poetry.

Aristotle, De Interpretatione,
17a, 1–8.

Of propositions and problems there are—to comprehend the matter in outline—three divisions: for some are ethical propositions, some are on natural philosophy, while some are logical.

Aristotle, Topica, 105b, 19–22.

The language of political inquiry, like language in general, serves a multiplicity of purposes. We have occupied ourselves with language insofar as it is employed to tender knowledge claims, to claim to know, to opine, to describe, to deduce, to induce, and to explain. In the process of coming to know we entertain conceptual schemata, we axiomatize, we define, criterially characterize and typify. We invoke unproblematic assumptions and auxiliary hypotheses. As a consequence of all this we make confident or guarded knowledge claims. We make strong or weak claims—and we recognize that all of them, strong or weak, are in principle corrigible. We admit that our only indefeasible certainty is the certainty that attends logically true assertions—and that such assertions are empirically empty. They inform us about the appropriate use of language, but tell us nothing descriptive about the nonlinguistic world. We recognize that our normative utterances, in the last analysis, can be unpacked into general sentiments of attraction and repulsion conjoined with factual or analytic claims—and that whatever truth they involve is a function of the truth of their constituent propositional components—the warranted truth of the analytic or synthetic assertions that constitute their cognitive content.

We have also suggested that language serves other than cognitive purposes as well. We employ language for performative, ritual, and expressive purposes. When we make a formal declaration of intention, as in a marriage ceremony or in taking an oath, declaring war or surrendering, we are employing language for performative purposes. Such performances can be faulted by failing to meet the conditions which render them binding.

Ritual or ceremonial language performs still other tasks. When introduced to someone, we ask the ritual question, "How do you do?" and most assuredly do not expect a reply that would catalogue the circumstances surrounding the state of psychic or physical health of our new acquaintance. We are *not* making a medical or clinical inquiry. Ritual language provides verbal cues that constitute part of the elaborate pattern of interpersonal expectations that make social life possible—but it is, in and of itself, noncognitive. It gives some (generally) unintended indication of the fact that we are familiar with the etiquette expected in social intercourse. It serves to provide evidence of our social rectitude. In itself, it constitutes a verbal cue which permits our *alter* to reasonably anticipate how we might subsequently behave. It suggests to him that we are to be numbered among those whose behavior is "normal." Through the use of ceremonial or ritual language we afford others some preliminary evidence that we will fulfill other patterned expectations and that our interactions will be governed by mutually understood rules of conduct.

Expressive language, in turn, provides us with the occasion to reduce intrapsychic tension. We lament, declaim, expostulate, and exult—we give expression to our feelings—and feel all the better for it. Similarly, we often speak of art as being "expressive." The artist "expresses" himself in his work, on his canvas or in his music. As long as art is so construed, its function is purely expressive and manifestly noncognitive. The measure of its utility would be the degree of satisfaction it produces for the artist, but as such would be neither true nor false. It might well be appropriate or inappropriate—just as laughing would be an appropriate expression of felt humor, or smiling an appropriate expression of good will, but laughing, smiling and weeping are neither true nor false.

Performative or ritual language can be appropriate or inappropriate, successful or unsuccessful in a similar manner—but it is neither true nor false. Ascriptions of truth or falsity can be responsibly made only to analytic or synthetic propositions. We can, of course, say that the conditions that make a performative utterance binding are satisfied—and *that* would be a cognitive utterance. Under such circumstances we have studied the conditions which make performative utterances binding and find that those conditions are fulfilled in one or another circumstance. But the performative utterance, in and of itself, is neither true nor false. Similarly, we can say that weeping is an appropriate expression of anguish—and *that* would be a cognitive claim. We have studied the circumstance of one or another culture, or of the generic dispositions of men, and found that when men are sad they tend to cry. Crying serves as an indicator of distress. But crying, grimacing, laughing, smiling, declaiming, exulting, expostulating, cursing, whistling, and humming are, in and of themselves, neither true nor false.

Noncognitive Language and Political Inquiry

This kind of analysis suggests several things with respect to the import of noncognitive language use within political inquiry. One can systematically study noncognitive language, make a variety of characterizing knowledge claims concerning its use, the occasions for its employment, its relationship to a system of socially sanctioned norms. We can subject it to content analysis. Noncognitive utterances can be utilized for manipulative or predictive advantage—but it should be clear that noncognitive language cannot be itself employed to make knowledge claims. A noncognitive utterance is noncognitive—and whatever we do with it, we cannot use it to utter a truth.

As is the case with all serious issues of language use, it is relatively easy to draw a distinction by choosing clear cases. It is evident that ceremonial and performative language is, in and of itself, noncognitive. It is equally clear in many instances of expressive use. But there are any number of instances in which a clear distinction cannot, without argument, be made. We all are prepared to recognize that the individual who refers to another as a "bastard," is not using the language for specifically cognitive purposes. He is primarily expressing disdain. To ask him what the measure of a "bastard" is, is largely inappropriate. Similarly, terms like "Fascist pig," "racist," and "the Establishment," have little cognitive content, but emphatic expressive force. But it seems equally clear that such cases may not be *purely* expressive. One can, in many instances, draw cognitive information from the agents of such utterances if one has the opportunity and the patience. One can, under certain conditions, appropriately ask, "What do you mean when you call someone a 'bastard,' . . . 'a Fascist pig,' . . . 'a racist'?" It is even remotely possible that one's interlocutor had some specific cognitive meaning in mind *before* employing such locutions.

There are whole classes of linguistic utterances that seem to be largely, if not exclusively, noncognitive and yet in and of themselves may have, and often have been credited with, significant cognitive import. Myths, phantasies and imaginings have been suggested as being among them. We do talk of daydreams as phantasies and thereby attribute to them an all but exclusive expressive function. Similarly, we speak of wish fulfillment in our imaginings, and we tend to think of myths as some kind of collective phantasy. And yet there are a number of political thinkers who attribute some special cognitive merit to the linguistic products they identify as myth, imaginings and phantasy.

Early in the present century, for example, Georges Sorel maintained that only "myth" could give us "global knowledge" of complex political phenomena.[1] More recently (as we have seen) Russell Kirk has insisted that it is "imagination" alone that can make social science scientific.[2] Mulford Sibley, in turn, has maintained that "unscientific truths" govern political wisdom—and Herbert Marcuse contends that "phantasy" and "intuition" are in some sense cognitively critical to political inquiry.[3]

Such claims are interesting for a variety of reasons, but primarily because they focus attention on an ill-defined class of linguistic performances that are very difficult to analyze. What sort of "truths" are "unscientific truths"? Does "intuition" have an unequivocal cognitive function? Are "phantasy" and "imagination" necessary adjuncts to the enterprise we recognize as scientific? The questions involve, of course, a variety of issues that can only be alluded to, but there is one central issue which demands attention, not only because there have been some prominent representatives of the tradition it represents, but because it is a major theme in one of the contemporary student subcultures. That issue is whether there can be a "political science" or a "science of society" at all.

We are all familiar with most of the mock arguments advanced in support of the privative claim that there can be no "science" of society (and inferentially no political "science"). Our concern here will be restricted to the argument advanced by Sorel, because central to his argument is his insistence that "myths" rather than science afford us special social and political truths that are truer than true.

Sorel simply insisted that a "science of society" was, in principle, impossible. Not only could predictions about the political future not be tendered, but he went on to insist that we are simply incapable of determining "whether one hypothesis about it is better than another."[4] The claims made by Kirk, Sibley and Marcuse, and those in much the same tradition, are far more muted, more defensible, and, in general, more complex than those made by Sorel. They are in substantial agreement, however, insofar as all claim that political inquiry can never be a "science" as long as it confines itself to "positivistic" devices—that is, as long as it treats political matters as though they can be analyzed into concerns within the three domains of discourse: the analytic, the synthetic and the normative—as long as men insist that questions about man's individual and collective political behavior can be answered by employing the techniques of analytic, linguistic, and experimental precision, and controlled and public interpretation. All insist that some "extrascientific" adjunct is necessary. In the case of Sorel, the "myth" is invoked. In the case of Kirk and Sibley appeal is made to religious or poetic "faith." Marcuse makes recourse to "phantasy," "intuition" and the "concrete dialectic" to supplement the "positivistic" devices of contemporary social science.

The familiar linguistic products of "faith," "imagination," "phantasy," and "intuition" are at best interstitial with respect to the cognitive and noncognitive ranges of discourse. We tend to characterize imaginings and phantasies as "wish fulfillments," essentially expressive. We identify faith with profound *feelings*. And yet, in some sense, we want to attribute cognitive merit to at least some of the linguistic by-products of faith and phantasy—which may suggest that we use such terms loosely, to cover a wide variety of performances and a disparate collection of linguistic entities. Whatever the case, it is *not* the case that imaginings, phantasies, and intuitions are *exclusively* productive of noncognitive consequences. The question is whether their products are anything more than *tangentially* cognitive, whether they can serve as special "extrascientific" sources of social and political wisdom.

Sorel's work anticipated a great deal of the "anti-behavioralist" and "anti-positivist" criticism that has come to characterize the work of scholars like Marcuse, Kirk and Sibley. In a sense, Sorel has been father to a long line of critics, each equally dubious about the merits of social science—and each prepared to supplement standard science with special cognitive tools ranging from myths to mystic insights. Sorel shares other features with his heirs—his work is particularly difficult to analyze. On the one hand, he was, by his own and almost everyone else's judgment, a notoriously bad writer whose prose more often followed psychological, rather than logical, order.[5] On the other hand, because he disdained "precision" and deplored "the artificial rigor of intellectualism," it is, more often than not, extremely difficult to reconstruct his arguments with any confidence whatsoever. Sorel simply failed to articulate all the premises of his arguments and therefore his discussions are frequently perplexingly elliptical. For at least these reasons, Sorel could be, at one time or another, a defender of the proletariat, an advocate of an insistent, if transmogrified, Marxism, and a protagonist of bourgeois virtues—a defender of radical libertarianism and an anti-Semite—a radical revolutionary and a traditionalist—a socialist and a defender of monarchism—an enthusiast of Lenin and Mussolini as well. His writings have been understood to have influenced Marxism-Leninism, National Socialism, and Fascism.[6] As is the case with works of art, everyone seems to "interpret" Sorel's work in accordance with his own lights.

It would be simple enough to interpret Sorel's work as "art" or "poetry," having primarily, if not exclusively, expressive function— to say that the author employed his prose as a vehicle to ventilate his sentiments and that his readers have subsequently and similarly ventilated themselves in reading it, each coming away from Sorel with nothing more than they brought to him. No cognitive exchange has taken place. But such an appraisal hardly seems to do justice to the serious thought one finds in Sorel. The question is whether the serious content of Sorel's account involves any appeal to other than standard cognitive elements and procedures. Is it true, in effect, that Sorel's analysis of political life involves an appeal that is "transcientific," that his "myth" is a necessary supplement to the analytic and empirical devices available to normal science?

If one considers Sorel's work in its entirety, it is obvious that his disclaimers concerning the possibility of a "science of politics" are by and large directed against "scientific socialism," the "science of society" touted by the "orthodox Marxists" of the turn of the century.[7] He insisted that Marx, himself, had made "many and sometimes enormous" errors. He argued that Marx, as well as his orthodox protagonists, had employed vague and ambiguous formulations in theory construction which afflicted their arguments with equivocations. Moreover, it was obvious, in many instances, that wherever a truth claim was made by Marxists without equivocation, empirical fact had infirmed them.

It is clear that whatever objections Sorel might legitimately (or illegitimately) raise against Marxism as a "positive social science," those objections could hardly serve to invalidate *all* and *any* efforts at constructing an adequate social or political science. For Sorel to warrant the claim that we are in no position to discuss whether one rather than another theory about the future of society is more or less credible would require more evidence than that one or another theory about the future was wrong. As a matter of fact even the most elementary inventory of the truth claims made by Sorel indicates that he, himself, claimed to have not only a more comprehensive, but a more *competent* theory about social futures than any alternate candidate theory.

The fact is that Sorel attempted a special empirical *theory* of individual and collective motivation. His theory of society and political behavior was predicated on a collection of general knowledge claims concerning the behavior of man. "To say that we are acting," Sorel maintained, "implies that we are creating an imaginary world placed ahead of the present world and composed of movements which depend entirely on us."[8] To have advanced such an assertion is to claim that before men act they entertain anticipated outcomes, "imaginary worlds," which guide their performance. This is clearly an empirical knowledge claim and is confirmed or disconfirmed by collecting empirical evidence. Do men, in fact, invoke "imaginary worlds" before they act? Do they *always* do this? Under what circumstances *do* they—if they don't undertake such invocations universally?

These "imaginary worlds," for Sorel, constitute conjectured outcomes which guide the acts of individual men—when they become collective imaginings they constitute a "myth." Sorel maintained that "science" did not understand the function of such imaginings and such myths, and consequently "science" could afford only a "misleading idea of the forces which really move men."[9] All of which may be perfectly true, but takes us not one step toward confirming the contention that a "science of society" is in principle impossible or that science requires some exotic adjuncts to issue significant knowledge claims.

To have said that one account of the forces that move men is wrong or inadequate implies that some other account is correct or more adequate. It would seem, therefore, that one *can* distinguish more or less adequate hypotheses about man's social and political future. If two sets of propositions are advanced to account for man's past and present political behavior, and one which includes an account of the role of "myths" is more adequate, it would follow that a hypothesis which employed "myths" for predictive leverage would be inductively more creditable. Unless we are completely mistaken about induction and the advantages it affords for prediction, an adequate explanation of man's political behavior would give us predictive advantage. If Sorel is saying anything at all, he is claiming that his account, which includes an appreciation of the function of "myth," is a more adequate account than any competitor and consequently any anticipation of futures would have to entertain knowledge of the "myths" which mobilize men to collective effort. A "myth" would be nothing more than a collection of symbols or signs that represent "all the strongest inclinations of a people, of a party or of a class, inclinations which recur to the mind with the insistence of instincts in all the circumstances of life" through which men "reform their desires, passions, and mental activity."[10]

Thus the "myth" itself may be a symbolic figuration, a noncognitive expression of "inclinations," but as such would be neither true nor false, is no special supplement to normal science, and would hardly qualify as the source of "global" or "synoptic" knowledge. A "myth," as Sorel employs the term, is a device which taps "inclinations," and if it is successful it mobilizes men to some sort of reasonably specific action. But to anticipate its success we would have to know what "inclinations" are harbored by a people, a party or a class. In retrospect we can reconstruct those "inclinations." All such activity is obviously empirical—and it is just such activity that we characterize as "standard science."

To define a myth as that linguistic device, that "body of images which, by intuition alone, and before any analyses are made, is capable of evoking as an undivided whole the mass of sentiments of a party, sect or class," is to make an analytic and empirical knowledge claim. There is such a thing as a myth, defined in a specific manner, which does, in fact, evoke in men an undivided mass of sentiments. This is an empirical proposition in motivational psychology and is subject to the evidence conditions which govern truth ascriptions in that universe of discourse. Men who act as a consequence of compelling myths do not themselves "analyze" any more than the individual who uses expressive language "analyzes" before employing it or being aroused by it. Expressive language either successfully or unsuccessfully evokes sentiments in others—but it is, in itself, neither true nor false. Neither purely expressive language nor myth, so understood, is cognitive. We can, as Sorel does, make cognitive claims *concerning* myths. Whether any myth does in fact evoke "as an undivided whole the mass of sentiments" of a party, faction or people is an empirical question—and is answered by standard empirical techniques.

Myths, as Sorel construes them, are not "paralogical" or "transcientific" adjuncts to the scientific enterprise. As he understands them, they constitute complex and essentially expressive utterances which are employed to invoke certain determinate behavioral responses. They, in and of themselves, are neither true nor false. Truth or falsity can be responsibly assigned only to Sorel's claim that he has correctly identified the psychological forces that move men to act. This is a straightforward, if complex, empirical claim and is subject to the common tests of standard science. If the claim is true, Sorel has contributed to the science of politics and the science of society. Moreover, he has, wittingly or unwittingly, shown that his disclaimers—that one cannot have such a science and that one cannot determine the merit of alternate predictions about the future of political and social man—are unfounded. His very efforts deny his own contentions. Sorel contributed to political and social science, and nothing he said indicates that in making that contribution Sorel employed anything other than the standard procedures of analytic and empirical inquiry.

This is, of course, precisely how Vilfredo Pareto understood Sorel's enterprise. Sorel's "myth" was no more than a special case of what Pareto called a "derivation" in the *Trattato*. The "myth" was a condensed symbol, a collection of images, which lent expression to the sentiments which moved men to act. "Myth," itself, was a descriptive concept in a specific theory of political motivation, the merit of which could be assessed by normal experimental techniques.[11]

Noncognitive Language and Contemporary Analysis

This interpretation of "myth" seems to be, as a matter of fact, tacitly or explicitly accepted in contemporary discussions of political motivation. Thus Murray Edelman's intersting account of the *Symbolic Uses of Politics* speaks of "myths" which have a "powerful emotional pull" and which function to provide a sense of community among a determinate collection of men, as well as a "powerful means of expression for mass publics." "Myths" are composed of "condensation symbols" which derive their "meanings" from the "psychological needs of the respondents"; they "condense into one symbolic event, sign, or act, patriotic pride, anxieties, remembrances of past glories or humiliations, promises of future greatness: some one of these or all of them."[12] Such symbolic or mythic locutions either assist in "social adjustment" or serve to "externalize" individual or collective psychological problems. Some men come to understand symbolic or mythic language use and employ it instrumentally, to further their own special interests—which means that while symbolic or mythic language is, in and of itself, expressive, it can be both cognitively assessed, and cognitively employed as well. In and of itself symbolic or mythic language is neither true nor false, but as a component of a more extended theory of human motivation, "symbols" and "myths" serve as descriptive and/or theoretical concepts—subject to the truth conditions governing any significant knowledge claims.

Clifford Geertz's discussion of "symbol systems" follows the same analysis. Geertz's account turns on alternate interpretations of symbolic language that have been offered—and he dismisses some as too "rudimentary to cope with the complexity of the interaction among social, psychological, and cultural factors" involved. Geertz offers an outline of a more comprehensive *theory* of symbolic language and its functions in political and social circumstances. Such language employments, in and of themselves, have something of the species traits of analogy, metaphor, trope, pun or paradox, and are deployed to suggest more complex meanings than those of "the tempered language of science." Symbolic language serves to afford a "template for the organization of social and psychological processes . . . in situations where the particular kind of information they contain is lacking, where institutionalized guides for behavior, thought, or feeling are weak or absent." As such, symbolic or mythic language is neither true nor false. It is either effective or ineffective. What is subject to cognitive scrutiny is the explicit and empirical theory of symbolic or mythic language.[13] As such, "myth" and "symbolic language" can be absorbed without remainder into the body of social science. It is not a "paralogical" or "transempirical" supplement, but a relatively specific theory of individual or collective motivation, a special theory within the confines of empirical psychology—and possessed of as much truth as is contained in the well-confirmed inductive and lawlike generalizations upon which it rests.

If Sorel's "myths" can, and have been, so accommodated, Kirk's "imagination" and Sibley's "prescientific" and "postscientific" knowings are still (as has already been suggested) more easily assimilated. Whatever "imagination," "intuition," "insight," and "transcientific" knowings are understood to be, everyone is prepared to admit that the pursuit of knowledge begins with something loosely called "intuition" or "imagination." We intuit similarities between things in generating our first preliminary conceptual schemata with which we learn to orient ourselves in the world. We employ imagination in order to generate speculative hypotheses about the world of things and the world of men. We have already suggested, several times, that there is no determinate logic of discovery. Men go about discovering relations between variables in strange, complex, and curious fashions. *However* they hit upon such relations, such relations cannot be advanced as *true* until they have been made subject to empirical test. Intuition and imagination, no matter how confidently felt or insistently defended, can never, in themselves, warrant the truth of any knowledge claim. The mathematician may hit upon a solution to a complex mathematical problem in his sleep, but the certification of its truth will not be the consequence of sleeping. He will not recommend sleeping to his audience as a truth certifying technique—what he will do will be to publicly calculate the answer to his problem by employing the standard techniques of mathematical proof in order to establish the merit of his initial "intuition." Any other effort would be dismissed as inconsequential. Similarly, we may intuit or imagine the relationship between some specific kind of family environment and a disposition to enlist oneself in one or another political organization, but our intuition or imagination cannot, in and of themselves, produce the truth warrant that would compel responsible cognitive assent on the part of any rational audience.

Marcuse's appeal to "phantasy" and "intuition" is no less subject to the same assessment. It is very difficult, of course, to determine what Marcuse means to say since he has, like Sorel before him, very little sympathy with the demand for linguistic precision. His language is that of neo-Hegelianism—a language that has not been particularly noteworthy for its clarity and specificity. Our concern here, however, is with his claim that "phantasy" is, in some determinate sense, essential to political inquiry.

Marcuse seems to be arguing that "phantasy" is essential to political inquiry because "phantasy" is "imagination," and "imagination" "denotes a considerable degree of independence from the given, of freedom amid a world of unfreedom. In surpassing what is present, it can anticipate the future."[14]

This is curious indeed. If we must employ imagination or phantasy to anticipate the future, certainly some anticipations are better than others. Some anticipations are simply wish-fulfillments, others are predicated on false assumptions, others are simply stupidities, and still others are projections made on the basis of reasonably well confirmed tendencies in act. All anticipations of the future (individual or collective, natural as well as social) are in some sense independent of the given, and all of them involve a logical leap warranted only by a regularity analysis of the past and present— all of them are undertaken with some hazard—and all of them exemplify "freedom" in *that* sense in a "world of unfreedom." But all of us recognize that anticipations which are *totally* "free" from the "given" (whatever that is supposed to mean), are not "free" but irresponsible. When Marcuse tells us that "phantasy" can provide us with "answers" that "would be very close to the truth, certainly closer than those yielded by the rigorous conceptual analyses of philosophical anthropology," for it would "determine what man is on the basis of what he really can be tomorrow," he can hardly mean that *any* phantasy will do. The phantasy he seems to be advocating is that which is very much akin to the intuition employed by a skilled and knowledgable scientist, who knows his subject very well and can thus make credible, if probabilistic, projections within his universe of inquiry. The merit of those projections will be determined by the available total evidence concerning "potentialities" operative in that universe, and those potentialities can only be determined by systematic empirical assessment. Only then can futures be anticipated with the "certainty of a reasoned and reasonable chance. . . ."[15] In such determinations "phantasy," "imagination," and "intuition" will function in an essential preliminary, but tightly controlled, cognitive fashion. Their specific cognitive merit can only be determined by standard empirical techniques.

Only when preliminary moves employing "phantasy" and "intuition" assist in the construction of viable social science theory can they gain admission—and then only as *propaedeutic* to the knowledge enterprise. Marcuse seems to at least intuit such a requirement, for when he characterizes his work as "critical theory," a theory employed to "explain the totality of man and his world in terms of his social being," he contends that its truth is certified not by phantasy or imagination, but by "demonstration" that proceeds "on empirical grounds." He talks of fulfilling man's "possibilities" in terms of "definable goals of practice," goals which are expressive of "an actual tendency" empirically determinable. He characterizes his theory as something which is clearly not the product of "mere speculation." It is a viable theory "grounded on the capabilities of the given society." Moreover, it has explanatory and predictive pretensions. In 1937 he maintained that his theory could have "easily" "comprehended and predicted" the "social situation expressed in the authoritarian states" that had appeared in Germany and Italy.[16] No mean achievement—but one which could only be accomplished by standard science.

All of which means, if it means anything at all, that Marcuse advances, as intrinsic to his enterprise, a social science theory having explanatory and predictive function—whose only tests of truth would be logical consistency, and empirically confirmed descriptive and explanatory power. That this theory is conjoined with a collection of familiar unproblematic and *prima facie* values (Marcuse offers, as we have seen, "freedom," "happiness," "truth," "reason," "fulfillment," and "authenticity" as candidates) makes it normative in intention. Marcuse's work gives expression to a complex normative argument. It generates the predictable collection of prescriptions, proscriptions, recommendations, exhortations, and warnings. But his injunctions have as much force as his definitions have consistency and his knowledge claims have truth. When critical terms are given a variety of definitions, each of which is not self-evidently compatible with the other, it is difficult to say that we have, in fact, "definable goals." If "freedom" is identified with "reason," and then we are told that "freedom is the truth of *necessity*," and yet "reason means shaping life according to men's *free* decision . . . ,"[17] we cannot help being puzzled—not because we do not share Marcuse's values, or fail to enjoy enough "phantasy," but because it becomes increasingly difficult to know what he means to say. If we are told that "the *totality* of human relations" must be "liberated," we can hardly be sure what we are enjoined *to do* or, as the case might be, *not do*—no matter how much "intuition" we can conjure up.

When, however, Marcuse claims that "the labor process" causes the "laborer's organs [to] atrophy and [be] coarsened . . ." and that the "unpurified, unrationalized release of sexual relationships would be the strongest release of enjoyment as such and the total devaluation of labor for its own sake . . . ,"[18] these are serious (if confused) *factual* and *causal,* i.e., *empirical,* claims. The question that urges itself upon one is, how can they be verified? The most singular thing about Marcuse's work in this respect, is the impressive lack of empirical evidence for *any* of his claims. His references are almost invariably to discursive, rather than experimental, literature. Even in the one instance where appeal is made to the clinical literature of psychoanalysis, he opts to reject most of the prevailing judgments of practicing clinicians and therapists and makes recourse to Freud's "metapsychological" conjectures—invoking, for his purposes, singular speculations, like the "death instinct," to explain individual and collective phenomena. We find ourselves back with the least creditable Freud—with his conjectural "prehistoric domestic drama" and his fables about "racial memories"— and a theory of society which sees collective life "rooted in instincts."[19]

One has difficulty with Marcuse not because one resists "freedom," "happiness," "authenticity," and "fulfillment" as values, or because one lacks the requisite "phantasy" or "intuition," but because one simply does not know what to make of what Marcuse means to say, how much of what he says is to be taken seriously, or what is implied by what he does succeed in saying, given the vague, rambling and paradoxical characterizations he offers. It is doubtful if any appeals to "phantasy," "imagination," or "intuition" will make the task any easier. If it is true, as Marcuse contends, that there is a "truth" "beyond science and logic,"[20] it is incumbent upon him to exhibit that he has attained it, can give expression to it, and can characterize its evidence conditions—in other words that he can credibly establish that his enterprise is a cognitive one. Marcuse makes a special effort to satisfy just such a demand in undertaking recourse to one final putative extrascientific adjunct: "dialectical logic."

Appeals to something vaguely called the "dialectic" are commonplace in political science literature. The "dialectic" has been pressed into service on a variety of occasions and is understood to satisfy a variety of functions. The central issue is whether it ever performs a *cognitive* function. To this question no definitive answer can be attempted here—given obvious restrictions of space, intention and disposition. It can be said, however, that the "dialectic" has had an unfortunate history.

Originally, in antiquity, the term "dialectics" simply meant the "art of dispute and debate (*dialektike techne*)" through which a more adequate understanding of anything was obtained by tendering, inspecting and attempting to resolve questions concerning it, advanced from conflicting points of view. It was German Idealism that elevated the dialectic to a special place in the inventory of epistemic devices. Its special virtues have long been sung—but efforts to characterize its application, or catalogue its achievements, have produced little of substance. J. N. Findlay, one of the most knowledgeable commentators on Hegel (the dialectic owes its contemporary renaissance to the followers of Hegel), characterizes the dialectic in the following way:

> Exactly what is meant by calling [Hegel's] philosophy "dialectical" is . . . far from clear, nor whether it is a good or a bad manner of philosophizing. The meaning and worth of the Hegelian Dialectic is, in fact, teasingly obscure even to those who have studied Hegel longest and most sympathetically, who have brooded deeply over the discrepant accounts he gives of his method, and on the Protean tricks through which he operates it. If one starts by thinking Dialectic easy to characterize, one often ends by doubting whether it is a method at all, whether any general account of it can be given, whether it is not simply a name covering any and every of the ways in which Hegel argues. And if one tries to distinguish between the way in which the method *should* be used, and the way in which Hegel actually uses it, one soon finds that his practice provides no standards by means of which its detailed working can be tested.[21]

There is nothing to indicate that the nature and merit of Marcuse's "dialectic" is any more apparent. For one thing, it is almost impossible to determine what Marcuse understands the dialectic to be. Sometimes he speaks of it as a "logic," but it is obvious that it is a most singular "logic," a logic which "reveals and expresses that which really is—as distinguished from that which appears to be (real)."[22] It would thus be a "logic" with empirical and ontological pretensions. A most singular "logic." Furthermore, it is a "logic" which takes seeming delight in semantic vagueness. It is a "logic," for example, that reveals to us that "Truth" (dignified with the capital T) is the equivalent of "Being" (equally dignified, as one might expect, with a capital B). It tells us, moreover, that "in their completed form both happiness and reason coincide."[23] "Dialectical logic," as we have already observed, identifies Reason and Freedom, and conjoins that intelligence with the formula "Reason = Truth = Reality,"[24] which permits us to assert, if "dialectical logic" means anything at all, that Truth is equal to Being and Being is equal to Happiness and Happiness is equal to Reason and Reason is equal to Freedom and Freedom is equal to Reality and Reality is equal to Truth and Truth is . . ., and around once again. But this is not all it accomplishes. We are informed that we must defend all these insights against the threat of "Nothing" (also endowed with the substantive capital)—which is "a potentiality and a threat to Being." Since Nothing is a potentiality and a threat to Being, it is a potentiality and threat to Truth, it is a potentiality and a threat to Happiness, and since it. . . .

No charge of inconsistency or contradiction can be sustained against such a "logic," since it not only does nothing to avoid the semantic and syntactic vagueness of ordinary speech—it incorporates and expands upon them. The "dialectic" is a "logic" which has empirical pretensions, is semantically vague and syntactically obscure, and concerning which no judgment of consistency can be scrupled. A most singular "logic."

Lewis Carroll (himself a logician), in his adventure of *Alice in Wonderland,* provides us with what is perhaps an instructive sequence. Alice, among the quaint company of the inhabitants down the Rabbit Hole, found herself faced with the prospect of participating in a "Caucus-race." When she asked what a "Caucus-race" might be, she was told that in order to come to know what it was one really ought to do it. A circle was laid out—it really didn't matter whether it was a circle or not—there are no rules for this sort of thing. Then everyone was placed *somewhere* along the course and took up running at will. After a while when everyone was tired, the "race" was stopped—and then a decision had to be made as to who had won. After long deliberation it was decided that since everyone had put so much effort into the activity—*everyone* had won. The only question that remained was who was to provide the prizes. It was inevitable, it seems, that Alice was made to shoulder the burden.

The "dialectic" seems very much like a "Caucus-race"—there doesn't seem to be any identifiable body of rules that subtend the entertainment. Everyone takes up the activity wherever he chooses and continues until he is tired. At its conclusion everyone has won— and the reader must provide the prizes. One cannot help feeling that something has gone amiss.

The "dialectic" has, in fact, had a doleful history in the one place where it was taken seriously: in the Soviet Union. It was originally touted as a "logic" that opposed "idealistic formal logic" (what Marcuse calls, with Hegel, "abstract logic"). Formal logic, it was held, was simply a bourgeois snare (for Marcuse "formal or symbolic logic" is part of the "logic of domination"—a Marcusean transliteration of the Marxist "bourgeois oppression"). "Dialectical logic," to a generation of Soviet thinkers (as it is to Marcuse), was a "logic" that revealed the "essences" of things, the "fundamental and immutable laws of thought" and of "evolution of social and mental life." It "reflected" the real world and made "thinking and being identical." Being the source of so many good things, Soviet thinkers stoutly defended it against the impostures of formal logic. Formal logic being "abstract" (for them as it is to Marcuse), it failed to recognize the "real contradictions" that inhabit reality. The great advantage of "dialectical logic" was that it was a "logic of contradictions," and thereby captured the "contradictory essence" of "reality" (something it does for Marcuse as well). All of this was embodied in the work of Engels and Lenin and Plekhanov. In the first edition of the standard *Brief Philosophical Dictionary,* published during the Stalin period, it was insisted that "the laws of formal logic oppose themselves to the laws of dialectical logic," and Soviet mathematicians and logicians were enjoined to develop a "proletarian dialectic to replace the "empty" logic of "Bourgeois idealism." Marcuse has been equally eloquent in characterizing the poverty of "abstract logic," and admonishes American philosophy to seek out his "contradictory two-dimensional logic" to replace the "one-dimensional thinking" of formal logic. Formal logic "dominates"—dialectical logic "liberates."

One need but review the history of the controversy concerning the "logic of contradictions" as it developed in the Soviet Union in order to appreciate its signal failure.[25] Every responsible Soviet thinker today recognizes that it is especially absurd to hold that contradiction exists not only in thought and language but also in "reality," since it is the distinguishing trait of a self-contradictory utterance that it describes nothing whatever. A contradiction is *always* false—and says *nothing* at all.[26] Marxist-Leninists have been quick to reinterpret "contradiction," to mean no more than the presence of "conflicting or opposing tendencies" in "reality." But such a redescription empties the term "contradiction" of any independent meaning. If one means to say, as Marcuse does on occasion, that there is an "opposition of forces, tendencies, elements, which constitutes the movement of the real . . . ,"[27] then that is what one ought to say. There is no merit in baptizing a perfectly consistent description of trends and countertrends, opposing forces and countervailing tendencies tendentiously as "contradictions."

It is not at all clear that the "dialectic," and its "logic of contradiction," serves *any* independent cognitive purpose that escapes normal cognitive techniques. If one were not generous, one might characterize its specific function as obscuring gaps in arguments, camouflaging impaired reasoning, affording a semblance of credibility to vague and unsupported factual claims, making illicit transitions from matters of fact to ascriptions of value and in general providing a noncognitive linguistic recreation.

When Marcuse tells us that "the dialectical definition defines the movement of things from that which they are not to that which they are," he can only mean that he is attempting to characterize the development of something in terms of confirmed historic or systematic process laws. When he says that the "object of dialectical logic is neither the abstract, general form of objectivity, nor the abstract general form of thought—nor the data of immediate experience," he is doing little else than (in his own language style) saying that a historic or systematic process law, conjoined with initial conditions, provides an adequate account of development—

and such an account is neither simply "abstract, general, of thought or of immediate experience."[28] It involves concrete inductive generalizations covering a reasonably well-defined class of concrete objects understood to operate within specified or specifiable boundary conditions. None of which involves a "logic of contradictions," a "dialectic," or *any* exotic adjunct to standard scientific techniques.

If all one wishes to do is to indicate that language has a variety of functions—that no single description, no matter how complex, exhausts reality, that variables frequently interact in a complex system of interdependencies, that unanticipated consequences follow from our most carefully rehearsed social acts, that much of the detail of our natural and social world is contingent and evanescent, that confirmed lawlike regularities afford us only approximations of outcomes, that all our synthetic knowledge is corrigible—then appeal to a mysterious "dialectic logic," the rules of which are at best opaque, and whose influence has done more to engender than reduce confusion, is simply not necessary. Imagination, intuition, phantasy, the dialectic and poetry can, like preliminary conceptual schemata, serve as *heuristic* devices critical to the knowledge enterprise—but they are not its substitute. Nor do they constitute indifferent substitutes for the language of cognition. To make knowledge claims commits us to linguistic precision, specified or specifiable rules of evidence, a public characterization of meaning and an intersubjective test of truth. We cannot satisfy these commitments with imagination, intuition, phantasy, the dialectic or poetry.

Our account thus far has pursued the outlines of an analysis calculated to distinguish the cognitive from the noncognitive employments of the language. Whatever cognitive utility "the dialectic," "imagination," "phantasy," and "intuition" have is the consequence of their function as sometimes necessary preliminaries to significant cognitive enterprise. "Imagination," "phantasy," and "intuition," whatever they are taken to mean, at best *suggest* lines of inquiry in very much the same fashion as analogy and metaphor. Every research scientist and scholar employs them in order to orient himself with respect to his subject matter. Only when such "insights" mature into relatively precise test hypotheses, open to public scrutiny, do they enter into the knowledge enterprise itself.

Only when they are confirmed directly by some finite set of observations or indirectly within the confines of a systematically related set of propositions—only when they have warranted confirmed or systemic meaning—do they enter as material truths into the body of credibilities.

Ideologies and Noncognitive Language

While the discussion thus far has suggested a strategy which might accomodate a variety of claimants for interstitial cognitive status, there remains, inevitably, an imposing body of material outside the confines of the account. Political ideologies, for example, have received extensive consideration in political science literature, to which our brief discussion of "myths" hardly makes contribution. If Sorel tended to treat "myths" as noncognitive locutions, such a characterization is simply inadequate to accomodate ideological thinking in general. A more fruitful analysis might be one which made "myths," as Sorel conceived them, instantiations of a special subset of a more inclusive class of complex linguistic entities. The inclusive class might be identified as "ideologies," with "myths" as limiting cases.

Ideologies, in general, and myths as special cases, can be understood to perform the same noncognitive political and social functions in at least one respect. They can be used to mobilize sentiment, provide rationalizations for organizational purpose, serve as recruitment aids, recharge flagging enthusiasm—in effect perform manipulative and expressive, and only tangential cognitive, functions. In this capacity they are, by and large, neither true nor false. We all immediately recognize that the Marxist-Leninist who claims that the "truth" of Marxism is confirmed by its ability to mobilize revolutionary sentiment has advanced a bogus argument.[29] That Christianity has found billions of adherents in the course of two millennia does not serve to confirm a single one of its doctrinal utterances. Christianity has enjoyed enormous success and has gathered into its fold untold millions of non-Christians in what used to be seen as a triumphal inevitability. All of which tells us interesting things about the sociology of mass behavior, the satisfaction of individual emotional needs, and the processes that govern the dissemination of ideas and the techniques effectively employed in proselytization—but nothing about the truth or falsity of any of the utterances that have issued forth from Christian theologians since the death of Christ.

Success in expressive employments constitutes no evidence of truth. The most patently absurd collection of simplisms can enjoy, and have in fact enjoyed, the most astonishing political success. All of which simply admonishes us to distinguish the truth of any linguistic performance from its emotive and pragmatic effect. The fact is that political ideologies can be understood, generically, as complex normative arguments—and as such are essentially cognitive artifacts. They are, at their best, composed of argued beliefs about matters of fact, conjoined with a finite set of analytic statements and value commitments. At times such complex arguments can be synoptically and stenographically expressed. On such occasions we might talk of condensed language. The assumption would be that such language could be suitably expanded upon request. "Myths," as Sorel employed the term, might appropriately refer to condensed formulations that *cannot* be expanded or, if expanded, are known to be false. Such formulations might then be appropriately referred to as couched in symbolic or mythic language—and such formulations, as Sorel seemed to appreciate, might be all but expressive. They would be noncognitive.

Commentators on political affairs have made us all aware of the fact that when ideologies are taken up by political constituencies they find expression in ordinary language and generally make an appearance in locutions that are lax in precision, that are deductively defective and cognitively flawed. Some analysts have gone so far as to construe such defective performances as symptomatic of ideological thinking in and of itself. Thus, for example, Talcott Parsons identifies what he calls the "essential criteria of an ideology" as "deviations from social science objectivity." Ideology contains statements about society which can be shown, by the methods of social science, to be positively in error and involves a manifest bias in selectivity—only those truths that suit his purpose are entertained by the ideologist.[30] The ideologist, in effect, is a biased purveyor of falsehoods. Werner Stark has similarly characterized ideological thought as "a mode of thinking which is thrown off its proper course . . . something shady, something that ought to be overcome and banished from our mind"—thought that is somehow "deformed"—ideological ideas are "like a dirty river, muddied and polluted by the impurities that have flooded into it."[31]

Should we accept such characterizations, ideologies should be dismissed as having significant social functions, but possessed of only grossly impaired cognitive import. Ideological thinking, by definition, would be defective cognitive thought. Such an account is manifestly inadequate.[32] Ideological arguments are a special class of complex normative arguments—and normative arguments, as we have suggested, are as true or as false as the truth or falsity of their constituent statemental components. Marx as an ideologist did not simply generate defective arguments impaired by false descriptive propositions. Whatever faults one can find in Marx (and there are, no doubt, many) are faults common to *any* cognitive undertaking. Similarly, neither Giovanni Gentile nor Alfred Rosenberg could be reasonably conceived to have been nothing more than calculating deceivers. Gentile's attempt to vindicate Fascism, and Rosenberg's attempt to vindicate National Socialism were serious attempts to provide the normative, and consequently cognitive, rationale for Fascist and National Socialist policies and institutions. Should their arguments prove defective, should their credibility be undermined, they can no longer serve as *vindications*— although they may serve manipulative and persuasive purpose very effectively.

That ideologies serve noncognitive purpose, that they lend themselves to the manipulation of masses, that they come to serve as rationalizations for brutalities and stupidities is common knowledge—but such functions do not *characterize* "ideological thinking." Some men use drama or poetry to gull the innocent. Some use art. Some use science. The fact that poetry, art and science can be put to such noncognitive purpose is not their defining property.

If a distinction is to be made between ideologies and their flawed progeny—that is to say a distinction is entertained between the reasoned arguments of social and political philosophers of the

caliber of Marx and Gentile and the grossly simplified versions
that pass into doctrinal catechisms or serve exclusively expressive or
evocative function—we might speak of "ideologies" and "myths"
(elsewhere I have suggested the term "doctrine" might be invoked
to refer to the "relatively loose collection of [ideological theses]"
which are "essentially action related" and "contain a program and
a strategy for its fulfillment" and "provide a belief system for
organizations that are built around them").[33] The distinction would
be between argued beliefs that are intended to serve essentially
cognitive purpose and the shadow of those beliefs, or their formulation in expressive or evocative language, that serve essentially or
exclusively pragmatic (organizational, strategic or manipulatory)
purpose. The distinction would reflect the distinction between the
language and intention of Marx and Mao, between Gentile and
Mussolini, between John Locke and Richard Nixon, between
Herbert Spencer and Barry Goldwater.

When normative argument is processed for popular consumption
—to serve the organizational, strategic and recruitment purposes of
a political faction of whatever persuasion—what results is very
often something that looks, for all the world, like "thinking thrown
off its proper course," discourse undertaken to project one's psychological problems on the world, to give expression to intrapsychic
strain, to alleviate one's personal emotional indisposition or evoke
collective sentiments. We have all been exposed to such counterfeit
efforts at political persuasion and been subject to such mobilizing
techniques—the simple employment of invective, gross exaggera-
tion, unqualified declamation, diatribe, exhortation and empty
rhetoric. We are all familiar with the catalogue of abuses rehearsed
in political argument—and we are all painfully aware that when
language has devolved to this, its simplest noncognitive employment,
the reasoned resolution of problems, is impossible. Mythic or doctrinal language is the language of "confrontation," the preparation
for inevitable, because provoked, conflict—an invocation to arm
for Armageddon. The employment of such primitive linguistic
devices constitutes clear evidence that language has failed its cognitive purpose. Mythic or doctrinal language is a verbal grimacing,
a spoken gesture language, a language employed all but exclusively

to invoke, excite and express emotion. It is an exacerbated form of expressive language, vague in intention, imprecise in formulation, uncertified by any conceivable public test. It is the language of outrage—and it portends violence. It dichotomizes the world into the morally exalted and the morally irredeemable, the chosen and the damned, the progressives and the reactionaries, the capitalists and the proletariat, the oppressed and the oppressors, the Gentile and the Jew, the Black and the White, the good guys and the bad. In such a universe violence becomes a predictable necessity. Mythic or doctrinal language is the most perverse form of noncognitive discourse—because those who invoke it are prepared to have *us* pay the price of its use.

Notes

1 Cf. G. Sorel, *Reflections of Violence* (New York: Free Press, 1950), pp. 140, 144f.

2 R. Kirk, "Is Social Science Scientific," in N. W. Polsby, R. A. Dentler, and P. A. Smith (eds.) *Politics and Social Life* (Boston: Houghton Mifflin, 1963), pp. 60–64.

3 M. Q. Sibley, "The Limitations of Behavioralism," in J. Charlesworth (ed.), *Contemporary Political Analysis* (New York: Free Press, 1967), pp. 51–71; H. Marcuse, *Negations: Essays in Critical Theory* (Boston: Beacon, 1968), pp. 154f.

4 Sorel, *Reflections,* p. 142.

5 Cf. *Ibid.,* pp. 31–34.

6 Cf. H. Barth, *Masse und Mythos* (Hamburg: Rowohlt, 1959), pp. 10ff., 18f.

7 Cf. particularly G. Sorel, "La necessita e il fatalismo nel Marxismo," in *Saggi di critica del Marxismo* (Milan: Sandron, 1903), pp. 59–94.

8 Sorel, *Reflections,* pp. 55f.

9 *Ibid.,* p. 52.

10 *Ibid.,* p. 142.

11 V. Pareto, "Georges Sorel," *La Ronda* (1922), p. 542.

12 M. Edelman, *The Symbolic Uses of Politics* (Urbana, Ill.: Univ. of Illinois, 1967), ch. 1.

13 C. Geertz, "Ideology as a Cultural System," in D. Apter (ed.), *Ideology and Discontent* (New York: Free Press, 1964), pp. 47–76.

14 Marcuse, *Negations,* p. 154.

15 H. Marcuse, "Repressive Tolerance," in R. Wolff, B. Moore, Jr., and H. Marcuse, *A Critique of Pure Tolerance* (Boston: Beacon, 1965), p. 87.

16 Marcuse, *Negations,* pp. 134f., 144; *One Dimensional Man* (Boston: Beacon, 1964), pp. xi, xv.

17 Marcuse, *Negations,* pp. 137, 138, 141.

18 *Ibid.,* pp. 185, 187.

19 H. Marcuse, *Eros and Civilization* (New York: Random House, 1955), particularly pp. 5f.

20 Marcuse, "Repressive Tolerance," in Wolff, Moore, and Marcuse, *op. cit.,* p. 98.

21 J. N. Findlay, *Hegel: A Reexamination* (New York: Collier, 1962), p. 55.

22 Marcuse, *One Dimensional Man,* p. 124.

23 Marcuse, *Negations,* p. 199.

24 Marcuse, *One Dimensional Man,* p. 123.

25 A. J. Gregor, "Changing Concepts of Logic in Soviet Philoso-

phy," *Duquesne Review,* Fall (1966), pp. 87–100, and *A Survey of Marxism* (New York: Random House, 1965), pp. 57–71, 122–128.

[26] Cf. the various collections of discussions by Soviet thinkers on this and related issues in A. Kosing and E. Kosing (eds.), *Ueber formale Logik und Dialektik* (Berlin: Kultur und Fortschritt, 1952); N. Lobkowicz (ed.), *Das Widerspruchsprinzip in der neueren sowjetischen Philosopie* (Dordrecht: Reidel, 1959).

[27] Marcuse, *One Dimensional Man,* pp. 140f.

[28] *Ibid.,* p. 141.

[29] T. J. Blakeley, *Soviet Scholasticism* (Dordrecht: Reidel, 1961), pp. 34f.

[30] T. Parsons, "An Approach to the Sociology of Knowledge," *Transactions* (1959), 25.

[31] W. Stark, *Sociology of Religion* (London: Routledge, 1966), I, pp. 90f.

[32] Cf. N. Harris, *Beliefs in Society: The Problem of Ideology* (London: Watts, 1968), chap. 1.

[33] A. J. Gregor, *Contemporary Radical Ideologies* (New York: Random House, 1968), pp. 9f.

Suggested Readings

Gregor, A. James. *Contemporary Radical Ideologies.* New York: Random House, 1968. Chap. 1.

Lasswell, Harold D. "The Language of Politics," in H. D. Lasswell and N. Leites (eds.), *Language of Politics.* Cambridge, Mass.: MIT, 1965.

Ogden, C. K., and Richards, I. A. *The Meaning. of Meaning.* New York: Harcourt, Brace, 1923. Chapter Ten.

11

Conclusion

The White Rabbit put on his spectacles. "Where shall I begin, please your Majesty?" he asked.

"Begin at the beginning," the King said, very gravely, "and go on till you come to the end: then stop."

Lewis Carroll

There is little that can be said at the conclusion of a book of this kind that would add substantively to what has gone on before. Our concern has been with the talk of the talk of political inquiry. Political scientists have developed a language style and a vocabulary, particularly over the past generation, that requires considerable analysis. However one defines the political scientist's universe of inquiry—and many ways have been suggested by just as many people—it is the political scientist's talk about that universe that recommends itself to therapeutic scrutiny. One cannot always see through the political scientist's speech to the cognitive import of what he intends. The study we have just concluded is an effort to characterize some of the rule-governed strategies that can be understood as implicitly governing the talk of political scientists.

The recourse, at this point, to the conditional "can be understood" suggests that the measure of success enjoyed by the effort can be gauged only by a judgment that is essentially normative and pragmatic. It is normative because it makes no necessary claim to characterize what political scientists in fact *do* in the course of their work, but rather serves to articulate what would serve to legitimize

343

what they *do* do. In effect, the study constitutes a sustained recommendation concerning language employments. Like all recommendations it offers justificatory argument in its support. Its justification is, ultimately, in terms of yield. If practitioners succeed in going about their business with greater dispatch and precision—if the steps in the generation of empirical and normative theory are rendered more apparent—if the promise of more abundant theoretical yield is realized—if we find ourselves more effectively equipped to provide the rationale for our chosen strategies—and if some confusions are dissipated—because we have, in some small measure, profited by pursuing the discussion contained in this work, the recommendations contained herein are, in that measure, felicitous.

Even if this introduction were maximally effective—what we have accomplished is little more than an introduction. There are so many issues as yet interred in the language of political inquiry that no single work could resolve them. What has been suggested has been a critical and analytic strategy thought to offer maximal promise.

A beginning has been made with respect to the perennial problem of the relationship of science to political inquiry. An effort has been made to distinguish between the domains of language most critically the concern of the student. Some specification has been offered that characterizes their domain variant and invariant truth conditions and the relationship of simpler to more complex linguistic artifacts. Some time has been spent attempting to unpack portmanteau concepts like "understanding" and "explanation," and science-specific concepts like "law," "theory" and "model." How successful any of this has been is difficult to establish. What can be said with some confidence is that such problems cannot be cavalierly dismissed. Political inquiry is an arduous undertaking, and in undertaking it the student of political inquiry assumes intellectual obligations of compelling complexity.

The fact is that political inquiry can no longer be conducted in the unself-conscious and nondeliberative manner that characterized the works of the traditional masters of the discipline. Whatever our persuasion, the "truths" of political inquiry will have to meet the minimum requirements of truth certification—and these requirements have to be catalogued, displayed and publicly vindicated. James Rosenau has somewhere suggested that the sciences of human behavior, like countries in the twentieth century, pass through diverse stages as they approach "modernization." They pass through a traditional stage in which there is reliance on funded common-sense knowledge, couched in the vaguenesses and ambiguities of ordinary speech, only to enter into a transitional "take-off" in which a science begins to become cumulative and commences a process which is self-generative, self-regulative and self-corrective.

But before that stage is attained, the practitioners of "innovative" and "modernizing" trends become involved in frenetic activity, often disorganized and sometimes undisciplined.

Like the leaders of protest movements in traditional societies . . . the modernizing practitioners are not able to contain their revolutionary fervor once they overcome the forces of tradition and shoulder the responsibilities of leadership. The surge of innovative activity is too exciting and the vision of its ultimate potential too exhilarating to temper enthusiasm with perspective, involvement with restraint, and creative formulations with scientific procedures. In the name of greater discipline the field comes to be marked by undisciplined inquiry. Freed of the traditional rules and as yet unconcerned about the need for modern ones, its newly ascendant practitioners are receptive to almost any innovative framework, irrespective of whether it is capable of yielding reliable empirical findings. Despite the welter of activity, therefore, knowledge is no more cumulative in the take-off stage than in the preceding one. Rather than building on each other's work and converging around accepted concepts and standardized procedures, the practitioners support each other's innovativeness even as they pursue their own.

As the process runs its course, however, "innovative frameworks are scaled down to manageable proportions, the new concepts are rendered operational, and the resulting hypotheses are tested, revised and tested again." As a consequence, the "schools of thought," the "perspectives" and the "paradigms" give way to empirical findings, the "grandiose theory to the rigorous study, the propositional inventory to the research design . . . and the all encompassing insight to the precise formulation. . . . And, with this greater discipline, the practitioners begin to take cognizance of each other's hypotheses, to use each other's methods, to carry each other's work one step further, to replicate each other's findings—in short, to build on each other's research."[1]

Should political inquiry have embarked on such a process—what is required at this point is careful and protracted epistemological and metalinguistic analysis, a sorting out of cognitive strategies, a close inspection of alternatives. That task is best characterized as metapolitical. What has been attempted here has been an introduction to that service function which does not, in itself, enhance our substantive knowledge of our universe of inquiry, but clears away some of the linguistic confusion that obscures its outlines.

Philosophy and Political Inquiry

One of the principal functions of philosophy, since it made its appearance as a distinguishable human activity, is to encourage participants in the knowledge enterprise to sort out, catalogue and characterize the truth conditions governing the kinds of claims advanced by rational agents. Christian Bay's admonition that political scientists should avoid the elementary errors that afflicted traditional inquiry into politics is a summary recognition that traditional political scientists "had not learned to distinguish between verifiable *descriptive* statements, statements of *normative* positions, and (empirically empty and normatively neutral) *analytical* statements, including definitions and other equations."[2]

This sorting, cataloguing and assaying is itself a special kind of cognitive activity—a second-order concern with first-order questions. Engaged in this kind of pursuit, men ask questions about questions and they talk about talk. Philosophy, as this kind of activity, is a necessary antecedent to the serious development of any body of credible information.

Construed in such guise, philosophical activity is understood as critical to, but distinct from, political inquiry as a substantive undertaking. Philosophy is an analytic ancillary to the knowledge enterprise. To conceive philosophy as a special quest for a special wisdom, a "quest for universal knowledge, for knowledge of the whole"[3]—would not only constitute a special intellectual arrogance, but would be fundamentally mistaken as well. Few philosophers today could, in good conscience, claim a special perceptive faculty that would permit them to limn a special knowledge—knowledge of the "whole." "Understanding" and "knowing" of either parts or wholes must meet specific evidence conditions. The most comprehensive "knowing" is an "understanding" which is both systemic and standard, which entertains maximally reliable credibilities conjoined with publicly defensible evaluations. Such understanding is not, cannot be, the special possession of philosophers. It is the conjoint product of standard science and normative assessment. To possess knowledge of the "whole," to understand most comprehensively, is to pursue science broadly conceived and responsibly discharged.

Philosophy is today generally recognized as a critical and analytic activity that performs a variety of metafunctions—it is serious and insistent analysis of the language of inquiry. It has revealed itself to be largely, if not exclusively, a preoccupation with language. The distinctive trait of twentieth-century philosophy is, as a matter of fact, a sustained and incisive preoccupation with language— ordinary language and reconstructed language—the rule-governed symbolic exchanges between language users, between purveyors of ordinary speech and those employing the exalted speech of poetry, metaphysics and "theory," as well as those invoking the stipulative utterances of standard science. The conviction is that the study of language can yield insight into such matters, or at least materially reduce the measure of confusion that characterizes the discussions about them. Since at least the time of Frege and Russell, the concern has become increasingly deliberative and insistent. Language is recognized as the vehicle of truth claims, a vehicle that effectively transports whatever intellectual baggage we have accumulated, but a vehicle that must be continually refashioned and reshaped in transit. In growing up within the confines of a given language environment we acquire, by virtue of thinking in inherited semantic and syntactical grooves, funded conceptual categories which we must, ultimately, modify if we are to generate a maximally reliable, and internally supportive, system that adequately characterizes our world and its denizens. In the course of coming to know that world— in coming to fashion the linguistic artifacts capable of characterizing it—we move from language level to language level. Our ordinary language transforms itself from common utterances to academic and literary locutions, from the academic and literary to the eristic, symbolic, propositional and formal. We come to understand the world by reconstructing our language. We commence with our unproblematic and procedural "tacit" knowings and we generate our complex, propositional and "explicit" knowings. We commence with our empathic, and end with our systemic and evaluative, under-standings.

It is doubtful whether philosophy serves anything other than a critical service function in the generation of such substantive and systemic understanding. Philosophers have no special faculty for perceiving some special omnibus "whole," nor does it seem likely that they have a special capacity for generating, confirming and purveying "normative" knowledge. References to the "whole" can only have complex theories as their objects—and it is more than doubtful whether there is some singular knowledge that could be characterized as "normative." One simply does not undertake to *discover* the *truth* about what is right or wrong. One can, it would seem, try to determine what *is* right or wrong—but it seems implau-sible to suggest that someone might discover at some time or another whether "Treat men as ends, never as means" is either true or false. One simply does not request, nor expect to receive, grants to finance field research into such problems—which suggests that normative issues are domain specific and differ significantly from descriptive and formal issues. At best, thinkers preoccupied with normative issues are specially competent in a special language domain—which means that normative "theorists" can best be construed as possessed of special analytic and critical skills. What-ever knowledge they possess is essentially, if not exclusively, procedural and metalinguistic.

If political philosophers have knowledge of the "whole," a special comprehension of politics, then they command a comprehensive theory of politics—substantive understanding that is both systematic and evaluative. If political philosophers are primarily concerned with the traditional treatment of such understanding—their knowledge is descriptive, essentially archival and scholarly. If their concerns are specifically contemporary and exclusively normative, they command procedural and systematic language skills.

Unless political philosophers command encyclopedic knowledge of the universe of inquiry, conjoined with special analytic and critical linguistic skills, their principal function is in a service capacity. They keep empirical theorists aware of their intellectual responsibilities—they ventilate confusions, expose ambiguities, reduce vagueness, and identify flawed argument. Most frequently their influence is felt in those instances when their colleagues confound disparate cognitive domains, confuse formal, empirical and normative issues. In such a capacity political philosophers are becoming increasingly influential.[4]

Metalinguistics and Political Inquiry

If "metapolitics" identifies a range of concerns that is essentially analytic and critical, and all but exclusively linguistic, the immediate objection that its practitioners must parry is that its preoccupations are "trivial." One is, it is said, concerned with "real," not with "verbal," issues when one studies political matters. There is an all but indefeasible conviction among some students of political inquiry that to consider linguistic aspects of research problems, to undertake critical and analytic assessment of the various domains of discourse, is to trivialize serious issues. Such persons celebrate this judgment by referring to such preoccupations as "merely verbal" or "simply matters of language." The implication is that one should not concern oneself with "merely verbal," but with "serious" and "significant," issues.

The ten preceding chapters have attempted to make clear the insubstantiality of such objections. If one considers the bulk of "serious" and "significant" problems which agitate political scientists, one realizes that in most, if not all, cases a preliminary assessment of linguistic usage materially aids in their solution. When

Hans Morgenthau maintained that " . . . if one looks at the cold war as it actually developed in the aftermath of World War II, one realizes that it has not been the result of the willful machinations of certain individuals or groups of individuals, but that it arose inevitably out of objective conflicts of interests which could not be accommodated by the diplomatic means which both sides were willing to use"[5]—the judgment was a "serious" and "significant" one. Conceiving the judgment as a linguistic problem neither reduces its seriousness nor its significance—and has the advantage of making clear what would count as evidence of its truth. One realizes, for example, that Morgenthau's account contains a negative claim, i.e., the cold war was *not* the result of the willful machination of individuals or groups of individuals—a claim that as a linguistic problem would be rephrased as "What evidence would be required to confirm the judgment, 'The cold war was not the result of the machinations of certain individuals or groups of individuals'?" Similarly, the clause devoted to the "causes" that "inevitably" produced the cold war would be construed as a linguistic problem of the following sort, "What evidence would be required to confirm the deterministic claim, 'The cold war was the inevitable result of objective conflicts of interest which could not be accommodated by the diplomatic means which both sides were willing to use'?"

The truth conditions governing negative claims, and those governing attributions of "inevitability" are very exacting. To know that is to make "significant" progress in the direction of resolving "serious" and "significant" issues. To realize that the complex phrase "objective conflicts of interest" requires analysis as a constructum whose evidence conditions require an ultimate appeal to some criterially or contextually defined referents is to outline a "serious" and "significant" research strategy calculated to answer a "serious" and "significant" question.

One is no less "committed," "concerned," or "humanistic," nor are one's activities any less "relevant," "serious," or "significant" by construing political issues, initially, as linguistic problems. One of the principal difficulties that besets political inquiry is not only the extent to which "significant" questions are empirical, formal or normative, but to what extent they are linguistic. To identify a political society as a "system" may not only conceal empirical, formal and normative elements, but the locution may suffer a degree of vagueness and ambiguity that renders it intractable. Utterances, for example, that make reference to the "national interest," or to a putative "conflict of interest" raise a flurry of linguistic problems. Similarly, when Harold Laski told his students that the "state" is "an organization for enabling the mass of men to realize social good on the largest possible scale" and that "social good" "consists in the unity our nature attains when the working of our impulses results in a satisfied activity,"[6] he conjured up a host of linguistic problems that required resolution before any truth determinations could be attempted. Not only were his claims qualitative (and thus difficult to confirm), but they invoked an indeterminate number of normative, formal and empirical issues that required antecedent metalinguistic treatment—treatment that would move inquiry far along the process of truth determination.

All this is not to say that *all* linguistic problems are serious and significant. There are many linguistic issues that are trivial—just as there are many empirical, formal and normative issues that are equally trivial. We have here rehearsed standard arguments for the seriousness of the enterprise only to establish the implausibility of treating metalinguistics (and metapolitics by entailment) contemptuously.[7]

Linguistic Precision and Political Inquiry

Still another objection is to be found in the catalogue of objections to metapolitics. Briefly stated, the objection is that "neopositivistic" and "behavioristic" "reduction" of concepts "eliminate" "troublesome concepts" from the universe of political inquiry, and thus serve to "dominate" our minds, impair our critical faculties, and provide a "totalitarian logic" that serves the *status quo*.[8]

To such an objection one can only reply that unless meaning can be specified, truth cannot be responsibly assigned. There are features of our universe of inquiry which require identification, that are not, as it were, simply thrust upon us. They are identified and characterized only by self-conscious and deliberate activity by men. These relatively covert aspects of experience are identified in the conceptual language of science. Elements of the object world that we identify as "power," "class," "repression," "alienation," "anomie," and "system" do not impinge upon us as do "hunger," "red," "solid" and "pain." Much of ordinary language is composed of the latter unproblematic concepts—but even in ordinary language signs appear which require some specification of meaning before they can be used effectively. Only by deliberating upon them can we begin to specify the recognitors that will count as their meaning, and determine their felicitous use.

To characterize a society as "repressive" requires a specification of how people in circumstances characterized by specific initial conditions do or would behave as against situations which are "non-repressive." The term is a dispositional one—at any given time a repressive society need not be repressing, any more than an elastic material need always be stretched nor a malleable piece of iron need always be bending. In order to tell if a society is, in fact, possessed of a dispositional attribute, such an attribution must be defined not lexically, nor by necessary and sufficient conditions, but by a complex determination (in the form of a complex proposition in the subjunctive mood) of the observable conditions by virtue of which a proposition containing the sign is considered true. The determinations of meaning and truth are made via conditional or if-then sentences. The antecedent clause specifies the circumstances in which the observations are to be made and the consequent clause indicates the behavior which, under the specified conditions, will count as instances of the sign being defined. The entire complex conditional statement constitutes an "operationalization" which specifies determinant meaning and establishes the conditions for truth ascription. Such "operationalization" does not exhaust the conceivable meaning of a concept. Criterial definitions, like contextual definitions, both operationalizable, are "porous," "open textured." They do, however, indicate the meaning of the concept as it is employed in any specific case, and they do so by focusing on observable properties. They commence with an antecedent clause which specifies initial conditions which must hold, either as necessary or sufficient or necessary and sufficient conditions, for the consequent to hold.[9]

All such complex, conditional and partial specifications of meaning are statements about the felicitous use of signs. The effort to determine which conditions and consequent observations shall be included in an interpretation of meaning is one of the most exacting tasks in theory construction. As a critical effort no concept is excluded. No sign, no matter how threatening to the *status quo,* to established elites, is simply excluded from such considerations.

The social scientist, attempting to exhibit meanings and establish truth, necessarily invokes other than ordinary speech. This means that his concepts will have special, often stipulative meaning, which deprives ordinary language concepts of the multiplicity of meanings that attend them in common parlance. To construe this as a shortcoming, rather than a special virtue, is a prejudice common to a variety of critics. A concept can only be understood to mean what its definition says it means. It is only necessary that that definition be sufficiently precise so that we can, with some degree of assurance, determine when we do or when we do not have an instance of it. Not having met that necessary condition we can only say that the concept has been inadequately defined. To maintain that the proferred definition does not "really" define the concept is to offer a counterdefinition—which, in its own turn, must meet the necessary condition of specificity. Definitions are conventions, warranted by their function within complex linguistic artifacts called theories. The only thing critics can mean when they insist that "positivistic" and "behavioristic" definitions "distort" the universe of inquiry is that they, the "nonpositivists" and "nonbehaviorists," can more adequately define concepts, house them more coherently in complex linguistic artifacts that better predict and explain the object world with which they are concerned.

Concepts like "the power elite," and "the repressive society" are not suspect because they threaten the *status quo,* but because they are never defined with the specificity requisite to their use as scientific terms. It is not enough to insist that ordinary persons intuitively know what the "power elite" or the "repressive society" is. Such an affirmation may very well tell us more about the mythopoetic convictions of ordinary people than they tell us about our object of inquiry. If either concept is a serviceable concept, it is not because of its compatibility or consonance with common and intuitive "sense," but because we can identify its referents with reliability and because we can affirm with reasonable probability its connection with other attributes and behaviors. No scientific concept can be devoid of directly or indirectly observable reference. It is that reference which conveys meaning and permits the determination of truth. Marcuse, for example, defines "repressive society" in terms of "needs," and he distinguishes between "real" and "fictive" needs—all of which cries out for analysis—not because such concepts threaten the *status quo*, but because such terms are intolerably vague and ambiguous.

It is reasonably clear that contemporary treatments of scientific concepts do not preclude the assessment of *any* candidate concept whether the candidate is quantitative or qualitative. At the present stage in the development of political inquiry any suggestion that the enterprise deal *only* with quantified or quantifiable concepts is clearly restrictive. But the treatment of qualitative concepts should be made as rigorous as each case allows—with a recognition that the employment of concepts can serve didactic and heuristic as well as predictive and explanatory purpose.

Most of the objections raised by "antibehavioralist" authors turn on a consideration of concepts employed for heuristic purpose. The substance of these objections is that when one commences inquiry one entertains a "conceptual framework"—what we have here identified as ordinary language or preliminary conceptual schemata—that is characteristically imprecise. All of which is patently true. The thrust of the discussion here is not that such initial strategies should be eschewed, but that they should be recognized for what they are. One can begin with the vaguest and most imprecise formulations in the effort to orient oneself in a special range of concerns or to reorient oneself in a familiar range, but at some point one must leave off such preliminary strategies and proceed to standardize meaning, formalize putative relations, and confirm truth claims. Even the most insistent critics of "one-dimensional" thought recognize that at some point their "multidimensional" claims must be warranted—and it turns out that their claims must have "objective validity" and the demonstration of truth "has to proceed on empirical grounds."[10]

In effect, the negative criticism of efforts at semantic and syntactic rigor originate either in confusion or in a disposition to gull the unsophisticated. One can admire the candor with which those who knowledgeably exploit vagueness and ambiguity for suasive effect go about their business[11]—but one can only lament the confusion which afflicts those whose commitment is to the knowledge enterprise. The suggestion that our language must be imprecise in order to capture "reality" or truth is a studied deception or a thoughtless error. One simply does not "capture" "reality" in language. Capturing "reality" is not a function of speech. One does not capture "reality" in speech—or in poetry—or in art. The language of science attempts to identify recurrent features of experience in order to afford retrodictive, predictive and explanatory leverage. With such cognitive products at our disposal we come to understand, in a comprehensive and systematic fashion, political phenomena. Exalted speech in poetry and drama may convey feelings and those feelings may correspond to those which attend some one or another political phenomenon. If they succeed we have attained a kind of empathic understanding—we have "dwelt within" phenomena. If we have direct experience with complex phenomena, we entertain private states of mind and can be said to have an intuitive appreciation of the experience. But in no case can we be said to have captured "reality." To capture any "reality" is to duplicate it—a process which seems to be, in principle, impossible—and were it not impossible, it would be pointless. The purpose of inquiry is not to duplicate experience, but to understand it. And to understand it in any sense we must undertake one or another or all the linguistic strategies we have, in broad outline, rehearsed. Without recourse to them we cannot say that we *know* anything, much less that we know any *truths,* about "reality."

Values and Political Inquiry

No discussion of the relationship between linguistic analysis and political inquiry would be complete without at least a summary treatment of some of the most celebrated and recurrent problems concerning the putative relationship that obtains between "values" and inquiry. Our brief analysis of normative discourse addressed itself to general concerns of that language domain—the present discussion occupies itself with the claim that "science" and/or the "scientific method" is inextricably caught up in "values" that not only determine 1) what the researcher chooses to study; 2) they afflict him with a selective perception that structures his findings; and 3) they determine what will count as evidence in truth accreditation.

We have already considered one of the most prominent attempts to support such claims—the monograph by Thomas Kuhn, *The Structure of Scientific Revolutions.* But there are any number of alternate candidate arguments available in abundance in specifically political science literature. Arguments by Leo Strauss, Robert Strausz-Hupé and Henry Kariel constitute an inventory of claims concerning the putative relationship of values to inquiry.[12] Unfortunately, most of the arguments tendered are fragile and sometimes fugitive. They, nonetheless, provide the occasion for a reconsideration of serious issues and an opportunity to characterize in preliminary outline the relationships between "values" and inquiry as they can be reasonably understood to obtain.

First (but not foremost), it is true, but trivial, that anyone who pursues inquiry is *motivated* to do so—which is generally taken to mean that the agent has some *interest* in doing so—which, in turn, means that the agent is prepared to see some *value* in the enterprise. A human being has only limited time and energy resources at his disposal and is compelled, as a matter of fact, to allocate them selectively. This having been said, several things are reasonably clear: 1) "values" can, in this sense, serve as motives; 2) the "values" can be good, bad or indifferent as long as they provide the energy for undertaking inquiry; 3) precisely the same relationship between "values" and inquiry apply to all and any inquiry, in the natural as well as the social sciences; 4) these motivating value considerations are *extrinsic* to scientific inquiry *per se*.

We have already suggested that an individual may opt to pursue some range of inquiry because he entertains some political values— he may be a Fascist, a Marxist, a conservative or a liberal. But having opted for that inquiry, he is confined by the institutionalized norms, the *intrinsic* norms of his pursuit. The search for maximally reliable truth claims is *not* the simple commitment to a "value"—that can be simply taken up or left off at the individual's discretion. The search for truth is not the consequence of a *preference*. The pursuit of truth, the exercise of rationality, is, as we have already suggested, the most compelling *instrumental* good. Whatever goal values we pursue, whatever extrinsic values we harbor, they are served best, in fact, by the truth. Inquiry is governed by the *intrinsic* norms of truth accreditation. Truth claims, invoked to serve extrinsic values, are maximally serviceable (whatever those extrinsic values), only if they meet domain and interdomain specific intrinsic norms. This is as true of the social as it is of the natural sciences.

The logician who pursues the information sciences may do so for the basest motives—the lust for wealth, to obtain status, to impress young ladies—but to achieve his purpose, he must meet the intrinsic norms of that pursuit. Hitler's scientists, who sought to bomb England into submission (whatever their ultimate intentions), were compelled to pursue the sciences of ballistics, rocketry and propulsion in conformity with the intrinsic norms of adequacy governing those sciences.

When critics like Leo Strauss insist that "positivists" and "behavioralists" seek to "avoid value judgments altogether" and that they insist that "moral obtuseness is the necessary condition for scientific analysis," their claims are tendentious. The actual posture is that a distinction must be made between extrinsic value judgments and the application of intrinsic norms (that is to say between normative argument and the application of scientific standards of adequacy). To confuse the two serves no cognitive purpose. To further suggest, as Strauss does, that the scientist is the prey of his "preferences," one of which is the "preference" for truth (presumably as opposed to a "preference" for falsehood), is hardly credible. Anyone pursuing any line of inquiry, for whatever extrinsic value, has good and sufficient reason for pursuing truth. It is not simply a preference—it is an argued judgment for which there is good and compelling vindication. The effective achievement of any purpose requires an inventory of maximally reliable credibilities. Only the pursuit of truth can provide them.

Much the same can be said of pursuing a select line of research within a universe of inquiry. Some students of political inquiry will undertake study in international relations, some local politics, some comparative politics and some normative theory. Whatever motivates them—psychological predispositions, special competences, perversity or the desire to enhance freedom and well-being—judgments of their competence rest not on the extrinsic motives or values that direct their energies, but their capacity to meet the domain and interdomain specific norms of adequacy intrinsic to their range of concerns.

The second claim, that values render the student of politics selectively perceptive so that he tends to notice, record and concern himself with only select aspects of complex phenomena—aspects which tend to support his preconceptions—is probably true. We know enough about human beings to know that they suffer an inordinate number of handicaps that make the pursuit, discovery, articulation and acceptance of truth so difficult. But all this means is that science, whether natural or social, physics or political science, must be prepared to scrutinize every truth claim, that every truth claim be articulated with as much precision as possible, that vagueness and ambiguity not be permitted to serve as insulation against counterevidence, that heartfelt conviction, linguistic handicap, foolishness and hyperbole not be permitted to substitute themselves as evidence conditions. That a man fails to overcome his preconceptions is understandable—but that we be gulled by his performance, or imagine that biases are undetectable, is inexcusable.

As has already been suggested, behavioral science has provided compelling evidence that perception and thought is materially influenced by an impressive array of extrinsic factors—class, status, political persuasion, education, sex and race-related interests among others. But the fact that we can identify and isolate those influences indicates that they can, in principle, be offset. One of the principal concerns of corrigible science is just such identification and redress of bias. Bias is the identifiable influence of prejudgments on the collection, processing and interpretation of data. Obviously some biases may regularly escape our attention—but this can only mean that social scientists should apply the intrinsic norms of science more fastidiously. It cannot mean that objective research must forever and inextricably carry the burden of bias. We have already argued that if such should be the case no one could ever consistently argue that all truths were so afflicted—for to make the claim would defeat the claim. If it is true that all truth claims are inevitably biased, then the truth claim that all truth claims are inevitably biased is inevitably biased. The claim would be self-stultifying.

The final claim, that values determine what will count as evidence in truth accreditation, is the most interesting and is, in a very qualified sense and over a restricted range of concerns, probably true. Richard Rudner and Ernest Nagel have both argued that judgments of adequacy with respect to "statistical hypotheses" involve *intrinsic value judgments* (rather than the application of intrinsic domain specific *norms*).[13] Theoretical statistics, so the argument proceeds, employs levels of statistical significance; commonly there are three: 1 percent, 5 percent and 0.3 percent. Levels of significance address themselves to the probability of error. In no case, science being what it is, can the adequacy of either significance level *insure* the investigator against error. He is therefore compelled to make a choice between chancing to commit one or another error. If he rejects a hypothesis, he may be rejecting a truth; if he accepts the hypothesis, he may be harboring a falsehood. Even given a determined statistical significance level, the investigator must make a choice. That choice will be, at least in part, determined by the *importance* (in the sense of a *value judgment*) of the issues involved. It is intuitively obvious that a judgment of adequacy of evidence will be more readily forthcoming if the statistical hypothesis deals with a concern that invokes little human interest than if it involves one of emphatic weight. If the statistical hypothesis has to do with the toxic side effects of a new drug when used on human beings, the question of what is to count as adequacy becomes urgent and the importance of making an error in accepting or rejecting a statistical hypothesis is a cause of grave ethical concern. The intrinsic norms of science, alone, do not afford the leverage for making the requisite decision. What seems to be involved is a value judgment *intrinsic* to science.

It seems that at critical junctures within science an investigator must make *ascriptive value judgments* which are *intrinsic* to the enterprise. But it must be noted that this circumstance is not restricted to the social, but involves the natural sciences as well.

The real question is whether such a consideration can be generalized over more concerns than those dealing with statistical hypotheses. There appear to be, in fact, analogous circumstances in a variety of political science concerns. In broad policy matters political scientists seem to concern themselves with assessments, projections and weighing of evidence, that turn, at best, on measures of subjective probability. In characteristic instances we are not dealing with statistical probabilities at any level of mensurable significance. We find ourselves confronted with subjective judgments of probable outcomes. Will, for example, maintenance of the *status quo* in Latin America, with only incremental reforms, ultimately maximize the welfare benefits of a greater number of persons than a massive revolution now? Would the United States of America face more hazards by unilaterally disarming now rather than by maintaining a defense capability that may act as a deterrent?

These are obviously important human concerns, and they engage interest in the sense that they turn on characteristically normative matters ("happiness," "well-being," "survival").

Framed in such fashion, the discussion is obviously germane to issues that preoccupy students of political inquiry. It is equally clear that, so framed, the question involves a number of complex issues. Are the judgments required in such policy matters intrinsically normative (as seems to be the case with respect to the decision-making process with regard to statistical hypotheses) or are such "forced" judgments the result of a paucity of evidence, an inadequate data base and faulted communication?

It seems fairly clear that much of the "normative" and "judgmental" character of such deliberations *is* a consequence of an inadequate information base. We simply cannot undertake responsible cost accounting or make defensible projections when the issues involved are so complex and our information is so inadequate. Thus we tend to mask our inadequacies and screen our ignorance behind a profusion of expressive declamations, *ad hoc* proclamations, moral pronouncements and condensed ceremonial and ritual utterances. We are often faced with forced, living and momentous decisions when we have only the most circumscribed information at our disposal.

In such a context recourse to value judgments may be little more than a flight from responsibility. What we require is a more systematic, rigorous and well-confirmed inventory of truths about our world and the men in it. If we could fully characterize the probability of risk run in maintaining a defense establishment against the probability of risk run in unilateral disarmament, much of the pointless and tedious discussion that attends such issues would be deflated. What we would find, as has already been suggested, is that the vast majority of men invoke unproblematic, universalizable, intelligent and intelligible values to vindicate their decisions. The critical constituent in such vindications are the statemental elements, the constative truths that only standard science can warrant.

It seems relatively clear that values: extrinsic and intrinsic value judgments, intrinsic norms, and instrumental values, interact in complex ways in inquiry—but it is equally transparent that all require a systematic sorting out. Because there are reasonably clear instances in science, both natural and social, where intrinsic value judgments must be made cannot constitute a license to disregard instances where decision making requires not value judgment, but adequate information as a base for responsible choice. Because the decision governing truth ascription with regard to, as far as we know, a restricted class of statistical hypotheses seems to require intrinsic value judgments, it cannot serve as an unrestricted warrant to solve complex issues by appeal to "values." These considerations suggest, at best, that instances where recourse to intrinsic value judgments are legitimate be specifically identified. They cannot be construed to mean that wherever the individual is faced with inadequate data and a poverty of information, he should take refuge in subjective "value" judgment. What is required, more frequently than not in political inquiry, is more information, more adequate analysis of costs, and an assessment of the prospects of success—rather than increased "commitment."

To address oneself to the vindication of judgments and norms, the verification of descriptive and the validation of formal claims, in order to responsibly undertake decision, is to assume a rigorous and demanding obligation. There is no way of responsibly discharging the task without preliminary linguistic analysis, the sorting out, cataloguing and assessment of domain variant truth claims—without scrutinizing and making public defense of one's normative commitments and without doing the substantive empirical and formal work without which all would be to no effect.

The Prospects for Political Inquiry

For more than a generation now the study of politics, political systems, political culture, political institutions, and political behavior has developed with impressive rapidity. That the development has not been simply cumulative, that efforts have been frequently flawed, that the information produced has been partial and the understanding fostered fragmentary, is all true. But if one pauses to reflect that factor analysis, complex statistical analyses, multivariate assessments, as well as a host of research techniques and cognitive strategies are less than half a century old—if one considers the only recent development of computer capabilities, the storage, algorithmic and retrieval potential of such technological adjuncts of behavioral science—one can be reasonably sanguine about the prospects of the discipline. What the substitution of a new symbolic system did for mathematics, the substitution of arabic for roman numerals, suggests the potential that may well be concealed in contemporary computer capabilities.

Development in the field of research strategies and techniques is proceeding with the same remarkable rapidity and with the same impressive prospects. Institutions throughout the country are training students of political inquiry in the most effective techniques of data collection, processing and interpretation. Courses in research methods, quasi-experimental and experimental designs are now becoming standard throughout the discipline.

Where development is not equally impressive is in the domain of specifically normative inquiry. Traditional political "theorists" have been, as a matter of fact, ill-disposed to innovate, to embark on serious critical and analytic assessment of their language domain. Where philosophers have made systematic attempts to come to grips with *praxiology,* the systematic study of practical reasoning, and the logic of decision and action, attempting to systematically and formally analyze the structure of normative argument,[14] political "theorists" have been, by and large, content to restrict their concerns to intellectual history, to the tendentious ventilation of putative "core" values, the issuance of empty directives ("expand the range of undefined freedom," "enhance the social good," or "improve the human condition"), or the conveyance of vague generalities. Political "theorists"—or more appropriately political philosophers—have a number of tasks before them, tasks with which they have, as yet, only become peripherally involved: 1) linguistic analysis, and 2) a convincing account of the informal and formal logic of normative discourse. Without the systematic discharge of these obligations the generation of responsible normative argument is all but impossible. Linguistic analysis means, minimally, a sorting out of truth claims and a characterization of their truth conditions. An account of the formal and informal logic of normative discourse requires at least a convincing interpretation of normative meaning, a systematic treatment of praxiology, and ideally metapraxiological considerations, as well as at least a nodding acquaintance with deontic logic, the formal syntax of normative discourse. Conjoined with these insights, under the present institutional structure of political science, the political philosopher is further expected to have almost encyclopedic knowledge of the state of his discipline. He must have access to information from sociology, psychology, economics, history and descriptive linguistics. In effect, the obligations tacitly or explicitly assumed by the political philosopher are no less demanding, no less challenging and certainly no less exciting than those assumed by those who pursue empirical and formal truths.

To construe all this as anything other than science broadly conceived, an activity both rigorous and public, intelligent and intelligible, productive of maximally reliable truth, is to threaten our world and our time with a new obscurantism that could serve only the interests of those moved by dark or shapeless motives. Political inquiry offers us the opportunity of controlling our own destiny. It is a control that can be purchased only at the cost of dedication and considerable sacrifice.

Notes

[1] J. N. Rosenau, "The Premises and Promises of Decision-Making Analysis," in J. C. Charlesworth (ed.), *Contemporary Political Analysis* (New York: Free Press, 1967), pp. 190f.

[2] C. Bay, "Politics and Pseudopolitics," H. Eulau (ed.), in *Behavioralism in Political Science* (New York: Atherton, 1969), p. 112.

[3] L. Strauss, "What is Political Philosophy?" in *ibid.,* p. 94.

[4] For an intersting discussion of developments in "political theory," cf. N. A. Mc Donald and J. N. Rosenau, "Political Theory as Academic Field and Intellectual Activity," in M. D. Irish (ed.), *Political Science: Advance of a Discipline* (Englewood Cliffs, N.J.: Prentice-Hall, 1968), pp. 21–54.

[5] H. J. Morgenthau, "The Impact of the Cold War on Theories of International Law and Organization," in A. A. Said (ed.), *Theory of International Relations: The Crisis of Relevance* (Englewood Cliffs, N.J.: Prentice-Hall, 1968), p. 177.

[6] H. Laski, *The Grammar of Politics* (5th ed. London: George Allen & Unwin, 1967), pp. 24, 25.

[7] R. Rudner, *Philosophy of Social Science* (Englewood Cliffs, N.J.: Prentice-Hall, 1966), pp. 8f.

[8] H. Marcuse, *One Dimensional Man* (Boston: Beacon Press, 1964), *passim,* but particularly pp. 11–18.

[9] R. H. Ennis, "Operational Definitions," in L. Krimerman (ed.), *The Nature and Scope of Social Science* (New York: Appleton Century-Crofts, 1969), pp. 431–444.

[10] Marcuse, *op. cit.,* p. xi.

[11] ". . . clarity, alas, is not one of our goals. Confusion is mightier than the sword!" Free (A. Hoffman), *Revolution for the Hell of It* (New York: Dial, 1968), p. 26.

[12] L. Strauss, *What is Political Philosophy?* (New York: Free Press, 1959), pp. 18–26; R. Strausz-Hupé, "Social Science Versus the Obsession of 'Scientism,'" in H. Schoeck and J. Wiggins (eds.), *Scientism and Values* (New York: Van Nostrand, 1960), pp. 219–234; H. S. Kariel, "Social Science as Autonomous Activity," in *ibid.,* pp. 235–260; cf. also H. R. G. Greaves, "Political Theory Today," in C. A. McCoy and J. Playford (eds.), *Apolitical Politics*

(New York: Crowell, 1967), pp. 232–246.

[13] R. Rudner, "No Science can be Value-Free," in Krimerman, *op. cit.,* pp. 754–758; E. Nagel, *The Structure of Science* (New York: Harcourt Brace & World, 1961), pp. 496–498.

[14] Cf., for example, T. Kotarbinski, "Praxiological Sentences and How They are Proved," in E. Nagel, P. Suppes, and A. Tarski (eds.), *Logic, Methodology and Philosophy of Science* (Stanford: Stanford University, 1962), pp. 211–223; N. Rescher (ed.), *The Logic of Decision and Action* (Pittsburgh: University of Pittsburgh, 1967).

Suggested Readings

Brodbeck, M. "General Introduction," in M. Brodbeck (ed.), *Readings in the Philosophy of the Social Sciences.* New York: Macmillan, 1968.

Lasswell, Harold D. *The Future of Political Science.* New York: Atherton, 1964.

Leys, Wayne A. R. "Political Philosophy—in Quotation Marks," in M. B. Parsons (ed.), *Perspectives in the Study of Politics.* Chicago: Rand McNally, 1968.

Nagel, Ernest. *The Structure of Science.* New York: Harcourt, Brace & World, 1961. Chapter 13.

Glossary

This glossary is offered as a didactic and mnemonic aid. The brief definitions that follow words which may be unfamiliar to the reader attempt to begin to characterize their meaning. Regrettably and inevitably such brief definitions are equivocal and less felicitous than one might desire. Many of them, furthermore, are stipulative and cannot be construed as prescriptive.

Absolute reliability (see "Reliability")

Academic language (see "Language")

Analogical (or substantive) model (see "Models")

Analogue (or formal) model (see "Models")

Analytic conceptual schema (see "Conceptual schemata")

Analytic domain   That domain of discourse in which the truth of a proposition is determined by analysis and logical inference, i.e., the truth conditions governing truth status are intralinguistic, formal, and not empirical.

Analytic proposition   A proposition whose truth follows (with the assistance of definitions) from the principles of logic alone and whose denial involves a contradiction.

Argument   A systematic arrangement of propositions in which certain propositions, called premises, constitute the bases for inferring other propositions, called conclusions.

Sound argument   An argument which is both valid (in the formal sense) and in which the premises supporting the conclusion are true assertions.

Valid argument   When the premises of a deductive argument guarantee the truth of the conclusion, and that guarantee is the consequence of the fact that the argument instantiates a standard valid form, the argument is said to be valid. Validity does not insure either the material truth of any constituent premise or the conclusion.

Auxiliary assumption   An assumption implicitly or explicitly unproblematically entertained which attends and is essential to the attempt to determine the truth status of a problematic proposition, or set of propositions, under scrutiny.

Axiomatic system   A logically ordered set of propositions in which a
subset of propositions is selected as basic, i.e., axioms, and the remainder
constitute derivative theorems. The theorems are derived from the
axioms employing a specific set of transformation rules (with definitions understood to be a subset of transformation rules). An uninterpreted axiomatic system is a calculus.

Categoric generalization (see "Generalization")
Classificatory conceptual schema (see "Conceptual schemata")
Coextensive relation (see "Relations")
Cognitive language (see "Language")

Concept   A sign that refers to groups, categories or collections of things
or events, or the relations between them. When concepts are conceived
to share functional relationships, they are spoken of in empirical inquiry
as "variables."

Conceptual schemata   Any collection of propositions calculated to order
experience in some intelligible fashion: in political science literature,
conceptual schemata of varying degrees of sophistication are referred
to as "conceptual frameworks" or "approaches."

  Analytic conceptual schema   A conceptual schema composed of sets
  of definitions (a definitional schema) conjoined with a set of analytic
  or logically true sentences. The *truth* of such a schema is determined
  by inspection of its logical properties; its *utility* is determined by the
  uses to which such a schema can be put in empirical inquiry.

  Classificatory conceptual schema   A conceptual schema generated to
  provide classificational categories for elements in the universe of inquiry.
  If the classificatory schema provides for the necessary and sufficient
  conditions for the applicability of each of the classifying terms, the
  schema is definitional. If only some of the classifying terms are afforded
  adequate characterization, one has an incomplete definitional schema
  or a classificatory conceptual schema. Complete or incomplete classificatory schemata provide the basis for taxonomies, classifications
  and typologies.

  Ordinary language conceptual schema   A conceptual schema produced
  by, and inhabiting, ordinary language. The concepts characteristically
  found in such schemata are relatively imprecise and ambiguous and
  only vaguely suggest testable propositions. Such schema are adapted

to ordinary contexts, but their imprecision necessitates systematic efforts at reducing semantic and syntactical variance before they can be put to responsible scientific purpose.

Preliminary conceptual schema A conceptual schema in which some systematic efforts at reducing semantic and syntatical variance have been undertaken. At least one indigenous concept or relationship has been rigorously characterized. Such schemata are, in principle, capable of supporting some verification studies and are formulated in academic or, more characteristically, eristic language.

Concretum "Concreta" refer to what in ordinary language are spoken of as "concrete objects," e.g., chairs, tables, houses—objects whose existence and character are directly evidenced by unproblematic and direct observations.

Congruence Congruence is measured by the degree to which an indeterminate, but finite, set of recognitors (empirical indicators) serve as consistently symptomatic of a given empirical referent.

Construct A "construct," as the term is employed here, refers to a compound and/or complex abstraction, e.g., "the state" or "the presidency," whose meaning is partially or exhaustively explicated in terms of concreta (e.g., the specific acts of role encumbents, documents which catalogue the conventions or rules which provide for patterned expectations that characterize institutionalized behaviors, etc.).

Contextual definition (see "Definition")

Contingent relation (see "Relation")

Correlation A calculation that indicates that variations in the values assumed by one or more elements in the universe of inquiry are matched in the same (positive correlation) or in the opposite (negative correlation) direction by variations in one or more others.

Counterfactual (contrary to fact) conditional A conditional that asserts what would be the case if a condition, which in fact is not or was not realized, were or had been realized.

Criterial (or range) definition (see "Definition")

Deductive model of explanation (see "Explanation")

Definition An explanation of the meaning of a linguistic expression.

Contextual definition A definition which provides the meaning of the *definiendum* (the expression to be defined) by indicating how sentences containing it can be translated into synonymous sentences that do not contain the expression to be defined.

Criterial (or range) definition A definition in terms of an indeterminate, but finite, number of properties or attributes some element in the universe of inquiry might display to be counted in the class of elements. The elements in the class are said to display a "family resemblance," sharing one or more of the defining properties or attributes although no specific one is logically necessary.

Explicit definition A definition which provides the necessary and sufficient conditions for the employment of a sign, and which will not change (as a consequence) the truth status of the sentence in which the sign appears when the substitutable sign or signs are inserted. The *definiens* is the logical equivalent of the *definiendum*.

Implicit definition A term is implicitly defined by a set of propositions which reveal the term's denotation and its constitutive relations.

Lexical (verbal) definition The *definiendum* is declared synonymous with a better known term or terms (the *definiens*) and best characterized in reconstructed languages as explicit definitions.

Operational definition A procedure (which might be characterized as an "experimental procedure") which establishes the meaning of the *definiendum* in terms of observable recognitors.

Ostensive definition Conveyance of the meaning of a term by exhibiting an example of the class of elements to which it is applicable.

Recursive definition A rule for eliminating the *definiendum* through a finite number of symbolic transformations.

Stipulative definition An arbitrary restriction on the denotation of a term by rendering it more precise (more fully characterizing its intension).

Demonstration In logic to demonstrate a conclusion is to show that it is a valid inference from other propositions which serve as premises. A demonstration provides absolute reliability in truth ascription.

Denotation A word is said to denote the class of entities to which it is applicable by virtue of its intension (the sum of the attributes implied by the term).

Dependent variable That variable to be explained, e.g., variable vote choice, attribute, or behavior, conceived as influenced by, the consequence of, to depend on, or to be explained by some variable or variables spoken of as independent.

Descriptive truth A truth claim which makes reference to empirical matters.

Deterministic relation (see "Relations")

Diachronic relation (see "Relations")

Direct inference (see "Inference")

Disposition explanation (see "Explanation")

Domain of discourse A domain of discourse is defined in terms of techniques for truth determination: the *formal* domain, which delivers absolute truth determination; the *synthetic* domain, which provides for maximal reliability; and the *normative* domain which provides reasoned vindications.

Domain variant and/or invariant criteria   The criteria employed to warrant truth claims in the various language domains: the formal domain is governed by logical, i.e., intralinguistic, criteria; the synthetic by evidence, i.e., extralinguistic, criteria; and the normative by both, conjoined with the plausibility of one, or a set of, unproblematic "principles." Some criteria are "domain invariant," i.e., consistency— whether one makes claims that are formal, synthetic, or normative inconsistency (equivocation or contradiction) would fault them.

Emotive (or expressive) language (see "Language" and "Meaning")

Epistemic level   Truth claims concerning concrete, observable objects, the evidence conditions of which are direct and unproblematic observations, are tendered on the lowest or most elemental epistemic level. Truth claims concerning logical constructs or theoretical entities, the evidence conditions of which involve complex auxiliary assumptions and sophisticated language use, are tendered at higher or more complex epistemic levels.

Eristic language (see "Language")

Evidence conditions   Those conditions, the presence of which once established, provide the warrant for truth claims.

Explanandum event   The variable behavior, natural or social, individual or collective, to be explained.

Explanans   The collection of propositions conceived as providing an explanation for the *explanandum* event (the event to be explained).

Explanation   In ordinary language an "explanation" is any linguistic response made to a question that serves to abate puzzlement.

Deductive model of explanation   An explanation having the form of a logical demonstration in which the *explanandum* is the deductive consequence of holding one or more general laws conjointly with some determinate set of initial conditions which together, as the *explanans,* constitute the premises of the deduction.

Disposition explanation   A scientific explanation of variable behavior (the *explanandum* event) in terms of a "disposition to behavior," i.e., when an individual's behavior is explained in terms of a disposition: "anger," "intelligence" conjoined with a statement of conditions which invoke the disposition (the *explanans*).

Genetic explanation   An explanation, historic in character, that provides an explanation of the *explanandum* in terms of a series, chain or "colligation" of antecedent events which make the *explanandum* "intelligible."

Semantic explanation   A technique for making clear the literal meaning of a sign or symbol. A lexical definition would, in this sense, provide an explanation for a word.

Explication   The process of analyzing (explicating) a concept in order to reduce semantic variance.

Extended language (see "Language")

Extensional generalizations (see "Generalization")

External validity (empirical)   Questions of "external validity" address themselves to the generalizability or representativeness of scientific findings. Can the results of some specific systematic inquiry be effectively generalized (i.e., have the threats to external validity been maximally reduced; has the sample employed been established as random)?

Extrinsic (or instrumental) goods   Those elements or actions that are productive of some intrinsic good, i.e., goods recognized as valuable in and of themselves (e.g., money is instrumental in producing happiness, which is recognized as valuable in and of itself).

Formalization   The process of reducing syntactical variance.

Formalized disciplines   Those disciplines in which discourse is conducted in formal language, i.e., in which syntactical variance has been maximally reduced.

Formal language (see "Language")

Generalizations   Locutionary acts which purport to make truth claims which refer or apply to any of possibly many things and/or the relations between them. Generalizations support inferences.

Categoric generalization   A generalization that affirms a law of interaction that states that values of a unit, or units, are regularly associated with values of another or others. An example of such a generalization (a simple inductive generalization) would be: "Juvenile delinquents tend to come from broken homes." The category "delinquency," its frequency and rate, is associated with homes that are "broken."

Extensional generalization   A generalization extended from observations made on individuals, not to the class of individuals but to related classes, e.g., from the simple generalization that all instances of iron inspected have melting points, we make the extensional generalization that all metals have a melting point. This is spoken of as a "cross inductive generalization."

Simple generalization   A generalization made on the basis of the inspection of a number of instances in a discrete class of elements, e.g., when we assert that all mothers of autistic or introspective children are overprotective as a consequence of having inspected a representative number of children and their mothers. Such generalizations are spoken of as "simple inductive generalizations."

Syndromatic generalization   A generalization which asserts that some entity X, possessed of attribute a is also possessed of a syndrome of attributes $b, c \ldots n$ as well.

Theoretical generalization   A generalization extended not to related classes but to apparently unrelated and disparate classes of elements in the universe of inquiry, e.g., systems theorists impute "prerequisites" and "requisites" to societies, polities, organisms, cells and cybernetic mechanisms among other things on the basis of confirmed generalizations made on physiological systems.

Implicative meaning (see "Meaning")

Implicit definition (see "Definition")

Independent variable   That variable conceived as being the "cause," or part of the "cause," understood to effect variation in the dependent variable.

Inference   The passage from one or more accepted premises to the consequent acceptance of a conclusion.

Direct inference   An inference made from a population to a sample of it, e.g., if *all* men are mortal, any single or determinate number of men, *must* be mortal.

Extensional inference (see "Extensional generalization")

Inverse inference   An inference made from a sample of a population to the total population. An inverse inference is supported by a simple inductive generalization.

Predictive inference   An inference made from a sample to an individual outside it.

Theoretical inference (see "Theoretical generalization")

Instrumental goods (see "Extrinsic goods")

Interdependency relation (see "Relations")

Internal validity (empirical)   This refers to the interpretability of an experimental treatment. In order to interpret the results of any experiment it is necessary to attempt to control threats to interpretation, that is to say one should be in a position to determine the influence upon the dependent variable of any factors other than the experimental treatment (e.g., the influence of events other than the experimental exposure that might account for results, the influence of processes occurring within experimental subjects independently of any experimental manipulation and so on).

Intrinsic goods   Values that are held to be good in and of themselves, e.g., happiness.

Intrinsic norms of science   Those time variant adequacy criteria employed in judging the truth status of claims made by practicing scientists. In the formal domain the prevailing intrinsic norms are logical; in the empirical domain, evidence; and in the normative domain both—conjoined with the initial or argued plausibility of assertions of value. If science is restricted to the empiriological activities of scientists, the adequacy criteria are those of logic and evidence—and normative criteria may be treated as "extrinsic."

Irreversible relation (see "Relations")

Justificatory argument   Any argument (see "Argument") employed to produce the truth warrant for an empirical, formal or normative truth claim.

Language   In ordinary language the term "language" refers, in general, to any formalized and conventionalized set of spoken, written, or gesticulated signs which are employed in encoding, transmitting and decoding feelings and thoughts.

Academic language   A variant of literary language in which a relatively systematic, but informal, effort is made to reduce semantic variance (i.e., academic language is partially standardized).

Ceremonial language   A variant of performative language in which one addresses another by title, evidences awareness of status or displays knowledge of conventional etiquette.

Cognitive (or constative) language   Language in which truth claims are tendered. In general, an utterance is said to have cognitive character if it is employed to articulate a proposition.

Emotive (or expressive) language   Noncognitive language in which feelings or emotions are expressed.

Eristic language   That language with which partial formalization and partial standardization have been undertaken in order to permit the articulation of descriptive and verificational propositions.

Extended language   When conventional language is extended to unusual contexts, as when we speak of music or art as a "language" (i.e., the "language" of art) or we employ reasonably well understood terms to apply to unusual referents (e.g., when we speak of God as a "person").

Formal or artificial language   A language which provides for maximal syntactic invariance by (1) being uninterpreted (i.e., having no semantic interpretation), (2) providing rules for sentence formation and rules for transformation (with definitions understood as a subset of transformation rules).

Literary language   Literary language is relatively sophisticated ordinary language use (sophisticated in this context refers primarily to an increased range of vocabulary). (See "Academic language.")

Noncognitive language   Those utterances which do not, in principle, tender knowledge claims or which could be assigned truth status (e.g., performative and expressive utterances).

Normative language   Language in which evaluation, prescription and proscriptions, and arguments in their support, are tendered.

Performative language   Language in which one performs rather than issues knowledge claims. Placing a bet, declaring war, making a promise would involve performative language use.

Perlocutionary language   Language employed, essentially (whatever else it accomplishes), to produce some effect in and influence an audience or (when one deliberates) the speaker himself. As employed here, normative arguments are construed as essentially perlocutionary, undertaken, in principle, to exercise influence. Normative arguments may be construed as cognitive because of the presence in them of constative utterances (formal and synthetic propositions). Conjoined with such cognitive elements are specifically normative utterances which may be simply emotive, but which provide the perlocutionary force of the performance.

Postulational language   Language in which systematic and formal or informal efforts are made to establish the logic of proof. The emphasis is on the systematic (in the logical sense) character of a set of propositions in terms of derivation.

Protocol language   Any set of unproblematic knowledge claims that serve as the basic epistemic units of more complex claims made at more sophisticated linguistic and epistemic levels.

Symbolic language   A language in which systematic and formal efforts at reducing semantic variance are undertaken by using symbols (stipulative notational devices) rather than natural language to refer to variables and characterize putative relations. Problems and solutions are formulated in formal language. Alternately, in political science literature, "symbolic language" has also been used to refer to language in which some of the terms employed are "condensed symbols" having connotative (in the nonlogical sense) significance—nonliteral meanings which, for an audience, are determined by collective or individual variations in life experience, interests, psychological disposition or attitudes.

Lawlike In ordinary language any statement of an invariance, either a uniform sequence of events, a uniform coexistence of properties, or a correlation of simultaneous events, is spoken of as "lawlike," and if confirmed, a "law." As employed in this discussion, it has a more restricted meaning: it refers to a contingent, unrestricted (as to time and place) general proposition that supports subjunctive and/or counterfactual conditionals and finds a place in a deductive system that serves to explain and predict (see "Relations").

Linguistic level "Levels" of language are determined by the degree of sophistication with which language is employed, e.g., ordinary language is employed in a nondeliberative, relatively nonstandardized and non-formalized manner. Transit to different levels is marked by efforts at standardization and formalization (the reduction of semantic and syntactical invariance). There is a rough, but general, correspondence between epistemic and language levels.

Locutionary act Any speech utterance.

Logical truth A logical principle or any proposition that derives from logical principles alone; contrasted with empirical or synthetic truths.

Maximal reliability (see "Reliability")

Meaning The "meaning" of a sign or symbol is provided by characterizing its use or function in language.

  Cognitive meaning The cognitive meaning of a proposition is revealed in the conditions governing its truth status (e.g., if the cognitive meaning of a proposition is formal its truth conditions involve only intralinguistic matters—if the cognitive meaning is empirical or synthetic, its truth conditions involve extralinguistic states of affairs, i.e., its operational or systemic meaning).

  Emotive (or expressive) meaning Emotive meaning is construed as a variant of psychological meaning having as referent some emotional state or states of an individual or group.

  Implicative meaning The meaning of a sign or symbol in terms of what it implies (both logically and/or pragmatically). The meaning is revealed in the set of logical and/or causal propositions in which those implications are drawn out.

  Operational meaning The meaning conveyed in terms of conditional experimental observations (some discrete or finite, but indeterminate set of recognitors).

  Pragmatic meaning All public uses to which language can be put, perlocutionary and noncognitive that can be characterized as having "utility," or being "appropriate," rather than aspiring to specific truth status, as well as the personal psychological effect of language use.

Psychological meaning   The significance of an utterance in terms of the responses made to a sign or symbol by an audience. Such meaning can be audience or individual variant and dependent. A subset of pragmatic meaning.

Semantic (denotative, referential or designative) meaning   The extralinguistic state of affairs to which a proposition refers; the extralinguistic state of affairs that must exist if the proposition is to be true (its evidence conditions).

Syntactical meaning   The use or function of a sign or symbol, or sign-complex or symbol complex, in intralinguistic contexts, i.e., in relation to each other.

Systemic (or theoretic) meaning   The meaning of a sign or sign-complex which derives from its function in a collection of propositions. A sentence, for example, or a theoretical entity, may have cognitive meaning and yet not have, in and of itself, direct operational meaning—its meaning is governed by the indirect contribution it makes to the collection of propositions of which it is a constituent (e.g., if the presence of a sentence in some collection of propositions alters the meaning in terms of expectations or explanatory consequences—the sentence has systemic, and only in such systemic combination, indirect operational meaning).

Metalanguage   The language employed to speak about the object language. (Metapolitics employs a metalanguage employed to talk about political talk.)

Model   In ordinary language a standard for imitation or comparison (normative use) or a pattern (cognitive use).

  Analogical (or substantive) model   An analogical extension of some features of one range to another.

  Analogue model   A formal model in which structural features of one range are imputed to another; the theory and the model are in some specific respects isomorphic.

  Replica (micromorphic or macromorphic) model   An iconic copy of some aspects of one entity in some other.

Necessary and sufficient condition   Given the antecedent X, the consequent Y is always present, and conversely, given Y, X is always present.

Necessary condition   A condition predictable of both propositions and properties. Something is a necessary condition for something else if the latter cannot be true unless the former is true; but the former can be true without the latter being true (e.g., the necessary condition of John's graduation is that he is enrolled in the school—but the fact that he is enrolled in school, while a necessary condition of his graduation, is not a sufficient condition for his graduation).

Necessary relation (see "Relations")

Normative language (see "Language")

Normative proposition (see "Propositions")

Observation (or protocol) sentences (or propositions) Reports of unproblematic observations, involving only a minimum of interpretive components (auxiliary assumptions).

Open-textured (or porous) concepts Concepts defined in terms of observables (recognitors). Since experience is ongoing, such concepts may take on new or extended meaning as a consequence of new experience and consequently have systematically variant meaning.

Operational definition (see "Definition")

Operationalization The process by which some finite (if indeterminate) set of observables (recognitors) are held to provide the meaning of a term. Operationalization, as a consequence, specifies what the truth or evidence conditions of an empirical knowledge claim are; it establishes the semantic, denotative, designative or referential meaning of a descriptive or synthetic term.

Operational meaning (see "Meaning")

Performative language (see "Language")

Perlocutionary language (see "Language")

Persuasive redefinition A redefinition of a term in such a manner that its emotive meaning is preserved but its cognitive meaning is altered (e.g., when "freedom" is redefined as "law-governed behavior" rather than "absence of restraint." The term "freedom" still enjoys high positive emotional salience, but has significantly changed its implicative and descriptive meaning).

Postulational language (see "Language")

Pragmatics The systematic study of the actions implied, the psychosocial circumstances surrounding such action, and the personal psychological significance which obtains on the occasions of linguistic use.

Procedural knowledge The ability to do certain sorts of things rather than the knowledge or ignorance of this or that propositional truth. The ability to perform tasks.

Proposition A sentence that can be assigned truth status.

Analytic (or logical) proposition A statement whose denial involves a self-contradiction; whose truth follows directly, or derivately from the principles of logic, i.e., whose truth conditions and truth warrant involve only intralinguistic properties rather than any reference to the object world.

Normative proposition (or utterance) A characteristically normative proposition (or utterance) would be one whose "truth" would be conventional or entrenched; as a consequence it might be more accurate to characterize such speech performances as "utterances" since they, in and of themselves, are treated in this account as not having any specific intersubjective truth conditions analogous to synthetic and logical propositions.

Synthetic (empirical, descriptive) proposition A statement which is neither analytic nor self-contradictory, whose truth status is determined by direct or indirect reference to the object world (i.e., whose truth conditions are extralinguistic).

Propositional knowledge A cognitive repertoire; knowledge of propositional truths.

Protocol language (see "Language")

Protocol sentence (see "Observation sentence")

Randomization Minimally, the procedure by virtue of which a sample of a population is drawn so that each member of the population has an equal chance of being selected; or more accurately, the process by which a sample is drawn in which every possible combination of n elements of a population has the same probability of being selected.

Range Specifies the entities over which theories and generalizations are deployed.

Recognitor A discriminable feature of the object world used as symptomatic of some object or class of objects.

Referent In ordinary language, that to which a sign refers.

Reification The disposition, predicated on the archaic notion that every word is the name of something extralinguistic, to treat abstract concepts as concrete things.

Relations (between variables in empirical inquiry) The "connections" or "linkages" postulated or "discovered" to obtain between categorized elements in the universe of inquiry.

Contingent relation If X, then Y, but only if certain attendant conditions obtain.

Coextensive relation If X, then also Y.

Deterministic relation If X, then always Y.

Interdependency relation A combination of reversible, sequential and contingent relations.

Irreversible relation If X, then Y, but if Y no conclusion about X.

Necessary relation   If *X*, then, and only then *Y* (see "Necessary condition").

Reversible relation   If *X*, then *Y*, and if *Y*, then *X*.

Sequential (or diachronic) relation   If *X*, then later *Y*.

Stochastic relation   If *X*, then *Y* to some degree of probability.

Substitutable relation   If *X*, then *Y;* but if *Z*, then also *Y* (*Z* is the "functional equivalent" of *X*, i.e., productive of the same consequence).

Sufficient relation   If *X*, then *Y*, irrespective of anything else (see "Sufficient condition").

Reliability   In ordinary language "reliability" refers to the degree of confidence one can invest in a claim, personality traits, and truth status attributions.

Reliability (in empirical inquiry)   Minimally, the provision of procedures establishing the congruence, precision and objectivity of findings (as distinguished from procedures providing for internal and external validity).

Absolute reliability   The confidence which can be invested in the conclusion of a valid deductive argument.

Maximal reliability   When empirical inquiry meets criteria of reliability, internal and external (empirical) validity, recognizing that all synthetic claims are inextricably corrigible, it is said to be maximally reliable.

Replica model (see "Models")

Reversible relations (see "Relations")

Science   That dynamic and self-corrective cognitive activity calculated to produce propositional knowledge enjoying maximal domain variant reliability.

Scope   Specifies the set of all those properties or relations over which a generalization may be deployed (compare "Range").

Semantics   The systematic study of the meaning of signs.

Semantic variance   The vagueness and ambiguity which characteristically attends sign use in ordinary language; the variability in semantic meaning.

Semiotics   The general theory of signs, understood here (after Morris) to include (1) syntactics, (2) semantics, and (3) pragmatics.

Sentence (or sentential) variable   A variable whose values are sentences.

Sentence token   The employment of a sentence type in a particular circumstance.

Sentence type   The fact that a sentence (e.g., "It is raining") can be used on a variety of occasions and its truth status will vary with each employment, requires that a distinction be made between a sentence as a sentence in general (a "type") and its specific context-dependent employment (its "token" use).

Sequential relation (see "Relations")

Sign   Any physical thing which stands in conventional correspondence to other physical things (e.g., the sign "house" stands in conventional correspondence—when the sign is felicitously used—to certain symptomatic perceptions we identify as a house in the object world).

Significance   The private and consequently variable meaning of a sign or sign complex.

Signification   The public meaning of a sign or sign-complex; its denotation covers all utterances which can, in principle, meet public evidence conditions.

Sign token   When a sign-type is employed in a specific speech act it is referred to as a sign token; the instantial use of a sign type.

Sign type   A sign that can be employed in a multiplicity of complex speech acts, having as a consequence systematically variant meaning in each specific use (e.g., the sign type "dog" can appear in a variety of well-formed sentences and in each of its sign token uses it will have specific, but systematically variant meaning).

Sound argument (see "Argument")

Standardization   Any effort undertaken to reduce semantic variance in sign use.

Stipulative definition (see "Definition")

Stochastic relation (see "Relations")

Subjunctive conditional   Assertion of the type: "If X were the case; Y would be its consequence."

Substitutable relations (see "Relations")

Sufficient condition (for an event)   Whenever X is present Y is invariably present although Y may be present when the antecedent X is absent (e.g. restriction of oxygen for a determinate period of time is the sufficient condition of a determinate organism's death; wherever there is that deprivation there will be death; but death can come to an organism for reasons other than oxygen starvation).

Sufficient relation (see "Relations")

Symbol   Symbols are a subclass of signs that have "condensed meaning" (i.e., a flag is a symbol having a finite, but indeterminate, and variable number of meanings–meaning being in large part determined by the life experience and psychological states of the various symbol interpreters), or arbitrarily chosen signs employed in symbolic languages.

Symbolic language (see "Language")

Symptom sentence   An assertion of the presence of a recognitor that serves as an indicator for, or part of the meaning of, an individual member of a determinate class of entities, or a construct or theoretical entity.

Synchronic When events occur at the same time, they are said to be synchronic.

Syntactical variance The vagueness and imprecision that attend ordinary language use in specifying the relations understood to obtain between signs.

Syntactics The systematic study of the relations of signs to signs in abstraction from the meaning function of signs and the relations of signs to interpreters.

Synthetic proposition (see "Proposition")

Systemic (or theoretical) meaning (see "Meaning")

Theorem (see "Axiomatic system")

Theoretical entity This refers to "inferred entities," entities having "systemic meaning" and "theoretical truth status"; entities introduced to enhance the theoretical yield of a collection of propositions.

Theoretic yield The ability of a proposition, or a set of propositions, to provide a number of directly or indirectly testable propositions or cover a range or scope of hitherto seemingly unrelated phenomena within the universe of inquiry.

Theory A systematically related set of propositions, including one or more lawlike assertions, that is directly or indirectly testable. A "normative theory" would be a "theory" that supports the issuance of prescription, proscription, recommendations, warnings, urgings or counsel.

Truth conditions The domain variant conditions which govern the ascription of truth status to a proposition (formal truth conditions for analytic propositions and evidence truth conditions for synthetic propositions).

Truth status The negative, positive or indeterminate cognitive status assigned a proposition (true, false or indeterminate).

Truth warrant The confirmed truth conditions which legitimate truth ascriptions.

Verification The process of confirming the evidence conditions for synthetic (descriptive) truth claims.

Vindication A non-demonstrative argument, involving both analytic and synthetic constituents, offered in support of normative injunctions, appraisals, prescriptions and recommendations.

Warrant (see "Truth warrant")

Index

Abatement of puzzlement, 203-4, 209

Abelson, Robert, 99

"Acceptance" criterion, 203-5, 222

Adequacy
  genetic explanations and criteria of, 205-10, 231-32
  intrinsic norms of, 356-57

Alice in Wonderland (Carroll), 332-33

"All things being equal" (*ceteris paribus*) clause, 63
  in historic process laws, 209
  Johnson's use of, 175-76

American Behavioral Scientist (publication), 19

Analogy, *see* Arguments—analogical; Models—analogical

Analysis
  linguistic, 7-10
  noncognitive language and contemporary, 325-36
  See also Analytic philosophy

Analytic conceptual schemata, *see* Conceptual schemata—analytic

Analytic domain, definition of, 366

Analytic philosophy, 56-64, 240-42
  evidence conditions and, 62-64, 58-60
  protocol sentences and, 56-57
  reliability and, 58-60, 62
  See also Analysis—contemporary

Analytic proposition, definition of, 366, 377-78

Analytic truth, 50-52, 88

Analytic/synthetic distinction, 51, 73-74

Apter, David, 170, 183

Arendt, Hannah, 132

Arguments
  analogical, 107-13
    defective, 110-11
    generalizations and, 109-10
    inductive logic and, 111
    See also Models—analogical
  definition of, 366
  definition of justificatory, 373
  normative, 288-92
    attitudes and, 305-6
    cognitive activity and, 304-6
    ideology as, 336-39
    See also Discourse—normative
  sound, 90-96
    definition of, 366
  valid, 90-96
    connectives and, 94-95
    definition of, 366
    form of, 95
    mathematics and, 91-94

Aristarchus, 33

Aristotle, 10, 171, 254, 315

Art, 317

Assertions
  descriptive, 51-55
  lawlike, 163-70
    Marx's use of, 164-66, 168
    See also Laws—systematic process

Assumptions, 107-13
  definition of auxiliary, 367
Atomic sentences, 59
Attitudes
  normative discourse and, 284,
      288, 298, 305-6, 309
  sentiments compared to, 304-6
Auden, W. H., 17
Austin, John L., 241, 264
Authority, appeal to, 59
Auxiliary assumption, definition
      of, 367
Axelrod, Robert, 144
Axiomatic system
  definition of, 367
  theories and, 178, 182
  uninterpreted, *see* Calculus
Axiomatization, partial, 96-100
  of conceptual schemata, 140-46
  Simulmatics Project and,
      99-100
Axioms, 180
Ayer, A. J., 9, 241, 264
  on normative language, 283-84

Bay, Christian, 17, 215, 346
"Because," uses of, 124-25
Behavior
  explanations of, 210-17,
      221-22
  variables and, 125-26, 163
Behavioral Science (publication),
      19
Behavioralism, 17-23
  criticisms of, 17-18, 215,
      353-54, 357
  Marxism and, 17, 39
  science and, 18-23
Behavioralists, criterial definition
      of, 19-20
Believing, understanding and,
      260-64
Bentham, Jeremy, 214

Berelson, Bernard, 96
Bergmann, Gustav, 209
Bertalanffy, Ludwig von, 189-90
Black, Max, 160, 199
Blanshard, Brand, 282
Braybrooke, David, 144
Brecht, Arnold, 1
Brezezinski, Z. K., 131-32
Brief Philosophical Dictionary
      (Soviet Union), 333
Brodbeck, May, 198
Brown, Robert, 226
Brown, Roger, 201
Butow, Robert, 211-12, 216

Calculus, models and, 178-80,
      187-90, 193
"Canons of Induction" (Mill),
      146-50
Carnap, Rudolf, 8, 57, 116, 241
Carroll, Lewis, 332-33, 343
Castro, Fidel, 166
Certainty
  of empirical assertions, 102-4
  practical and logical, 88
Ceteris paribus clause ("all things
      being equal"), 63
  in historic process laws, 209
  Johnson's use of, 175-76
Children, ordering of experience
      by, 120-21, 123-24, 170
Chisholm, Roderick, 264
Claims
  descriptive, 51-55
    corrigibility of, 64-65, 87-88
    observation and, 51-55, 61
  knowledge, *see* Knowledge
      claims
  truth, *see* Truth claims
Classification, *see* Conceptual
      schemata—classificatory
Cognitive activity, normative
      argument and, 304-6

Cognitive truth, 87-90
Cohen, Morris, 58
Colligation, 202, 204-5, 207, 209
Communist Manifesto (Marx and
    Engels), 164
Competence, linguistic, 46-48
Computer programming, 99-100
Computer simulations, 99-101
Concept
    definition of, 122, 367
    descriptive, 135-36
    dispositional, 135
    open-textured or porous
        definition of, 377
        explication and, 134-35
Concept formation, conceptual
        schemata, generalizing
        knowledge claims and,
        119-59
Conceptual schemata, 119-59
    analytic, 128, 170-75
        axiomatization and, 140-41
        classification and, 170-73
        definition of, 367
        process laws and, 174-75
        theory construction and,
            181-82
    axiomatized, 5, 140-46
    of children, 120-21, 123-24,
        170
    classificatory, 5, 140, 170-73
        definition of, 367
        Mill's "Canons of Induction"
            and, 146
        theory construction and, 182
    definition of, 367
    ordinary language, 123-27
        axiomatization and, 140,
            143-45
        definition of, 367
        science and, 29-30
        theory construction and,
            181-82

See also Language—
    ordinary
    partially axiomatized, 140-46
    preliminary, 126-27, 140-46
        analogical models and, 191
        definition of, 30, 368
        evidence requirements of, 33
        formal theory and, 33-34
        intuition and, 32-33
        Mill's "Canons of Induction"
            and, 149
        theory construction and,
            30-33, 181-82
        spontaneous, 123-24
        theory construction and, 182-85
        variables and, 125-26, 142, 146
Concreta
    definition of, 368
    synthetic truths and, 51
Condition
    evidence, *see* Evidence
        conditions
    necessary, 176
        definition of, 376-77
    necessary and sufficient, 176-77
        definition of, 376
    sufficient, 176
        definition of, 380
Conditional, counterfactual
    definition of, 368
    lawlike generalizations and,
        168
Conduct of Inquiry, The
    (Kaplan), 11
Confirmation
    of generalizations, 149, 152,
        162-63, 215-17
    intersubjective, 53
    of intuition, 215
Congruence
    definition of, 368
    of ordinary languages, 155
    of recognitors, 150

Connectives
  deductive logic and, 94-95
  syntactical rules for, 87-90
Consensus, 151-52
Consistency, 162
  formal logic and, 90
  linguistic precision and, 70
  of observation statements, 272
  science and, 25, 26
Construct
  definition of, 368
  synthetic truths and, 51
Contemporary analysis,
        noncognitive language
        and, 325-36
  See also Analytic philosophy
Contingent statements, 87, 89
"Contradiction," 334-35
Correlation
  definition of, 368
  intergenerational, 150-51
Counterfactual conditional
  definition of, 368
  lawlike generalizations and, 168
"Covering law model" of
        explanation, 232-33
Criteria
  "acceptance," 203-5
  adeqacy, 205-10, 231-32
  domain variant and/or
        invariant, 263-65
    definition of, 370
  objective, 205-10

Dahl, Robert, 17, 18, 136, 168-69
Debray, Régis, 166
Deductive logic, see Logic—
        deductive
Deductive model of explanation,
        definition of, 370
Definiendum, 52, 127-28
Definiens, 52, 128

Definition, 126-40, 353
  contextual, 136-37, 352
    definition of, 368
  criterial (or range), 128, 352
    of "behavioralists," 19-20
    contextual definition
        compared to, 136-37
    definition of, 368-69
    explication and, 133-35
    Johnson's use of, 175
    of "politics," 6
    rules for use of, 131-33
  definition of, 368
  explicit, 127-28
    definition of, 369
  implicit, 128-30, 157
    explication and, 133-35
  lexical (or verbal or nominal),
        138-41
    definition of, 369
  nonoperating, 139-40
  operational, 139, 178
    definition of, 369
  ostensive, definition of, 369
  persuasive, 290
  "real," 133, 138-40
  recursive, 128
    definition of, 369
  reductive, 96-98
  stipulative, 128
    definition of, 369
    of "good" and "right,"
        289-91
    use of, 137-38
  truth by, 49-50
De Interpretatione (Aristotle),
        315
Demonstration, definition of, 369
Denotation, definition of, 369
Dependent variable
  conceptual schemata and,
        125-26, 142, 145-46
    definition of, 369

Descriptive assertions (or claims)
  corrigibility of, 64-65, 87-88
  observation and, 51-55, 61
  See also Observation statements
Descriptive discourse, 284
Descriptive sentences, truth conditions for, 82
Descriptive truth, 51-53
  definition of, 369
De Sola Pool, Ithiel, 99
Deutsch, Karl, 139-40
Dialectic, 330-35
Dilthey, Wilhelm, 210-11, 215
DiRenzo, Gordon, 214
Disagreement, normative, 291-304
  primary (ultimate) values and, 291-92, 294-95, 297-304, 309, 311
  resolution of, 295-304
  See also Discourse—normative
Disanalogy, 110-11
Discourse
  descriptive, 284
  noncognitive, 315-42
    dialectical logic as, 330-35
    ideologies and, 336-40
    imagination and, 318-20 326-28, 335
    intuition and, 319-20, 326-28, 335
    Marcuse and, 319-20, 327-35
    myths and, 318-21, 323-26, 336
    phantasy and, 318-20, 327-28, 335
    Sorel and, 319-25
  normative, 36, 282-314
    arguments using, 288-92
    attitudes in, 284, 288, 298, 305-6

cognitive activity and, 304-6, 308-9
    definition of, 282-83
    descriptive discourse and, 284, 289
    formal language and, 304
    logic and, 307-8
    objectivity and, 306-11
    as perlocutionary, 283-88
    primary (ultimate) values and, 291-95, 297-304, 307-11
    resolution of disagreement in, 295-304
    sentiments in, 284, 286, 288, 304-6
    See also Language—normative
  perlocutionary, 283-88
Dispositions
  directive, 211
  explanations via intentions, reasons and, 210-17, 220-23
Domain
  definition of analytic, 366
  definition of formal, 369-70
  definition of normative, 370
  definition of synthetic, 370
Domain of discourse, definition of, 369-70
Domain variant and/or invariant criteria, 263-65
  definition of, 370
Domain variant truth conditions, 113-14
Donagan, Alan, 200, 211
Downs, Anthony, 128-30, 157
Dray, William, 204

Easton, David, 1, 86, 181, 190
Economic Theory of Democracy, An (Downs), 128

Edelman, Murray, 325

Elections, computer simulations of, 100

Empirical generalization, explanation via, 226-28

Empirical statements, 102-4

Engels, Friedrich, 164-66, 168, 333

Epistemic level, definition of, 370

Essays on the Scientific Study of Politics (Storing), 17

Ethics, science, political science and, 35-37

Evidence
  best, 34-35
  domain variant and/or invariant, 263-65
  total, 111, 267-68
  truth and, 265, 267-75

Evidence conditions, 58-64
  analytic philosophy and, 58-60, 62-64
  of analytic truths, 50
  definition of, 370
  feelings as, 261
  intersubjective, 64
  knowing and, 262-67
  problematic, 62-64
  public, 69-71
  of synthetic truths, 51
  unproblematic, 58-60
  See also Truth conditions

Experience
  discriminable recognitors and, 120-23
  intersubjective, 57-60, 62
  knowledge claims and, 154-56
  language and ordering of, 54-55, 120-24, 154-56, 170
  pure, 57, 58
  See also Observation

Explanandum event

definition of, 370

in genetic explanations, 202-3, 206, 209

Explanans, definition of, 370

Explanations, 198-237
  of behavior, 210-17, 221-22
  "covering law model" of, 232-33
  definition of, 370
  definition of deductive model of, 370
  disposition, 210-17
    definition of, 370
  via empirical generalizations, 226-28
  functional, 223-26
  genetic, 201-10
    colligation in, 202, 204-5, 207, 209
    definition of, 370-71
    generalizations in, 206-9
    as incomplete, 208-9
    "linking" of propositions in, 203-6
    objective criteria for, 205-10, 231-32
    as partial, 208-9
  historic, *see* Explanation—genetic
  via intentions, reasons and dispositions, 210-17, 220-23
  intuitive, 215, 217
  meanings of, 199-200
  objective criteria for, 205-10
  as partial, 230-31
  prescriptive model of, 228-33
  psychological, 213-15, 221
  reason analysis, 217-18
  scientific, 200-1
  semantic, definition of, 371
  theory compared to, 233
  of "unique" events, 217-19

Explanatory "uniqueness" of
 social science, 217-22
Explication
 definition of, 371
 of ordinary language, 133-35
External validity, 149
 definition of, 371
Extrinsic (or instrumental)
 goods, definition of, 371

"Faith"
 cognitive function of, 320
 Kuhn and, 32-34
 primary (ultimate) values and,
  292, 309, 311
 "synoptic vision" and, 255-56
 understanding and, 255-56,
  276
 See also Intuition
Fascism, 294
Feelings, understanding and,
 258-62, 267
Festinger, Leon, 213
Field, G. Lowell, 141, 170, 172,
 180, 183
Findlay, J. N., 331
Fogelin, Robert, 263, 268
Formal language, *see* Language—
 formal, artificial or
 reconstructed
Formal logic, *see* Logic—formal
Formal theory, *see* Theory—
 formal
Formalization, 239, 241
 definition of, 371
 as linguistic precision, 70-71
 of natural (ordinary)
  language, 74
Formalized disciplines,
 definition of, 371
Frege, Gottlob, 25
Friedrich, Carl, 131-32
Fromm, Erich, 299

Functions
 explanation via, 223-26
 latent, 223-24
 manifest, 223

Game theory, 192, 310
Garma, Angel, 247
Geertz, Clifford, 325-26
General terms, 121-23
Generalizations, 156
 analogies and, 109-10
 assumptions and, 107-8
 behavioral, 214-17
 commonsense, 161-62, 168-69
 confirmation of, 149, 152,
  162-63, 215-17
 definition of, 371
 definition of categoric, 371
 definition of extensional, 371
 descriptive, 167, 169, 171
 explanation via empirical,
  226-28
 in genetic explanations, 206-9
 inductive, 5, 107, 111-13,
  162-63, 167
  See also Logic—inductive
 language as instrument for,
  121-23
 lawlike, 167-69
  in genetic explanations,
   206-9
  nonevents and, 219-20
  process laws as, 173-76
  See also Lawlike assertions
 ordinary language, 156, 161-63
 psychological, 214-17
 simple, 371-72
 syndromatic, 170-73
  definition of, 372
 theoretical, definition of, 372
 "unique" events and, 218-19
Generalizing knowledge claims,

see Knowledge claims—
    generalizing
Genetic explanations, *see*
    Explanations—genetic
Gentile, Giovanni, 290, 294, 338
German Ideology (Marx), 142
Germino, Dante, 131-32
"Good," definitions of, 289-91
Goodman, Nelson, 271-72
Guevara, Ernesto "Ché," 166

Haas, Ernst, 223, 236
Hart, H. L. A., 301
Hegel, G. W. F., 331
Hempel, C. G., 134, 205
Heuristics, logic, precision and,
    96-101
Historic process laws, 173-77,
    209, 218-19
Historical explanation, *see*
    Explanation—genetic
Hitler, Adolf, 290
    analogical arguments of, 110
    primary values and, 294, 301
    on stratification, 108
Hoffmann, Abbie (Free), 364
Homans, George, 139, 144, 168
Homologies, 189-90
Hughes, H. Stuart, 132
*Human Behavior: An Inventory
    of Scientific Findings*
    (Berelson and Steiner), 96
Hume, David, 286
Hypotheses
    assumptions, analogical
        argument and, 107-13
    null, 154

Ideology
    definition of, 23-24
    noncognitive discourse and,
        336-40
    as normative argument, 336-39

science as, 23-27
    See also Myths
Imagination, 318-20, 326-28, 335
Independent variable
    conceptual schemata and,
        125-26, 142, 145-46
    definition of, 372
Induction, *see* Generalizations—
    inductive; Logic—inductive
"Induction, Canons of" (Mill),
    146-50
"Indwelling," understanding by,
    257-59
Inference
    causal, 108
    definition of, 372
    definition of direct, 372
    definition of inverse, 372
    definition of predictive, 372
    extensional, *see* Generalization
        —extensional
    extensional predictive, 109-10
    inductive, 108, 111-14, 167
        See also Generalizations—
        inductive; Logic—inductive
    inverse, 110
Inquiry, political, *see* Political
    Inquiry
Insight
    as cognitive tool, 321, 326
    in political inquiry, 275-77
    primary (ultimate) values and,
        309-10
    "understanding" as, 243,
        250-51, 256, 276
        See also Faith; Intuition
Instrumental (extrinsic) goods,
    definition of, 371
Intelligence, rationality and,
    160-61
Intentions, explanations via
    reasons, dispositions and,
    210-17, 220-23

Intercorrelation, *see* Correlation
Internal validity, 149
  definition of, 372-73
Interpretation, "understanding,"
  theory and, 247-53
Intersubjective confirmation,
  descriptive truth and, 53
Intersubjective observation, 24,
  57-59
Intrinsic goods, definition of, 373
Intrinsic norms of adequacy,
  356-57
Intrinsic norms of science,
  definition of, 373
Intuition
  cognitive function of, 319-20,
    326-28, 335
  explanatory, 215, 217
  in informal discourse, 242
  in mathematics, 205
  primary (ultimate) values and,
    309-10
  as "understanding," 243,
    252-53, 256, 259-60, 269,
    276
  unreliability of, 59
  See also Faith; Insight
Invariance, putative, *see* Lawlike
  assertions
Isomorphism, 187-89
Is/ought dichotomy, 288, 290,
  292, 312

James, Henry, 77
Jennings, M. Kent, 151
Johnson, Chalmers, 174-76
Johnston, R. E., 98
Justificatory argument, definition
  of, 373

Kapital, Das (Marx), 142, 164,
  166
Kaplan, Abraham, 11, 119, 134,
  136-37, 239

Kariel, Henry, 293, 356
Kassof, Allen, 132
Katz, Jerrold, 74, 241
Kautsky, Karl, 166
Kessen, William, 58-59
Kim, K. W., 218-20
Kirk, Russell, 17, 243, 319, 320
Knowing, 238-81
  "understanding" distinguished
    from, 244-47, 249-50,
    262, 266, 268
Knowledge
  intersubjective, 71-72
  in political inquiry, 275-77
  procedural
    children and, 124
    definition of, 377
    rationality and, 161
    "understanding" and, 249,
      251-54, 262, 269
  propositional
    definition of, 378
    rationality and, 161
    "understanding" and, 249,
      251-54, 262, 269
  systemic, 247-48, 250-54, 262
Knowledge claims
  contextual dependency of,
    58-59
  descriptive, 75
  generalizing, 176-77
    concept formation,
      conceptual schemata and,
      119-59
    lawlike assertions and,
      166-67
    syndromatic generalizations
      and, 173
  induction and empirical,
    150-53
  inferential, 70
  ordinary language, experience
    and sophisticated, 154-56

See also Observation—
    sophisticated
  substantive, 50
Kuhn, Thomas S., 28-34, 356

Language
  academic, 140, 239-41
    definition of, 373
  ceremonial (or ritual), 5,
    316-18
    definition of, 373
  children and, 120-21, 123-24
  creative use of, 47-48
  definition of, 8, 373
  definition of cognitive (or
    constative), 373
  definition of extended, 373
  emotive (or expressive), 5
    definition of, 373
    in noncognitive discourse,
      317-19, 324, 339, 340
    simple, 283
  eristic, 141-43, 239-40
    definition of, 373
  experience and, 54-55, 120-24,
    154-56
  formal, artificial or
    reconstructed
    definition of, 373-74
    normative disourse and, 304
    observation and, 53
    philosophy and, 347-48
    semantic invariance of,
      239-40
    synthetic/analytic
      distinction of, 73
    use of definitions in, 127-28
  as generalizing instrument,
    121-23
  as historic deposit, 54-55, 61-62
  literary, 140, 239-42
    definition of, 374
  mythic (or doctrinal), 339-40

noncognitive
  contemporary analysis and,
    325-36
  definition of, 374
  ideologies and, 336-40
  political inquiry and, 318-25
  See also Discourse—
    noncognitive
normative, 4-5, 348-49
  definition of, 282-83, 374
  "value-free" science and,
    306-11
  See also Discourse—
    normative
observation and, 53-65
ordinary (natural), 242
  concept formation in, 30,
    123-27
  confirming generalizations
    in, 152
  experience and, 54-55,
    120-24, 154-56
  explication of, 133-35
  generalizations in, 156,
    161-63
  as historic deposit, 54-55,
    61-62
  "knowing" as used in,
    244-47
  nondeliberative nature of,
    127, 144-45, 154-56, 352
  pragmatics and, 66-67
  rationality and, 161
  rules of, 78-79
  semantic and syntactical
    variance in, 89-90
  synthetic/analytic
    distinction in, 73-74
  "understanding" as used in,
    242-47
  See also Conceptual
    schemata—ordinary
    language

performative, 317-18
    definition of, 374
perlocutionary
    definition of, 374
    See also Discourse—
        perlocutionary
phenomenalistic, 60-61
philosophy's preoccupation
    with, 347-49
postulational, 239-40
    definition of, 374
protocol, 155
    definition of, 374
    See also Protocol sentences
sense-data, 60-61
sensory experience and, 120-23
symbolic (or mythic), 239-40,
    325-26
    definition of, 374-75
theory load of, 58
thing-predicate, 60-61
Laski, Harold, 351
Lasswell, Harold D., 136, 137,
    139, 214
Lawlike, definition of, 375
Lawlike assertions, 163-70
    Marx's use of, 164-66, 168
Laws
    historic process, 173-77, 209,
        218-19
    normative characterization of,
        169-70
    systematic process, 173-77,
        218-19
    theories, models and, 160-97
Lazarsfeld, Paul, 145
Lenin, V. I., 166, 290, 294, 333
Level, definition of linguistic, 375
Linguistic analysis, political
        inquiry and, 7-10
    See also Analysis—
        contemporary; Analytic
        philosophy

Linguistic competence, 46-48
Linguistic level, definition of, 375
Linguistic performance, 46-48
Linguistic philosophy, 240-42
Linguistic precision
    criticisms of, 351-55
    logic, heuristics and, 96-101
    meaning, truth and, 68-72
    political inquiry and, 351-55
"Linking" of propositions in
        genetic explanations,
        203-7
Locutionary act, definition of,
        375
Logic
    Aristotelian, 25
    deductive, 101-7
        connectives and, 94-95
        inductive logic compared to,
            101-7
        semantics, syntactics and,
            85-87
        See also Logic—formal
    dialectical, 330-35
    formal
        computer simulations and,
            100-1
        consistency and, 90
        dialectical logic and, 333-34
        as heuristic device, 100
        incorrigibility of, 101
        inductive logic compared to,
            101-2, 104-5
        science and, 25-26
        See also Logic—deductive
    inductive, 101-7
        analogies and, 111
        deductive logic compared to,
            101-7
        empirical knowledge claims
            and, 150-53
        generalizations and, 107,
            111-13

Mill's canons of, 146-50
precision, heuristics and,
    96-101
predicate, 25
propositional, 90
sentential, 25
values and, 307-8
Logical Syntax of Language
    (Carnap), 116
Logical truth,
    definition of, 375
    empirical truth and, 116
Lubell, Samuel, 202-3
Luxemburg, Rosa, 166

McCarthy, Joseph, 202-3, 206
McClosky, Herbert, 151-52
Macdonald, Margaret, 9
Mackenzie, W. J. M., 1, 16
Macromorph, 186
Mandler, George, 58-59
Mannheim, Karl, 27
Mao Tse-tung, 166
Marcuse, Herbert, 354
    dialectical logic and, 330-35
    noncognitive discourse and,
        319-20, 327-28, 329-35
    normative discourse and, 289,
        296-97, 329
Martin, R. M., 241
Marx, Karl
    lawlike assertions of, 164-66,
        168
    normative argument and, 305
    schemata of, 142-43
    use of variables by, 126,
        164-66
Marxism, 23
    Behavioralism and, 17, 39
    dialectical logic and, 333-34
    noncognitive discourse and,
        321-22, 333-34, 336
    primary values of, 294

Sorel on, 321-22
Mathematics, 99
    explicit definitions in, 127-28
    formal validity and, 91-93
    intuition in, 205
    understanding of, 255, 265-66
Meaning, 42-76
    definition of, 375
    definition of cognitive, 375
    definition of emotive (or
        expressive), 375
    explication of, 133-34
    implicative, 47
        definition of, 375
    operational, 56
        definition of, 375
    pragmatic, 43-44, 69
        definition of, 375-76
    psychological, 47, 64
        definition of, 376
    public, 45
        definitions and, 130-31
        semantic meaning and, 82
    referential, 63-64, 69-70
    semantic (denotative or
        designative), 68, 81-84
        definition of, 43, 44, 376
        synthetic truth and, 51
    syntactical, 50, 84-85
        definition of, 43-44, 376
    systemic (or theoretic), 63-64,
        68-70
        definition of, 376
    truth, linguistic precision and,
        68-72
Meehan, Eugene, 11, 12
Megarians, 25
Merton, Robert, 145-46, 223
Metaethics, 8, 283
Metalanguage, definition of, 8,
    376
Metalinguistics, political science
    and, 349-51

Metalogic, 8
Metamathematics, 8, 205
Metaphors
  analogical models as, 193
  Marx's use of, 126, 165-66
  as "understanding," 249, 257
  See also Arguments—analogical
Metapolitics, 1-14
Metascience, 8
Metatheorum, 8
Metatheory, 9
Micromorph, 186
Mill, John Stuart, 109
  "canons of induction" of,
    146-50
Miller, James, 189
Mitrany, David, 223
Models, 160-97
  analogical (or substantive),
    189-94
    definition of, 376
  analogue (or formal), 186-91,
    193
    definition of, 376
  for calculi, 178-80, 187-90,
    193
    definition of, 180, 188, 376
  laws, theories and, 160-97
  mathematical, 192
  as propadeutic to theory
    construction, 183-85
  replica, 185-86, 189-90, 193
    definition of, 376
  theories and, 177-85, 188-89,
    193-94
  See also Conceptual schemata
Moore, Barrington, 201-2, 294
Morgenthau, Hans, 82-84, 350
Morris, Charles W., 115-16, 241
Motivation, *see* Explanations—via
    intentions, reasons and
    dispositions
Murphy, Joseph, 8-9

Mussolini, Benito, 294
Mystic insight, *see* Insight
Myths, 318-21, 323-26, 336-37,
  339

Nagel, Ernest, 58, 200, 359
National Socialism, 23, 294
Nationalsozialistische
    Monatshefte (periodical),
    294
Needs, satisfaction of
  normative disagreement and,
    297-303
  truth and, 284-87
Neumann, Sigmund, 132
New Science (Vico), 211
Newton, Isaac, 33
Niemi, Richard G., 151
Nonevents, explanation of,
  219-20
Normative argument, *see*
    Arguments—normative
Normative disagreement, *see*
    Disagreement—normative
Normative discourse, *see*
    Discourse—normative
Normative language, *see*
    Language—normative
Normative theories, 255-56
Null-hypotheses, 154
Numbers, formal validity and,
  93-94

Objective criteria for explanatory
    adequacy, 205-10
Objective truth, science and,
  27-35
Objectivity
  definition of, 24
  normative discourse and,
    306-11
  observation language and,
    61-65

primary (ultimate) values and, 307-11
of recognitors, 150
Observation
descriptive claims and, 51-55, 61
intersubiective, 24, 57-59
language and, 53-61
naive, 53
reliability and, 59-62, 65
sophisticated, 53
symptomatic recognitors and, 55-56, 149-50
synthetic truths and, 51, 60
Observation sentences (or propositions), 57-58, 61, 270-74
definition of, 57, 377
Ogden, C. K., 43, 54, 58
Olson, Robert, 282
Open-textured (or porous) concepts
definition of, 377
explication and, 134-35
Operationalization, 352
of conventional signs, 62
definition of, 377
explication of meaning and, 134-35
identification of recognitors and, 56, 182
theory construction and, 182
Oppenheim, Felix, 282
Osgood, C. E., 43

Pap, Arthur, 241
Paradigm, Kuhn's discussion of, 28-34
Pareto, Vilfredo, 325
Parsons, Talcott, 130, 144, 157, 171, 182, 327
Peirce, Charles Sanders, 54-55
Performance, linguistic, 46-48

Perlocutionary discourse, 283-88
primary (ultimate) values and, 293
Perry, Ralph Barton, 287
Persuasive redefinition, definition of, 377
Peters, R. S., 211
Phantasy, 36, 318-20, 327-28, 335
Philosophy
analytic, see Analytic philosophy
linguistic, 240-42
political inquiry and, 346-49
Philosophy of Language (Katz), 74
Piaget, Jean, 124
Plato, 109
Plekhanov, Georgi, 333
Poincaré, Henri, 250
Polanyi, Michael, 238, 250, 252
Political inquiry, 318-25, 346-63
linguistic analysis, 7-10
linguistic precision and, 351-55
metalinguistics and, 349-51
metapolitics and, 10-14
noncognitive language and, 318-25
philosophy and, 346-49
prospects for, 362-63
semantic variance in, 72
understanding, knowledge and "insight" in, 275-77
values and, 355-62
Political science
concerns of, 35-37
ethics, science and, 35-37
informality of, 35-37, 72
language of, 4-7
science and, 17-41
"understanding" and, 243-44
"Politics," definition of, 6-7
Polsby, Nelson, 136

Popper, Karl, 233
Positivism, 70, 292, 320, 357
"Power," definitions of, 136-37,
        139-40, 169
Pragmatics, 66-68, 78, 115
  definition of, 44, 377
Pratt, R. C., 291, 292
Precision, linguistic, *see*
        Linguistic precision
Predicate logic, 25
Prepositions, 84-85
Prescriptive model of
        explanation, 228-33
Primary (or ultimate) values
  cognitive activity and, 308-9
  faith and, 292, 309, 311
  intuition and, 309-10
  nature of, 293-95
  normative disagreement and,
        291-95, 297-304, 309, 311
  objectivity and, 307-11
Primer of Political Analysis
        (Strickland, Wade and
        Johnston), 98
Principles, ultimate, *see* Primary
        (or ultimate) values
Procedural knowledge
  children and, 124
  definition of, 377
  rationality and, 161
  "understanding" and, 249,
        251-54, 262, 269
Process laws, *see* Laws—historic
        process; Laws—systematic
        process
Pronouns, 84
Propositional knowledge
  definition of, 378
  rationality and, 161
  "understanding" and, 249,
        251-54, 262, 269
Propositions
  basic, 102

definition of, 377
definition of analytic (or
        logical), 366, 377-78
generic, 170
genetic explanations and
        "linking" of, 203-7
logically true, *see* Arguments—
        valid
normative, definition of, 378
partial axiomatization of, 96-98
protocol, *see* Protocol
        sentences
reduction of, 96-98
synthetic, definition of, 378
Protocol sentences (or
        propositions), 280
  definition of, 377
  intersubjective observation
        and, 56-57
  science and, 58-59
Public evidence conditions, 69-71
Public meaning, *see* Meaning—
        public
Public Opinion Quarterly, 19
Purdue Opinion Panel, 112-13
Purposes, understanding of,
        253-56
Puzzlement, abatement of, 203-4,
        209

Quine, W. V., 73

Randomization, 147
  definition of, 378
Range, definition of, 378
Rapoport, Anatol, 184-85
Rationality, 59, 160-62, 213-16
Reasons, explanations via
        intentions, dispositions
        and, 210-17, 220-23
Recognitors
  discriminable, 120-23, 144

symptomatic, 182
  definition of, 378
  observation and, 55-56,
    149-50
  reliability and, 149-50
Reduction
  definitional, 96-98
  proposition, 96-98
Referent, definition of, 378
Reichenbach, Hans, 57
Reification, definition of, 378
Relations
  coextensive, 125, 163
    definition of, 378
  contingent, 125, 164-65
    definition of, 378
  definition of, 378
  deterministic, 125, 163, 165
    definition of, 378
  interdependency, 125, 165
    definition of, 378
  irreversible, 125, 163, 165
    definition of, 378
  necessary, 125, 163-65
    definition of, 379
  reversible, 125, 163
    definition of, 379
  sequential (or diachronic),
    125, 163, 165
    definition of, 379
  stochastic, 125, 163, 165
    definition of, 379
  substitutable, 125, 163-66
    definition of, 379
  sufficient, 125, 164-65
    definition of, 379
Reliability
  absolute
    definition of, 379
    science and, 22-24, 59
  analytic philosophy and, 58-60
    62
  consistency and, 25

definition of, 379
in empirical inquiry
  definition of, 379
  observation and, 59-62, 65,
    149-50
maximal
  definition of, 379
  of science, 21-24, 26, 59
of recognitors, 149-50
science and, 21-26, 71-72
Replica model, 185-86, 189-90,
  193
  definition of, 376
Republic (Plato), 109
Revolution for the Hell of It
  (Hoffman), 364
Richards, I. A., 43, 54, 58
Rickert, Heinrich, 210-11, 215
Rokeach, Milton, 214
Rosenau, James, 345-46
Rosenberg, Alfred, 338
Rosenberg, Morris, 145
Rudner, Richard, 359
Russell, Bertrand, 139
Ryle, Gilbert, 238, 241

Scepticism, absurdity of, 66
Scheffler, Israel, 264
Schemata, *see* Conceptual
  schemata
Schlick, Moritz, 57
Schmidt, C., 165
Schoeck, Helmut, 17
Schulze, Robert O., 153
Science, 17-41
  behavioralism and, 18-23
  definition of, 21-23, 379
  ethics, political science and,
    35-37
  explanations in, 200-1
  formal logic and, 25-26
  as "ideology," 23-27
  objective truth and, 27-35

objectivity of, 24, 306-7
political science and, 17-41
protocol sentences and, 58-59
reliability and, 21-26, 71-72
as self-corrective, 23-24
signification and, 69
theories and models in
    maximally formalized,
    178-80
theories in natural, 178
as "value-free," 306-11
Scientific method, definition of,
    21-23
Scope, definition of, 379
Scriven, Michael, 169, 204
Searle, John, 312
Self-recommending values, *see*
    Primary (or ultimate)
    values
Semantic rules, 97-99
  inductive logic and, 106
  of theories, 178
Semantic variance, 70
  definition of, 379
  definitional reduction and,
    97-98
  formal language and, 239-40
  of ordinary language, 89-90
  political inquiry and, 72
  propositional reduction and,
    98-99
Semantics, 77-118
  definition of, 44, 379
Semiotics, definition of, 379
Sentences
  atomic, 59
  descriptive, 82
  protocol, 280
    definition of, 377
    intersubjective observation
      and, 56-57
    science and, 58-59
  symptom, definition of, 380-81

Sentence token, definition of, 379
Sentence type, definition of, 379
Sentence variable, definition of,
    379
Sentential logic, 25
Sentiments
  attitudes compared to, 304-6
  normative discourse and, 284,
    286, 288, 304-6
Set, definition of, 52
Sheldon, Richard, 182
Sibley, Mulford, 17, 40, 243,
    291-92, 319-20
Sign token, 81
  definition of, 380
Sign type, 81
  definition of, 380
Signs
  conventional, 62, 82
  definition of, 380
  felicitous use of, 79-81, 122
Significance, 69
  definition of, 115, 380
Signification, 69, 82
  definition of, 380
Signification and Significance
    (Morris), 115
Similarity, extensional predictive
    inferences and, 109-10
Simon, Herbert, 181
Simulations, computer, 99-101
Simulmatics Project, 99-100
*Social Origins of Dictatorship
    and Democracy* (Moore),
    201-2
Social science, explanatory
    "uniqueness" of, 217-22
Sophisticated knowledge claims,
    ordinary language,
    experience and, 154-56
Sophisticated observation, 53
Sorel, Georges, 319-26, 336-37

Sound argument, 90-96
  definition of, 366
Speculative hypotheses,
    assumptions, analogical
    argument and, 107-13
Spontaneous conceptual
    schemata, 123-24
Stalin, Josef, 166
Standardization, 239, 241
  consistency and, 70-71
  definition of, 380
  of natural (ordinary)
    language, 74
Stark, Werner, 328
Starkenburg, H., 165, 168
Statements
  contingent, 87, 89
  necessary, 87-89
    See also Truth—necessary
  observation, 57-58, 61, 270-74
    definition of, 57, 377
  protocol, 280
    definition of, 377
    intersubjective observation
      and, 56-57
    science and, 58-59
  tautologous, 86-89
Steiner, Gary, 96
Stevenson, C. L., 284
Stimuli, see Recognitors
Stipulation, see Definition—
    stipulative
Stoicism, 25
Storing, Herbert, 17
Strauss, Leo, 356, 357
Strausz-Hupé, Robert, 40, 213,
    356
Strickland, D. A., 98
Structure of Scientific
    Revolutions, The (Kuhn),
    28, 356
Subjunctive conditional, 168
  definition of, 380

Substitution rules, see Syntactical
    rules
Suci, G. J., 43
Sufficient condition, 176
  definition of, 380
Suppes, Patrick, 241
Symbol, definition of, 380
Symbolic language, 239-40,
    325-26
  definition of, 374-75
Symbolic Uses of Politics
    (Edelman), 325
Symptom sentence, definition of,
    380-81
Symptomatic recognitors, 182
  definition of, 378
  observation and, 55-56, 149-50
  reliability of, 149-50
Synchronic, definition of, 381
"Synoptic vision,"
    "understanding" as,
    249-50, 253-57, 269
Syntactical rules, cognitive truth
    and, 87-90
Syntactical variance, 70
  definition and, 128
  definition of, 381
  of ordinary language, 89-90
  political inquiry and, 72
Syntactics, 77-118
  definition of, 381
Syntax, definition of, 43-44
Synthetic truth
  definition of, 51
  observation and, 60
Synthetic/analytic distinction,
    51, 73-74
System, axiomatic
  definition of, 367
  theories and, 178, 182
  uninterpreted, see Calculus
Systematic process laws, 173-77,
    218-19

Systematization, *see* Conceptual
    schemata—classificatory

Tannenbaum, P. H., 43
Tarski, Alfred, 241
Tautologies, 86-89
Tawney, R. H., 136
Taxonomy, 170-73
Testability and Meaning
    (Carnap), 57
Theorems, 143, 180
Theoretic yield, definition of, 381
Theoretical entity
    definition of, 381
    synthetic truth and, 51
Theories, 160-97
    calculi and, 178-80, 187
    conceptual schemata
        contrasted to, 33-34,
        182-83
    definition of, 177, 381
    empirical, 255-56
    formal, 178
        evidence requirements of, 33
        preliminary conceptual
        schemata and, 33-34
    formal proof, 205
    game, 192, 310
    isomorphic, 187
    models and, 177-85, 188-89,
        193-94
    normative, 255-56
    partially axiomatized schemata
        and, 143
    partially formalized, 180
    "understanding,"
        interpretation and, 244-47
    See also Conceptual schemata
Theory construction
    computer simulations and,
        100-1
    conceptual schemata and,
        182-85

Theory load, 58
Tinder, Glenn, 243-44
Togo, Shigenori, 212
Topica (Aristotle), 315
Totalitarian society, criterial
    definitions of, 131-33
*Toward a General Theory of
    Action* (Parsons), 171
Trattato (Pareto), 325
"Truth," 42-76
Truth
    analytic, 50-52, 88
    cognitive, 87-90
    contingent, 87, 89
    by definition, 49-50
    descriptive (empirical or
        synthetic), 51-53
        definition of, 369
    empirical, 51-53
        logical truth and, 116
        recognitors for, 56
        warranting, 154
    evidence and, 265, 267-75
    logical
        definition of, 375
        empirical truth and, 116
    meaning, linguistic precision
        and, 68-72
    necessary
        cognitive truth and, 87-89
        empirical assertions and,
        102-4
        valid arguments and, 94
    needs satisfied by, 284-87
    objective
        science and, 27-35
    synthetic
        definition of, 51
        observation and, 60
Truth claims, warranting
    empirical, 154
Truth conditions
    definition of, 381

domain variant, 113-14
  language and, 60
  semantic meaning and, 82
Truth status, definition of, 381
Truth warrant, definition of, 381
Tucker, Robert, 176
Typology, 170-73

Ultimate values, *see* Primary (or
    ultimate) values
"Understanding," 238-81
  animal, 251-52, 254
  believing and, 260-64
  feelings and, 258-62, 267
  by "indwelling," 257-59
  interpretation, theory and,
    244-47
  intuition as, 243, 252-53, 256,
    259-60, 269, 276
  "knowing" distinguished from,
    244-47, 249-50, 266, 268
  machine, 251-53
  metaphors and, 249, 257
  mystic insight and, 243, 250-51
  nature of, 256-62
  in ordinary language, 242-47
  philosophy and, 347
  in political inquiry, 275-77
  in political science, 243-44
  public testing of, 258-60, 262
  of purposes, 253-56
  as "synoptic vision," 249-50,
    253-57, 269
  theoretical infrastructure of,
    247-49, 252-56
  uses of, 244-47
"Unique" events, explanation of,
    217-22
Utility, 66
Utterances
  constative (or cognitive), 284
    normative assumption of,
    285-88

protocol, *see* Protocol sentences
  See also Discourse; Language

Valid argument, 90-96
  connectives and, 94-95
  definition of, 366
  form of, 95
  mathematics and, 91-94
Validity
  external, 149
    definition of, 371
  formal, *see* Valid argument
  internal, 149
    definition of, 372-73
  verification and, 90
"Value-free" science, 306-11
Values
  definition of, 285
  logic and, 307-8
  needs and, 299
  political inquiry and, 355-62
  primary, *see* Primary (or
    ultimate) values
  universalizable, 303-4
Van Dyke, Vernon, 11, 181,
    291-92
Variables
  classificatory schemata and, 170
  definition of, 145-46
  dependent
    conceptual schemata and,
      125-26, 142, 145-46
    definition of, 369
  independent
    conceptual schemata and,
      125-26, 142, 145-46
  Marx's use of, 126, 164-66
  Mill's "Canons of Induction"
    and, 146-50
  personality, 176
  in process laws, 173-74
  relations between, 163-66, 173
  sentence, definition of, 379

Verifications
   definition of, 381
   validity and, 90
Vico, Giambattista, 211
Vindication, definition of, 381
Vocabulary of Politics, The
      (Weldon), 9
Voting (book), 96
Vygotsky, Lev, 119

Wade, L. L., 98
Walsh, W. H., 209

Weber, Max, 172, 220
Weldon, T. D., 9
Whorf, Benjamin, 155
Wiggins, James, 17
Willer, David, 144
Windelband, Wilhelm, 210-11,
   215
Wiseman, H. V., 138
Wittgenstein, Ludwig, 42, 241
World Politics (publication), 19

Zetterberg, Hans, 96-98, 163-65,
   172